WHERE GOD AND SCIENCE MEET

Recent Titles in
Psychology, Religion, and Spirituality
J. Harold Ellens, Series Editor

Married to an Opposite: Making Personality Differences Work for You
Ron Shackelford

Sin against the Innocents: Sexual Abuse by Priests and the Role of the
Catholic Church
Thomas G. Plante, editor

Seeking the Compassionate Life: The Moral Crisis for Psychotherapy and
Society
Carl Goldberg and Virginia Crespo

Psychology and the Bible: A New Way to Read the Scriptures, 4 Volumes
J. Harold Ellens and Wayne E. Rollins, editors

Sex in the Bible: A New Consideration
J. Harold Ellens

WHERE GOD AND SCIENCE MEET

How Brain and Evolutionary Studies
Alter Our Understanding of Religion

VOLUME 3
The Psychology of Religious Experience

Edited by Patrick McNamara

PRAEGER PERSPECTIVES

Psychology, Religion, and Spirituality

J. Harold Ellens, Series Editor

PRAEGER
Westport, Connecticut
London

Library of Congress Cataloging-in-Publication Data

Where God and science meet : how brain and evolutionary studies alter our understanding of religion / edited by Patrick McNamara.

    p. cm. — (Psychology, religion, and spirituality, ISSN 1546–8070)

   Includes index.

   ISBN 0–275–98788–4 (set) — ISBN 0–275–98789–2 (v. 1) — ISBN 0–275–98790–6 (v. 2) — ISBN 0–275–98791–4 (v. 3)

   1. Psychology, Religious. 2. Genetic psychology. 3. Evolutionary psychology. 4. Experience (Religion) 5. Neurology. I. McNamara, Patrick H.

   BL53.W511 2006

   200.1'9—dc22   2006021770

British Library Cataloguing in Publication Data is available.

Library of Congress Catalog Card Number: 2006021770

ISBN: 0–275–98788–4 (set)

     0–275–98789–2 (vol. 1)

     0–275–98790–6 (vol. 2)

     0–275–98791–4 (vol. 3)

ISSN: 1546–8070

First published in 2006

Praeger Publishers, 88 Post Road West, Westport, CT 06881

An imprint of Greenwood Publishing Group, Inc.

www.praeger.com

Printed in the United States of America

The paper used in this book complies with the Permanent Paper Standard issued by the National Information Standards Organization (Z39.48–1984).

10 9 8 7 6 5 4 3 2 1

CONTENTS

VOLUME 3
THE PSYCHOLOGY OF RELIGIOUS EXPERIENCE

Series Foreword

The interface between psychology, religion, and spirituality has been of great interest to scholars for a century. In the last three decades a broad popular appetite has developed for books which make practical sense out of the sophisticated research on these three subjects. Freud expressed an essentially deconstructive perspective on this matter and indicated that he saw the relationship between human psychology and religion to be a destructive interaction. Jung, on the other hand, was quite sure that these three aspects of the human spirit, psychology, religion, and spirituality, were constructively and inextricably linked.

Anton Boisen and Seward Hiltner derived much insight from both Freud and Jung, as well as from Adler and Reik, while pressing the matter forward with ingenious skill and illumination. Boisen and Hiltner fashioned a framework within which the quest for a sound and sensible definition of the interface between psychology, religion, and spirituality might best be described or expressed.[1] We are in their debt.

This series of General Interest Books, so wisely urged by Greenwood Press, and particularly by its editors, Deborah Carvalko and Suzanne I. Staszak-Silva, intends to define the terms and explore the interface of psychology, religion, and spirituality at the operational level of daily human experience. Each volume of the series identifies, analyzes, describes, and evaluates the full range of issues, of both popular and professional interest, that deal with the psychological factors at play (1) in the way religion takes shape and is expressed, (2) in the way spirituality functions within human persons and shapes both religious formation and expression, and (3) in the ways that spirituality is shaped and expressed by religion. The interest is psycho-spiritual. In terms of the rubrics of the disciplines and the science of psychology and spirituality this series of volumes investigates the *operational dynamics* of religion and spirituality.

The verbs "shape" and "express" in the above paragraph refer to the forces which prompt and form religion in persons and communities, as well as to the manifestations of religious behavior (1) in personal forms of spirituality, (2) in acts of spiritually motivated care for society, and (3) in ritual behaviors such as liturgies of worship. In these various aspects of human function the psychological and/or spiritual drivers are identified, isolated, and described in terms of the way in which they unconsciously and consciously operate in religion, thought, and behavior.

The books in this series are written for the general reader, the local library, and the undergraduate university student. They are also of significant interest to the informed professional, particularly in fields corollary to his or her primary interest. The volumes in this series have great value for clinical settings and treatment models, as well.

This series editor has spent an entire professional lifetime focused specifically upon research into the interface of psychology in religion and spirituality. These matters are of the highest urgency in human affairs today when religious motivation seems to be playing an increasing role, constructively and destructively, in the arena of social ethics, national politics, and world affairs. It is imperative that we find out immediately what the psychopathological factors are which shape a religion that can launch deadly assaults upon the World Trade Center in New York and murder 3,500 people, or a religion that motivates suicide bombers to kill themselves and murder dozens of their neighbors weekly, and a religion which prompts such unjust national policies as pre-emptive defense; all of which are wreaking havoc upon the social fabric, the democratic processes, the domestic tranquility, the economic stability and productivity, and the legitimate right to freedom from fear, in every nation in the world today.

This present set of three volumes, the project on religion and the brain, is an urgently needed and timely work, the motivation for which is surely endorsed enthusiastically by the entire world today, as the international community searches for strategies that will afford us better and deeper religious self-understanding as individuals and communities. This project addresses the deep genetic and biological sources of human nature which shape and drive our psychology and spirituality. Careful strategies of empirical, heuristic, and phenomenological research have been employed to give this work a solid scientific foundation and formation. Never before has so much wisdom and intelligence been brought to bear upon the dynamic linkage between human physiology, psychology, and spirituality. Each of these three aspects has been examined from every imaginable direction through the illumining lenses of the other two.

For fifty years such organizations as the Christian Association for Psychological Studies and such Graduate Departments of Psychology as those at Boston University, Fuller, Rosemead, Harvard, George Fox, Princeton, and the like, have been publishing significant building blocks of empirical, heuristic, and phenomenological research on issues dealing with religious behavior and psycho-spirituality. In this present project the insights generated by such patient and careful research are synthesized and integrated into a holistic psycho-spiritual world view, which takes the phenomenology of religion seriously.

Some of the influences of religion upon persons and society, now and throughout history, have been negative. However, most of the impact of the great religions upon human life and culture has been profoundly redemptive and generative of great good. It is urgent, therefore, that we discover and understand better what the psychological and spiritual forces are which empower people of faith and genuine spirituality to give themselves to all the creative and constructive enterprises that, throughout the centuries, have made of human life the humane, ordered, prosperous, and aesthetic experience it can be at its best. Surely the forces for good in both psychology and spirituality far exceed the powers and proclivities toward the evil that we see so prominently perpetrated in the name of religion in our world today.

This series of Greenwood Press volumes is dedicated to the greater understanding of *Psychology, Religion and Spirituality,* and thus to the profound understanding and empowerment of those psycho-spiritual drivers which can help us transcend the malignancy of our earthly pilgrimage and enormously enhance the humaneness and majesty of the human spirit, indeed, the potential for magnificence in human life.

J. Harold Ellens

NOTE

1. Aden, L., & Ellens, J. H. (1990). *Turning points in pastoral care: The legacy of Anton Boisen and Seward Hiltner.* Grand Rapids, MI: Baker.

ACKNOWLEDGMENTS

I would like to thank Debbie Carvalko from Greenwood Press for her advocacy of this project, for her help at every step of the way, and for her advice and encouragement at critical junctures of the project. I would also like to thank J. Harold Ellens for his belief in the importance of this project and for his sage advice throughout. Our advisory board members—Ray Paloutzian, Kenneth Pargament, Harold Koenig, Andrew Newberg, Scott Atran, and Donald Capps—in addition to their help in identifying topics to be covered also helped us to find the best authors to cover them! Advisors also kept the editor from making mistakes that could have cost the project dearly. In short, these advisors have immeasurably increased the quality of these volumes. I would also like to thank Lena Giang, Pattie Johnson, Anna Kookoolis, Jocelyn Sarmiento, and Sarah Varghese for their help with editing and formatting the references for all the chapters in the series—a thankless task at best, but these assistants did it both conscientiously and carefully. Finally, I would like to thank Ms. Erica Harris, my head research assistant, who helped out on all aspects of this project. Her organizational help has meant all the difference throughout. She did yeoman's work on the project Web site, kept track of correspondence with authors, and generally kept the project running smoothly and on schedule.

PREFACE

In recent years, several lines of evidence have converged on the conclusion that religiousness is associated with a specific and consistent set of biological processes. Religion appears to be a cultural universal. There may be a critical period (adolescence) during the life cycle of normally developing persons when religiousness is best transmitted from an older to a younger generation (see volume II, chapter 4). Individual differences in religiosity are associated with consistent health benefits (see volume I, chapter 7; volume III, chapter 2) as well as unique health risks (see volume III, chapters 4 and 8). Twin studies have shown that religiousness is moderately to highly heritable (see volume I, chapter 3). Genetic studies have implicated specific genes in religiousness (mostly genes that code for regulatory products of monoamine transmission in limbic-prefrontal networks; for reviews, see Comings, Gonzales, Saucier, Johnson, & MacMurray, 2000; D'Onofrio, Eaves, Murrelle, Maes, & Spilka, 1999; Hamer, 2004; see also volume I, chapter 3). Consistent with these preliminary genetic studies, neurochemical and neuropharmacologic studies have implicated limbic-prefrontal serotoninergic and dopaminergic mechanisms in mediation of religious experiences (see volume II, chapters 1 and 2; volume III, chapters 1 and 10). Neuroimaging and neuropsychologic studies have implicated a consistent set of neurocognitive systems and brain activation patterns in religious activity (mostly limbic-prefrontal networks (see volume II, chapters 2, 3, 8, and 9; volume III, chapter 7). A cognitive psychology of religious belief has revealed both the unique aspects of religious cognition as well as its commonalities with other basic cognitive processing routines (see volume I, chapters 6, 9, and 10; volume II, chapter 10). Finally, changes in self-reported religious experience by individuals suffering from obsessive-compulsive disorder; schizophrenia, Parkinson's disease, and temporal lobe epilepsy are in the expected direction if the previously mentioned neurocognitive networks (limbic-prefrontal) do in fact mediate core aspects of religiousness (see volume II, chapters 1 and 8; volume III, chapter 1).

Although the array of previously mentioned findings suggests to some investigators that it is reasonable to speak about potential neurocognitive specializations around religiosity, caution is in order when attempting to interpret the findings (see volume II, chapters 3, 5, 6, and 8; and all three commentaries). As in every other scientific enterprise, what is investigated in any given study is not the whole phenomenon of interest but rather only a small constituent part of the whole. The previously cited studies could not investigate "religion" per se. That is too vast a phenomenon to be studied in a single project. Instead, they tried to operationalize religiousness in various ways—with everything from a score on an inventory about religious practices to measurements on those practices themselves. Thus, we are reduced to making inferences about the nature of religiousness from data we collect via these questionnaire and observational/experimental methods. Making inferences about the nature of religion as a whole from neurobiologic correlations of one aspect of religiosity is, of course, fraught with danger (as all three commentators and several of our authors point out), but there is simply no other way to proceed. Inference and extrapolation from observations you collect on operationalized measures of the phenomenon you are interested in is necessary if you want to make progress. What is all-important, however, is to extrapolate, infer, and proceed with caution and humility. Constraints on incautious claims and inferences can often be obtained if you have a good theoretical framework from which to generate inferences about data meanings and from which you can develop falsifiable hypotheses. When it comes to biologic correlates of religiousness, the best available theory is evolution. Thus, several of the essays in these volumes discuss potential evolutionary and adaptive functions of religion.

Claims, however, about potential adaptive functions of religiousness also need to be treated with great caution and tested against the evidence. Several authors in these volumes address the question of whether religiousness can be considered an evolutionary adaptation (see volume I, chapters 1, 4, 5, 7, 8, and 10; volume II, chapter 4; volume III, chapter 6; and all three commentaries). For those scientists who think the evidence supports some variant of an adaptationist position (see volume I, chapters 4, 5, 7, and 10; volume II, chapter 4; volume III, chapter 6), the questions shift to what part of religiousness is actually adaptive and what functions might religiousness enact? Some theorists suggest that it is reasonable to speak about a "common core" religious experience fundamental to all forms of religiosity (see volume I, chapter 7; volume III, chapters 5 and 6). Some investigators suggest that the aspect of religiousness that was "selected" over evolutionary history was the capacity for trance, placebo responding, or altered states of consciousness, or ASC (see volume I, chapters 5 and 7; volume III, chapter 6). The capacity for trance, placebo responding, and ASC, of course, would yield both health benefits and arational or even irrational belief states over time. Other theorists (see volume I, chapters 4 and 5; volume II, chapter 4) suggest that the aspect of religiousness that was selected over evolutionary history was its ability, primarily via ritual displays and other "costly signals" (see volume I, chapters 2, 4, and 5; volume II, chapter 10), to solve the free-rider problem (where unscrupulous individuals exploit the benefits of group cooperation without paying any of the costs of that cooperation) and thereby promote cooperation among individuals within early human groups. Other theorists who tilt toward some kind of adaptationist position emphasize both costly signaling theory as well as gene–culture interactions to explain particular associations of religiosity, such as its ability to promote character strengths (volume I, chapter 2), its ability to protect against death-related fears (volume I, chapter 9; volume III, chapter 8), its ability to generate life meanings (volume III, chapter 3), its ability to address attachment needs (volume I, chapter 8; volume II, chapter 6), its links with the sources and phenomenology of dreams (volume III, chapter 9), and its similarities with special perceptual capacities of the aesthetic sense (volume II, chapter 7).

Although it has to be admitted that all these investigators have marshaled an impressive array of evidence to support their claims concerning religion's potential adaptive functions, all the authors of these theories realize that it is nearly impossible to demonstrate conclusively that some biopsychologic process is an adaptation, in the classical sense of that term. Several authors in these volumes have pointed out just how easy it is to get muddled when attempting to think through evolutionary approaches to a phenomenon as complex as religiousness (see volume I, chapters 1, 8 and 10; volume II, chapter 6; and all three commentaries). It is all too easy to overlook the harmful (and presumably nonadaptive) aspects of religiousness (see volume I, chapters 1 and 6; volume III, chapters 4 and 8). Ignorance of the complexity of religious phenomena, an underappreciation of the pervasive effects of social learning and cultural transmission on cognitive functions, and confusion around technical terms in evolutionary biology (such as adaptation, exaptation, and so forth) all militate against progress in this new science of the biology of religion.

To help think through problems of evolutionary change and adaptations in animals, the evolutionary biologist has often utilized the principles and methods of cladistics and phylogenetic analysis. Debates on potential adaptive functions of religion may benefit by taking a look at these methods. Cladistic methodology is used to analyze phylogenetic relationships in lineages that are recognized by the presence of shared and derived (advanced) characteristics. When cladistic methodology is supplemented with the advanced statistical tools of "phylogenetic analysis," you get precise and powerful techniques for reconstructing evolutionary history. These techniques have now been successfully used in the cultural arena, as in analyzing biocultural changes (e.g., language evolution). Scholars of ritual and religious practices have now amassed a huge amount of data on the historical development of ritual practices and on ritual practices in premodern human groups. There may therefore be enough data to reconstruct the evolutionary history of ritual practices in certain human lineages. If there is also enough data available on the history of various forms of healing practices of cooperative enterprises (e.g., farming or herding), it may be possible to assess change in ritual practices against change in these other forms of human activity. By superimposing phenotypic features (e.g., ritual practices) over accepted language phylogenies, one can reconstruct the history of evolutionary change in ritual practices as well as potential correlated change in health or in cooperative practices. Thus, hypotheses about potential adaptive functions of key aspects of religiousness may be tested quantitatively using these sorts of methods. With these sorts of methods, one could also potentially assess whether some aspect of religiousness (e.g., ritual practices) fit criteria for an adaptation or an exaptation. An adaptation involves the modification of a phenotypic feature (e.g., a particular ritual practice) that accompanies or parallels an evolutionary acquisition of a function (new healing practices or new forms of cooperation). However, in exaptation, the feature originates first rather than in parallel and only later is co-opted for the function in question. In short, because phylogenetic analysis involves quantitative reconstruction and analysis of histories of shared and derived traits, it provides powerful methods for identification of potential adaptive functions of religion. I draw attention to these techniques only to point out their potential. They have significant limitations, and they have not yet been applied to many problems in biocultural evolution. In particular, phylogenetic techniques have not yet been brought to bear on questions of the evolutionary history of religious practices. Nevertheless, they may be one way to shed some light on the problem of potential adaptive functions of religion.

The fact that reasonable speculations about potential adaptive functions of religion can be advanced at all is partly due to the startling consistency of the evidence summarized in these volumes on the neurobiologic correlates of religiousness. While tremendous progress has been made in identifying neurobiologic correlates of religiousness, it will be a challenge to place these findings in new theoretical frameworks that can do justice to the richness and complexity of the religious spirit. The essays in these volumes provide the necessary first tools to do just that.

Patrick McNamara

REFERENCES

Comings, D. E., Gonzales, N., Saucier, G., Johnson, J. P., & MacMurray J. P. (2000). The DRD4 gene and the spiritual transcendence scale of the character temperament index. *Psychiatric Genetics, 10,* 185–189.

D'Onofrio, B. M., Eaves, L. J., Murrelle, L., Maes, H. H., & Spilka, B. (1999). Understanding biological and social influences on religious attitudes and behaviors: A behavior genetic perspective. *Journal of Personality, 67,* 953–984.

Hamer, D. (2004). *The God gene: How faith is hardwired into our genes.* New York: Doubleday.

CHAPTER 1

The Neuropharmacology of Religious Experience: Hallucinogens and the Experience of the Divine

David E. Nichols and Benjamin R. Chemel

INTRODUCTION AND DEFINITIONS

Despite the considerable diversity of the world's religions, at the core of each is a set of beliefs that defines the place of humans in the universe. These beliefs form the foundations of peoples' worldviews, and, in doing so, they provide a basis for relating to and interacting with the world around them. The beliefs, practices, dogma, and infrastructure of religious systems should ultimately be rooted in the primary transcendent experience of the divine. Accounts of these deeply spiritual experiences inspire the framework of religion and provide answers to the fundamental questions of human existence, such as "Who am I?" "Why are we here?" "What is morally right?" "Is there an afterlife?" The capacity for this type of experience seems to be an inherent trait of our species that can be traced back to prehistory. For much of human history, the exploration of spiritual realms was the domain of shamans, mystics, philosophers, monks, and poets, yet modern scientists are developing new experimental approaches to probe the biological nature of religious experiences. Considering the ubiquity and global impact of spiritual and religious tendencies, this knowledge is essential for a complete understanding of the mind, and of our species, in its totality.

The belief that science and religion are mutually exclusive has, until very recently, hindered the pursuit of research on the fundamental nature of religious experiences. In Western culture, there is a long history of dispute between the beliefs held by "the church" and discoveries of natural phenomena by scientists. Science is based on empirical exploration of the quantifiable aspects of the world around us, whereas religion deals with the supernatural and relies on intuition rather than rationale. The worldviews promoted by science and religion are not always compatible, yet they do sometimes overlap.

The mind is one place where science and religion meet. Because the current paradigm of neuroscience considers the entire spectrum of human consciousness to be the result of complex events within the nervous system, it stands to reason that if research can help us to understand the neurochemical processes associated with memory and perception, it also should be able to shed light on the underlying causes and physiological nature of religious experiences. As far as we know, mystical states of consciousness depend on processes of neuronal translation that are similar, if not identical, to those responsible for converting stimuli from our everyday environment into conscious perception. This reductionist approach does not preclude the existence of a higher power, nor does it assume that religious episodes are all in the mind; rather, it simply states that the *experience* of a supernatural reality, like any other experience, is dependent on natural processes within the human body.

These reductionist approaches of modern neuroscience allow little or no room for faith and belief, and it seems likely that extensive scientific study of religious experience could lead to one of the next great confrontations between science and religion. Fortunately, or unfortunately, depending on the reader's perspective, significant funding is not likely to be available for such studies in the foreseeable future. Nevertheless, research results that bear on this question are beginning to appear as the tools of neuroscience become ever more sophisticated.

This chapter focuses on one main component of human spirituality—the primary experience of God or a higher reality. These so-called religious experiences seem to be the seeds from which the myriad manifestations of religion arose, and they are also arguably the aspect of religion that is best suited for empirical exploration. Although the supernatural aspects of these experiences may lie beyond the scope of science, there is increasing interest in exploring their biological nature and origin.

Defining the religious experience is a difficult task that often is likely to please only the defining party. The diversity of personally held religious beliefs and the variety of subjective states confound any attempt to create an all-encompassing description. In an effort to unify the many views of religion, Walter Houston Clark (1958), a highly respected religious scholar, has defined the religious experience as "the inner experience of an individual when he senses a beyond, especially as evidenced by the effect of this experience on his behavior when he actively attempts to harmonize his behavior with the Beyond" (p. 22). This broad definition is well suited for comparing the various forms of religious experiences, regardless of how they are produced.

Because of the spontaneous and usually nonreproducible nature of the religious experience, research exploring its neuropsychological basis is severely limited by the lack of an experimental model. For that reason, a condition or agent that is capable reliably of producing similar experiences becomes an invaluable tool for study. Thus, in an attempt to deepen our understanding of the mind, researchers have begun to examine the mental states associated with prayer, fasting, meditation, mental disorders such as epilepsy or schizophrenia, and the ingestion of psychoactive substances (Saver & Rabin, 1997). This latter topic is the central theme of this chapter.

PSYCHEDELIC/HALLUCINOGENIC AGENTS

We start this section with a definition of the substances we intend to discuss. Although these substances are generally known to modern science by the catchall name "hallucinogens," they also have been referred to by the terms psychedelic, psychotomimetic, and entheogenic—generally taken to mean mind manifesting, mimicking psychosis, and generating the god within, respectively. We use these terms interchangeably. Curiously, these descriptors suggest that certain aspects of consciousness may be shared by mental illness, religious inspiration, and hallucinogen-induced mind states. The definition of these substances that best sets the stage for the ensuing discussion appeared in perhaps the most authoritative reference book on pharmacology known popularly as "Goodman and Gilman." There one reads, "the feature that distinguishes psychedelic agents from other classes of drugs is their capacity reliably to induce or compel states of altered perception, thought, and feeling that are not (or cannot be) experienced otherwise except in dreams or at times of religious exaltation" (Jaffe, 1985, pp. 563–564). Readers should keep this unusual definition in mind as we proceed.

The complex range of phenomena produced by hallucinogens varies more so than for any other class of drugs and is highly influenced both by the mental state and expectations ("set"), and external environment ("setting") of the user. As a result of these sources of variability, one of the most striking characteristics of the subjective effects produced by hallucinogens is that they differ considerably from person to person and even in the same individual on different occasions. Nevertheless, the following effects are commonly produced by hallucinogenic drugs: altered perception of reality and self; intensification of mood; visual or auditory hallucinations, including vivid eidetic imagery and synesthesia; distorted sense of time and space; enhanced profundity and meaningfulness; and a ubiquitous sense of novelty.

At higher doses, however (but sometimes even at lower doses), perception of ordinary reality may suddenly cease, and an alternate reality or "visionary state" can appear. Following the loss of an objective physical framework with which to compare this experience, such visionary states seem, for all intents and purposes, completely real. Without external environmental cues to serve as reference points, they are perceived as outside the framework of time and space. Often referred to as a "peak experience," it is this state, rather than simple alterations of sensory perceptions, that leads to the experience of transcendental or mystical states. These peak experiences do not routinely occur following hallucinogen ingestion, and in fact are relatively rare, but they are the type of drug effect that most closely mimics spontaneous visionary states and are of greatest relevance to our discussion.

The late Daniel X. Freedman (1968), one of the foremost pioneers of clinical LSD (d-lysergic acid diethylamide) research, gained the impression from his many studies that:

> one basic dimension of behavior latently operative at any level of function and compellingly revealed in LSD states is "portentousness"—the capacity of the mind to see more than it can tell, to experience more than it can explicate, to believe in and be impressed with more than it can rationally justify, to experience boundlessness and "boundaryless" events, from the banal to the profound. (p. 331)

Further, "The sense of truth is experienced as compellingly vivid but not the inclination to test the truth of the senses" (p. 331). In essence, Freedman is saying that LSD produces profound experiences, accompanied by a belief in their truth.

The idea that hallucinogens are capable of inducing religious experiences in those who ingest them is sure to be met with stiff resistance by some readers. For some, the notion of a drug-induced spiritual encounter is by definition invalid, inauthentic, or superficial; for them, only through spontaneous rapture can one truly experience the nature of the divine. The notable religious scholar, Huston Smith (1964), refuted such skeptics by stating:

> refusal to admit that drugs can induce experiences descriptively indistinguishable from those which are spontaneously religious is the current counterpart of the seventeenth century theologians' refusal to look through Galileo's telescope or, when they did, their persistence in dismissing what they saw as machinations of the devil. When the fact that drugs can trigger religious experiences becomes incontrovertible, discussion will move to the more difficult question of how this new fact is to be interpreted. (p. 524)

THE IMPACT OF PSYCHEDELIC AGENTS ON RELIGIOUS THOUGHT

With that brief background, we examine how these substances have had an impact on religion. Throughout history, humans have ingested psychoactive materials, principally plants and plant extracts, to provide altered states of consciousness (ASC). The contemporary shamanic uses of approximately 150 psychoactive plants have been verified by field research conducted early in the last century (Schultes & Hofmann, 1992). It seems quite probable that many eons ago, at the dawn of human existence, our early ancestors discovered the mind-altering potential of certain plants during the exploration of their environment for food. The psychological effects produced by the ingestion of these substances could have impacted the worldview of sentient ancient humans in profound ways. Although it must remain a matter for speculation, some believe that spiritual thought arose as a direct result of the prehistoric use of mind-altering plants.

The use of psychoactive plants in healing and spiritual practices is deeply rooted in numerous indigenous cultures around the globe. In many tribal societies that have retained their traditional ways, matters of health and spirit are considered inseparable. In contrast to the Western medical paradigm, those cultures commonly believe that various illnesses are the result of spiritual rather than physical causes. For this reason, shamans routinely ingest substances or practice rituals that enable them to access the "spirit world" in order to diagnose and cure. In many cases, these plants have been deified and revered for their unique impact on the human psyche.

Historical evidence suggests that the use of hallucinogens almost certainly predates written history and also may have played a role in the development of modern civilization. These theories were largely promoted by the amateur ethnomycologist, R. Gordon Wasson. He and others put forth the idea that a hallucinogenic brew was the basis of the Eleusinian mysteries of the classical Greeks (Wasson, Hofmann, & Ruck, 1978). This highly regarded cult inspired many of the most notable citizens of Greece for nearly two millennia. The secret of the mysteries was known only by a select few hierophants and was protected by threat of death. Despite this secrecy, a few historical accounts exist that suggest the mysteries were revealed to pilgrims after breaking a fast by drinking a brew called *kykeon*, the central component of which appears to have been barley. Wasson and colleagues presented a compelling case that this brew was made from grain that had been infected by the parasitic ergot fungus (*Claviceps purpurea*). The purple, finger-like dormant forms, or sclerotia, of this fungus contain ergot alkaloids that are capable of producing powerful LSD-like mind-altering effects.

Another ethnohistorical claim made by Wasson was that the mythical soma of the Aryan *Rig Veda* was a psychoactive species of mushroom, *Amanita muscaria*, or fly agaric (Wasson, 1968). During the second millennia B.C., in what now stretches from northern India to Iran, a plant and brew, both named soma, were regarded as a god. Hymns devoted to the sacred, and indisputably psychoactive soma fill an entire volume of the Vedic texts. Although the absolute identity of the substances that once formed the basis of soma and the Eleusinian mysteries may be permanently lost, these ancient practices beg us to recognize that humankind has a longstanding relationship with psychoactive drugs.

More conclusive evidence of the ritualistic ingestion of hallucinogenic plants comes from the many explorers and anthropologists who have reported the intact use of psychoactive plants into present times. These indigenous uses seem to be vestiges of ancient traditions, which, until their rediscovery in the past century, largely existed in secrecy. Practitioners often suffered centuries of religious and political repression by Europeans, who displayed contempt for native shamanic practices, believing them to be inspired by the devil (Schultes & Hofmann, 1992). The most detailed contributions to this field of study come from the famed Harvard ethnobotanist, Richard Evans Schultes, as he built on the ethnobotanical work of his predecessors. By exhaustively studying the enthnographic uses of plants in Mexico and the Amazon Basin, he became the world's foremost expert on the anthropological use of psychoactive plants in the New World. His collections rekindled interest in these substances and formally introduced them to the modern world for the first time. Three of these shamanic plants will be briefly reviewed here to provide historical perspective on their ritual use.

Recent archaeological evidence suggests that peyote (*Lophophora williamsii*) has a history of use that can be traced more than three thousand years (Schultes & Hofmann, 1992). Spanish conquistadors in the sixteenth century reported the use of this cactus, called *peyotl* by the Aztecs, making peyote one of the first plant hallucinogens of the New World to be recognized by Europeans. This small spineless cactus grows in the desert regions of northern Mexico and southern Texas. In Mexico, the Huichol are the most prominent among the tribes who still practice the archaic shamanic use of peyote. To this day, the Huichol make annual pilgrimages over hundreds of miles to their ancestral homelands where they collect the tops of this cactus for ceremonial use. For these people, peyote forms a holy trinity with deer and corn. The symbolic imagery revealed by its ritual ingestion is reflected in their intricate artwork and inspires many aspects of tribal life (Furst, 1972).

In the latter part of the nineteenth century, the use of peyote spread throughout many tribes living on reservations in the United States. This practice was commonly met with opposition from local authorities and religious leaders, although the exclusive use of peyote by native peoples is now protected by the Religious Freedom Restoration Act of 1993. As many as two hundred thousand individuals from over forty different tribes belong to what is now known as the Native American Church (Stewart, 1987). Although customs and practices vary from tribe to tribe, ceremonies consist of syncretic elements that combine native spirituality and Christian religion. The use of peyote in this context has been a vital means of preserving tribal traditions and customs in a world of rapidly encroaching modernization. By creating a social framework and a means of personal growth for its adherents, the use of peyote in the Native American Church provides a viable, nonaddictive alternative to alcohol (Stewart, 1987). Sven Liljeblad (1972), an American anthropologist, reported a belief commonly held by Native Americans that peyote "has come to the Indians to lead them to Him as Christ came to the whites. As God reveals Himself in Peyote, it becomes a sacrament whereby communion is established with Him or with the spiritual world in general" (p. 103).

The pre-Colombian use of hallucinogenic mushrooms was also recorded in the writings of Spanish chroniclers. In the language of the Aztecs, the name for these fungi was *teonanácatl*, meaning "God's flesh." The exact identity of this sacrament was a mystery until the middle of the last century, when, to the surprise of modern scholars, intact mushroom cults were discovered in Oaxaca, Mexico. There, and elsewhere in Mexico, many species of mushrooms, primarily from the genus *Psilocybe*, are still routinely ingested by shamans and other villagers during social occasions and nighttime ceremonies (Schultes & Hofmann, 1992). Under such influences, shamans are said to gain access to spirit realms and are thus able to act as liaisons between the human and supernatural worlds. It is worth noting that Wasson, in pursuing the ethnobotanical leads provided by Viktor and Pablo Reko, Robert Weitlaner, and Richard Evans Schultes, was probably the first white person ever to ingest the sacred *teonanácatl* in 1955 (Hofmann, 1978). An account of his experience captivated the world when it was published in a 1957 issue of *LIFE* magazine (Wasson, 1957).

Similar to the effects produced by peyote, hallucinogenic mushrooms provide a powerful spiritual experience. In the words of one contemporary healer:

> The more you go inside the world of Teonanácatl, the more things are seen. And you also see our past and our future, which are there together as a single thing already achieved, already happened. . . . I knew and saw God: an immense clock that ticks, the spheres that go slowly around, and inside the stars, the earth, the entire universe, the day and the night, the cry and the smile, the happiness and the pain. He who knows to the end the secret of Teonanácatl can even see that infinite clockwork. (Schultes & Hofmann, 1992, p. 149)

Another sacred hallucinogen recorded by the Spanish was known by the name *ololiuqui*, which means "round things." This decoction, made from the ground seeds of various morning glory species (*Ipomoea violacea, Rivea corymbosa*, etc.), is administered for medicinal purposes and is ingested by shamans so that they may diagnose and treat illness. It was said to be substituted for *teonanácatl* when weather conditions were unfavorable for the mushrooms. In the sixteenth century, it was reported by a Spanish physician that shamans who ingested this plant could communicate with gods (Schultes, 1941). Like *teonanácatl*, the true botanical identity of *ololiuqui* was forgotten to science, even though the use of this plant persisted in secrecy into modern times. It was conclusively identified less than a century ago by Richard Evans Schultes (1941), who collected and identified specimens of this legendary medicine. The botanical work that Schultes performed in the deserts and jungles of the Americas was furthered in the laboratory of Swiss chemist Albert Hofmann, who was the first to isolate and identify the active components in many of the hallucinogenic plants used by shamans. After his accidental discovery of the potent hallucinogen, D-lysergic acid diethylamide (LSD; LSD-25), Hofmann became interested in natural products that shared the visionary potential of LSD. He demonstrated, through isolation from the plants, a certain degree of personal experimentation, and subsequent chemical synthesis that psilocybin and certain ergot alkaloids similar in structure and activity to LSD were the principal active components in *teonanácatl* and *ololiuqui*, respectively (Wasson, 1978). By doing so, he opened the door to scientific study of these substances.

EARLY SCIENTIFIC STUDY OF PSYCHEDELIC AGENTS

In the decades following this period of ethnobotanical discovery, hallucinogens fell out of the hands of shamans into the experimental designs of researchers in disciplines as varied as psychology, theology, neuroscience, and medicine. The discovery of the psychoactive properties of LSD in 1943 led to a new area of study of the mind, what might be called a "golden age" of psychedelic research. During the 1950s and early 1960s, hallucinogens, primarily LSD, were administered to thousands of volunteers in hundreds of clinical research applications, notably for psychotherapy, treatment of alcoholism, and to relieve suffering in terminally ill patients (Grinspoon & Bakalar, 1979).

Although most of this research was conducted in a manner that was appropriate for the times, a subset of primarily academic researchers, after experiencing the effects of these compounds firsthand, abandoned accepted research approaches. They adopted nontraditional methodologies of working with psychedelics and became outspoken advocates for their mass use. Knowing what we do about the profound effects of these substances, perhaps such a turn of events should not be too surprising. The widespread use of hallucinogens quickly became a highly charged political issue, accompanied by popularly held negative attitudes that were often promoted by the media and strengthened by the irresponsible use of psychedelics.

Scientific interest in human experiments with hallucinogens rapidly declined when commercial access to these chemicals was restricted in 1963. Concern over the safety and alleged risks to society posed by hallucinogens eventually resulted in the passing of federal legislation in 1970 that outlawed the possession of many hallucinogens. Today, most hallucinogens are classified as schedule I controlled substances, which by legal definition have a high potential for abuse, a lack of demonstrated safety, and no accepted medical uses. These restrictions had profound effects on how society, science, and medicine approached these substances. The simple fact of being classified as illegal drugs has cast a heavy pall over any possible value they may be seen to have by ordinary citizens.

The 1960s and 1970s were decades marked by cultural revolution, which in various ways was intertwined with the use of psychedelic drugs. Many people used psychoactive plants and synthetic compounds recreationally, often citing reasons that included personal and spiritual exploration. Anecdotal reports of mystical experiences induced by hallucinogens were incorporated into the popular lore surrounding these compounds, which inspired both contempt and admiration.

Perhaps more reliable support for the idea that hallucinogens are capable of producing transcendent visionary or spiritual states has been provided as a by-product of several academic studies. One such study was designed to treat alcoholics with large doses of LSD. It was thought that a high-dose experience induced by LSD might resemble delirium tremens and could essentially frighten alcoholics into a reevaluation of their habits (Aaronson & Osmond, 1970). Although the efficacy of these treatments has been questioned by subsequent research (Ludwig, Levine, Stark, & Lazar, 1969), many subjects reported transcendent experiences of a mystical nature, and it has been reported that the greater the psychedelic experience, the greater and more lasting was the improvement (Fox, 1967). Additional, more generalized studies, which were designed to evaluate the range of effects produced by psychedelics (primarily LSD and mescaline), suggest that anywhere from 24 to 95 percent of the personal accounts included religious components (Batson & Ventis, 1982).

One of the more well-documented examples of the ability of psychedelics to provoke mystical experiences took place in the spring of 1962. Walter Pahnke, then a Harvard PhD student, conducted a groundbreaking scientific study designed to examine the similarities between psychedelic and spontaneous religious experiences. In what later came to be known as "the Good Friday experiment," 20 graduate students of theology, who were naïve to psychedelic drug use, volunteered to participate in a double-blind, placebo-controlled experiment. Pahnke hypothesized that the hallucinogen psilocybin (from *teonanácatl*), when administered in a religious setting to those who were religiously inclined, could reliably induce experiences that were indistinguishable from spontaneous mystical experiences (Pahnke, 1963). In the basement chapel of a Boston University church, pills containing either an active placebo (nicotinic acid) or 30 mg of synthetic psilocybin were randomly distributed to the test subjects. As the experiment proceeded, the subjects listened to the Good Friday church service that was being conducted directly above them. Following the service, the subjects were interviewed about their personal experiences. A written account, accompanied by an extensive questionnaire, was provided by each of the subjects in the days following the experiment. Similar techniques were used as means of evaluation six months after the experiment.

Using common characteristics of mystical experiences derived by reviewing either published accounts or reviews of spontaneous religious experiences, Pahnke trained objective evaluators to discriminate written descriptions of authentic mystical experiences (Pahnke & Richards, 1969). The personal accounts of the test and control subjects were then assessed by this method. Additionally, nine distinct characteristics were carefully chosen in an attempt to define universally the mystical experience. These were largely derived from the work of earlier religious scholars (notably William James and W. T. Stace) and guided the formation and evaluation of the questionnaire used in the short (one-week) and long-term (six-month) follow-up evaluations. The characteristics of religious experience used in this study were feelings of unity or ego-loss, transcendence of space and time, a deeply felt positive mood, sacredness, a noetic sense of an ultimate truth or reality, paradoxicality, ineffability, transiency, and a persistent integration of the experience into one's life. Pahnke (1963) reported that in every measure, the subjects who received psilocybin scored significantly higher on the mystical scale than the control group.

The difference between the two groups was even more apparent at the six-month follow-up. At that point, all but one of the experimental subjects, and none of the control subjects, reported having an experience that was decided to be indistinguishable from primary accounts of spontaneous experiences (the one experimental subject whose experience was not classified as such stated that he had intended that outcome) (Pahnke & Richards, 1969). Additionally, it appeared that the experimental group was much more likely to have integrated aspects of the experience into their lives in a beneficial way.

Although many scientists and theologians acknowledge the importance of this study, some important critiques have been made. Pahnke's evaluation technique employed a discrete method of classification whereby aspects of the subject's experiences were categorized as being either mystical or nonmystical. This dichotomy may have over-reported the incidence of mystical aspects, in that profound altered states of consciousness of a psychedelic rather than religious nature would have been classified as being mystical rather than ordinary (Batson & Ventis, 1982). Furthermore, the double-blind nature of the trial was surely compromised at the onset of the effects of psilocybin. Another important critique of the study is that Pahnke displayed a tendency to overemphasize the positive aspects of the experimental subject's experiences and downplay the negative (Doblin, 1991).

More than two decades after the original experiment, follow-up interviews were performed on 16 of the original 20 subjects (Doblin, 1991). Although finding that none of the subjects displayed any long-term negative effects from their psychedelic experience, this follow-up demonstrated that positive effects of psilocybin had, in some cases, also been accompanied by psychological turmoil. This study suggests that the state induced by hallucinogens (if one can generalize) is not simply one of bliss and ecstasy, but also can be accompanied by intense psychological struggle. All seven of the experimental subjects in the psilocybin group who participated in the 20-year follow-up reported that they ultimately considered their experience to be positive and of a spiritual nature, despite any acute difficulties. This finding supports the commonly held belief that the outcome of such sessions can be largely mediated by attending to the set and setting of the individual. Doblin (1991) states that all of the seven psilocybin subjects reported positive, long-lasting contributions to their spiritual lives by what they considered to be authentic mystical states. A few of them even reported that their hallucinogenic experience was the strongest spiritual event of their lives. None of the placebo subjects reported similar impacts on their lives.

Religion is also concerned with the end of life and the possibility of existence beyond death. Here is another area where the therapeutic use of psychedelics has demonstrated spiritual implications. In the mid-1950s, a Chicago internist named Eric Kast was evaluating the analgesic effects of LSD compared to traditional opiates in dying patients. He found that LSD had an acute analgesic effect that was comparable to that of opiates. Surprisingly, however, in some patients he discovered that LSD had a persistent analgesic effect that extended for weeks beyond the acute effects of the drug. In one study of 80 patients, nearly 75 percent of them experienced "metaphysical reactions," with a happy, oceanic feeling that extended up to 12 days in some patients. Kast (1966) further noted that philosophical and religious attitudes toward death and dying changed as well, although those attitudinal changes were not captured in the data. There was a general improvement in the patient's feelings, and sleep patterns improved for approximately 12 to 14 days.

These early studies by Kast were expanded on in the late 1960s by a group of physicians at Maryland's Spring Grove state hospital that included Walter Pahnke, Al Kurland, Sandy Unger, Charles Savage, and Stanislav Grof. In a series of studies, this group reported on the effects of LSD in terminal cancer patients (Pahnke et al., 1969; Pahnke, Kurland, Unger, Savage, & Grof, 1970; Grof, Goodman, Richards, & Kurland, 1973). In the studies, LSD produced a positive change in scores of depression, emotional tension, psychological isolation, fear of death, and amount of pain medication required. In approximately one-half of the patients, the improvement was dramatic, and patients who had the most profound experiences tended to show the most benefit.

Although the degree of response varied, it was clear that some patients experienced a positive transcendent state. One patient who experienced positive ego transcendence felt that

> she had left her body, was in another world, and was in the presence of God which seemed symbolized by a huge diamond-shaped iridescent Presence. She did not see Him as a person but knew He was there. The feeling was one of awe and reverence, and she was filled with a sense of peace and freedom. (Pahnke et al., 1970, p. 70)

This type of encounter, noted earlier as what has been called a "peak experience," led to the most profound improvement in quality of life.

Although we have made no attempt to provide a thorough review of all the studies employing hallucinogens in dying patients, it should suffice to say that this use is perhaps the most well-documented and successful modern application of these substances in medicine. As a result of his extensive experience conducting LSD sessions, including his work with the Spring Grove group, Stanislav Grof wrote a number of books and essays describing the effects of LSD. In particular, he proposed that a "confrontation with death in a ritual context" can both eliminate the fear of death and lead to personal transformation. The experiences of death and rebirth that can be induced by psychedelics can sometimes lead to radical changes in the patient's attitude toward death and dying, resulting in relief of pain and distress and spiritual opening (Grof & Grof, 1980). These changes largely parallel those that are observed following a so-called near-death experience (Noyes, 1980) and further emphasize the potential similarity between an actual physical encounter with death and the perception of one that may be induced by a hallucinogen.

We have discussed how hallucinogens may be able to catalyze changes in consciousness that can lead to religious experiences, although their use alone is not sufficient to generate these effects reliably in every individual. As shown in Pahnke's Good Friday experiment, suitable preparation and a proper environment are also essential. Under such conditions, these substances may help to regenerate the soul and transform personality, effects that are not without therapeutic implications. Nonetheless, despite the promise generated by research studies, exploration of the effects of hallucinogens in humans essentially ceased. In 1966, 70 active research projects investigating the clinical effects of hallucinogens were being conducted; by 1970 only six remained; by the 1980s they were virtually nonexistent. The focus of the few remaining hallucinogen research programs shifted from the clinic to the research laboratory, where these substances became pharmacological tools to explore brain neurochemistry.

HALLUCINOGENS AND CONSCIOUSNESS

We now shift the focus of this chapter from historical and psychological phenomena to the neuropharmacology of hallucinogens and, specifically, how transcendent or mystical experiences might be produced from a neurochemical perspective. We examine brain structure and neuropharmacology in an attempt to rationally explain how hallucinogens might evoke visionary experiences. We should caution readers, however, that the ice beneath our feet is thin as we move in that direction.

Unfortunately, most of what we know about the human pharmacology of hallucinogens dates from about 50 years ago, and almost none of that is mechanistic. Clinical trials were fairly rudimentary, cognitive science was nonexistent, and there were few pharmacologically specific drugs with which to probe the mechanistic basis for the effects of hallucinogens. The vast majority of mechanistic studies on hallucinogens have been carried out in rodents, but fortunately there are a number of parallels in brain function between humans and lower mammals. Although admittedly we are still in the dark with respect to our understanding of the mind, there are certain aspects of the brain that are well enough understood to discuss in this context.

The major problem that we confront at the very outset is understanding the nature of human consciousness. How can one possibly discover how drugs alter consciousness without an understanding of consciousness itself? Although the study of consciousness is now gaining vogue, there is still no clear understanding of what it is and how it originates out of brain structures. Nevertheless, there seems to be a consensus that an intact thalamocortical system is necessary for consciousness (Plum, 1991; Tononi, 2004). We use this idea as a basic foundation for the subsequent discussion.

Tononi (2004) has proposed that consciousness arises from the brain's ability to integrate information in a way that is contingent on the connectivity within functionally specialized regions of the thalamocortical system. He further argues that the *quality* of consciousness is determined by the informational relationships that causally link its elements and the distinct activity states of these elements at any given moment. Massimini and colleagues (2005) have recently provided evidence in support of this hypothesis by showing that the loss of consciousness that occurs during sleep may be related to a breakdown in cortical effective connectivity.

In largely parallel reasoning, Vollenweider and Geyer (2001) propose that hallucinogens disrupt information processing in cortico-striato-thalamo–cortical (CSTC) feedback loops, leading to an inability to screen out, or "gate," extraneous stimuli and to attend selectively to salient features of the environment—features that to some extent may parallel those seen in the very early stages of schizophrenia. They propose that nonphysiological disruptions of thalamic gating of sensory and cognitive information leads to an overload of the processing capacity of the cortex and that hallucinogens may alter thalamocortical transmission by stimulation of 5-HT$_{2A}$ receptors located in several components of the CSTC, including the prefrontal cortex, striatum, nucleus accumbens, and thalamus.

We extend this reasoning to suggest that a religious experience represents an altered, or qualitatively different, state of consciousness that results from changes in the activity states of the interacting elements. Thus, even if we do not understand how a thalamocortical network might generate consciousness, we can still discuss ways that hallucinogens may alter processing in interacting brain structures that impinge on the network, and from that knowledge perhaps construct a framework within which to relate what is known about the psychopharmacological effects of hallucinogens.

It is widely recognized that the complexity of the cortex is what sets humans apart from the great apes. It is in the frontal cortex that executive decisions are made and important elements of personality are determined. Incoming sensory information as well as affective tags and access to memories all converge in the frontal cortex, where the totality of incoming data is continuously integrated in some way to form what we experience as consciousness.

Earlier, we cited conclusions by Daniel Freedman on the effects of LSD in humans. Freedman (1968) also noted that one of the effects of these hallucinogens was to heighten the sense of witnessing one's own experience in the context of a lucid, unclouded awareness. In essence, the ego remains intact and is an observer of the experience as it unfolds; whereas during poisoning or a toxic psychosis, consciousness is clouded, confused, or disoriented, and there may be no memory of the events. Thus, we can draw one clear distinction between the effects of hallucinogens and other substances that may alter consciousness: the effects of hallucinogens are typically remembered quite clearly and vividly.

During a visionary experience, consciousness and the self also remain intact, memory continues to function, and one is aware of what is happening even if it lies outside the realm of ordinary experience. Afterward, during ordinary consciousness, the subject can remember and report on the subjective details. These characteristics apply irrespective of whether the experience is spontaneous or induced by a psychedelic. Based on Tononi's concepts, it seems reasonable to infer that the basic integrative process of consciousness has not been disrupted, but rather some of the interactive brain elements involved in producing consciousness have been altered.

In ordinary waking consciousness, the incoming sensory streams bring information about the external environment. We are hardwired to respond to changes in the environment that represent survival cues, threats, sexual opportunities, occasions to gather food, and so on. Adaptive responses to the environment are necessary for survival of the species, and, as such, we would expect that coincident but irrelevant sensory cues will largely be absent at the level of our conscious awareness, having been filtered out of the information that is integrated into our consciousness. The nature of this filtering or gating process is of some interest as we discuss the actions of hallucinogens. We noted its importance in the ideas of Vollenweider and Geyer, cited above, and later we see that this gating concept is probably fundamental to religious experience.

How can we relate these functions to mystical states? First and foremost, one can anticipate that if the incoming information for integration into consciousness is diverted from environmental responses to interoceptive or subjective cues, then the nature of consciousness will change. The *quality* of consciousness will be altered because the informational relationships have changed that causally link the elements of the thalamocortical network (Tononi, 2004). That is, the quality of consciousness will change in a way that represents a shift from an external adaptive state of consciousness to one that is internally reflective and driven by hopes, feelings, dreams, memories, and imagination. We will remain conscious, but the *quality* of our consciousness will change.

Thus, if consciousness is normally focused on the everyday world, then any direct awareness of our subjective state, in place of its object, would be experienced as anomalous. A psychedelic model consistent with this reasoning would view altered states of consciousness as the subjective reflections or by-products of general mental activity, resulting when the "known object" of focal awareness is replaced by features of the "knowing medium" (Hunt & Chefurka, 1976). This point is reminiscent of the meditative techniques used by many Eastern religious traditions.

We posit that even if we alter the informational relationships of the elements involved in generating consciousness, what we experience may still be perceived as completely real. As a consequence of certain types of brain lesions, through the effects of pharmacological agents or in forms of psychiatric disorders such as schizophrenia, this reality may differ significantly from the nature of what might be called a "consensus" reality. Nevertheless, it may still be experienced as real by the subject, and indistinguishable from consensus reality because there is no objective relativistic framework with which to compare it.

Probably the only way that one might be able to recognize that an altered state of consciousness was being experienced at any given moment would be if there was an internal observer that remained objective and dissociated or unaffected by the processes that had changed the quality of consciousness. Such a postulate would require a sort of consciousness overseer that could retain a memory of what objective reality was like. This sort of dualism has been firmly rejected by modern cognitive neuroscience. Thus, one characteristic of a genuine mystical experience is that it must be perceived as being completely real.

If the memory of an altered-state experience remains intact during ordinary waking consciousness, the subject will be able to assess the extent to which the altered state differed from waking consciousness. A useful analogy would be to consider the memory of a dream. In the midst of a dream, no matter how real it may seem at the moment, we may not recognize that we are dreaming, but if we remember the dream when we awaken, we will clearly realize that we were dreaming. It might be added that, although lucid dreams are those in which subjects are aware they are dreaming, that recognition can only occur because they are not completely absorbed in the "reality" of the dream.

We have attempted to convey the idea that it is possible to alter one's perception of reality through a variety of means, and that during the experience it may not be perceived as anything other than real. A visionary or transcendental state must be perceived as completely real for it to be considered authentic. It is important to accept this premise, because if a transcendent or religious experience did not have the quality of seeming completely real, it would be perceived as illusion or hallucination and would have no lasting impact.

Transcendental or visionary states have the quality of being ineffable; there is no language that can adequately convey the richness of the experience. Similarly, Daniel Freedman often focused on the fact that hallucinogens produce a feeling of portentousness. That is, psychedelics can produce a powerful and profound sense that something ominous or momentous is about to occur or is occurring, producing awe and amazement. These descriptors are the same as those we might attach to a visionary experience, and they resemble Rudolph Otto's "numinous" (Otto, 1958).

We propose that a feeling of portentousness is a product of frontal cortical activity. It is well accepted that the behavior of other mammals (at least nonprimates) is driven primarily by reflexes and instincts, with little or no ability to make conscious choices. If we reject the Skinnerian notion that humans have no free will, then it is only in humans where reflection and introspection can occur and conscious decisions can be made to carry out specific behaviors. That is, the rationale for making complex decisions will be based on subjective comparisons of the predicted outcomes of different choices and a ranking of the acceptability of those outcomes in the context of one's value systems. Some choices will have more profound implications than others, and it is through our understanding of those consequences that we make such decisions.

Therefore, if we assume that the ability to place experiential events into Freedman's continuum, ranging from the banal to the profound, results from comparisons derived through cortical functions, it would then seem logical that attaching a sense of portentousness to an experience—a descriptor that must lie at the extreme end of the ranking system—must derive from processes that involve the frontal cortex.

From a neuropharmacology perspective, one can envision that exogenous substances such as psychedelics might alter cortical processing and sensory gating to produce experiences that are ineffable or are perceived as portentous. We can explore how this might happen by examining the targets of these molecules in mammalian systems and how these targets might affect relevant brain areas.

THE NEUROPHARMACOLOGY OF HALLUCINOGENS

Based on their chemical structures, hallucinogens are classified into three structural groups: tryptamines, phenethylamines, and ergolines. Tryptamines include psilocybin, psilocin, and *N,N*-dimethyltryptamine (DMT), and they bear a close structural similarity to serotonin (see Figure 1.1). LSD and related compounds are called ergolines and can be considered special cases of tryptamines because they have a tryptamine as their core framework. Mescaline, DOI, and 2-CB are examples of phenethylamines. Although these latter types do not resemble serotonin in structure, all three structural classes of hallucinogens seem to exert their effects on human consciousness by interacting with similar targets.

Figure 1.1   Chemical Structures of the Neurotransmitter Serotonin and Several Psychedelics

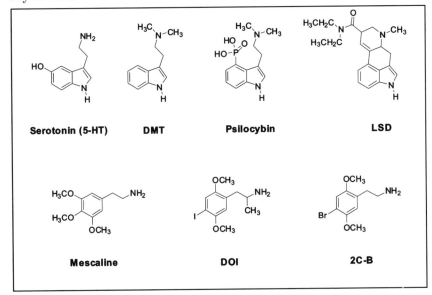

Note: DMT, psilocybin, and mescaline occur naturally in certain plants and fungi. LSD is semi-synthetic, being produced by chemical processes from ergot alkaloids. DOI and 2C-B are examples of totally synthetic psychedelic molecules.

It is not our objective here to provide a comprehensive review of neuropharmacology. Rather, we attempt to integrate what is known about the molecular effects of hallucinogens and their influence on particular brain circuits with how those actions could lead to mystical experiences. The neurotransmitter system of special importance to the present discussion involves serotonin as the chemical transmitter substance. Serotonin (5-hydroxytryptamine, or 5-HT) is an evolutionarily ancient neurotransmitter, occurring in snails and mollusks. In the mammalian brain, it originates from small groups of cells in a phylogenetically old area of the upper brain stem known as the raphe nuclei. These raphe cells send projections to higher brain centers, releasing serotonin into terminal fields of a variety of important structures.

At the molecular level, there is a fairly clear consensus that the key site for hallucinogen action is a particular type of serotonin receptor known as the 5-HT_{2A} subtype (Aghajanian & Marek, 1999; Branchek, Adham, Macchi, Kao, & Hartig, 1990; Ebersole, Visiers, Weinstein, & Sealfon, 2003; Egan, Herrick-Davis, Miller, Glennon, & Teitler, 1998; Krebs-Thomson, Paulus, & Geyer, 1998; McKenna & Saavedra, 1987; Nelson, Lucaites, Wainscott, & Glennon, 1999; Nichols, 1997, 2004; Pierce & Peroutka, 1989; Sadzot et al., 1989; Scruggs, Patel, Bubser, & Deutch, 2000; Smith, Barrett, & Sanders-Bush, 1999; Smith, Canton, Barrett, & Sanders-Bush, 1998; Titeler, Lyon, & Glennon, 1988). This conclusion was initially developed by, among other approaches, correlation of rat behavioral responses to hallucinogenic amphetamines with their affinities and efficacies at the 5-HT_2 receptor (Glennon, Titeler, & McKenney, 1984; Glennon, Titeler, & Young, 1986; Glennon, Young, & Rosecrans, 1983; Nichols & Glennon, 1984; Rasmussen, Glennon, & Aghajanian, 1986; Sanders-Bush, Burris, & Knoth, 1988). More compelling evidence for this conclusion recently has been provided by two clinical studies that demonstrated that the hallucinogenic effects of psilocybin could be blocked by preadministration of 5-HT_{2A}-selective antagonists (Carter et al., 2005; Vollenweider, Vollenweider-Scherpenhuyzen, Babler, Vogel, & Hell, 1998).

The earliest hypothesis for the cellular action of hallucinogens was based on the observation that LSD dramatically reduced the firing rate of raphe cells. One characteristic of these cells is that they fire in a regular rhythmic rate that is correlated with the level of vigilance. During sleep their firing rate decreases, and during REM sleep they cease firing altogether. Early experiments had shown that LSD potently suppressed the firing of cells in the dorsal raphe nucleus (Aghajanian, Foote, & Sheard, 1968, 1970; Aghajanian, Haigler, & Bloom, 1972). Other tryptamine hallucinogens, such as DMT, also inhibited dorsal raphe cell firing (Aghajanian et al., 1970; Aghajanian & Haigler, 1975; deMontigny & Aghajanian, 1977). Thus, Aghajanian and Haigler (1975) hypothesized that this suppressant effect on raphe cells might be the underlying basis for the action of hallucinogens.

This idea was very attractive because the raphe cells send serotonergic projections throughout the forebrain and are the source of serotonin afferents in the prefrontal cortex (Moore, Halaris, & Jones, 1978). It was also inferred that the connection between reduced raphe firing and REM sleep was somehow related to the action of LSD.

Nevertheless, problems soon developed with this hypothesis, largely because the phenethylamine hallucinogens such as mescaline lacked this effect (Aghajanian et al., 1970; Haigler & Aghajanian, 1973). Furthermore, a nonhallucinogenic ergoline called lisuride also potently suppressed raphe cell firing (Rogawski & Aghajanian, 1979). Ultimately it was discovered that the suppression of raphe cell firing was mediated by stimulation of somatodendritic serotonin 5-HT$_{1A}$ receptors. This hypothesis for the mechanism of action of hallucinogens was, therefore, not tenable.

Although the suppression of raphe cell firing may not be a primary mechanism for hallucinogens, one cannot conclude that it has no consequences at all. The firing of raphe cells is responsible for serotonin release in the cortex, and any change in firing rate would alter cortical serotonergic tone. The main effect of physiologically released serotonin in the prefrontal cortex is to inhibit pyramidal cells (Puig, Artigas, & Celada, 2005). Thus, a reduction in the rate of raphe cell firing would lead to increased excitability of cortical pyramidal cells, sensitizing them to 5-HT$_{2A}$ receptor activation by hallucinogens.

The observations that raphe cell firing ceases during REM sleep and that LSD also suppresses raphe cell activity may have relevance to an interesting study reported nearly four decades ago that has been virtually forgotten. Clara Torda (1968) recorded EEGs and obtained dream records from two subjects during 11 consecutive nights. During control nights, the subjects received 10-minute intravenous saline infusions, which started 30 minutes after the onset of their third REM episode. On alternate nights, intravenous infusion of 5 micrograms per minute of LSD was given. Subjects were awakened during their fourth and fifth REM episodes and asked to report what was on their mind. In all cases, subjects reported they were dreaming. On control nights, the average latency to the fourth REM period and dreaming was about 90 minutes. With LSD infusion, however, the latency to this REM episode was 10 to 19 minutes.

Although this study was too small to reach significant conclusions, it does suggest that LSD, at least in small doses, can initiate REM sleep and dreaming. If similar neurochemical events are evoked by LSD in the waking state, it would certainly provide a basis for the belief that psychedelics can produce effects that resemble dreams. It may be that cessation of raphe cell firing is a contributing, but not sufficient, condition for an altered state to be perceived as dreamlike.

Most recent attention on the mechanism of action of hallucinogens has been focused on the frontal cortex. After in vitro and animal behavioral experiments indicated that serotonin 5-HT$_2$ sites might be the biological targets for these drugs, numerous anatomical localization studies demonstrated that 5-HT$_{2A}$ receptors appear to be expressed most highly in cortical regions of rats and humans (e.g., McKenna & Saavedra., 1987; Pazos, Cortes, & Palacios, 1985; Pazos, Probst, & Palacios, 1987). In the rat prefrontal cortex, these receptors were primarily localized to pyramidal and local circuit interneurons (Miner, Backstrom, Sanders-Bush, & Sesack, 2003). Interestingly, 5-HT$_{2A}$ receptors were also expressed on the surface of dendritic neuronal outgrowths in regions that did not form direct synaptic junctions. The authors suggested that serotonin within the prefrontal cortex may exert at least some of its actions through volume transmission mechanisms. That means simply that some serotonin axon terminals release serotonin into the fluid around the cells, and it diffuses throughout the adjacent region. Based on their results, and previous data, Miner et al. (2003) proposed that cortical 5-HT innervation is largely nonjunctional and that the entire cortical volume may be within reach of this neurotransmitter. Thus, it is hypothesized that some of the physiological actions of 5-HT in the cortex may be constantly exerted, with more or less efficacy at the various 5-HT receptors, providing widespread, global, and/or sustained influence in the neocortex. Electrophysiological studies have confirmed that 5-HT$_{2A}$ receptors localized on cortical pyramidal cells have excitatory effects on projection neurons in the neocortex (Araneda & Andrade, 1991; Ashby, Edwards, & Wang, 1994). Hallucinogens increase both spontaneous and electrically evoked responses in cortical neurons, and they appear to affect primarily cortico-cortico interactions.

It is also becoming clear that hallucinogens enhance the release of the neurotransmitter glutamate in the cortex. Significant controversy still centers on the details of the mechanism whereby hallucinogens increase cortical glutamate following activation of 5-HT$_{2A}$ receptors, but it is believed that the glutamate is released from thalamic afferents to the cortex. Following these lines of reasoning, Scruggs et al. (2000) hypothesized that hallucinogens exert a direct effect, by acting through 5-HT$_{2A}$ receptors located on thalamocortical afferents to increase glutamate release onto nonpyramidal glutamatergic cells. Alternatively, Lambe and Aghajanian (2001) proposed an indirect role for 5-HT$_{2A}$ receptor modulated glutamate release that involves the release of a retrograde messenger. Such a substance could be produced as a result of receptor activation, diffuse out from the postsynaptic membrane, and block K^+ channels on presynaptic terminals of glutamatergic neurons, leading to depolarization and glutamate release.

One of the two known major signaling events following 5-HT$_{2A}$ receptor activation is stimulation of phospholipase A2 (PLA$_2$), leading to mobilization and release of arachidonic acid. Behavioral effects of hallucinogens in rodents do not correlate with the ability of 5-HT$_{2A}$ receptor agonists to activate the other major 5-HT$_{2A}$ receptor signaling pathway mediated by phospholipase C (PLC), and it has been suggested that the generation of arachidonic acid may be the more relevant second messenger for the actions of hallucinogens (Kurrasch-Orbaugh, Watts, Barker, & Nichols, 2003). It is interesting, therefore, that arachidonic acid is an extracellular blocker of K$^+$ channels (Poling, Karanian, Salem, & Vicini, 1995; Poling, Rogawski, Salem, & Vicini, 1996). Thus, a plausible scenario is that hallucinogens activate postsynaptic 5-HT$_{2A}$ receptors on pyramidal cells, leading to the formation of arachidonic acid, which diffuses to adjacent presynaptic glutamatergic thalamic afferents, causing depolarization and release of glutamate.

These cellular actions would stimulate activity in cortical cells and lead to increased demand for oxygen. As would be predicted by this discussion, hallucinogens have been shown to increase cerebral metabolic rate. In studies by Franz Vollenweider and his colleagues at the Psychiatric University Hospital Zurich, positron emission tomography studies with [^{18}F]fluorodeoxyglucose were coupled with Dittrich's APZ questionnaire (Dittrich, 1998), a rating scale for altered states of consciousness. Various changes in mood and perception were correlated with changes in cerebral metabolic rate of glucose (CMRglu) (Vollenweider & Geyer, 2001; Vollenweider et al., 1997, 1998). Administration of psilocybin produced a global increase in CMRglu bilaterally in areas of the cortex that are known to express a high density of 5-HT$_{2A}$ receptors. Their data indicate that 5-HT$_{2A}$ receptor activation leads to a hyperfrontal metabolic pattern, which was correlated with a depersonalization/derealization syndrome, thought disturbances, and mania-like symptoms.

TRYING TO FIT ALL THE PIECES TOGETHER

How does all this information fit together in a model of hallucinogen effects on cortical function? Although the functional circuitry of the cortex is not yet well understood, results by Sanchez-Vives and McCormick (2000) from experiments using ferret prefrontal cortical slices have suggested that the basic operation of cortical networks is the generation of self-maintained depolarized states that are tightly regulated through interaction with local GABA-ergic neurons and intrinsic membrane conductances. They further postulated that the ability of cortical networks to generate persistent and recurring activities even in the absence of ongoing subcortical inputs could be a process that underlies perceptual influences on sensory information processing. Clearly, changes in cortical cell sensitivity induced by 5-HT$_{2A}$ receptor activation, as well as glutamate release, whether by activation of presynaptic excitatory 5-HT$_{2A}$ receptors or by retrograde release of a transmitter, would dramatically affect these cortical networks.

Serotonin 5-HT$_{2A}$ receptors are also localized in areas of the thalamus, the reticular nucleus of the thalamus, and the ventral tegmental area. Although few functional studies with hallucinogens have been carried out in any of these areas, the thalamus may be the second most important site of action for hallucinogens. The thalamus, along with the amygdala, represents the major source of glutamate afferents innervating the neocortex, and, as we have seen, hallucinogens increase glutamate levels in the cortex. The thalamus processes not only somatosensory inputs, but also receives afferents from both the raphe nuclei and the locus coeruleus (Asanuma, 1992). A functioning thalamocortical network is essential for consciousness, and glutamate release from thalamic afferents in the cortex appears to be one of the salient features of hallucinogen pharmacology.

In rat brain, significant levels of 5-HT$_{2A}$ receptor mRNA are found in the reticular nucleus of the thalamus (Cyr, Landry, & Di Paolo, 2000). This region of the thalamus is of particular interest here because it is thought to serve as a sort of gate for processing signals to the cortex. Synaptic inputs to the reticular nucleus arise from the other thalamic nuclei, and it sends inhibitory projections back into the thalamus, apparently serving a negative-feedback regulatory role in thalamic function. It has been proposed to be a sort of "searchlight" of attention (Crick, 1984; Sherman & Guillery, 1996) and to control elements of signal-to-noise or the quality of information being sent to the cortex (see Vollenweider & Geyer, 2001, and references therein). In particular, the thalamic reticular nucleus can direct "attention" through its inhibitory GABA-ergic input to all other thalamic nuclei and assists in organizing activity in specific thalamic nuclei according to characteristics of sensory input and attentional demands (Behrendt, 2003; Smythies, 1997). It is thus in the thalamus, and in particular the reticular nucleus of the thalamus, that we find what might be the gate or filter for determining which information is sent to the cortex. We have already noted that such a gate has been implicated in altered states of consciousness.

A number of studies have shown that 5-HT$_{2A}$ receptors often activate inhibitory GABA interneurons, leading to speculation that 5-HT$_{2A}$ receptor activation in the reticular thalamic nucleus might indeed increase the level of inhibitory input to relay cells. Dysfunction of the reticular nucleus would lead to loss of sensory-specific inhibition of specific thalamic nuclei and further impairment of the signal-to-noise ratio. Noise could then predominate over stimulus-specific activity, with relay cells being recruited into thalamocortical circuits without receiving adequate sensory input. The combination of increased thalamic relay cell excitability and reticular thalamic nucleus dysfunction could lead to activation of thalamocortical circuits and the formation of coherent assemblies of thalamocortical oscillations that would be independent of afferent sensory inputs, potentially giving rise to underconstrained perception, such as hallucinations or dream imagery (Behrendt, 2003).

Although mediodorsal thalamic projections would normally fire in response to sensory information processed by the thalamus, a direct action of hallucinogens on these terminals would evoke glutamate release in the absence of appropriate sensory input. Because pyramidal cells would now be hyperexcitable, the effects of extracellular glutamate would be potentiated.

In addition to many studies that point to the frontal cortex and thalamus as key sites for the action of hallucinogens, the locus coeruleus (LC) may also be an important player. This possibility is intriguing because the LC is a point of convergence for widely ranging somatosensory and visceral sensory inputs from all regions of the body. The LC has been likened to a "novelty detector" for salient external stimuli (Aston-Jones & Bloom, 1981; Cedarbaum & Aghajanian, 1978). This group of cells sends noradrenergic projections diffusely to all parts of the forebrain, as well as the cerebral cortex (Aghajanian & Marek, 1999), and is the sole source of norepinephrine in the cortex. Within the cortex, 5-HT_{2A} and α_1-adrenergic receptors share a similar regional and laminar distribution (see Marek & Aghajanian, 1999, and references therein). Furthermore, activation of either 5-HT_{2A} or $_1$-adrenergic receptors modulates cortical pyramidal cells and interneurons in a parallel fashion (Marek & Aghajanian, 1994, 1996, 1999).

Systemic administration of LSD, mescaline, or other phenethylamine hallucinogens to anesthetized rats decreased spontaneous activity of LC cells, but enhanced the activation of LC neurons evoked by sensory stimuli (Aghajanian, 1980; Chiang & Aston-Jones, 1993; Rasmussen & Aghajanian, 1986; Rasmussen, Glennon, & Aghajanian, 1986). Suppression of LC firing was blocked by local infusion of GABA antagonists, and the enhanced responses to external stimuli were blocked by an NMDA antagonist. These results led Chiang and Aston-Jones (1993) to propose that systemic administration of 5-HT_{2A} agonists suppressed LC firing indirectly by tonic activation of an inhibitory GABA-ergic input to the LC. They proposed that the facilitating effect on sensory inputs was mediated through excitatory amino acid receptors in the LC.

In its role as a "novelty detector," the LC has been thought to enhance the signal-to-noise ratio in modulating postsynaptic activity throughout the brain, and the suppression of basal activity with enhanced responding to external sensory stimuli would amplify this effect (see Marek & Aghajanian, 1998, and references therein). Thus, hallucinogens might alter sensory processing in all parts of the brain, but their effects on LC neurons might suggest that sensory events ordinarily not considered unusual could be perceived as having increased novelty. Indeed, it is a well-known anecdote that under the influence of hallucinogens ordinary objects can seem new or novel, fascinating, and highly interesting.

Because the LC sends noradrenergic projections to the cortex, where α_1-adrenergic and serotonin 5-HT_{2A} receptors have both a similar laminar distribution and similar actions on pyramidal cells, changes in LC firing would also affect pyramidal cell excitability. Although the major site of action of hallucinogens may be 5-HT$_{2A}$ receptors localized in prefrontal cortical areas, it would be very surprising if enhanced LC firing induced by hallucinogens did not also modulate the direct effects of 5-HT$_{2A}$ agonists on cortical cells.

Another area where 5-HT$_{2A}$ receptors are highly expressed is the ventral tegmental area (VTA), dopaminergic cell bodies that receive serotonergic afferents from the raphe nuclei (see Doherty & Pickel, 2000, and references therein). These dendrites commonly showed 5-HT$_{2A}$ receptor immuno-reactivity and tyrosine hydroxylase colocalization. Thus, 5-HT$_{2A}$ receptor activation may directly affect local dendritic release of dopamine (DA) as well as release of DA in mesocortical and mesolimbic terminal fields. A substantial number of 5-HT$_{2A}$-labeled dendrites were also detected that did not contain tyrosine hydroxylase immunoreactivity, suggesting 5-HT$_{2A}$ receptor modulation of other nondopaminergic, perhaps GABA-ergic, interneurons in the VTA.

A recent study by Nocjar, Roth, and Pehek (2002) suggested that activation of 5-HT$_{2A}$ receptors by hallucinogens would be expected to modulate dopaminergic activity of VTA cells directly, or indirectly through nondopaminergic neurons, and affect DA release from projections in cortical and limbic structures. If, as recently suggested by Lisman and Grace (2005), there is a functional hippocampal-VTA loop designed to detect novelty that regulates entry of information into long-term memory, activation of the VTA would also affect memory and could contribute to the perception of novel states of consciousness induced by hallucinogens. This process also may be relevant to the fact that hallucinogen users typically have strong memories of their experiences.

To summarize, hallucinogens appear to exert their effects at the molecular level mainly by stimulating serotonin 5-HT$_{2A}$ receptors. In the prefrontal cortex, these receptors are localized on the proximal portion of apical dendrites and dendritic spines on pyramidal cells. Activation of these receptors leads to membrane depolarization and increased sensitivity of cortical cells.

All serotonin in the brain is produced by the raphe nucleus, which sends serotonin projections to all forebrain structures, including the prefrontal cortex. Hallucinogens reduce firing of raphe cells either directly by stimulation of 5-HT$_{1A}$ receptors or indirectly by 5-HT$_{2A}$ receptor activation of inhibitory GABA interneurons. Cessation or reduction of raphe cell firing would lead to a disruption of normal serotonergic tone, which would include reduced activation of inhibitory cortical 5-HT$_{1A}$ receptors, further enhancing cortical cell excitability.

Many thalamic nuclei as well as the reticular nucleus express 5-HT$_{2A}$ receptors. Essentially all incoming sensory information is processed through the thalamus, with modulation by the reticular nucleus of the thalamus, which has afferents from specific thalamic nuclei and associated cortical areas. Alterations in the firing mode of thalamic neurons are associated with dramatic changes in the neuron's responsiveness to peripheral stimuli (McCormick & Bal, 1997). The thalamus sends excitatory glutamate projections to the cortex. Hallucinogens not only perturb thalamic functioning, but also lead to increased release of glutamate from thalamic afferents to the cortex. Thus, hallucinogens reduce the signal-to-noise ratio in the information stream arriving at the cortex from thalamic terminals.

Both the LC and VTA express 5-HT_{2A} receptors and receive input from the raphe. The LC sends excitatory noradrenergic projections to both the thalamus and cortex. Hallucinogens potentiate burst firing in LC neurons in response to novel stimuli. Stimulation of α_1-adrenergic receptors in the cortex enhances pyramidal cell sensitivity and appears to share a common molecular signaling pathway with 5-HT_{2A} receptors. VTA cells are depolarized by activation of 5-HT_{2A} receptors, which leads to enhanced DA release in the cortex.

One can now appreciate that the overall effect of hallucinogens on brain function is extremely complex, involving multiple interactive systems. We should also keep in mind that these discussions are at a very rudimentary level of understanding. But we can nevertheless conclude that hallucinogens produce marked alterations within all three of the ascending brain-stem monoamine activating systems, produce changes in cortical cell excitability and cortico-cortico interactions, perturb thalamic gating functions, and induce action potentials in cortical cells through increased glutamate release.

One could envision, therefore, that hallucinogens greatly enhance the sensitivity and excitability of cortical processing, while at the same time inducing glutamate release from thalamic afferents that normally signal incoming sensory information to be processed. That is, the signal-to-noise ratio in the cortex for incoming sensory inputs from the thalamus would be very low. Such reasoning is generally consistent with empirical observations that the low-dose effects of hallucinogens include greatly amplified or distorted incoming sensory stimuli.

In the context of a religious or transcendent experience, the most important idea to keep in mind is that the cortex is hyperexcitable, attempting to process and integrate information, while at the same time the normal sensory information that it should be processing has been reduced or, at high doses, possibly eliminated by changes in thalamic gating functions. We posit that the cortex will fill in or extrapolate missing information, creating sensory constructs where none exist. In contrast to a computer, where nothing will be processed without input, the brain remains conscious with full data integration capacity and processing functions. Indeed, these functions would seem to be more active and responsive than during ordinary consciousness. What quality of consciousness will be generated under these conditions?

We would propose that affective components derived from elements of the limbic system such as the hippocampus and amygdala will replace sensory information. Signals arising from introspective and interoceptive processes would normally be at a low level during waking consciousness, flooded by external sensory data, but with the effects of a hallucinogen will represent a significant portion of the incoming data available for processing. Memories, emotions, and ideas will rise to the level of conscious awareness. Indeed, the external world may be effectively shut out, creating a sensory vacuum. With the cortex in a hyperexcitable state but receiving data only from limbic structures, memory stores, and phylogenetically old brain structures in the core of the brain, what will fill this void?

We now arrive at the limits of our ability to speculate, and we reach a place of conflict between reductionist science and religion. Absolute reductionists may say that the perception of a god arises out of some primordial emotional need in our limbic system, a desire not to be alone in the universe. Or, reductionism may propose that the ego is so fixed on survival that when faced with annihilation of the ordinary world, manifested through the cessation of familiar sensory information, it creates another reality where it survives annihilation, seen constructed as an afterlife with physical attributes. If God does not exist, must humans invent one?

CONCLUSIONS

Science cannot say whether God exists any more than science can say what existed before the big bang. Science also cannot presently explain how a visionary experience occurs, either spontaneously or when induced by a psychedelic. What we can say, however, is that the two experiences appear to be very similar or identical. We can also be certain that psychedelics perturb the key brain structures that inform us about our world, tell us when to pay attention, and interpret what is real. Psychedelics activate ancient brain systems that project to all of the forebrain structures that are involved in memory and feeling; they sensitize systems that tell us when something is novel and when to remember it. We may not be able to explain how the neurochemical brain changes induced by psychedelics produce a visionary experience, but perhaps we should not be too surprised that they do.

The mind is truly one of the last great frontiers of science. It is unfortunate that hallucinogens cannot be more easily used in research to help elucidate the neurochemical basis of consciousness. Coupled with measures of subjective states, cognitive tests, and new brain scanning technologies, hallucinogens could be extremely powerful tools to help us understand who we are and how that identity is tied to the functions of our brains. Sadly, delving too deeply into these questions may provide knowledge that many people simply do not wish to know, and perhaps that is part of the fear of these substances.

When this chapter was being written, there was a case pending before the United States Supreme Court of a small syncretic Brazilian church with a branch in the United States that was fighting to be allowed to continue its use of a psychoactive substance known as hoasca. This church, the Centro Espirita Beneficente União do Vegetal, ingests a sacramental brew made of two Amazonian plants, one of which contains a hallucinogenic substance known as DMT. Followers fervently believe that hoasca is an essential link to the divine and that denying them the right to use it would certainly have destroyed their religion. Despite use of these substances for thousands of years and scientific studies demonstrating their relative safety when used properly, there was a chance that these believers would be denied the practice of their religion because of the misguided notion that hallucinogens are dangerous drugs under all circumstances and at all times. As this book is going to press, we now can say that the Court decided to allow this church to continue using its sacrament.

As a modern society we must be open to the possibilities presented by these substances, not only for research on consciousness, but also for their ability to reconnect us with primary spiritual experiences that are largely absent from modern religions. The recitation of ancient verses and the practice of formalized rituals will never have the power of a single visionary experience to inspire. This fact certainly represents a threat to most established religions, yet Walter Houston Clark, the noted religious scholar, believes that, "Millions of Americans, if they are ever to enjoy profound religious experience, will only do so through psychedelic drugs" (Clark, 1968, p. 91).

Decisions about the use of these substances should not be based on irrational fears and intimidation. Rather, the appreciation of their value must be based on honest information, free of distortions, and a willingness to accept the possibility that even though these substances have ancient origins, they still may have much to teach us about the mind and their ability to inspire religious faith. As a modern society, we have waited too long to explore these fascinating materials.

REFERENCES

Aaronson, B. S., & Osmond, H. (1970). *Psychedelics: The uses and implications of hallucinogenic drugs.* Garden City, NY: Anchor Books.

Aghajanian, G. K. (1980). Mescaline and LSD facilitate the activation of locus coeruleus neurons by peripheral stimuli. *Brain Research, 186*, 492–498.

Aghajanian, G. K., Foote, W. E., & Sheard, M. H. (1968). Lysergic acid diethylamide: Sensitive neuronal units in the midbrain raphe. *Science, 161*, 706–708.

Aghajanian, G. K., Foote, W. E., & Sheard, M. H. (1970). Action of psychotogenic drugs on single midbrain raphe neurons. *Journal of Pharmacology and Experimental Therapy, 171*, 178–187.

Aghajanian, G. K., & Haigler, H. J. (1975). Hallucinogenic indoleamines: Preferential action upon presynaptic serotonin receptors. *Psychopharmacology Communication, 1,* 619–629.

Aghajanian, G. K., Haigler, H. J., & Bloom, F. E. (1972). Lysergic acid diethylamide and serotonin: Direct actions on serotonin-containing neurons in rat brain. *Life Science International, 11,* 615–622.

Aghajanian, G. K., & Marek, G. J. (1999). Serotonin and hallucinogens. *Neuropsychopharmacology, 21,* 16S–23S.

Araneda, R., & Andrade, R. (1991). 5-Hydroxytryptamine2 and 5-hydroxytryptamine 1A receptors mediate opposing responses on membrane excitability in rat association cortex. *Neuroscience, 40,* 399–412.

Asanuma, C. (1992). Noradrenergic innervation of the thalamic reticular nucleus: A light and electron microscopic immunohistochemical study in rats. *Journal of Comparative Neurology, 319,* 299–311.

Ashby, C. R., Jr., Edwards, E., & Wang, R. Y. (1994). Electrophysiological evidence for a functional interaction between 5-HT$_{1A}$ and 5-HT$_{2A}$ receptors in the rat medial prefrontal cortex: An iontophoretic study. *Synapse, 17,* 173–181.

Aston-Jones, G., & Bloom, F. E. (1981). Norepinephrine-containing locus coeruleus neurons in behaving rats exhibit pronounced responses to non-noxious environmental stimuli. *Journal of Neuroscience, 1,* 887–900.

Batson, C. D., & Ventis, W. L. (1982). *The religious experience: A social-psychological perspective.* New York: Oxford University Press.

Behrendt, R. P. (2003). Hallucinations: Synchronisation of thalamocortical gamma oscillations underconstrained by sensory input. *Conscious Cognition, 12,* 413–451.

Branchek, T., Adham, N., Macchi, M., Kao, H. T., & Hartig, P. R. (1990). [3H]-DOB (4-bromo-2,5-dimethoxyphenylisopropylamine) and [3H] ketanserin label two affinity states of the cloned human 5-hydroxytryptamine2 receptor. *Molecular Pharmacology, 38,* 604–609.

Carter, O. L., Pettigrew, J. D., Hasler, F., Wallis, G. M., Liu, G. B., Hell, D., et al. (2005). Modulating the rate and rhythmicity of perceptual rivalry alternations with the mixed 5-HT$_{2A}$ and 5-HT$_{1A}$ agonist psilocybin. *Neuropsychopharmacology, 30,* 1154–1162.

Cedarbaum, J. M., & Aghajanian, G. K. (1978). Activation of locus coeruleus neurons by peripheral stimuli: Modulation by a collateral inhibitory mechanism. *Life Science, 23,* 1383–1392.

Chiang, C., & Aston-Jones, G. (1993). A 5-hydroxytryptamine2 agonist augments gamma-aminobutyric acid and excitatory amino acid inputs to noradrenergic locus coeruleus neurons. *Neuroscience, 54,* 409–420.

Clark, W. H. (1958). *The psychology of religion: An introduction to religious experience and behavior.* New York: Macmillan.

Clark, W. H. (1968). Religious aspects of psychedelic drugs. *California Law Review, 56,* 86–115.

Crick, F. (1984). Function of the thalamic reticular complex: The searchlight hypothesis. *Proceedings of the National Academy of Sciences, 81,* 4586–4590.

Cyr, M., Landry, M., & Di Paolo, T. (2000). Modulation by estrogen-receptor directed drugs of 5-hydroxytryptamine-2A receptors in rat brain. *Neuropsychopharmacology, 23,* 69–78.

de Montigny, C., & Aghajanian, G. K. (1977). Preferential action of 5-methoxytryp-tamine and 5-methoxydimethyltryptamine on presynaptic serotonin receptors: A comparative iontophoretic study with LSD and serotonin. *Neuropharmacology, 16,* 811–818.

Dittrich, A. (1998). The standardized psychometric assessment of altered states of consciousness (ASCs) in humans. *Pharmacopsychiatry, 31*(Suppl. 2), 80–84.

Doblin, R. (1991). Pahnke's "Good Friday experiment": A long-term follow-up and methodological critique. *Journal of Transpersonal Psychology, 23,* 1–28.

Doherty, M. D., & Pickel, V. M. (2000). Ultrastructural localization of the serotonin 2A receptor in dopaminergic neurons in the ventral tegmental area. *Brain Research, 864,* 176–185.

Ebersole, B. J., Visiers, I., Weinstein, H., & Sealfon, S. C. (2003). Molecular basis of partial agonism: Orientation of indoleamine ligands in the binding pocket of the human serotonin 5-HT2A receptor determines relative efficacy. *Molecular Pharmacology, 63,* 36–43.

Egan, C. T., Herrick-Davis, K., Miller, K., Glennon, R. A., & Teitler, M. (1998). Agonist activity of LSD and lisuride at cloned $5HT_{2A}$ and $5HT_{2C}$ receptors. *Psychopharmacology Berlin, 136,* 409–414.

Fox, R. (1967). Is LSD of value in treating alcoholics? In H. A. Abramson (Ed.), *The use of LSD in psychotherapy and alcoholism* (pp. 477–495). New York: Bobbs-Merrill.

Freedman, D. X. (1968). On the use and abuse of LSD. *Archives of General Psychiatry, 18,* 330–347.

Furst, P. T. (1972). Peyote among the Huichol Indians of Mexico. In P. T. Furst (Ed.), *Flesh of the Gods: The ritual use of hallucinogens* (pp. 180–181). New York: Praeger.

Glennon, R. A., Titeler, M., & McKenney, J. D. (1984). Evidence for 5-HT2 involve-ment in the mechanism of action of hallucinogenic agents. *Life Science, 35,* 2505–2511.

Glennon, R. A., Titeler, M., & Young, R. (1986). Structure-activity relationships and mechanism of action of hallucinogenic agents based on drug discrimination and radioligand binding studies. *Psychopharmacology Bulletin, 22,* 953–958.

Glennon, R. A., Young, R., & Rosecrans, J. A. (1983). Antagonism of the effects of the hallucinogen DOM and the purported 5-HT agonist quipazine by 5-HT2 antago-nists. *European Journal of Pharmacology, 91,* 189–196.

Grinspoon, L., & Bakalar, J. B. (1979). *Psychedelic drugs reconsidered.* New York: Basic Books.

Grof, S., Goodman, L. E., Richards, W. A., & Kurland, A. A. (1973). LSD-assisted psy-chotherapy in patients with terminal cancer. *International Pharmacopsychiatry, 8,* 129–144.

Grof, S., & Grof, C. (1980). *Beyond death: The gates of consciousness.* London: Thames and Hudson.

Haigler, H. J., & Aghajanian, G. K. (1973). Mescaline and LSD: Direct and indirect effects on serotonin-containing neurons in brain. *European Journal of Pharmacology, 21,* 53–60.

Hofmann, A. (1978). History of the basic chemical investigations on the sacred mush-rooms of Mexico. In J. Ott & J. Bigwood (Eds.), *Teonanacatl hallucinogenic mush-rooms of North America* (pp. 47–64). Seattle: Madrona.

Hunt, H. T., & Chefurka, C. M. (1976). A test of the psychedelic model of altered states of consciousness. The role of introspective sensitization in eliciting unusual subjective reports. *Archives of General Psychiatry, 33*, 867–876.

Jaffe, J. H. (1985). Drug addiction and drug abuse. In A. G. Gilman, L. S. Goodman, T. W. Rall, & F. Murad (Eds.), *Goodman and Gilman's the pharmacological basis of therapeutics* (7th ed., pp. 532–581). New York: Macmillan.

Kast, E. (1966). LSD and the dying patient. *Chicago Medical School Quarterly, 26*, 80–87.

Krebs-Thomson, K., Paulus, M. P., & Geyer, M. A. (1998). Effects of hallucinogens on locomotor and investigatory activity and patterns: Influence of $5-HT_{2A}$ and $5-HT_{2C}$ receptors. *Neuropsychopharmacology, 18*, 339–351.

Kurrasch-Orbaugh, D. M., Watts, V. J., Barker, E. L., & Nichols, D. E. (2003). Serotonin 5-hydroxytryptamine 2A receptor-coupled phospholipase C and phospholipase A2 signaling pathways have different receptor reserves. *Journal of Pharmacology and Experimental Therapy, 304*, 229–237.

Lambe, E. K., & Aghajanian, G. K. (2001). The role of Kv1.2-containing potassium channels in serotonin-induced glutamate release from thalamocortical terminals in rat frontal cortex. *Journal of Neuroscience, 21*, 9955–9963.

Liljeblad, S. (1972). *The Idaho Indians in transition, 1805–1960*. Pocatello: Idaho State University.

Lisman, J. E., & Grace, A. A. (2005). The hippocampal-VTA loop: Controlling the entry of information into long-term memory. *Neuron, 46*, 703–713.

Ludwig, A., Levine, J., Stark, L., & Lazar, R. (1969). A clinical study of LSD treatment in alcoholism. *American Journal of Psychiatry, 126*, 59–69.

Marek, G. J., & Aghajanian, G. K. (1994). Excitation of interneurons in piriform cortex by 5-hydroxytryptamine: Blockade by MDL 100,907, a highly selective $5-HT_{2A}$ receptor antagonist. *European Journal of Pharmacology, 259*, 137–141.

Marek, G. J., & Aghajanian, G. K. (1996). Alpha 1B-adrenoceptor-mediated excitation of piriform cortical interneurons. *European Journal of Pharmacology, 305*, 95–100.

Marek, G. J., & Aghajanian, G. K. (1998). Indoleamine and the phenethylamine hallucinogens: Mechanisms of psychotomimetic action. *Drug and Alcohol Dependence, 51*, 189–198.

Marek, G. J., & Aghajanian, G. K. (1999). $5-HT_{2A}$ receptor or α_1-adrenoceptor activation induces excitatory postsynaptic currents in layer V pyramidal cells of the medial prefrontal cortex. *European Journal of Pharmacology, 367*, 197–206.

Massimini, M., Ferrarelli, F., Huber, R., Esser, S. K., Singh, H., & Tononi, G. (2005). Breakdown of cortical effective connectivity during sleep. *Science, 309*, 2228–2232.

McCormick, D. A., & Bal, T. (1997). Sleep and arousal: Thalamocortical mechanisms. *Annual Review of Neuroscience, 20*, 185–215.

McKenna, D. J., & Saavedra, J. M. (1987). Autoradiography of LSD and 2,5-dimethoxyphenylisopropylamine psychotomimetics demonstrates regional, specific cross-displacement in the rat brain. *European Journal of Pharmacology, 142*, 313–315.

Miner, L. A., Backstrom, J. R., Sanders-Bush, E., & Sesack, S. R. (2003). Ultrastructural localization of serotonin2A receptors in the middle layers of the rat prelimbic prefrontal cortex. *Neuroscience, 116*, 107–117.

Moore, R. Y., Halaris, A. E., & Jones, B. E. (1978). Serotonin neurons of the midbrain raphe: Ascending projections. *Journal of Comparative Neurology, 180*, 417–438.

Nelson, D. L., Lucaites, V. L., Wainscott, D. B., & Glennon, R. A. (1999). Comparisons of hallucinogenic phenylisopropylamine binding affinities at cloned human 5-HT_{2A}, 5-HT_{2B} and 5-HT_{2C} receptors. *Naunyn Schmiedebergs Archives of Pharmacology, 359*, 1–6.

Nichols, D. E. (1997). Role of serotoninergic neurons and 5-HT receptors in the action of hallucinogens. In H. G. Baumgarten & M. Gothert (Eds.), *Serotoninergic neurons and 5-HT receptors in the CNS* (pp. 563–585). Berlin Heidelberg: Springer-Verlag.

Nichols, D. E. (2004). Hallucinogens. *Pharmacology and Therapeutics, 101*, 131–181.

Nichols, D. E., & Glennon, R. A. (1984). Medicinal chemistry and structure-activity relationships of hallucinogens. In B. L. Jacobs (Ed.), *Hallucinogens: Neurochemical, behavioral, and clinical perspectives* (pp. 95–142). New York: Raven Press.

Nocjar, C., Roth, B. L., & Pehek, E. A. (2002). Localization of 5-HT(2A) receptors on dopamine cells in subnuclei of the midbrain A10 cell group. *Neuroscience, 111*, 163–176.

Noyes, R., Jr. (1980). Attitude change following near-death experiences. *Psychiatry, 43*, 234–242.

Otto, R. (1958). *The idea of the holy: An inquiry into the non-rational factor in the idea of the divine and its relation to the rational* (J. W. Harvey, Trans.). New York: Oxford University Press.

Pahnke, W. N. (1963). *Drugs and mysticism. An analysis of the relationship between psychedelic drugs and the mystical consciousness.* Unpublished doctoral dissertation, Harvard University, Cambridge, MA.

Pahnke, W. N., Kurland, A. A., Goodman, L. E., & Richards, W. A. (1969). LSD-assisted psychotherapy with terminal cancer patients. *Current Psychiatric Therapies, 9*, 144–152.

Pahnke, W. N., Kurland, A. A., Unger, S., Savage, C., & Grof, S. (1970). The experimental use of psychedelic (LSD) psychotherapy. *Journal of the American Medical Association, 212*, 1856–1863.

Pahnke, W. N., & Richards, W. A. (1969). Implications of LSD and experimental mysticism. In C. T. Tart (Ed.), *Altered states of consciousness* (pp. 399–428). New York: Wiley.

Pazos, A., Cortes, R., & Palacios, J. M. (1985). Quantitative autoradiographic mapping of serotonin receptors in the rat brain. II. Serotonin-2 receptors. *Brain Research, 346*, 231–249.

Pazos, A., Probst, A., & Palacios, J. M. (1987). Serotonin receptors in the human brain—IV. Autoradiographic mapping of serotonin-2 receptors. *Neuroscience, 21*, 123–139.

Pierce, P.A., & Peroutka, S.J. (1989). Hallucinogenic drug interactions with neurotransmitter receptor binding sites in human cortex. *Psychopharmacology Berlin, 97*, 118–122.

Plum, F. (1991). Coma and related global disturbances of the human conscious state. In A. Peters & E. G. Jones (Eds.), *Normal and altered states of function* (pp. 359–425). New York: Plenum Press.

Poling, J.S., Karanian, J.W., Salem, N., Jr., & Vicini, S. (1995). Time- and voltage-dependent block of delayed rectifier potassium channels by docosahexaenoic acid. *Molecular Pharmacology, 47*, 381–390.

Poling, J.S., Rogawski, M.A., Salem, N., Jr., & Vicini, S. (1996). Anandamide, an endogenous cannabinoid, inhibits shaker-related voltage-gated K^+ channels. *Neuropharmacology, 35*, 983–991.

Puig, M.V., Artigas, F., & Celada, P. (2005). Modulation of the activity of pyramidal neurons in rat prefrontal cortex by raphe stimulation in vivo: Involvement of serotonin and GABA. *Cerebral Cortex, 15*, 1–14.

Rasmussen, K., & Aghajanian, G.K. (1986). Effect of hallucinogens on spontaneous and sensory-evoked locus coeruleus unit activity in the rat: Reversal by selective 5-HT2 antagonists. *Brain Research, 385*, 395–400.

Rasmussen, K., Glennon, R.A., & Aghajanian, G.K. (1986). Phenethylamine hallucinogens in the locus coeruleus: Potency of action correlates with rank order of 5-HT2 binding affinity. *European Journal of Pharmacology, 132*, 79–82.

Rogawski, M.A., & Aghajanian, G.K. (1979). Response of central monoaminergic neurons to lisuride: Comparison with LSD. *Life Science, 24*, 1289–1297.

Sadzot, B., Baraban, J.M., Glennon, R.A., Lyon, R.A., Leonhardt, S., Jan, C.R., & Titeler, N. (1989). Hallucinogenic drug interactions at human brain 5-HT2 receptors: Implications for treating LSD-induced hallucinogenesis. *Psychopharmacology Berlin, 98*, 495–499.

Sanchez-Vives, M.V., & McCormick, D.A. (2000). Cellular and network mechanisms of rhythmic recurrent activity in neocortex. *Nature Neuroscience, 3*, 1027–1034.

Sanders-Bush, E., Burris, K.D., & Knoth, K. (1988). Lysergic acid diethylamide and 2,5-dimethoxy-4-methylamphetamine are partial agonists at serotonin receptors linked to phosphoinositide hydrolysis. *Journal of Pharmacology and Experimental Therapy, 246*, 924–928.

Saver, J.L., & Rabin, J. (1997). The neural substrates of religious experience. *Journal of Neuropsychiatry and Clinical Neuroscience, 9*, 498–510.

Schultes, R.E. (1941). *A contribution to our knowledge of Rivea corymbosa: The narcotic ololiuqui of the Aztecs.* Cambridge, MA: Harvard Botanical Museum.

Schultes, R.E., & Hofmann, A. (1992). *Plants of the gods: Their sacred, healing, and hallucinogenic powers.* Rochester, VT: Healing Arts Press.

Scruggs, J.L., Patel, S., Bubser, M., & Deutch, A.Y. (2000). DOI-induced activation of the cortex: Dependence on 5-HT$_{2A}$ heteroceptors on thalamocortical glutamatergic neurons. *Journal of Neuroscience, 20*, 8846–8852.

Sherman, S.M., & Guillery, R.W. (1996). Functional organization of thalamocortical relays. *Journal of Neurophysiology, 76*, 1367–1395.

Smith, H. (1964). Do drugs have religious import? *Journal of Philosophy, 61*, 517–530.

Smith, R. L., Barrett, R. J., & Sanders-Bush, E. (1999). Mechanism of tolerance development to 2,5-dimethoxy-4-iodoamphetamine in rats: Down-regulation of the 5-HT$_{2A}$, but not 5-HT$_{2C}$, receptor. *Psychopharmacology Berlin, 144*, 248–254.

Smith, R. L., Canton, H., Barrett, R. J., & Sanders-Bush, E. (1998). Agonist properties of N,N-dimethyltryptamine at serotonin 5-HT2A and 5-HT2C receptors. *Pharmacology Biochemistry and Behavior, 61*, 323–330.

Smythies, J. (1997). The functional neuroanatomy of awareness: With a focus on the role of various anatomical systems in the control of intermodal attention. *Consciousness and Cognition, 6*, 455–481.

Stewart, O. C. (1987). *Peyote religion: A history.* Norman: University of Oklahoma Press.

Titeler, M., Lyon, R. A., & Glennon, R. A. (1988). Radioligand binding evidence implicates the brain 5-HT2 receptor as a site of action for LSD and phenylisopropylamine hallucinogens. *Psychopharmacology Berlin, 94*, 213–216.

Tononi, G. (2004). An information integration theory of consciousness. *BMC Neuroscience, 5*, 42.

Torda, C. (1968). Contribution to serotonin theory of dreaming (LSD infusion). *New York State Journal of Medicine, 68*, 1135–1138.

Vollenweider, F. X., & Geyer, M. A. (2001). A systems model of altered consciousness: Integrating natural and drug-induced psychoses. *Brain Research Bulletin, 56*, 495–507.

Vollenweider, F. X., Leenders, K. L., Scharfetter, C., Maguire, P., Stadelmann, O., & Angst, J. (1997). Positron emission tomography and fluorodeoxyglucose studies of metabolic hyperfrontality and psychopathology in the psilocybin model of psychosis. *Neuropsychopharmacology, 16*, 357–372.

Vollenweider, F. X., Vollenweider-Scherpenhuyzen, M. F., Babler, A., Vogel, H., & Hell, D. (1998). Psilocybin induces schizophrenia-like psychosis in humans via a serotonin-2 agonist action. *NeuroReport, 9*, 3897–3902.

Wasson, R. G. (1957). Seeking the magic mushroom teonanacatl. *Life, 42*, 100–120.

Wasson, R. G. (1968). *Soma: Divine mushroom of immortality.* New York: Harcourt Brace Jovanovich.

Wasson, R. G. (1978). The hallucinogenic fungi of Mexico: An inquiry into the origins of the religious idea among primitive peoples. In J. Ott & J. Bigwood (Eds.), *Teonanacatl hallucinogenic mushrooms of North America* (pp. 65–84). Seattle: Madrona.

Wasson, R. G., Hofmann, A., & Ruck, C. A. P. (1978). *The road to Eleusis: Unveiling the secret of the mysteries.* New York: Harcourt Brace Jovanovich.

CHAPTER 2

THE RELATIONSHIP BETWEEN RELIGION AND HEALTH

Andrew B. Newberg and Bruce Y. Lee

INTRODUCTION

The relationship between religion and health care has cycled between cooperation and antagonism throughout history. Some of the most advanced civilizations of ancient times (such as the Assyrians, Chinese, Egyptians, Mesopotamians, and Persians) attributed physical illnesses to evil spirits and demonic possessions, and treatment was aimed at banishing these spirits. Since then, physicians and other health care providers have been viewed by religious groups as everything from evil sorcerers to conduits of God's healing powers. Conversely, religion, from the perspective of physicians, scientists, and health care providers, has been viewed with interest, disinterest, and disdain.

In recent years, there has been a growing interest in understanding the effects of religion on health among the medical and scientific communities (Levin, 1996). Popular news magazines such as *Time* and *Newsweek* and television shows have devoted substantial coverage to the interplay of religion and health (Alternative Medicine, 2001; Begley, 2001a, 2001b; Woodward, 2001). Many spiritual activities aimed at improving or maintaining health such as yoga have become very popular (Corliss, 2001). Moreover, studies have clearly shown that many patients consider religion to be very important and would like their physicians to discuss religious issues with them. We will review what is currently known about clinical effects of religious and spiritual practices, and the challenges that researchers and health care practitioners may face in designing appropriate studies and translating results to clinical practice. We also will discuss future directions in the roles of religion and spirituality in health care.

THE IMPORTANCE OF RELIGION AND SPIRITUALITY TO PATIENTS AND PHYSICIANS

Studies have confirmed that religion and spirituality play significant roles in many people's lives. Over 90 percent of Americans believe in God or a higher power, 90 percent pray, 67–75 percent pray on a daily basis, 69 percent are members of a church or synagogue, 40 percent attend a church or synagogue regularly, 60 percent consider religion to be very important in their lives, and 82 percent acknowledge a personal need for spiritual growth (Bezilla, 1993; Gallup Report, 1994; Miller & Thoresen, 2003; Poloma & Pendleton, 1991; Shuler, Gelberg, & Brown, 1994). Studies have also suggested that patients are interested in integrating religion with their health care. Over 75 percent of surveyed patients want physicians to include spiritual issues in their medical care, approximately 40 percent want physicians to discuss their religious faith with them, and nearly 50 percent would like physicians to pray with them (Daaleman & Nease, 1994; King & Bushwick, 1994; King, Hueston, & Rudy, 1994; Matthews & Clark, 1998). Many physicians agree that spiritual well-being is an important component of health and that it should be addressed with patients, but only a minority (less than 20%) do so with any regularity (MacLean et al., 2003; Monroe et al., 2003). When physicians have been surveyed, they frequently blamed lack of time, inadequate training, discomfort in addressing the topics, and difficulty in identifying patients who want to discuss spiritual issues for this discrepancy (Armbruster, Chibnall, & Legett, 2003; Chibnall & Brooks, 2001; Ellis, Vinson, & Ewigman, 1999).

Educators have responded by offering courses, conferences, and curricula in medical schools, postgraduate training, and continuing medical education (Pettus, 2002). However, some question the relevance and appropriateness of discussing religion and spirituality in the health care setting, fearing that it gives health care workers the opportunity to impose personal religious beliefs on others. In addition, there is concern that necessary medical interventions may be replaced by religious interventions. A number of scholars have cautioned that it could be harmful if patients come to believe that their illnesses are due to poor faith (Sloan, Bagiella, & Powell, 1999). Others have cautioned that religion should not be considered to be an intervention because it is to be pursued for spiritual, not health-related, purposes. Moreover, there is considerable debate over how religion should be integrated with health care and who should be responsible, especially when health care providers are agnostic or atheist (Levin, Larson, & Puchalski, 1997).

THE ROLE OF RELIGION IN HEALTH CARE

Despite this controversy, there are many signs that the role of religion in health care is increasing. For instance, the Diagnostic and Statistical Manual of Mental Disorders, Fourth Edition, recognizes religion and spirituality as relevant sources of either emotional distress or support (Kutz, 2002; Lukoff, Lu, & Turner, 1992; Turner, Lukoff, Barnhouse, & Lu, 1995). Also, the guidelines of the Joint Commission on Accreditation of Healthcare Organizations require hospitals to meet the spiritual needs of patients (La Pierre, 2003; Spiritual Assessment, 2003). The literature has reflected this trend as well. The frequency of studies on religion and spirituality and health has increased over the past decade (Levin et al., 1997). Stefanek and colleagues reported a 600 percent increase in spirituality and health publications and a 27 percent increase in religion and health publications from 1993 to 2002 (Stefanek, McDonald, & Hess, 2004).

Some have recommended that physicians and other health care providers routinely take religious and spiritual histories of their patients to better understand their patients' religious background, determine how they may be using religion to cope with illness, open the door for future discussions about spiritual or religious issues, and help detect potentially deleterious side effects from religious and spiritual activities (Kuhn, 1988; Lo, Quill, & Tulsky, 1999; Lo et al., 2002; Matthews & Clark, 1998). It may also be a way of detecting spiritual distress (Abrahm, 2001). It is also important to understand whether there are religious beliefs that may affect how a person makes decisions about his or her health care. There also has been greater emphasis on integrating various religious resources and professionals into patient care, especially when the patient is near the end of life (Lo et al., 2002). Some effort has been made to train health care providers to listen appropriately to patients' religious concerns, perform clergy-like duties when religious professionals are not available, and better understand spiritual practices (Morse & Proctor, 1998; Proctor, Morse, & Khonsari, 1996).

METHODOLOGICAL ISSUES
WITH CLINICAL STUDIES

The study of religion and health has faced the same challenges that most nascent research areas have had to confront: lacks of adequate funding, institutional support, and training for investigators. This is part of the reason why a large percentage of the literature consists of anecdotes and editorials, which are helpful in generating discussions, formulating ideas, and fueling future studies but do not establish causality or scientific support of specific interventions. Of the scientific studies that have been performed, many have been correlational and have demonstrated interesting associations, but they have not always adjusted for all possible confounding variables such as socioeconomic status, ethnicity, and different life-styles or diets and as a result have not clearly established causality. In some cases, religious variables were included in a larger study that did not focus on the effects of religion. Because these studies were not necessarily designed and powered to primarily study the religious variables, results must be considered cautiously. There have been a limited number of randomized controlled trials (RCTs). For example, in a systematic review of studies from 1966 to 1999, Townsend and colleagues counted nine RCTs. But as the study of religion and health progresses, the number and sophistication of scientific studies should continue to grow.

There also are challenges inherent in the clinical study of religion. Understanding these challenges is crucial in designing appropriate studies and interpreting the results. Otherwise, inappropriate conclusions may be drawn, unnecessary and even dangerous interventions may be initiated, and further necessary research may be curtailed. Moreover, these challenges will help guide investigators in choosing areas needing further study. Several of these challenges are described below.

Defining Religion and Spirituality

Investigators have struggled to agree on formal definitions of religion and spirituality, two distinct and yet overlapping terms that have often been mistakenly used synonymously (Powell, Shahabi, & Thoresen, 2003; Tanyi, 2002). Even if universal definitions were established, which specific practices would be classified as either or neither? For example, where does one draw the line between religions and cults? In fact, the Merriam Webster dictionary defines a cult as "a religion regarded as unorthodox or spurious." What, then, is the criterion for being unorthodox and spurious? In fact, as history has often demonstrated, what formerly was considered a cult and spurious can eventually become a major religion, and vice versa.

Designing Studies with Sufficient Numbers of Subjects and Adequate Controls

It is difficult to control for the many possible confounders, as well as recruit and randomize subjects, because they may not be willing or able to alter their religious beliefs and practices for the study. In other words, one cannot simply take 100 religious individuals and assign half to maintain their religious practices and half to not maintain their religious practices. No one would be willing to participate. Since prayer and other religious activities can be private, silent, or disguised as social interactions, investigators may have trouble monitoring and ensuring that subjects comply with study requirements. Inadvertent noncompliance can easily occur, as patients may be influenced by visitors or their environment.

Measuring Religiousness and Spirituality

Religiousness can be measured in many different dimensions, and patients who score high in one dimension may not necessarily score high in others. For example, just because an individual feels that he or she is very religious (high *subjective religiosity*) does not mean he or she would score high on more objective measures (low *religious commitment/motivation*). An individual may not participate significantly in formal church, synagogue, or temple activities (low *organizational religiosity*) but may regularly perform private religious activities such as praying, reading religious scriptures, and watching religious television (high *nonorganizational religiosity*). A number of other potential measures exist, including how closely an individual's beliefs conform to the established doctrines of a religious body (*religious belief*), how knowledgeable or informed an individual is about his or her religion's doctrines (*religious knowledge*), and how well his or her actions, such as working for the church and acts of altruism, support his or her religion (*religious consequences*). Studies should always clearly state the exact measures used and avoid making claims about measures not used.

Determining Reliability and Validity of Measures

Some measures of religiousness may be determined by direct observation. For example, organizational religiosity can be established by noting over a period of time the frequency of church attendance, reading religious scriptures, and prayer. Measuring such activities can be challenging because quantity and quality might be difficult to differentiate. Subtle religious displays may be missed. Moreover, it is unclear how each activity should be counted. Is reading scriptures every day for one hour equivalent to reading scriptures five days a week for four hours? To establish a true cause-and-effect relationship, it would be helpful to determine whether increased religiosity corresponds to better health. Many studies simply divide patients into dichotomous groups (e.g., church membership or nonmembership), which does not account for significant variation within each of the two groups. Should certain religious activities be considered more important than others? Someone who does not belong to a church but regularly prays and follows religious doctrine may, in fact, have greater religious commitment than a person who belongs to a church but does not believe in or care to comprehend religious doctrine.

When direct observation is not possible, investigators must rely on self-report questionnaires or interviews. Therefore, the quality of the data depends on the quality of the instrument, and, unfortunately, many studies do not indicate whether and how their questionnaires or interviews were validated. Even well-validated instruments may be susceptible to a number of potential biases. For instance, patients may forget or be unwilling to admit lapses in religiousness.

Many existing measures are based on Western perspectives of religion and may not be applicable to traditions such as Buddhism or Hinduism.

Accounting for the Positive Externalities of Religion

Religion can provide many "positive externalities" that are potentially beneficial to health. Church groups can provide a social support network, and church activities may offer exercise and reprieves from unhealthy environments. People can meet future spouses, physicians, and other health care workers through church. Religious activities can offer retreats that take individuals away from daily stressors and provide time for reflection. Many religious doctrines suggest that participants observe specific dietary habits and avoid promiscuity, alcohol, and other high risk behaviors. Thus, when a study shows a positive effect of religion, it is not always clear what is responsible for the effect.

Determining the Direction of Causality

Is a patient's religious activity causing the observed effects on his or her health, or is the patient's health status affecting his or her religious activity? If an association is seen in a study, it may not be clear which side is the cause. In some cases, poor health can prevent or discourage patients from participating in religious and spiritual activities. In other cases, serious health problems may motivate patients to attend religious activities. Perhaps more importantly, health outcomes should never be tied to religion or spirituality. A person should not feel that health is related only to his or her religious behaviors, and religions should not be evaluated based on their potential for health benefits.

Accounting for Variations in Practices and Doctrines among and within Different Religions

Practices and doctrines vary significantly both within and across traditions. For example, prayers may be silent or vocal. Behaviors connoting minimum levels of religious commitment differ from one religion to another. For example, what may be proper dress in one denomination may be evidence of inadequate religious commitment in more orthodox denominations. A person's sense of well-being may depend on the degree of hierarchy in a religion and his or her place in that hierarchy. Moreover, a person's socioeconomic status, gender, and ethnicity can affect his or her acceptance by a given religious group.

Evaluating Effects of the Local Environment

Different religions hold different social statuses in different countries during different times. Practically all religions have been persecuted and deprived of resources at some time and place during history. Members of the dominant religion in a society may be more accepted, enjoy a stronger and more extensive social network, and have greater access to resources. All of these can have subtle psychological and physical consequences. In some severe cases, physical punishment may be inflicted on minority religious sects. Moreover, minority or fringe religious sects who are unable to convince mainstream individuals to join their cause may have to recruit among societal outcasts, many of whom could have psychological or physical illness. Therefore, any study of a specific religious sect should account for the location of the study group and the sect's relationship with the ambient society.

Determining the Proper Time Frame for the Study

How long should individuals or populations be observed before effects are expected to occur? Some spiritual activities such as prayer, yoga, and meditation have been found to have immediate effects on physical parameters such as heart rate and blood pressure. But these practices can also have long-term consequences that lead a person's spiritual journey. Furthermore, some religious experiences last for several moments and affect a person over a lifetime, and some experiences require a lifetime to occur. Therefore, studies that observe subjects over only a short period of time may miss findings. However, the longer the follow-up, the more costly and difficult the study is to perform, and the greater the chance that more confounders will enter the picture.

Bridging the Divide between Health Researchers and Religion Researchers

While interdisciplinary fields have the benefits of bringing together people with diverse interests, experiences, perspectives, and abilities, they also must confront communication hurdles. Health researchers and religion researchers often are not familiar with important publications in each others' specialty journals. Separate meetings, separate departments, different methodologies, and different lexicons have hindered collaboration. However, the emergence of interdisciplinary journals and conferences has begun to alleviate this problem.

THE POSITIVE EFFECTS OF RELIGION ON HEALTH

Disease Incidence and Prevalence

Various systematic reviews and meta-analyses demonstrate that religious involvement correlates with decreased morbidity and mortality (Ball, Armstead, & Austin, 2003; Braam, Beekman, Deeg, Smit, & Van Tilburg, 1999;

Brown, 2000; Kark, Carmel, Sinnreich, Goldberger, & Friedlander, 1996; Kune, Kune, & Watson, 1993; McCullough, Hoyt, Larson, Koenig, & Thoresen, 2000; McCullough & Larson, 1999; Oman, Kurata, Strawbridge, & Cohen, 2002), and high levels of religious involvement may be associated with up to seven years of longer life expectancy (Helm, Hays, Flint, Koenig, & Blazer, 2000; Hummer, Rogers, Nam, & Ellison, 1999; Koenig et al., 1999; Oman & Reed, 1998; Strawbridge, Cohen, Shema, & Kaplan, 1997). A study by Kark and colleagues over a 16-year period found that belonging to a religious collective in Israel was associated with lower mortality (Kark et al., 1996). In Comstock and Partridge's analysis of 91,000 people in a Maryland county, those who regularly attended church had a lower prevalence of cirrhosis, emphysema, suicide, and death from ischemic heart disease (Comstock & Partridge, 1972). Several studies have implied that religious participation and higher religiosity may have a beneficial effect on blood pressure (Armstrong, Van Merwyk, & Coates, 1977; Hixson, Gruchow, & Morgan, 1998; Koenig et al., 1998b; Walsh, 1998).

Some research findings have suggested that mortality and morbidity vary by religion, even when adjusting for major biological, behavioral, and socioeconomic differences (Rasanen, Kauhansen, Lakka, Kaplan, & Salonen, 1996; Van Poppel, Schellekens, & Liefbroer, 2002). However, as mentioned previously, the experience of individuals within a given religion can depend significantly on the local environment, so the results of such comparisons should be viewed guardedly. For instance, a study of contemplative monks in the Netherlands showed that their mortality compared with the general population varied with time during the 1900s (de Gouw, Westendorp, Kunst, Mackenbachh, & Vandenbroucke, 1995). Greater morbidity and mortality have been reported among Irish Catholics in Britain, which may be related to their disadvantaged socioeconomic status in that country (Abbotts, Williams, & Ford, 2001; Abbotts, Williams, Ford, Hunt, & West, 1997). A study in Holland suggested that smaller religious groups may be less susceptible to infectious disease because of social isolation (Van Poppel et al., 2002). In general, not enough studies have examined how mortality and morbidity for different religions vary over time and place. Moreover, many religions and religious sects have received little attention from investigators. Consequently, the body of literature comparing morbidity and mortality rates among religions is not large enough to draw any definitive conclusions. However, the results to date suggest that, under the right circumstances, religion can have a beneficial impact on health.

Disease and Surgical Outcomes

Studies also have reported that religiousness correlates with better outcomes after major illnesses and certain medical procedures. In Oxman and colleagues' analysis of 232 patients following elective open heart surgery, lack of participation in social or community groups and absence of strength and comfort from religion were consistent predictors of mortality (Oxman, Freeman, & Manheimer, 1995). Another study evaluated 30 elderly women after hip repair and found that religious belief was associated with lower levels of depressive symptoms and better ambulation status after surgery (Pressman, Lyons, Larson, & Strain, 1990). Contrada and colleagues found that in patients who underwent heart surgery, stronger religious beliefs were associated with shorter hospital stays and fewer complications, but attendance at religious services predicted longer hospitalizations (Contrada et al., 2004). On the other hand, Hodges and colleagues did not find spiritual beliefs to significantly affect recovery from spinal surgery (Hodges, Humphreys, & Eck, 2002).

Research has studied whether religiosity improves the survival of patients with different illnesses as well. In a study of African American women with breast cancer, patients who did not belong to a religion tended to have shorter survival rates (Van Ness, Kasl, & Jones, 2003). In a study by Zollinger and colleagues, Seventh Day Adventists had better breast cancer survival than non–Seventh Day Adventists, but this was likely due to earlier diagnosis and treatment (Zollinger, Phillips, & Kuzma, 1984). Several other studies of various cancers including colorectal, lung, and breast cancer showed no statistically significant effect of religious involvement on cancer survival (Kune, Kune, & Watson, 1992; Loprinzi et al., 1994; Ringdal, Gotestam, Kaasa, Kvinnsland, & Ringdal, 1996; Yates, Chalmer, St. James, Follansbee, & McKegney, 1981).

Behavior and Life-styles

Life-style differences may account for some of the observed effects in research on religion and health. Studies in Israel showed that secular residents had diets higher in total fat and saturated fatty acids (Friedlander, Kark, Kaufmann, & Stein, 1985) and higher plasma levels of cholesterol, triglyceride, and low-density lipoprotein (Friedlander, Kark, & Stein, 1987) than religious subjects. Oleckno and Blacconiere's study on college students revealed an inverse correlation between religiosity and behaviors that adversely affect health (Oleckno & Blacconiere, 1991). Religious involvement has been shown to be associated with greater use of seat belts (Oleckno & Blacconiere, 1991) and preventative services (Comstock & Partridge, 1972). Compared to the general population, Mormons and Seventh Day Adventists have been found to have a lower incidence of and mortality rates for cancers linked to tobacco and alcohol (Fraser, 1999; Grundmann, 1992).

Religion can affect alcohol and substance use at several stages. It may affect whether a person initiates use, how significant the use becomes, how the use affects the person's life, and whether the person is able to quit and recover (Miller, 1998). The attitudes of religions toward alcohol and substance use vary considerably. Some religious sects strictly prohibit alcohol and substance use, some allow the use of alcohol and incorporate drinking wine into their rituals, and others use psychoactive substances such as peyote, khat, and hashish to achieve spiritual goals (Lyttle, 1988). Most investigators study Judeo-Christian religious sects, which may allow the use of alcohol but tend to denounce alcohol abuse and illicit substance use. Therefore, conclusions from these studies may not apply to all religions.

Individuals involved in religion may be less likely to use alcohol and other substances (Heath et al., 1999; Luczak, Shea, Carr, Li, & Wall, 2002; Stewart, 2001). Even among those who use alcohol and drugs, religiously involved individuals are more likely to use them moderately and not heavily (Gorsuch & Butler, 1976; Miller, 1998). In a nationally representative sample of adolescents, Miller and colleagues determined that personal devotion (which they defined as a personal relationship with the divine) and affiliation with more fundamentalist denominations were inversely associated with alcohol and illicit drug use (Miller, Davies, & Greenwald, 2000). This effect was seen outside the United States as well, in Latin American regions (Chen, Dormitzer, Bejarano, & Anthony, 2004). A number of possible reasons exist for these findings. Religions can play a role in educating people about the dangers of alcohol and drugs and recommending against their use (Stylianou, 2004). Fear of violating religious principles and doctrines can have a powerful effect. Religious involvement and the accompanying positive externalities may keep people occupied and prevent idleness and boredom that can lead to substance abuse. There may be peer pressure from other members of the church to remain abstinent, and an absence of peer pressure to try alcohol and other substances. Moreover, religious involvement could be the effect rather than the cause. It may be that individuals less likely to engage in substance abuse are inherently more likely to be religious. Also, substance abuse may prevent religious involvement. Larson and Wilson noted that alcoholics compared to nonalcoholic subjects had less involvement in religious practices, less exposure to religious teachings, and fewer religious experiences (Larson & Wilson, 1980).

Many clinicians and researchers, as well as patients, feel that spirituality should play a large role in cessation programs (Arnold, Avants, Margolin, & Marcotte, 2002; Dermatis, Guschwan, Galanter, & Bunt, 2004). Indeed, spiritual ideas already permeate many established programs such as Alcoholics Anonymous (Brush & McGee, 2000; Forcehimes, 2004; Li, Feifer, & Strohm, 2000; Moriarity, 2001). Studies have suggested that religious and spiritual practices may aid recovery (Aron & Aron, 1980; Avants, Warburton, & Margolin, 2001; Carter, 1998). A significant number of recovering intravenous drug abusers turn toward religious healing, relaxation techniques, and meditation (Manheimer, Anderson, & Stein, 2003). Data suggest that patients often experience spiritual awakenings or religious conversion during recovery (Green, Fullilove, & Fullilove, 1998). However, not all studies have shown that religiously involved patients have better outcomes. The first RCTs failed to demonstrate sufficient clinical benefit from meditation (Murphy, Pagano, & Marlatt, 1986) or intercessory prayer (Walker, Tonigan, Miller, Corner, & Kahlich, 1997). In a study by Tonigan and colleagues, while subjects self-labeled as religious were more likely than agnostics and atheists to initiate and continue attending Alcoholics Anonymous meetings, their outcomes were not clearly better (Tonigan, Miller, & Schermer, 2002).

Religion may play a role in preventing risky sexual behavior that could potentially lead to sexually transmitted diseases and human immunodeficiency virus (HIV). In a study of African American adolescent females, religiosity correlated with more frank discussions about the risks of sex and avoidance of unsafe sexual situations (McCree, Wingood, DiClemente, Davies, & Harrington, 2003). Miller and Gur's study of over 3,000 adolescent girls found positive associations between personal devotion and fewer sexual partners outside a romantic relationship, religious event attendance and proper birth control use, and religious attendance and a better understanding of HIV or pregnancy risks from unprotected intercourse (Miller & Gur, 2002). But these findings are not universal. Some have found no relationship between religiosity and sexual practices (Dunne, Edwards, Lucke, Donald, & Raphael, 1994; McCormick, Izzo, & Folcik, 1985). In fact, religious traditions or environments may suppress open discussion of sex and contraception. Lefkowitz and colleagues found that adolescents who discussed safe sex with their mothers tended to be less religious (Lefkowitz, Boone, Au, & Sigman, 2003).

Some studies have looked at how religion and spirituality can promote exercise. Among Utah residents, people who attended church weekly were more likely to regularly exercise. However, differences in smoking and general health status seemed to account for this effect (Merrill & Thygerson, 2001). A study by McLane and colleagues suggested that incorporating faith-based practices in exercise programs may be attractive to certain people and improve participation in physical activity (McLane, Lox, Butki, & Stern, 2003).

Access to Health Care Resources

Along with encouraging healthy life-styles, religious groups may promote or provide access to better health care and sponsor health improvement programs (e.g., blood pressure screening, blood drives, soup kitchens, and food drives) (Heath et al., 1999; Koenig et al., 1998a; Stewart, 2001; Zaleski & Schiaffino, 2000). Groups such as the Catholic Church have substantial resources and positions that allow them to positively influence people in ways that many secular organizations cannot. Additionally, many hospitals and health care clinics are supported by, affiliated with, or owned by religious groups.

General Well-Being

A large number of studies have explored the relationship between religion and mental health. Studies have demonstrated religiosity to be positively associated with feelings of well-being in white American, Mexican American (Markides, Levin, & Ray, 1987), and African American populations (Coke, 1992). Krause (2003) observed that older African Americans were more likely than similarly aged white Americans to derive life satisfaction from religion. Religious service attendance was predictive of higher life satisfaction among elderly Chinese Hong Kong residents (Ho et al., 1995) and elderly Mexican American women (Levin & Markides, 1988). Members of religious kibutzes in Israel reported a higher sense of coherence and less hostility and were more likely to engage in volunteer work than nonmembers (Kark et al., 1996). Similar findings were reported in a population of nursing home residents (House, Robbins, & Metzner, 1982). Hope and optimism were higher among religious individuals than nonreligious individuals in some study populations (Idler & Kasl, 1997a, 1997b; Raleigh, 1992). Using religious attendance as one of the markers of social engagement, Bassuk and colleagues determined that social disengagement was linked with cognitive decline in the noninstitutionalized elderly (Bassuk, Glass, & Berkman, 1999).

A few studies have compared different religions. For example, one study showed that among elderly women in Hong Kong, Catholics and Buddhists enjoyed better mental health status than Protestants (Boey, 2003). However, not enough data exist to generate any definitive conclusions.

Depression

Several investigators have studied the effects of religion on depression. Prospective cohort studies have shown religious activity to be associated with remission of depression in Protestants and Catholics in the Netherlands (Braam et al., 1999) and in ill older adults (Koenig, George, & Peterson, 1998). Prospective studies have also found religious activity to be strongly protective against depression in Protestant and Catholic offspring who share the same religion as their mother (Miller, Warner, Wickramaratne, & Weissman, 1997) and weakly protective against depression in female twins (Kennedy, Kelman, Thomas, & Chen, 1996). Cross-sectional studies have yielded significant (Koenig et al., 1997) and nonsignificant (Bienenfeld, Koenig, Larson, & Sherrill, 1997; Koenig, 1998; Musick, Koenig, Hays, & Cohen, 1998) associations between different indicators of religiosity and a lower prevalence of depression in various populations.

Studies also have suggested an inverse correlation between religiosity and suicide. This was found to be the case in an analysis of the 1993 National Mortality Followback Survey data (Nisbet, Duberstein, Conwell, & Seidlitz, 2000) and also in an analysis of cross-sectional data of Judeo-Christian older adults from 26 countries (Neeleman & Lewis, 1999). Suicide may be less acceptable to people with high religious devotion and orthodox religious beliefs (Neeleman, Halpern, Leon, & Lewis, 1997; Neeleman, Wessely, & Lewis, 1998). But again, it is unclear whether suicidal individuals are less likely to hold strong religious beliefs, or individuals with strong religious beliefs are less likely to be suicidal.

Several RCTs have evaluated specific spiritual interventions and their impact on depression. One RCT demonstrated that directed and nondirected intercessory prayer correlated favorably with multiple measures of self-esteem, anxiety, and depression, but this study did not clearly state the randomization technique and did not account for multiple confounders (O'Laoire, 1997). Another RCT suggested that using religion-based cognitive therapy had a favorable impact on Christian patients with clinical depression, but the study may have contained too many comparison groups for strong cause-and-effect relationships to be established (Propst, Ostrom, Watkins, Dean, & Mashburn, 1992). Three RCTs suggest that religious (Islamic-based) psychotherapy speeds recovery from anxiety and depression in Muslim Malays, but the studies did not control for the use of antidepressants and benzodiazepines (Azhar & Varma, 1995; Azhar, Varma, & Dharap, 1994; Razali, Hasanah, Aminah, & Subramaniam, 1998). Thus, additional studies will be required to better elucidate the effects of spiritual practices on depression.

Coping with Medical Problems

Religious belief may provide meaning to and, in turn, help patients better cope with their diseases (Autiero, 1987; Foley, 1988; Patel, Shah, Peterson, & Kimmel, 2002). Although many major religions have deemed illness and suffering the result of sin, many believe that pain and suffering can be strengthening, enlightening, and purifying. According to various religious teachings, pain and suffering are inevitable and can be cleansing, test virtue, educate, readjust priorities, stimulate personal growth, and define human life (Amundsen, 1982).

Religions differ in how they confront suffering. Although generalizations are difficult to draw because considerable variability exists within and across religious traditions, many Buddhists believe in enduring pain matter-of-factly (Tu, 1980), many Hindus stress understanding and detachment from pain

(Shaffer, 1978), many Muslims and Jews favor resisting or fighting pain (Bowker, 1978), and many Christians stress seeking atonement and redemption (Amundsen, 1982).

Evidence suggests that religion provides more than just a distraction from suffering. The *diverting attention* and *praying* factors on the Coping Strategies Questionnaire have correlated with pain levels (Geisser, Robinson, & Henson, 1994; Swartzman, Gwadry, Shapiro, & Teasell, 1994; Swimmer, Robinson, & Geisser, 1992). The social network and support provided by religions may be associated with lower pain levels, and religious belief may improve self-esteem and sense of purpose (Hays et al., 1998; Musick et al., 1998; Swimmer et al., 1992). After following 720 adults, Williams and colleagues concluded that religious attendance buffered the effects of stress on mental health (Williams, Larson, Buckler, Heckmann, & Pyle, 1991). In another study of 107 women with advanced breast cancer, spirituality appeared to improve emotional well-being (Coward, 1991). Thus, religion and spirituality can provide important avenues toward coping.

THE NEGATIVE EFFECTS OF RELIGION ON HEALTH

Although most studies have shown positive effects, religion and spirituality also may negatively impact health. For example, religious groups may directly oppose certain health care interventions, such as transfusions or contraception, and convince patients that their ailments are due to noncompliance with religious doctrines rather than organic disease (Donahue, 1985). Asser and colleagues demonstrated that a large number of child fatalities could have been prevented had medical care not been withheld for religious reasons (Asser & Swan, 1998). After interviewing 682 North Carolina women, Mitchell and colleagues concluded that belief in religious interventions may delay African American women from seeing their physicians for breast lumps (Mitchell, Lannin, Mathews, & Swanson, 2002). In addition, religions can stigmatize those with certain diseases to the point that they do not seek proper medical care (Lichtenstein, 2003; Madru, 2003).

As history has shown, religion can be the source of military conflicts, prejudice, violent behaviors, and other social problems. Religions may ignore or ostracize those who do not belong to their church. Those not belonging to a dominant religion may face obstacles to obtaining resources and may experience hardships and stress that deleteriously affect their health (Bywaters, Ali, Fazil, Wallace, & Singh, 2003; Walls & Williams, 2004). Religious leaders may abuse church members physically, emotionally, or sexually (Rossetti, 1995; Tieman, 2002). And religious laws or dictums may be invoked to justify harmful, oppressive, and injurious behavior (Kernberg, 2003).

Additionally, perceived religious transgressions can cause emotional and psychological anguish, manifesting as physical discomfort. This religious or spiritual pain can be difficult to distinguish from physical pain (Satterly, 2001). In extreme cases, spiritual abuse (convincing people that they are going to suffer eternal purgatory) and spiritual terrorism (an extreme form of spiritual abuse) can occur either overtly or insidiously—that is, it can be implied, though not actually stated, that a patient will be doomed (Purcell, 1998a, 1998b). When a mix of religious, spiritual, and organic sources is causing physical illness, treatment can become complicated. Health care workers must properly balance treating each source.

THE EFFECTS OF SPECIFIC RELIGIOUS AND SPIRITUAL PRACTICES

Religious and spiritual practices have become highly prevalent and may be practiced in either religious or secular settings. Although many of these activities have been correctly or incorrectly linked to specific religions, practicing them does not necessarily connote certain beliefs. In fact, hundreds of variations of each spiritual activity exist, because many have been altered and combined with other nonreligious activities such as aerobics to develop hybrid techniques. As a result, some forms barely resemble the original versions. Thus, investigators must be very specific in describing the technique or activity that they are examining. Results from one form of meditation or yoga may not apply to other forms. A review of the literature shows that many studies do not clearly describe the form of spiritual activity under investigation.

Prayer

In Eisenberg and colleagues' survey of alternative medicine usage among Americans, one-fourth of respondents used prayer to cope with physical illness (Eisenberg et al., 1998). Evidence has been found that prayer may be associated with less muscle tension, improved cardiovascular and neuroimmunologic parameters, psychologic and spiritual peace, a greater sense of purpose, enhanced coping skills, less disability, and better physical function in patients with knee pain (Rapp, Rejeski, & Miller, 2000) and a lower incidence of coronary heart disease (Gupta, 1996; Gupta, Prakash, Gupta, & Gupta, 1997).

Poloma and Pendleton (1991) found that petitionary and ritualistic prayers were associated with lower levels of well-being and life satisfaction, while colloquial prayers were associated with higher levels. Leibovici (2001) reported on a double-blind RCT that showed remote, retroactive intercessory prayer was associated with shorter length of fever and hospital stay in patients with bloodstream infection. A very small, double-blind study showed that intercessory prayer used as adjunct therapy decreased mortality among children with leukemia (Collipp, 1969). In Byrd and colleagues' well-known double-blind study of patients admitted to a coronary care unit, intercessory prayer was linked to significantly more "good" outcomes (163 versus 147) than "bad" outcomes (27 versus 44) (Byrd, 1988). Harris and colleagues (1999) found similar outcomes with remote intercessory prayer. However, subsequent studies were not able to replicate these findings (Aviles et al., 2001; Matthews, Conti, & Sireci, 2001; Matthews, Marlowe, & MacNutt, 2000; Townsend, Kladder, Ayele, & Mulligan, 2002). Another issue arises in the interpretation of such studies. If prayer does work, does it prove that God exists; and if prayer does not work, does it prove that God does not exist? Perhaps these studies are evaluating something other than religion, such as the effects of human consciousness. Regardless, the effect of such distant prayer or distant intentionality is controversial.

Meditation

Meditation and meditation-related practices are widely used as alternative therapy for physical ailments (Eisenberg et al., 1998). Many physicians routinely recommend meditation techniques to their patients and include them as part of integrated health programs such as Dean Ornish's popular heart disease programs and a Stanford arthritis self-care course. Meditative and relaxation techniques are often part of childbirth preparation classes.

Although evidence is not yet definitive, preliminary studies suggest that meditation may have a number of health benefits, such as helping people achieve a state of restful alertness with improved reaction time, creativity, and comprehension (Domino, 1977; Solberg, Berglund, Engen, Ekeberg, & Loeb, 1996) and decreasing anxiety, depression, irritability, and moodiness and improving learning ability, memory, self-actualization, feelings of vitality and rejuvenation, and emotional stability (Astin, 1997; Astin et al., 2003; Bitner, Hillman, Victor, & Walsh, 2003; Solberg et al., 1996; Walton, Pugh, Gelderloos, & Macrae, 1995). Preliminary studies suggest that meditative practices may benefit and provide acute and chronic support for patients with a variety of health problems such as hypertension, psoriasis, irritable bowel disease, anxiety, and depression (Barrows & Jacobs, 2002; Carlson, Ursuliak, Goodey, Angen, & Speca, 2001; Castillo-Richmond et al., 2000; Kabat-Zinn et al., 1992; Kabat-Zinn et al., 1998; Kaplan, Goldenberg, & Galvin-Nadeau, 1993; Keefer & Blanchard, 2002; King, Carr, & D'Cruz, 2002; Manocha, Marks, Kenchington, Peters, & Salome, 2002; Reibel, Greeson, Brainard, & Rosenzweig, 2001; Williams, Kolar, Reger, & Pearson, 2001). Evidence also exists that meditation can improve chronic pain (Kabat-Zinn, 1982; Kabat-Zinn, Lipworth, & Burney, 1985). In a study by Kaplan and colleagues, all 77 men and women with fibromyalgia who completed a 10-week stress-reduction program using meditation had symptom improvement (Kaplan et al., 1993). Moreover, in several studies, meditators had better respiratory function (vital capacity, tidal volume, expiratory pressure, and breath holding), cardiovascular parameters (diastolic blood pressure and heart rate), and lipid profiles than nonmeditators (Cooper & Aygen, 1979; Wallace, Silver, Mills, Dillbeck, & Wagoner, 1983; Wenneberg et al., 1997).

Unfortunately, many studies did not specify or describe the type of meditation used. A wide variety of methods may be used, including some in which the body is immobile (e.g., Zazen, Vipassana), others in which the body is let free (e.g., Siddha yoga, the Latihan, the chaotic meditation of Rajneesh), and still others in which the person participates in daily activities while meditating (e.g., Mahamudra, Shikan Taza, Gurdjieff's "self-remembering"). So it is not clear which forms may be beneficial and what aspects of meditation are providing the benefits.

Although physically noninvasive, meditation can be harmful in patients with psychiatric illness, potentially aggravating and precipitating psychotic episodes in delusional or strongly paranoid patients and heightening anxiety in patients with overwhelming anxiety. Moreover, it can trigger the release of repressed memories. Therefore, all patients using meditative techniques should be monitored, especially when beginning to use meditation.

Yoga

Contrary to popular misconception, yoga predates Hinduism by several centuries, and, as the American Yoga Association emphasizes, because yoga practice does not specify particular higher powers or religious doctrines, it can be compatible with all major religions. In fact, many religions, including many Christian denominations, have adopted yoga techniques. Yoga is also widely used by the general public, often for regular exercise.

Yoga is based on a set of theories that have not been scientifically proven. Yoga practitioners believe that blockages or shortages of the life force can cause disease or decreased resistance to disease and that yoga can restore the flow of the life force to different parts of the body. They use a series of stretching, breathing, and relaxation techniques to prepare for meditation and use stretching movements or postures (*asanas*) that aim to increase blood supply and *prana* (vital force) as well as increase the flexibility of the spine, which is thought to improve the nerve supply. Yoga practices also incorporate breathing techniques (*pranayamas*) to improve brain function, eliminate toxins, and restore energy reserves in the solar plexus region.

The few limited clinical studies on yoga have been encouraging, showing reduced serum total cholesterol, low-density lipids, and triglyceride levels and improved pulmonary function tests in yoga practitioners (Arambula, Peper, Kawakami, & Gibney, 2001; Birkel & Edgren, 2000; Schell, Allolio, &

Schonecke, 1994; Selvamurthy et al., 1998; Stancak, Kuna, Srinivasan, Dostalek, & Vishnudevananda, 1991; Stanescu, Nemery, Veriter, & Marechal, 1981; Udupa, Singh, & Yadav, 1973). Studies have also suggested that yoga may be associated with acute and long-term decreases in blood pressure (Murugesan, Govindarajulu, & Bera, 2000; Sundar et al., 1984) and may benefit patients with asthma, hypertension, heart failure, mood disorders, and diabetes (Jain, Uppal, Bhatnagar, & Talukdar, 1993; Malhotra, Singh, Singh, et al., 2002; Malhotra, Singe, Tandon, et al., 2002; Manocha et al., 2002; van Montfrans, Karemaker, Wieling, & Dunning, 1990). Two small controlled but non–double-blind studies showed Hatha yoga to significantly alleviate pain in osteoarthritis of the fingers and in carpal tunnel syndrome (Garfinkel, Schumacher, Husain, Levy, & Reshetar, 1994; Garfinkel et al., 1998). However, yoga is not completely benign, because certain *asanas* may be strenuous and cause injury. In fact, yoga practitioners believe some *asanas* can cause disease.

More studies are needed to determine the benefits (and potential dangers) of yoga. Like meditation, many forms of yoga have emerged. Some involve significant aerobic exercise. Others involve significant strength and conditioning work. Many yoga practices include changes in diet and life-styles. Thus, it is difficult to distinguish between yoga and other practices that have established health benefits such as exercise. Therefore, future studies should focus on specific yoga forms and movements and avoid making general conclusions about all yoga practices.

Faith Healing

Faith healers use prayer or other religious practices to combat disease. Surveys have found that a substantial number of patients in rural (21%) and inner-city (10%) populations have used faith healers, and many physicians (23%) believe that faith healers can heal patients (McKee & Chappel, 1992). Despite numerous anecdotes of healing miracles, no consistent and convincing scientific proof has been reported that faith healers are effective (King & Bushwick, 1994). Additionally, it has not been determined whether faith healers affect patients psychologically or physiologically and what factors may make them effective. Conclusions cannot be drawn until further research is performed.

CONCLUSIONS AND FUTURE DIRECTIONS

In general, clinical studies of religion and spirituality on health are fraught with challenges. Designing studies that are able to establish cause-and-effect relationships is difficult. This is especially true in the study of religion and health, where many confounding factors abound. However, there is evidence that religion can provide health benefits. It is clear that religion can bring social and emotional support, motivation, healthy life-styles, and health care resources. Clinical studies are valuable in identifying possible associations, raising further questions, and guiding subsequent research. Clinical studies can also confirm possible cause-and-effect relationships elucidated by physiologic studies.

There are a number of future directions for research. Many of the accompanying and confounding factors need to be isolated to determine their relative roles. The clinical impact of findings from physiologic studies needs further investigation. Many diseases have not been studied. Many religious groups and sects have not been included in the early studies, and hence a broader impact of religion and religious behaviors needs to be surveyed. The effect of varying demographic parameters such as age, gender, and location also deserves further inquiry. Moreover, religious and spiritual activities may serve as adjunct therapy in various disease and addiction treatment programs. In the future, additional specific spiritual interventions may prove beneficial.

The findings to date have clinical implications. Religion is clearly important to many patients, and their religious concerns may need to be better addressed in the health care setting. Health care providers must be aware of how religious involvement can affect symptoms, quality of life, and patients' willingness to receive treatment. Perhaps more importantly, health care providers need to better understand how to manage these issues and deal with patients in which such issues play a prominent role.

The study of religion and health, as well as the integration of religion into the health care setting, is likely to grow. At the same time, new ways of researching this discipline may emerge and provide a substantial challenge to existing scientific methodologies. Unless the relationship between religion and health care cycles back to antagonism, many exciting new findings and approaches may appear.

REFERENCES

Abbotts, J., Williams, R., & Ford, G. (2001). Morbidity and Irish Catholic descent in Britain: Relating health disadvantage to socio-economic position. *Social Science Medicine, 52*(7), 999–1005.

Abbotts, J., Williams, R., Ford, G., Hunt, K., & West, P. (1997). Morbidity and Irish Catholic descent in Britain: An ethnic and religious minority 150 years on. *Social Science Medicine, 45*(1), 3–14.

Abrahm, J. (2001). Pain management for dying patients. How to assess needs and provide pharmacologic relief. *Postgraduate Medicine, 110*(2), 99–100, 108–109, 113–104.

Alternative medicine: A new breed of healers. (2001). *Time, 157*(15), 62–65, 68–69.

Amundsen, D. W. (1982). Medicine and faith in early Christianity. *Bulletin of Historical Medicine, 56*(3), 326–350.

Arambula, P., Peper, E., Kawakami, M., & Gibney, K.H. (2001). The physiological correlates of Kundalini yoga meditation: A study of a yoga master. *Applied Psychophysiological Biofeedback, 26*(2), 147–153.

Armbruster, C.A., Chibnall, J.T., & Legett, S. (2003). Pediatrician beliefs about spirituality and religion in medicine: Associations with clinical practice. *Pediatrics, 111*(3), 227–235.

Armstrong, B., van Merwyk, A.J., & Coates, H. (1977). Blood pressure in Seventh-day Adventist vegetarians. *American Journal of Epidemiology, 105*(5), 444–449.

Arnold, R., Avants, S.K., Margolin, A., & Marcotte, D. (2002). Patient attitudes concerning the inclusion of spirituality into addiction treatment. *Journal of Substance Abuse Treatment, 23*(4), 319–326.

Aron, A., & Aron, E.N. (1980). The transcendental meditation program's effect on addictive behavior. *Addictive Behaviors, 5*(1), 3–12.

Asser, S.M., & Swan, R. (1998). Child fatalities from religion-motivated medical neglect. *Pediatrics, 101*(4 Pt. 1), 625–629.

Astin, J.A. (1997). Stress reduction through mindfulness meditation. Effects on psychological symptomatology, sense of control, and spiritual experiences. *Psychotherapy and Psychosomatics, 66*(2), 97–106.

Astin, J.A., Berman, B.M., Bausell, B., Lee, W.L., Hochberg, M., & Forys, K.L. (2003). The efficacy of mindfulness meditation plus Qigong movement therapy in the treatment of fibromyalgia: A randomized controlled trial. *Journal of Rheumatology, 30*(10), 2257–2262.

Autiero, A. (1987). The interpretation of pain: The point of view of Catholic theology. *Acta Neurochirurgica Supplementum, 38*, 123–126.

Avants, S.K., Warburton, L.A., & Margolin, A. (2001). Spiritual and religious support in recovery from addiction among HIV-positive injection drug users. *Journal of Psychoactive Drugs, 33*(1), 39–45.

Aviles, J.M., Whelan, S.E., Hernke, D.A., Williams, B.A., Kenny, K.E., O'Fallon, W.M., et al. (2001). Intercessory prayer and cardiovascular disease progression in a coronary care unit population: A randomized controlled trial. *Mayo Clinic Proceedings, 76*(12), 1192–1198.

Azhar, M.Z., & Varma, S.L. (1995). Religious psychotherapy in depressive patients. *Psychotherapy and Psychosomatics, 63*(3–4), 165–168.

Azhar, M.Z., Varma, S.L., & Dharap, A.S. (1994). Religious psychotherapy in anxiety disorder patients. *Acta Psychiatrica Scandanavia, 90*(1), 1–3.

Ball, J., Armistead, L., & Austin, B.J. (2003). The relationship between religiosity and adjustment among African-American, female, urban adolescents. *Journal of Adolescence, 26*(4), 431–446.

Barrows, K.A., & Jacobs, B.P. (2002). Mind-body medicine. An introduction and review of the literature. *Medical and Clinical North America, 86*(1), 11–31.

Bassuk, S.S., Glass, T.A., & Berkman, L.F. (1999). Social disengagement and incident cognitive decline in community-dwelling elderly persons. *Annals of International Medicine, 131*(3), 165–173.

Begley, S. (2001a). Religion and the brain. *Newsweek, 137*(19), 50–57.

Begley, S. (2001b). Searching for the God within. *Newsweek, 137*(5), 59.

Bezilla, R. (Ed.). (1993). *Religion in America, 1992–1993*. Princeton, NJ: Princeton Religious Center (Gallup Organization).

Bienenfeld, D., Koenig, H. G., Larson, D. B., & Sherrill, K. A. (1997). Psychosocial predictors of mental health in a population of elderly women: Test of an explanatory model. *American Journal of Geriatric Psychiatry, 5*(1), 43–53.

Birkel, D. A., & Edgren, L. (2000). Hatha yoga: Improved vital capacity of college students. *Alternative Therapy and Health Medicine, 6*(6), 55–63.

Bitner, R., Hillman, L., Victor, B., & Walsh, R. (2003). Subjective effects of antidepressants: A pilot study of the varieties of antidepressant-induced experiences in meditators. *Journal of Nervous and Mental Disorders, 191*(10), 660–667.

Boey, K. W. (2003). Religiosity and psychological well-being of older women in Hong Kong. *International Journal of Psychiatric Nurse Residents, 8*(2), 921–935.

Bowker, D. (1978). Pain and suffering—Religious perspective. In W. T. Reich (Ed.), *Encyclopedia of bioethics* (pp. 1185–1189). New York: Free Press.

Braam, A. W., Beekman, A. T., Deeg, D. J., Smit, J. H., & Van Tilburg, W. (1999). Religiosity as a protective factor in depressive disorder. *American Journal of Psychiatry, 156*(5), 809; author reply 810.

Brown, C. M. (2000). Exploring the role of religiosity in hypertension management among African Americans. *Journal of Health Care Poor Underserved, 11*(1), 19–32.

Brush, B. L., & McGee, E. M. (2000). Evaluating the spiritual perspectives of homeless men in recovery. *Applied Nursing Research, 13,* 181–186.

Byrd, R. C. (1988). Positive therapeutic effects of intercessory prayer in a coronary care unit population. *Southern Medical Journal, 81*(7), 826–829.

Bywaters, P., Ali, Z., Fazil, Q., Wallace, L. M., & Singh, G. (2003). Attitudes towards disability amongst Pakistani and Bangladeshi parents of disabled children in the UK: Considerations for service providers and the disability movement. *Health and Social Care in the Community, 11*(6), 502–509.

Carlson, L. E., Ursuliak, Z., Goodey, E., Angen, M., & Speca, M. (2001). The effects of a mindfulness meditation-based stress reduction program on mood and symptoms of stress in cancer outpatients: 6-month follow-up. *Support Care Cancer, 9*(2), 112–123.

Carter, T. M. (1998). The effects of spiritual practices on recovery from substance abuse. *Journal of Psychiatric and Mental Health Nursing, 5*(5), 409–413.

Castillo-Richmond, A., Schneider, R. H., Alexander, C. N., Cook, R., Myers, H., Nidich, S., et al. (2000). Effects of stress reduction on carotid atherosclerosis in hypertensive African Americans. *Stroke, 31*(3), 568–573.

Chen, C. Y., Dormitzer, C. M., Bejarano, J., & Anthony, J. C. (2004). Religiosity and the earliest stages of adolescent drug involvement in seven countries of Latin America. *American Journal of Epidemiology, 159*(12), 1180–1188.

Chibnall, J. T., & Brooks, C. A. (2001). Religion in the clinic: The role of physician beliefs. *Southern Medical Journal, 94*(4), 374–379.

Coke, M. M. (1992). Correlates of life satisfaction among elderly African Americans. *Journal of Gerontology, 47*(5), 316–320.

Collipp, P. J. (1969). The efficacy of prayer: A triple-blind study. *Medical Times, 97*(5), 201–204.

Comstock, G. W., & Partridge, K. B. (1972). Church attendance and health. *Journal of Chronic Disorders*, *25*(12), 665–672.

Contrada, R. J., Goyal, T. M., Cather, C., Rafalson, L., Idler, E. L., & Krause, T. J. (2004). Psychosocial factors in outcomes of heart surgery: The impact of religious involvement and depressive symptoms. *Health Psychology*, *23*(3), 227–238.

Cooper, M. J., & Aygen, M. M. (1979). A relaxation technique in the management of hypercholesterolemia. *Journal of Human Stress*, *5*(4), 24–27.

Corliss, R. (2001). The power of yoga. *Time*, *157*(16), 54–63.

Coward, D. D. (1991). Self-transcendence and emotional well-being in women with advanced breast cancer. *Oncology Nursing Forum*, *18*, 857–863.

Daaleman, T. P., & Nease, D. E., Jr. (1994). Patient attitudes regarding physician inquiry into spiritual and religious issues. *Journal of Family Practices*, *39*(6), 564–568.

de Gouw, H. W., Westendorp, R. G., Kunst, A. E., Mackenbach, J. P., & Vandenbroucke, J. P. (1995). Decreased mortality among contemplative monks in The Netherlands. *American Journal of Epidemiology*, *141*(8), 771–775.

Dermatis, H., Guschwan, M. T., Galanter, M., & Bunt, G. (2004). Orientation toward spirituality and self-help approaches in the therapeutic community. *Journal of Addictive Disorders*, *23*(1), 39–54.

Domino, G. (1977). Transcendental meditation and creativity: An empirical investigation. *Journal of Applied Psychology*, *62*(3), 358–362.

Donahue, M. J. (1985). Intrinsic and extrinsic religiousness: Review and meta-analysis. *Journal of Personality and Social Psychology*, *48*, 400–419.

Dunne, M. P., Edwards, R., Lucke, J., Donald, M., & Raphael, B. (1994). Religiosity, sexual intercourse and condom use among university students. *Australian Journal of Public Health*, *18*(3), 339–341.

Eisenberg, D. M., Davis, R. B., Ettner, S. L., Appel, S., Wilkey, S., Van Rompay, M., et al. (1998). Trends in alternative medicine use in the United States, 1990–1997: Results of a follow-up national survey. *Journal of the American Medical Association*, *280*(18), 1569–1575.

Ellis, M. R., Vinson, D. C., & Ewigman, B. (1999). Addressing spiritual concerns of patients: Family physicians' attitudes and practices. *Journal of Family Practices*, *48*(2), 105–109.

Foley, D. P. (1988). Eleven interpretations of personal suffering. *Journal of Religion and Health*, *27*, 321–328.

Forcehimes, A. A. (2004). De profundis: Spiritual transformations in Alcoholics Anonymous. *Journal of Clinical Psychology*, *60*(5), 503–517.

Fraser, G. E. (1999). Associations between diet and cancer, ischemic heart disease, and all-cause mortality in non-Hispanic white California Seventh-day Adventists. *American Journal of Clinical Nutrition*, *70*(3 Suppl.), 532–538.

Friedlander, Y., Kark, J. D., Kaufmann, N. A., & Stein, Y. (1985). Coronary heart disease risk factors among religious groupings in a Jewish population sample in Jerusalem. *American Journal of Clinical Nutrition*, *42*(3), 511–521.

Friedlander, Y., Kark, J. D., & Stein, Y. (1987). Religious observance and plasma lipids and lipoproteins among 17-year-old Jewish residents of Jerusalem. *Preventive Medicine*, *16*(1), 70–79.

The Gallup Report: Religion in America: 1993–1994. (1994). Princeton, NJ: Gallup Poll.

Garfinkel, M. S., Schumacher, H. R., Jr., Husain, A., Levy, M., & Reshetar, R. A. (1994). Evaluation of a yoga based regimen for treatment of osteoarthritis of the hands. *Journal of Rheumatology, 21*(12), 2341–2343.

Garfinkel, M. S., Singhal, A., Katz, W. A., Allan, D. A., Reshetar, R., & Schumacher, H. R., Jr. (1998). Yoga-based intervention for carpal tunnel syndrome: A randomized trial. *Journal of the American Medical Association, 280*(18), 1601–1603.

Geisser, M. E., Robinson, M. E., & Henson, C. D. (1994). The Coping Strategies Questionnaire and chronic pain adjustment: A conceptual and empirical reanalysis. *Clinical Journal of Pain, 10*(2), 98–106.

Gorsuch, R. L., & Butler, M. C. (1976). Initial drug abuse: A review of predisposing social psychological factors. *Psychology Bulletin, 83*(1), 120–137.

Green, L. L., Fullilove, M. T., & Fullilove, R. E. (1998). Stories of spiritual awakening: The nature of spirituality in recovery. *Journal of Substance Abuse Treatment, 15*(4), 325–331.

Grundmann, E. (1992). Cancer morbidity and mortality in USA Mormons and Seventh-day Adventists. *Archives of Anatomy, Cytology, and Pathology, 40*(2–3), 73–78.

Gupta, R. (1996). Lifestyle risk factors and coronary heart disease prevalence in Indian men. *Journal of the Association of Physicians of India, 44*(10), 689–693.

Gupta, R., Prakash, H., Gupta, V. P., & Gupta, K. D. (1997). Prevalence and determinants of coronary heart disease in a rural population of India. *Journal of Clinical Epidemiology, 50*(2), 203–209.

Harris, W. S., Gowda, M., Kolb, J. W., Strychacz, C. P., Vacek, J. L., Jones, P. G., et al. (1999). A randomized, controlled trial of the effects of remote, intercessory prayer on outcomes in patients admitted to the coronary care unit. *Archives of Internal Medicine, 159*(19), 2273–2278.

Hays, J. C., Landerman, L. R., George, L. K., Flint, E. P., Koenig, H. G., Land, K. C., et al. (1998). Social correlates of the dimensions of depression in the elderly. *Journal of Gerontology Series B: Psychological Science and Social Science, 53*(1), 31–39.

Heath, A. C., Madden, P. A., Grant, J. D., McLaughlin, T. L., Todorov, A. A., & Bucholz, K. K. (1999). Resiliency factors protecting against teenage alcohol use and smoking: Influences of religion, religious involvement and values, and ethnicity in the Missouri Adolescent Female Twin Study. *Twin Research, 2*(2), 145–155.

Helm, H. M., Hays, J. C., Flint, E. P., Koenig, H. G., & Blazer, D. G. (2000). Does private religious activity prolong survival? A six-year follow-up study of 3,851 older adults. *Journal of Gerontology Series A: Biological Science and Medical Science, 55*(7), 400–405.

Hixson, K. A., Gruchow, H. W., & Morgan, D. W. (1998). The relation between religiosity, selected health behaviors, and blood pressure among adult females. *Preventive Medicine, 27*(4), 545–552.

Ho, S. C., Woo, J., Lau, J., Chan, S. G., Yuen, Y. K., Chan Y. K, et al. (1995). Life satisfaction and associated factors in older Hong Kong Chinese. *Journal of American Geriatric Society, 43*(3), 252–255.

Hodges, S. D., Humphreys, S. C., & Eck, J. C. (2002). Effect of spirituality on successful recovery from spinal surgery. *Southern Medical Journal, 95*(12), 1381–1384.

House, J.S., Robbins, C., & Metzner, H.L. (1982). The association of social relationships and activities with mortality: Prospective evidence from the Tecumseh Community Health Study. *American Journal of Epidemiology, 116*(1), 123–140.

Hummer, R.A., Rogers, R.G., Nam, C.B., & Ellison, C.G. (1999). Religious involvement and U.S. adult mortality. *Demography, 36*(2), 273–285.

Idler, E.L., & Kasl, S.V. (1997a). Religion among disabled and nondisabled persons I: Cross-sectional patterns in health practices, social activities, and well-being. *Journal of Gerontology Series B: Psychological Science and Social Science, 52*(6), 294–305.

Idler, E.L., & Kasl, S.V. (1997b). Religion among disabled and nondisabled persons II: Attendance at religious services as a predictor of the course of disability. *Journal of Gerontology Series B: Psychological Science and Social Science, 52*(6), 306–316.

Jain, S.C., Uppal, A., Bhatnagar, S.O., & Talukdar, B. (1993). A study of response pattern of non-insulin dependent diabetics to yoga therapy. *Diabetes Research and Clinical Practices, 19*(1), 69–74.

Kabat-Zinn, J. (1982). An outpatient program in behavioral medicine for chronic pain patients based on the practice of mindfulness meditation: Theoretical considerations and preliminary results. *General Hospital Psychiatry, 4*(1), 33–47.

Kabat-Zinn, J., Lipworth, L., & Burney, R. (1985). The clinical use of mindfulness meditation for the self-regulation of chronic pain. *Journal of Behavioral Medicine, 8*(2), 163–190.

Kabat-Zinn, J., Massion, A.O., Kristeller, J., Peterson, L.G., Fletcher, K.E., Pbert, L., et al. (1992). Effectiveness of a meditation-based stress reduction program in the treatment of anxiety disorders. *American Journal of Psychiatry, 149*(7), 936–943.

Kabat-Zinn, J., Wheeler, E., Light, T., Skillings, A., Scharf, M.J., Cropley, T.G., et al. (1998). Influence of a mindfulness meditation-based stress reduction intervention on rates of skin clearing in patients with moderate to severe psoriasis undergoing phototherapy (UVB) and photochemotherapy (PUVA). *Psychosomatic Medicine, 60*(5), 625–632.

Kaplan, K.H., Goldenberg, D.L., & Galvin-Nadeau, M. (1993). The impact of a meditation-based stress reduction program on fibromyalgia. *General Hospital Psychiatry, 15*(5), 284–289.

Kark, J.D., Carmel, S., Sinnreich, R., Goldberger, N., & Friedlander, Y. (1996). Psychosocial factors among members of religious and secular kibbutzim. *Israeli Journal of Medical Science, 32*(3–4), 185–194.

Kark, J.D., Shemi, G., Friedlander, Y., Martin, O., Manor, O., & Blondheim, S.H. (1996). Does religious observance promote health? Mortality in secular vs. religious kibbutzim in Israel. *American Journal of Public Health, 86*(3), 341–346.

Keefer, L., & Blanchard, E.B. (2002). A one year follow-up of relaxation response meditation as a treatment for irritable bowel syndrome. *Behavioral Research and Therapy, 40*(5), 541–546.

Kennedy, G.J., Kelman, H.R., Thomas, C., & Chen, J. (1996). The relation of religious preference and practice to depressive symptoms among 1,855 older adults. *Journal of Gerontology Series B: Psychological Science and Social Science, 51*(6), 301–308.

Kernberg, O.F. (2003). Sanctioned social violence: A psychoanalytic view. Part II. *International Journal of Psychoanalysis, 84*(Pt. 4), 953–968.

King, D. E., & Bushwick, B. (1994). Beliefs and attitudes of hospital inpatients about faith healing and prayer. *Journal of Family Practice, 39*(4), 349–352.

King, D. E., Hueston, W., & Rudy, M. (1994). Religious affiliation and obstetric outcome. *Southern Medical Journal, 87*(11), 1125–1128.

King, M. S., Carr, T., & D'Cruz, C. (2002). Transcendental meditation, hypertension and heart disease. *Australian Family Physician, 31*(2), 164–168.

Koenig, H. G. (1998). Religious attitudes and practices of hospitalized medically ill older adults. *International Journal of Geriatric Psychiatry, 13*(4), 213–224.

Koenig, H. G., George, L. K., Cohen, H. J., Hays, J. C., Larson, D. B., & Blazer, D. G. (1998a). The relationship between religious activities and cigarette smoking in older adults. *Journal of Gerontology Series A: Biological Science and Medical Science, 53*(6), 426–434.

Koenig, H. G., George, L. K., Hays, J. C., Larson, D. B., Cohen, H. J., & Blazer, D. G. (1998b). The relationship between religious activities and blood pressure in older adults. *International Journal of Psychiatry and Medicine, 28*(2), 189–213.

Koenig, H. G., George, L. K., & Peterson, B. L. (1998c). Religiosity and remission of depression in medically ill older patients. *American Journal of Psychiatry, 155*(4), 536–542.

Koenig, H. G., Hays, J. C., George, L. K., Blazer, D. G., Larson, D. B., & Landerman, L. R. (1997). Modeling the cross-sectional relationships between religion, physical health, social support, and depressive symptoms. *American Journal of Geriatric Psychiatry, 5*(2), 131–144.

Koenig, H. G., Hays, J. C., Larson, D. B., George, L. K., Cohen, H. J., McCullough, M. E., et al. (1999). Does religious attendance prolong survival? A six-year follow-up study of 3,968 older adults. *Journal of Gerontology Series A: Biological Science and Medical Science, 54*(7), 370–376.

Krause, N. (2003). Religious meaning and subjective well-being in late life. *Journal of Gerontology Series B: Psychological Science and Social Science, 58*(3), 160–170.

Kuhn, C. C. (1988). A spiritual inventory of the medically ill patient. *Psychiatric Medicine, 6*(2), 87–100.

Kune, G. A., Kune, S., & Watson, L. F. (1992). The effect of family history of cancer, religion, parity and migrant status on survival in colorectal cancer. The Melbourne Colorectal Cancer Study. *European Journal of Cancer, 28A*(8–9), 1484–1487.

Kune, G. A., Kune, S., & Watson, L. F. (1993). Perceived religiousness is protective for colorectal cancer: Data from the Melbourne Colorectal Cancer Study. *Journal of the Royal Society of Medicine, 86*(11), 645–647.

Kutz, I. (2002). Samson, the Bible, and the DSM. *Archives of General Psychiatry, 59*(6), 565; author reply 565–566.

La Pierre, L. L. (2003). JCAHO safeguards spiritual care. *Holistic Nursing Practices, 17*(4), 219.

Larson, D. B., & Wilson, W. P. (1980). Religious life of alcoholics. *Southern Medical Journal, 73*(6), 723–727.

Lefkowitz, E. S., Boone, T. L., Au, T. K., & Sigman, M. (2003). No sex or safe sex? Mothers' and adolescents' discussions about sexuality and AIDS/HIV. *Health Education and Resources, 18*(3), 341–351.

Leibovici, L. (2001). Effects of remote, retroactive intercessory prayer on outcomes in patients with bloodstream infection: Randomized controlled trial. *British Medical Journal, 323*(7327), 1450–1451.

Levin, J. S. (1996). How religion influences morbidity and health: Reflections on natural history, salutogenesis and host resistance. *Social Science and Medicine, 43*(5), 849–864.

Levin, J. S., Larson, D. B., & Puchalski, C. M. (1997). Religion and spirituality in medicine: Research and education. *Journal of the American Medical Association, 87*(9), 792–793.

Levin, J. S., & Markides, K. (1988). Religious attendance and psychological well-being in middle-aged and older Mexican Americans. *Sociological Analysis, 49,* 66–72.

Li, E. C., Feifer, C., & Strohm, M. (2000). A pilot study: Locus of control and spiritual beliefs in alcoholics anonymous and smart recovery members. *Addictive Behaviors, 25*(4), 633–640.

Lichtenstein, B. (2003). Stigma as a barrier to treatment of sexually transmitted infection in the American Deep South: Issues of race, gender and poverty. *Social Science and Medicine, 57*(12), 2435–2445.

Lo, B., Quill, T., & Tulsky, J. (1999). Discussing palliative care with patients. ACP-ASIM end-of-life care consensus panel. American College of Physicians-American Society of Internal Medicine. *Annals of International Medicine, 130*(9), 744–749.

Lo, B., Ruston, D., Kates, L. W., Arnold, R. M., Cohen, C. B., Faber-Langendoen, K., et al. (2002). Discussing religious and spiritual issues at the end of life: A practical guide for physicians. *Journal of the American Medical Association, 287*(6), 749–754.

Loprinzi, C. L., Laurie, J. A., Wieand, H. S., Krook, J. E., Novotny, P. J., Kugler, J. W., et al. (1994). Prospective evaluation of prognostic variables from patient-completed questionnaires. North Central Cancer Treatment Group. *Journal of Clinical Oncology, 12*(3), 601–607.

Luczak, S. E., Shea, S. H., Carr, L. G., Li, T. K., & Wall, T. L. (2002). Binge drinking in Jewish and non-Jewish white college students. *Alcoholism: Clinical and Experimental Research, 26*(12), 1773–1778.

Lukoff, D., Lu, F., & Turner, R. (1992). Toward a more culturally sensitive DSM-IV. Psychoreligious and psychospiritual problems. *Journal of Nervous Mental Disorders, 180*(11), 673–682.

Lyttle, T. (1988). Drug based religions and contemporary drug taking. *Journal of Drug Issues, 18,* 271–284.

MacLean, C. D., Susi, B., Phifer, N., Schultz, L., Bynum, D., Franco, M., et al. (2003). Patient preference for physician discussion and practice of spirituality. *Journal of General International Medicine, 18*(1), 38–43.

Madru, N. (2003). Stigma and HIV: Does the social response affect the natural course of the epidemic? *Journal Association Nurses AIDS Care, 14*(5), 39–48.

Malhotra, V., Singh, S., Singh, K. P., Gupta, P., Sharma, S. B., Madhu, S. V., et al. (2002). Study of yoga asanas in assessment of pulmonary function in NIDDM patients. *Indian Journal of Physiology and Pharmacology, 46*(3), 313–320.

Malhotra, V., Singh, S., Tandon, O. P., Madhu, S. V., Prasad, A., & Sharma, S. B. (2002). Effect of yoga asanas on nerve conduction in type 2 diabetes. *Indian Journal of Physiological Pharmacology, 46*(3), 298–306.

Manheimer, E., Anderson, B. J., & Stein, M. D. (2003). Use and assessment of complementary and alternative therapies by intravenous drug users. *American Journal of Drug and Alcohol Abuse, 29*(2), 401–413.

Manocha, R., Marks, G. B., Kenchington, P., Peters, D., & Salome, C. M. (2002). Sahaja yoga in the management of moderate to severe asthma: A randomized controlled trial. *Thorax, 57*(2), 110–115.

Markides, K. S., Levin, J. S., & Ray, L. A. (1987). Religion, aging, and life satisfaction: An eight-year, three-wave longitudinal study. *Gerontologist, 27*(5), 660–665.

Matthews, D. A., & Clark, C. (1998). *The faith factor: Proof of the healing power of prayer.* New York: Viking (Penguin-Putnam).

Matthews, D. A., Marlowe, S. M., & MacNutt, F. S. (2000). Effects of intercessory prayer on patients with rheumatoid arthritis. *Southern Medical Journal, 93*(12), 1177–1186.

Matthews, W. J., Conti, J. M., & Sireci, S. G. (2001). The effects of intercessory prayer, positive visualization, and expectancy on the well-being of kidney dialysis patients. *Alternative Therapy & Health Medicine, 7*(5), 42–52.

McCormick, N., Izzo, A., & Folcik, J. (1985). Adolescents' values, sexuality, and contraception in a rural New York county. *Adolescence, 20*(78), 385–395.

McCree, D. H., Wingood, G. M., DiClemente, R., Davies, S., & Harrington, K. F. (2003). Religiosity and risky sexual behavior in African-American adolescent females. *Journal of Adolescent Health, 33*(1), 2–8.

McCullough, M. E., Hoyt, W. T., Larson, D. B., Koenig, H. G., & Thoresen, C. (2000). Religious involvement and mortality: A meta-analytic review. *Health Psychology, 19*(3), 211–222.

McCullough, M. E., & Larson, D. B. (1999). Religion and depression: A review of the literature. *Twin Research, 2*, 126–136.

McKee, D. D., & Chappel, J. N. (1992). Spirituality and medical practice. *Journal of Family Practice, 35*(2), 201, 205–208.

McLane, S., Lox, C. L., Butki, B., & Stern, L. (2003). An investigation of the relation between religion and exercise motivation. *Journal of Perceptive Motor Skills, 97*(3 Pt. 2), 1043–1048.

Merrill, R. M., & Thygerson, A. L. (2001). Religious preference, church activity, and physical exercise. *Preventive Medicine, 33*(1), 38–45.

Miller, L., Davies, M., & Greenwald, S. (2000). Religiosity and substance use and abuse among adolescents in the National Comorbidity Survey. *Journal of the American Academic Child Adolescent Psychiatry, 39*(9), 1190–1197.

Miller, L., & Gur, M. (2002). Religiousness and sexual responsibility in adolescent girls. *Journal of Adolescent Health, 31*(5), 401–406.

Miller, L., Warner, V., Wickramaratne, P., & Weissman, M. (1997). Religiosity and depression: Ten-year follow-up of depressed mothers and offspring. *Journal of the American Academic Child Adolescent Psychiatry, 36*(10), 1416–1425.

Miller, W. R. (1998). Researching the spiritual dimensions of alcohol and other drug problems. *Addiction, 93*(7), 979–990.

Miller, W. R., & Thoresen, C. E. (2003). Spirituality, religion, and health. An emerging research field. *American Psychology, 58*(1), 24–35.

Mitchell, J., Lannin, D. R., Mathews, H. F., & Swanson, M. S. (2002). Religious beliefs and breast cancer screening. *Journal of Women's Health, 11*(10), 907–915.

Monroe, M. H., Bynum, D., Susi, B., Phifer, N., Schultz, L., Franco, M., et al. (2003). Primary care physician preferences regarding spiritual behavior in medical practice. *Archives of International Medicine, 163*(22), 2751–2756.

Moriarity, J. (2001). The spiritual roots of AA. *Minnesota Medicine, 84*(4), 10.

Morse, J. M., & Proctor, A. (1998). Maintaining patient endurance. The comfort work of trauma nurses. *Clinical Nursing Research, 7*(3), 250–274.

Murphy, T. J., Pagano, R. R., & Marlatt, G. A. (1986). Lifestyle modification with heavy alcohol drinkers: Effects of aerobic exercise and meditation. *Addictive Behaviors, 11*(2), 175–186.

Murugesan, R., Govindarajulu, N., & Bera, T. K. (2000). Effect of selected yogic practices on the management of hypertension. *Indian Journal of Physiological Pharmacology, 44*(2), 207–210.

Musick, M. A., Koenig, H. G., Hays, J. C., & Cohen, H. J. (1998). Religious activity and depression among community-dwelling elderly persons with cancer: The moderating effect of race. *Journal of Gerontology Series B: Psychological Science and Social Science, 53*(4), 218–227.

Neeleman, J., Halpern, D., Leon, D., & Lewis, G. (1997). Tolerance of suicide, religion and suicide rates: An ecological and individual study in 19 Western countries. *Psychological Medicine, 27*(5), 1165–1171.

Neeleman, J., & Lewis, G. (1999). Suicide, religion, and socioeconomic conditions: An ecological study in 26 countries, 1990. *Journal of Epidemiology and Community Health, 53*(4), 204–210.

Neeleman, J., Wessely, S., & Lewis, G. (1998). Suicide acceptability in African- and white Americans: The role of religion. *Journal of Nervous Mental Disorders, 186*(1), 12–16.

Nisbet, P. A., Duberstein, P. R., Conwell, Y., & Seidlitz, L. (2000). The effect of participation in religious activities on suicide versus natural death in adults 50 and older. *Journal of Nervous Mental Disorders, 188*(8), 543–546.

O'Laoire, S. (1997). An experimental study of the effects of distant, intercessory prayer on self-esteem, anxiety, and depression. *Alternative Therapies in Health and Medicine, 3*(6), 38–53.

Oleckno, W. A., & Blacconiere, M. J. (1991). Relationship of religiosity to wellness and other health-related behaviors and outcomes. *Psychological Reports, 68*(3 Pt. 1), 819–826.

Oman, D., Kurata, J. H., Strawbridge, W. J., & Cohen, R. D. (2002). Religious attendance and cause of death over 31 years. *International Journal of Psychiatry and Medicine, 32*(1), 69–89.

Oman, D., & Reed, D. (1998). Religion and mortality among the community-dwelling elderly. *American Journal of Public Health, 88*(10), 1469–1475.

Oxman, T. E., Freeman, D. H., Jr., & Manheimer, E. D. (1995). Lack of social participation or religious strength and comfort as risk factors for death after cardiac surgery in the elderly. *Psychosomatic Medicine, 57*(1), 5–15.

Patel, S. S., Shah, V. S., Peterson, R. A., & Kimmel, P. L. (2002). Psychosocial variables, quality of life, and religious beliefs in ESRD patients treated with hemodialysis. *American Journal of Kidney Diseases, 40*(5), 1013–1022.

Pettus, M. C. (2002). Implementing a medicine-spirituality curriculum in a community-based internal medicine residency program. *Academic Medicine, 77*(7), 745.

Poloma, M., & Pendleton, B. (1991). The effects of prayer and prayer experience on measures of general well being. *Journal of Psychology & Theology, 10,* 71–83.

Powell, L. H., Shahabi, L., & Thoresen, C. E. (2003). Religion and spirituality. Linkages to physical health. *American Psychology, 58*(1), 36–52.

Pressman, P., Lyons, J. S., Larson, D. B., & Strain, J. J. (1990). Religious belief, depression, and ambulation status in elderly women with broken hips. *American Journal of Psychiatry, 147*(6), 758–760.

Proctor, A., Morse, J. M., & Khonsari, E. S. (1996). Sounds of comfort in the trauma center: How nurses talk to patients in pain. *Social Science and Medicine, 42*(12), 1669–1680.

Propst, L. R., Ostrom, R., Watkins, P., Dean, T., & Mashburn, D. (1992). Comparative efficacy of religious and nonreligious cognitive-behavioral therapy for the treatment of clinical depression in religious individuals. *Journal of Consulting and Clinical Psychology, 60*(1), 94–103.

Purcell, B. C. (1998a). Spiritual abuse. *American Journal of Hospital Palliative Care, 15*(4), 227–231.

Purcell, B. C. (1998b). Spiritual terrorism. *American Journal of Hospital Palliative Care, 15*(3), 167–173.

Raleigh, E. D. (1992). Sources of hope in chronic illness. *Oncology Nursing Forum, 19*(3), 443–448.

Rapp, S. R., Rejeski, W. J., & Miller, M. E. (2000). Physical function among older adults with knee pain: The role of pain coping skills. *Arthritis Care and Research, 13*(5), 270–279.

Rasanen, J., Kauhanen, J., Lakka, T. A., Kaplan, G. A., & Salonen, J. T. (1996). Religious affiliation and all-cause mortality: A prospective population study in middle-aged men in eastern Finland. *International Journal of Epidemiology, 25*(6), 1244–1249.

Razali, S. M., Hasanah, C. I., Aminah, K., & Subramaniam, M. (1998). Religious-sociocultural psychotherapy in patients with anxiety and depression. *Australian and New Zealand Journal of Psychiatry, 32*(6), 867–872.

Reibel, D. K., Greeson, J. M., Brainard, G. C., & Rosenzweig, S. (2001). Mindfulness-based stress reduction and health-related quality of life in a heterogeneous patient population. *General Hospital Psychiatry, 23*(4), 183–192.

Ringdal, G. I., Gotestam, K. G., Kaasa, S., Kvinnsland, S., & Ringdal, K. (1996). Prognostic factors and survival in a heterogeneous sample of cancer patients. *British Journal of Cancer, 73*(12), 1594–1599.

Rossetti, S. J. (1995). The impact of child sexual abuse on attitudes toward God and the Catholic Church. *Child Abuse and Neglect, 19*(12), 1469–1481.

Satterly, L. (2001). Guilt, shame, and religious and spiritual pain. *Holistic Nursing Practices, 15*(2), 30–39.

Schell, F. J., Allolio, B., & Schonecke, O. W. (1994). Physiological and psychological effects of Hatha-yoga exercise in healthy women. *International Journal of Psychosomatics, 41*(1–4), 46–52.

Selvamurthy, W., Sridharan, K., Ray, U. S., Tiwary, R. S., Hegde, K. S., Radhakrishan, U., et al. (1998). A new physiological approach to control essential hypertension. *Indian Journal of Physiology and Pharmacology, 42*(2), 205–213.

Shaffer, J. A. (1978). Pain and suffering: Philosophical perspectives. In W. T. Reich (Ed.), *Encyclopedia of bioethics* (pp. 1181–1185). New York: Free Press.

Shuler, P.A., Gelberg, L., & Brown, M. (1994). The effects of spiritual/religious practices on psychological well-being among inner city homeless women. *Nurse Practitioners Forum, 5*(2), 106–113.

Sloan, R.P., Bagiella, E., & Powell, T. (1999). Religion, spirituality, and medicine. *Lancet, 353*(9153), 664–667.

Solberg, E.E., Berglund, K.A., Engen, O., Ekeberg, O., & Loeb, M. (1996). The effect of meditation on shooting performance. *British Journal of Sports Medicine, 30*(4), 342–346.

Spiritual assessment required in all settings. (2003). *Hospital Peer Reviews, 28*(4), 55–56.

Stancak, A., Jr., Kuna, M., Srinivasan, Dostalek, C., & Vishnudevananda, S. (1991). Kapalabhati-yogic cleansing exercise II. EEG topography analysis. *Homeostasis in Health and Disease, 33*(4), 182–189.

Stanescu, D.C., Nemery, B., Veriter, C., & Marechal, C. (1981). Pattern of breathing and ventilatory response to CO_2 in subjects practicing hatha-yoga. *Journal of Applied Physiology, 51*(6), 1625–1629.

Stefanek, M., McDonald, P.G., & Hess, S.A. (2004). Religion, spirituality and cancer: Current status and methodological challenges. *Psychooncology, 14*(6), 450–463.

Stewart, C. (2001). The influence of spirituality on substance use of college students. *Journal of Drug Education, 31*(4), 343–351.

Strawbridge, W.J., Cohen, R.D., Shema, S.J., & Kaplan, G.A. (1997). Frequent attendance at religious services and mortality over 28 years. *American Journal of Public Health, 87*(6), 957–961.

Stylianou, S. (2004). The role of religiosity in the opposition to drug use. *International Journal of Offender Therapy and Comparative Criminology, 48*(4), 429–448.

Sundar, S., Agrawal, S.K., Singh, V.P., Bhattacharya, S.K., Udupa, K.N., & Vaish, S.K. (1984). Role of yoga in management of essential hypertension. *Acta Cardiology, 39*(3), 203–208.

Swartzman, L.C., Gwadry, F.G., Shapiro, A.P., & Teasell, R.W. (1994). The factor structure of the Coping Strategies Questionnaire. *Pain, 57*(3), 311–316.

Swimmer, G.I., Robinson, M.E., & Geisser, M.E. (1992). Relationship of MMPI cluster type, pain coping strategy, and treatment outcome. *Clinical Journal of Pain, 8*(2), 131–137.

Tanyi, R.A. (2002). Towards clarification of the meaning of spirituality. *Journal of Advanced Nursing, 39*(5), 500–509.

Tieman, J. (2002). Priest scandal hits hospitals. As pedophilia reports grow, church officials suspend at least six hospital chaplains in an effort to address alleged sexual abuse. *Modern Healthcare, 32*(19), 6–7, 11, 14.

Tonigan, J.S., Miller, W.R., & Schermer, C. (2002). Atheists, agnostics and Alcoholics Anonymous. *Journal of Studies on Alcohol, 63*(5), 534–541.

Townsend, M., Kladder, V., Ayele, H., & Mulligan, T. (2002). Systematic review of clinical trials examining the effects of religion on health. *Southern Medical Journal, 95*(12), 1429–1434.

Tu, W. (1980). A religiophilosophical perspective on pain. In L.Y. Terenius (Ed.), *Pain and society* (pp. 63–78). Weinheim-Deerfield Beach, FL: Verlag Chemie.

Turner, R.P., Lukoff, D., Barnhouse, R.T., & Lu, F.G. (1995). Religious or spiritual problem. A culturally sensitive diagnostic category in the DSM-IV. *Journal of Nervous Mental Disorders, 183*(7), 435–444.

Udupa, K.N., Singh, R.H., & Yadav, R.A. (1973). Certain studies on psychological and biochemical responses to the practice in Hatha yoga in young normal volunteers. *Indian Journal of Medical Research, 61*(2), 237–244.

van Montfrans, G.A., Karemaker, J.M., Wieling, W., & Dunning, A.J. (1990). Relaxation therapy and continuous ambulatory blood pressure in mild hypertension: A controlled study. *British Medical Journal, 300*(6736), 1368–1372.

Van Ness, P.H., Kasl, S.V., & Jones, B.A. (2003). Religion, race, and breast cancer survival. *International Journal of Psychiatry and Medicine, 33*(4), 357–375.

Van Poppel, F., Schellekens, J., & Liefbroer, A.C. (2002). Religious differentials in infant and child mortality in Holland, 1855–1912. *Population Studies, 56*(3), 277–289.

Walker, S.R., Tonigan, J.S., Miller, W.R., Corner, S., & Kahlich, L. (1997). Intercessory prayer in the treatment of alcohol abuse and dependence: A pilot investigation. *Alternative Therapy and Health Medicine, 3*(6), 79–86.

Wallace, R.K., Silver, J., Mills, P.J., Dillbeck, M.C., & Wagoner, D.E. (1983). Systolic blood pressure and long-term practice of the Transcendental Meditation and TM-Sidhi program: Effects of TM on systolic blood pressure. *Psychosomatic Medicine, 45*(1), 41–46.

Walls, P., & Williams, R. (2004). Accounting for Irish Catholic ill health in Scotland: A qualitative exploration of some links between "religion", class and health. *Sociology of Health and Illness, 26*(5), 527–556.

Walsh, A. (1998). Religion and hypertension: Testing alternative explanations among immigrants. *Behavioral Medicine, 24*(3), 122–130.

Walton, K.G., Pugh, N.D., Gelderloos, P., & Macrae, P. (1995). Stress reduction and preventing hypertension: Preliminary support for a psychoneuroendocrine mechanism. *Journal of Alternative and Complementary Medicine, 1*, 263–283.

Wenneberg, S.R., Schneider, R.H., Walton, K.G., MacLean, C.R., Levitsky, D.K., Salerno, J.W., et al. (1997). A controlled study of the effects of the Transcendental Meditation program on cardiovascular reactivity and ambulatory blood pressure. *International Journal of Neuroscience, 89*(1–2), 15–28.

Williams, D.R., Larson, D.B., Buckler, R.E., Heckmann, R.C., & Pyle, C.M. (1991). Religion and psychological distress in a community sample. *Social Science and Medicine, 32*, 1257–1262.

Williams, K.A., Kolar, M.M., Reger, B.E., & Pearson, J.C. (2001). Evaluation of a wellness-based mindfulness stress reduction intervention: A controlled trial. *American Journal of Health Promotion, 15*, 422–432.

Woodward, K.L. (2001). Faith is more than a feeling. *Newsweek, 137*(19), 58.

Yates, J.W., Chalmer, B.J., St. James, P., Follansbee, M., & McKegney, F.P. (1981). Religion in patients with advanced cancer. *Medical and Pediatric Oncology, 9*, 121–128.

Zaleski, E.H., & Schiaffino, K.M. (2000). Religiosity and sexual risk-taking behavior during the transition to college. *Journal of Adolescence, 23*, 223–227.

Zollinger, T.W., Phillips, R.L., & Kuzma, J.W. (1984). Breast cancer survival rates among Seventh-day Adventists and non-Seventh-day Adventists. *American Journal of Epidemiology, 119*, 503–509.

CHAPTER 3

RELIGION, MEANING, AND THE BRAIN

Crystal L. Park and Patrick McNamara

INTRODUCTION

If you ask religious people why they believe in God or in many of the counter-intuitive or seemingly irrational tenets of religion, they will provide many and various reasons or justifications. Appeals to "meaning" and "purpose," however, will often be at the top of the list (Silberman, in press; Spilka, Hood, Hunsberger, & Gorsuch, 2003). Humans, for better or worse, require meaning and purpose in their lives, and religion addresses that fundamental need. The need for meaning may be a direct result of the large and complex brains that humans possess. Because of this complex brain, meaning is a central concern of humans. The brain evolved to process complex information and needs this kind of information so badly that, if deprived of information, it will produce information itself in order to process it. We contend that religion is a great source of complex information in the form of "meaning," which we describe more thoroughly below. In this restricted sense, then, the function of religion flows directly from the structure and complexity of the brain.

We take the notion that humans need meaning and purpose as a given (see Baumeister, 1991, and Wong & Fry, 1998, for detailed reviews of this contention). Thus, this chapter uses this claim as a starting point. What we seek to explore is how the mind/brain facilitates the extraction of meaning both with and without religion. By comparing the two operations we hope to shed some light on the unique contribution of religion to meaning.

The chapter begins with a description of what we mean by *meaning* and then summarizes why religion may be a particularly potent source of meanings. We need to set aside the problem of how people arrive at purpose in their lives, but we assume that our discussion of how people arrive at meanings will ultimately shed some light on the question of purpose. Next we consider the ways in which the mind/brain integrates and creates new meanings on a daily basis. We then illustrate how functional and potent these meanings are to the individual by reviewing cases of breakdown in the meaning system due to selective brain damage. Interestingly, we find some overlap in the neural networks that mediate meaning processes and those that are thought to mediate religious phenomena. After a brief comparison of the meanings created with and without religion, we conclude with a theory of how evolutionary forces might yield a form of religious ritual that would reliably produce surplus meanings that people rely on to function mentally from day to day and also, in many cases, to grow and flourish.

MEANING OF MEANING

Although the history of thought has oscillated between realist and nominalist approaches to meaning and concept formation, we take a practical approach by casting the problem of meaning construction alongside the problem of memory processing. A realist claims that the meanings of words and events are exhausted by their links to something real in the world. Nominalists, on the other hand, claim that the meanings of words are not exhausted by their links to the real world. Instead, words and concepts create new meanings of potential objects and states of affairs that may never have any link to the real world—think of all the imaginary beings that populate a child's or an artist's mind. Most people today believe that both the realists and the nominalists were correct in their own ways and that there is no essential contradiction between the two points of view. For real-world events, everyday meanings are extracted by a process of apprehension of the event and then an appraisal process of the significance of that event. For imaginary events, meaning construction proceeds without necessary reference to everyday constraints or rules. But even here the author of and the recipient (say, a reader of fiction) of the imaginary story/scenario will likely appraise the significance of the imaginary story according to some internal set of values and beliefs (Lazarus & Folkman, 1984). Thus, the appraisal process is central to meaning construction, as the transactional stress and coping perspective has been demonstrating for the past 40 years (see Aldwin, in press, for a review).

At least one part of meaning construction involves the integration, consolidation, and construction of new memories. Memories then act as filters or conceptual and schematic models through which any event is evaluated or appraised. Thus, memory is fundamental to meaning. If we can treat one piece of the meaning puzzle as part and parcel of the memory puzzle, we can bring into the discussion the enormous amount of scientific work done on the problem of memory during the last century as well as the breakthroughs occurring in the twenty-first century.

Meaning Is Constrained by a Hierarchy of Motivational Goals and Overarching Beliefs

The meaning or significance of an event always takes place within a previously given conceptual framework that is, in turn, built from innate preparatory or conceptual schemas and from memories. Innate schemas are the desires and propensities we are born with. They need to be triggered by the environment and are certainly shaped by the environment, but few will argue that a child is born with the same innate propensities as a rat. Humans come prepared to apprehend a three-dimensional world of objects and a caretaker's face, milk, warmth, and so forth. As the child grows and accumulates memories of significant experiences, these memories are shaped into concepts/frameworks and schemas of things that are highly important and significant and those that are less so. This memory-based conceptual framework, therefore, is determined largely by a hierarchy of motivational constructs (or what an organism desires and needs). Global meaning consists of a person's hierarchy of motivational goals, values, and ultimate sense of purpose within a global framework of order (Park & Folkman, 1997). Global meaning also influences which events we decide are relevant on a daily basis and the meaning or significance of those events (e.g., whether those occurrences are threats, losses, or challenges; Aldwin, in press). Further, global meaning influences appraisal of and coping with traumatic events, which involves reappraising both global meaning and the meaning of the event (i.e., searching for meaning) (Baumeister, 1991; Park, 2005).

Meaning Construction Occurs on a Moment-to-Moment Basis as an Appraisal Process

Moment-to-moment tagging of events as meaningful, while constrained or guided by a global, hierarchical meaning framework, proceeds psychologically as situation-specific "appraisals." An appraisal is a more or less immediate "online" or "on-the-spot" evaluation of the significance of an event to the well-being of the organism (Aldwin, in press). If the appraisal consists of a negative evaluation (that is, that the event is threatening or potentially harmful), defensive maneuvers (e.g., defense mechanisms, coping efforts) are initiated (Lazarus & Folkman, 1984), and if these maneuvers are unsuccessful, the organism may suffer serious physiological decline—regardless of the reality of the situation; such is the potency of the appraisal process. For example, if a young monkey is separated from its mother for even a day or two, it will conclude that its caretaker has disappeared and will not return, and the monkey will suppress its REM sleep, stop moving about, and stop eating (Reite, Kaemingk, & Boccia, 1989; Reite, Seiler, & Short, 1978).

Appraisals are not always veridical or accurate reflections of reality, nor do they need to be—even delusions can be helpful or adaptive under certain circumstances (e.g., when faced with extremely adverse situations, it may help to believe one will survive or flourish even if that is objectively unlikely). The placebo effect is a classic example of the beneficial effects of a nonveridical appraisal process yielding significant physiologic benefits for the organism. When a doctor gives a patient a sugar pill but tells him or her it is a special medication and assures the patient that it will help, the patient often does, in fact, feel better, at least for a little while (e.g., Sauro & Greenberg, 2005). Given the significant physiological impact of appraised meanings (e.g., that the sugar pill is real medicine) on health, we must assume that the brain/ mind systems that support belief, appraisal, and meaning construction are wired directly into immunologic, autonomic, and central nervous systems. Overwhelming evidence now exists for such direct functional links between these three systems, including the existence of receptors for neurotransmitters on immune system molecules and the projection of modulatory tracts that descend from the orbitofrontal cortex to hypothalamic and brain stem nuclei regulating autonomic nervous system responding. In other words, the thinking and feeling areas of the brain are directly connected to other centers and systems in the body that are directly responsible for maintaining health (Maier & Watkins, 2002). Thus, if one's thinking turns bad, his or her health often follows the downward spiral. There is now abundant evidence that pessimism is related to many aspects of poor health, including mortality (e.g., Maruta, Colligan, Malinchoc, & Offord, 2000; Schulz, Bookwala, Knapp, Scheier, & Williamson, 1996).

HOW DOES RELIGION PRODUCE MEANING?

To have a complete account of the religion-meaning-brain relationship, we need to investigate how religion is involved in producing meaning. In fact, religion can produce meaning in many different ways: (1) Religion provides an interpretive framework with which to assess the significance of events and thus guides the appraisal processes of many people. (2) Religion provides an interpretative framework that is comprehensive and ultimate, so religion allows for a greater number and range of appraisals of both mundane everyday events and events of rare significance, such as the death of a loved one. (3) Religion encompasses doctrines that are nonfalsifiable (thus, although many religious claims may seem contrary to reality, they cannot be proven false. For example, there is no way to measure the existence or actions of spiritual beings). (4) Religion uses mythopoetic imagery in its texts and rituals; such images, metaphors, and myths carry powerful affective meanings better than do abstract words and feelings. (5) Religion often relies on rituals, which are potent behavioral enactments of religious meaning systems. Each of these meaning-producing processes of religion is elaborated below.

Interpretative Framework

Religion often serves as an interpretative framework, a lens through which people's lives are experienced and understood. It can function as a kind of deductive top-down explanation for why things are the way they are. Why is there suffering? "Because God gave us free will and we often choose unwisely." Why do we choose unwisely? "Because original sin corrupted our mental faculties and to some extent our will" might be the answers proffered by a religious person. Such explanations that call on the divine or metaphysical can provide meaningful answers to any baffling or seemingly irredeemable experience, such as heinous crimes, painful illness and suffering, mental anguish, and profound loss.

Comprehensiveness

Of course, most religious explanations may not stand up to rigorous logical analysis. However, religious explanations can and often do appeal to an ultimate cause or purpose. Why did humans commit the original sin in the first place? Rational analysis would suggest that we must have already been somewhat corrupt or stupid to begin with (after all, who would rationally choose suffering over paradise and God?). The ultimate reasons for the "fall" and suffering are said to lie in the mysteries of free will and God's providence. Here we see the limitlessness of religious frameworks. In order for lower levels of these frameworks to work, they can appeal to ultimately comprehensive explanations for the ways things are (Emmons, 1999; Spilka, Shaver, & Kirkpatrick, 1997). Not only are these larger religious frameworks comprehensive, but they tend to be much more "existentially satisfactory" than secular explanations such as the hard, cold objectivity of science (Emmons, 1999; Pargament, Ano, & Wachholtz, 2005).

Nonfalsifiability of Religious Doctrine and Scriptures

Not only are religious frameworks able to accommodate and explain a wide variety of phenomena, they are capable of handling virtually any input or problem due to the flexibility of the system. From the scientific point of view, most religious tenets cannot be tested with standard scientific techniques, and thus the tenets are nonfalsifiable (e.g., Atran & Norenzayan, 2004). At the very least, one can refer to the ultimately inscrutable will of God. Beliefs that cannot be challenged or disproven are likely to be powerful influences on the appraisal process. Except for an exceptional few personalities, most people are uncomfortable with paradox and ambiguity (Loevinger, 1976; Loevinger, Wessler & Redmore,1970), and they prefer some definite evaluation system to a system that is unreliable. To the extent that religion claims access to eternal truths (or at least truths that cannot be falsified), then religion will function as a powerful meaning framework.

Mythopoetic Imagery

As important as rational and verbal meaning making is to humans, it is important to note that humans simultaneously process information using a second system as well—this one primarily emotional and experiential (see Chaiken & Trope, 1999, for a review). Religious meaning frameworks also provide for these very human needs for a deeper, less articulated but more impactful connection with the sacred and transcendent, much of which is conveyed through religion's mythopoetic imagery. Laughlin and Throop (2001) note that "mythopoetic imagery keeps the interpretive process in experience closer to the actual nature of reality than the rational faculties operating alone are able to do" (p. 709).

Rituals

The final source of religion's ability to produce meanings is in its behavioral manifestation: ritual. We turn now to a partial analysis of ritual as an unconscious process designed to produce meanings. We do not claim that ritual's only function is to produce meaning. Rather, we propose that looking at ritual from a "meaning" point of view may shed light on both religion and meaning.

Ritual has been defined as "the performance of more or less invariant sequences of formal acts and utterances not entirely encoded by the performers" (Rappaport, 1999, p. 24). According to anthropologists who study them, religious rituals exhibit the following features:

   a. apparently meaningless acts (e.g., walking around a temple seven times; sacrificing an animal; repetitious prayers or mantras)
   b. repetition (rituals are repeated in the same sequence over and over, sometimes daily for a worshipper and for thousands of years for a culture)
   c. intended purposes (can be propitiatory, commemorative, therapeutic, or some kind of rite of passage)
   d. may induce receptive attitude or trance states

Roy Rappaport's (1999) *Ritual and Religion in the Making of Humanity* provides a masterful summary of how religious ritual creates personal meanings for its practitioners as it links humans in cooperative groups and to a transcendent order. In his definition of ritual, the phrase "acts and utterances not encoded by the performers themselves" refers to the fact that the forms of the ritual were not invented by the people participating in the ritual. Instead they were handed down by ancestors or gods. Thus, participants in a ritual are linking themselves to an order (as inscribed in the acts and utterances of the ritual) that is ancient or even timeless and sanctioned by tradition and the highest authority.

Rappaport (1999) emphasizes that one does not need to believe in the truth value or claims of the ritual utterances in order to gain the benefits of ritual. Participation is all that is required (although belief can sometimes help). Participation implies some amount of acceptance of the ancient order referred to in the ritual performance. The connection to ancient inherited traditions carries with it access to meanings acquired from past generations.

Rappaport presents a detailed and nuanced view of the ritual processes that yield meaning. He begins by distinguishing between two kinds of messages that ritual conveys. The first is self-referential and concerns the current physical, psychic, or social states of the performers of the ritual. Most importantly, their presence at the ritual informs everyone present (including themselves) that they accept the invisible and sacred order referred to in the ritual. One's presence at the ritual, then, to some extent, delivers a message that he or she is open to the possibility of a transcendent order and all the other meanings of the ritual. Thus, one's presence at the ritual is said to be self-referential. In short, participation in ritual sends a message to oneself and the others present, and that message is something like this: "We have here a group of people gathered in a sacred space all of whom at least provisionally choose to entertain the idea that a transcendent and ancient order might exist and that that order can potentially impart meaning to daily life." That is a very powerful, almost unconscious, effect of religious ritual: It raises the question—the hope, really—that transcendent order exists and that that order will give meaning and purpose to daily life.

The second type of message encoded in ritual underlines this fact and the timeless order conveyed by ritual. These are the canonical messages such as sacred texts, prayers, incantations, and pronouncements. They are not encoded or created by the participants but are, instead, the relatively invariant messages about the nature of the world that participants take from the liturgy of the rite. Thus, in addition to the benefits of mere participation in the rite, religious participants also obtain the added benefit of the meanings conveyed by sacred texts, music, and prayers.

Rappaport notes that some terms and categories used in the field of linguistics might also profitably be put to use in the field of ritual studies. Two of these terms—"performatives" and "perlocutionary"—come from speech act theory. This is a branch of linguistics that deals with utterances that accomplish some action simply by pronouncing the utterance. For example, when a minister or priest utters the phrase "I now pronounce you man and wife" in the appropriate ritual context, the couple literally becomes man and wife. The utterance of the presiding minister is a performative, and the effect of the utterance on the couple is a perlocutionary. Or if someone says "I promise to . . . ", he or she in the act of uttering those words binds him- or herself to accomplish the act promised and thus utters a performative. The motivation to fulfill the promise is the perlocutionary effect on the person who made the promise.

Rappaport points out that rituals exhibit some of the properties of performatives. As performatives, rituals and their messages (self-referential and canonical) produce specific kinds of public signs that all can see and receive, and these signs, in turn, produce predictable kinds of perlocutionary effects on both the participants and observers. Because rituals, in their performative capacity, cause certain states to exist, those states become indexical signs (an indexical sign is an index of some other event; for example, smoke indicates fire, a footprint indicates a person has passed by). In contrast to symbols and icons, indexical signs are very reliable means of conveying accurate information about the persons in the ritual (i.e., that they are attempting to adhere to and accept a certain transcendent order). Ritual performance indexes information about the participants. For example, it can communicate that a couple has become married, that a boy has become a man, or that two groups have made peace.

By their participation in a ritual display, participants also to some extent display commitment to its outcome. This is a hard-to-fake signal of commitment to a given outcome and order. Thus, participation in ritual protects against free-riders and promotes trust among the participants in the group. Free-riders are people who want to enjoy the benefits of group participation without paying any of the costs associated with membership. A sincere religious believer can be seen at religious services and can expound indefinitely on religious doctrine and so forth. No free-rider would be willing to learn all of that doctrine. By publicly obligating or committing people and conveying information about the obligation indexically, ritual protects the group from free-riders (because free-riders will not pay the costs of attending the rituals). We discuss the issue of costly signals and free-riders further below. In addition to being a costly signal, rituals help individuals link their personal goals into a hierarchy of values that are linked to a transcendent order.

Interestingly, Rappaport points out that canonical messages are most often not indexical but rather are symbolic. These symbols give the self-referential messages their meaning by specifying that they are linked to a transcendent order or to what it is that the ritual achieves (e.g., a marriage or an initiation). It is the canon that defines the nature of the order it confers upon the participants.

In performing a ritual, Rappaport argues, a person accepts the canonical scheme governing the ritual and agrees to be bound by the obligations the ritual puts in place. A marriage is created, an initiation occurs, and so on, and all agree to be bound to the consequences of these newly established social orders. Crucially, this acceptance to be bound by the new order is not only something performers do in performing a ritual but also something they indexically convey to others, who can from then on consider them persons who have accepted that order.

In sum, Rappaport's explanation of how self-referential and canonical messages interact in ritual to produce new meanings illustrates a behavioral and often very social way that religion can produce meaning. Participation in religious rituals among other things sends messages to self and others about commitments, beliefs, and values of the participants. These messages are packed with guides regarding how to construct conceptual frameworks to engage in life-giving appraisals of both everyday and rare occurrences. Rappaport's description of how self-referential and canonical messages interact in ritual to virtually automatically produce new meanings illustrates a behavioral and often very social way that religion can generate meaning.

MIND/BRAIN CREATION OF MEANING

While religion is involved in the creation of meaning through a myriad of processes, this creation of meaning ultimately is mediated through the mind/brain. At this level, meaning is created largely through neural networks dedicated to (1) construction of the sense of self, (2) language, (3) concept formation, and, (4) surprisingly, sleep states. Interestingly, all of these functional domains (with the partial exception of sleep states) crucially involve the frontal lobes, so our review focuses on the role of the frontal lobes in meaning construction. A fair amount of information on how meaning is made by the mind/brain has accumulated. Where possible, we describe the potential religious correlates of this mind/brain construction, but, unfortunately, this cutting-edge research area of the confluence of religion, meaning, and the brain is still very new, and much remains unexplored (see Newberg & Newberg, 2005).

Self and Meaning

One of the most complex appraisal filters through which the brain evaluates events for their significance is the construct we call the Self. Virtually every event is evaluated in reference to the self: does it advance or hinder the aims of the self? It thus behooves us to briefly investigate brain mechanisms of this self.

Study of the self is important for the question of religion and meaning specifically because each self is unique and irreplaceable, and thus human dignity is linked with the sense of self we each experience. In addition, modern cognitive neuroscientific studies of the self indicate that virtually every higher cognitive function is influenced by the self: memories are encoded more efficiently when referred to the self; feelings and affective responses always include the self; fundamental attributions of intentionality, agency, and mind all concern selves in interaction with other selves and so on. Finally, study of the self is crucial for understanding many clinical disorders that involve breakdowns in the sense of self, including alterations in one's premorbid religious practices and religious orientation. Schizophrenia, obsessive-compulsive disorder, and some forms of temporal lobe epilepsy, for example, may heighten the sense of religiosity and may be associated with religious delusions. Parkinson's disease, on the other hand, may dampen the religious sense—at least in patients with frontal dysfunction. These disorders also involve dramatic breakdowns in the sense of self. More common disorders of self, such as depression or anxiety, can be accompanied by dramatic religious changes as well. In its capacity as "strength of character" or as a locus of virtues such as temperance, honesty, integrity, and trustworthiness (see below for further discussion of the role of character in religiousness), the self is intimately linked with religiosity insofar as religiosity is focused on building these character strengths. What, then, can neuroscience tell us about the roots and functions of the self?

The problem of the self has been somewhat intractable to analysis because the sense of self is so complex. The sense of self appears to draw on several psychological and neuropsychological domains such as autobiographical memory, emotional and evaluative systems, agency or the sense of being the cause of some action, self-monitoring, bodily-awareness, mind-reading or covert mimicking of other's mental states, subjectivity or perspective in perception, and, finally, the sense of unity conferred on consciousness when it is invested with the subjective perspective (Churchland, 2002; Gallagher, 2000; Metzinger, 2003; Northoff & Bermpohl, 2004). Any account of the psychology of self should at least be consistent with most or all of these properties.

In the absence of a theory that can account for all of the above properties of self, we argue that carefully considering the neuropsychological correlates of the sense of self will help narrow down key aspects of the self (see also LeDoux, 2002; Northoff & Bermpohl, 2004; Vogeley & Fink, 2003) that might help us identify links between self, religion, and meaning.

A number of investigators have suggested that the human sense of self depends crucially on prefrontal cortex (Craik, Moroz, & Moscovitch, 1999; McNamara et al., 1995; Miller et al., 2001; Vogeley, Kurthen, Falkai, & Maier, 1999). A review of the behavioral effects of prefrontal leucotomies led Weingarten (1999) to suggest that prefrontal lobes mediate some aspects of social sense of self and autonomy. Families of persons who sustain traumatic brain injury with orbitofrontal lesions invariably report that their relative's identity is profoundly altered, if not destroyed (Schnider & Gutbrod, 1999). Similarly, when a dementing process begins to invade basal forebrain and medial frontal sites, personality changes become marked and striking. Miller et al. (2001) reported that 7 of 72 patients with probable frontal-temporal dementing disorders exhibited a dramatic change in self. In 6 of these 7 patients, the selective dysfunction involved the right frontal region. In contrast, only one of the other 65 patients without selective right frontal dysfunction showed a change in self.

Experimental and functional imaging studies have pointed to the frontal lobes as crucial for the sense of self. Right frontal activation has been associated with experience of the self (Craik et al., 1999). Craik et al. showed that right frontal sites were activated whenever subjects processed or memorized materials referring to the self. Similarly, Fink et al. (1996) reported selective activation of right prefrontal cortical regions in subjects engaged in recall of personal versus impersonal long-term episodic memories. In a more recent functional imaging study, Kelley et al. (2002) confirmed that self-referential processing could be functionally dissociated from other forms of semantic processing within the human brain. Volunteers were imaged while making judgments about trait adjectives under three experimental conditions (self-relevance, other relevance, or case judgment). Relevance judgments, when compared to case judgments, were accompanied by activation of the left inferior frontal cortex and the anterior cingulate. A separate region of the medial prefrontal cortex was selectively engaged during self-referential processing, implying that medial prefrontal sites support self-related information-processing functions. In a seminal review of positron emission tomography (PET) studies on episodic encoding and retrieval processes, Wheeler, Stuss, and Tulving (1997; see also Nyberg et al., 1996) concluded that episodic retrieval of personal memories is associated with an increased blood flow in the right frontal cortex with no increased blood flow in the left frontal cortex; while episodic encoding is associated with the opposite pattern—that is, increased flow in left frontal cortex and no increased flow in right frontal cortex. They call this set of findings HERA, for hemispheric encoding/retrieval asymmetry.

Keenan, Nelson, O'Connor, and Pascual-Leone (2001) presented a series of pictures to a group of patients undergoing an intracarotid amobarbital test. The pictures represented faces generated by morphing the image of a famous person with the patient's own face, and participants were asked to remember what picture was shown during selective anesthesia of the right and the left hemispheres. Results indicated that most patients were unable to remember seeing their own face following an inactivation of the right hemisphere, whereas anesthesia of the left hemisphere did not interfere with recall of the self face. These results once again implicate right frontal cortex in support of the self.

The right frontal cortex (both at the orbito- and dorsalateral poles) differs from its left-sided counterpart in that it receives a more dense set of afferents coursing from the neostriatal and limbic systems, and it may also receive greater innervation from serotoninergic and noradrenergic cell groups in the brain stem (Bruder, 2003; Ongur & Price, 2000). Dopaminergic cell groups that project to the right prefrontal cortex display a more enhanced response to stress than dopaminergic cell groups projecting to the left prefrontal cortex (Berridge, Espana, & Stalnaker, 2003). These intriguing anatomical peculiarities suggest that the right frontal cortex is ideally positioned to integrate the wealth of emotional information delivered to it from subcortical limbic sites with high-level intentional and communicative functions of the frontal cortex.

In summary, a number of clinical, neuroimaging, and experimental studies of brain systems that contribute to the sense of self point to the frontal lobes as key. Right frontal cortex appears to be particularly important. Little is currently known about how religious aspects of the self are stored in the brain, but it is likely that the frontal lobes hold these representations of the religious self as well.

Language Networks and Meaning

Although meaning does not require language to function (after all, animals and humans who have lost core aspects of the language faculty nevertheless compute meanings), the development of language surely facilitated the expansion of the human meaning-making capacity. How do brain networks mediate core aspects of the language faculty? These core aspects include a lexicon, a grammar, and a set of rules linking lexical, grammatical, and semantic modules to produce sentences and utterances. Every sentence, for instance, assigns basic thematic roles (who did what to whom) to sentence constituents, and this theta role assignment process must, to some extent, intersect with the appraisal process discussed above.

Evidence for brain mediation of language function comes primarily from the clinic and from neuroimaging studies (Kertesz, 1999). We cannot review this vast field of studies here. Suffice it to say that left-sided frontal networks appear to mediate grammatical aspects of language, and left-sided posterior sites are important for language comprehension. Right-sided frontal networks are important for producing and understanding language in context, the pragmatic aspects of language use, including the appropriate use of speech acts mentioned above. Right-sided posterior sites are important for mediating prosodic aspects of speech or the emotional tone of a person's voice. These language functions are likely intimately tied to individuals' meaning-making processes, including those involving religious construals (Atran & Norenzayan, 2004).

Concept Formation

Much of our understanding of how the brain mediates concept formation comes from performances of brain-damaged subjects' performances on the Wisconsin Card Sort Test (WCST) of concept formation (Lezak, 1995, p. 61). In the basic setup of the WCST, the patient is given a pack of 60 cards on which are printed one to four symbols (e.g., a triangle or two stars or four circles). The symbols can also vary in color (red, green, yellow). The patient's task is to sort the 60 cards under four category cards (one red triangle; two green stars; three yellow crosses, and four blue circles). As the patient is attempting to guess what the sorting rule is for each category, the examiner informs him or her about whether each move is correct or incorrect. With enough trial and error sorts, the patient begins to form a concept of the rule that the examiner is using and, thus, what the correct rule is (e.g., "match all cards to the color of the category card and ignore the fact that it is also a triangle"). After 10 trials, the examiner secretly shifts the sort rule, and the patient must begin again to learn the correct sorting rule and thus learn the new concept the examiner is using as a rule. After six sorting trials, the examiner has a pretty good idea of how well the patient learns new concepts as well as the flexibility displayed by the patient in unlearning an old sorting rule and switching to a new one. Decades of use of the WCST suggests that patients with frontal lesions have the most difficulty with the test.

This process of concept formation, then, which occurs primarily in the frontal lobes, is a central component of meaning making. Concepts comprise the broad outlines of global meaning, discussed above. Regarding the links between religion, meaning, and the brain, the concepts more related to the supernatural—such as God, causality, morality, sin, suffering, and afterlife—clearly depend on these basic frontal lobe processes. Such concepts are apparently formed early (Boyatzis, 2005) but are subject to change throughout life as individuals confront experiences that may challenge their understanding of how the world works (Park, 2005).

Sleep-Associated Consolidation of Memories

We have argued that meaning is produced by the brain primarily via the accumulation of memories over time. It turns out that the sleeping brain plays a critical role in this process. Information gathered during the wake state appears to depend on hippocampal-cortical interactions that occur during both NREM (non–rapid eye movement) slow wave sleep (SWS) and REM (rapid eye movement) sleep and involve some sort of replay during REM sleep of learned associations acquired while awake (Buzsaki, 1996; Plihal & Born, 1997; Smith, 1995; Wilson & McNaughton, 1994). Wilson and McNaughton (1994), for example, showed that hippocampal cells that are active when rats learn a new maze are also active during subsequent sleep. Using PET and other scanning techniques, similar effects (re-activation of brain sites activated during learning) have been reported in humans (Laureys et al., 2001). Stickgold, Scott, Fosse, and Hobson (2001) have reported that learning a visual discrimination task was disrupted by selective deprivation of both REM and NREM. Similarly, Plihal and Born (1997) have reported that learning of paired associates and mental rotation tasks but not procedural memory tasks is dependent on subsequent NREM (early sleep) rather than REM (late morning sleep) periods for their consolidation. Although these studies are impressive, caution is required in interpreting many of the putative effects of sleep on memory systems. The role of REM sleep in memory consolidation, in particular, appears to have been somewhat overestimated. Nevertheless, the cumulative results from genetic, molecular, neuroimaging, and cognitive studies (Hairston & Knight, 2004; Hobson & Pace-Schott, 2002; Laureys et al., 2001; Maquet, Smith, & Stickgold, 2003; Walker, Brakefield, Hobson, & Stickgold, 2003) converge on the conclusion that sleep may be crucial for facilitating certain components of the processes of neural plasticity and for learning and memory.

Many authors have proposed that the hippocampus provides a rapidly encoded, but sparse, memory storage system ideal for the formation of distinct episodic memories. In contrast, the neocortex offers a slowly consolidating, dense memory storage system. Formation of independent memories within the neocortex results from frequent reactivation of the memory trace, either by reenactment of a sensorimotor pattern, as in most procedural learning paradigms, or by activation of a hippocampal representation of the memory, which would reactivate the cortical pattern. By using slow, automatic replay from the hippocampus (over days, weeks, or even years), high-density overlapping storage becomes feasible. Such replay may occur during SWS, when information is believed to flow from the hippocampus to the cortex and when there would be no competition from external sensory inputs. Such a model is supported by the findings of Plihal and Born (1997) noted above, suggesting a role for SWS in declarative memory consolidation.

While information appears to flow from hippocampus to cortex during SWS, theta rhythms are thought to support transfer of information in the opposite direction during REM sleep. Theta waves enhance hippocampal long-term potentiation (LTP), a candidate mechanism for memory formation. Interestingly, this synchronization with theta wave activity during REM sleep appears to shift from in-phase (i.e., correlating with the peak activity of the theta wave) to out-of-phase (correlated with the troughs of inactivity) over four to seven days of daily exposure to a new environment.

Such a shift could produce a switch from LTP and memory consolidation to memory erasure.

Together, these findings suggest a model of sequential memory processing in which different types or aspects of memories, including emotional memories, are processed progressively over the course of the night. In this model, specific memories from the recent past could be identified at sleep onset for subsequent reprocessing, and then stabilized or strengthened, possibly during NREM sleep, and integrated into cortical networks during REM. The model also suggests that meaning construction takes about seven days to coalesce. For episodic and emotional memories, cortical traces could be reactivated by hippocampal inputs during NREM and then linked in cortex during REM. The alternating REM and NREM periods would then permit several cycles of stabilization and integration, where the first cycle processes the memories reactivated at sleep onset and each subsequent cycle takes the products of memory integration from the preceding cycle as its starting point. The shift from predominantly SWS early in the night to REM late in the night would then reflect an underlying shift from an emphasis on stabilization and strengthening of waking memories early in the night toward the integration and establishment of new associative connections later in the night.

This knowledge of the mapping of the processes of memory consolidation and repeated elaboration and processing onto neurological substrates has not yet been applied to the meaning-making literature, but it clearly has important implications. In particular, the meaning-making literature notes that processes of repeated exposure and cognitive reappraisal are necessary to incorporate stressful events into one's global meaning system, sometimes over a period of years (Park & Folkman, 1997). Through this process of reappraisal, individuals are able to gain a new and more consistent understanding of the event (e.g., coming to see it as less aversive or problematic) or, sometimes, to change their global meaning system to accommodate the new information (e.g., changing their global beliefs in invulnerability or control) (Park, 2005). Although some of the intrusions and reappraisals occur during waking hours, it is likely that some important processing of this information also occurs during the processes of sleep. People with post-traumatic stress disorder, for example, often complain of intense dreams in which they essentially replay certain aspects of their original traumas. Hartmann (1998) has presented data that suggest that this replay of traumatic memories represents a process of slow integration of these unpleasant events into the long-term memory systems that ultimately serve as the basis of the meaning-making systems.

SYNDROMES OF MEANING LOSS

The brain is a pattern-detection device that operates on meaning; if no pattern is detectable, the brain seeks to create one. This is a truism throughout psychology, but neuropsychological syndromes provide particularly vivid illustrations of this search for meaning (e.g., Anton's syndrome, in which the patient is blind but does not believe he or she is blind, or confabulation syndrome after frontal lobe injury, in which the patient compulsively invents elaborate stories whenever unable to answer a simple question due to loss of memory).

Persons with right frontal lobe deficits, for example, may cling to an erroneous belief no matter how much evidence to the contrary is available (see articles in Christodoulou, 1986). In Capgras syndrome, for example, the patient believes his wife has been duplicated in every physical respect and thus is an imposter. He realizes it is a fantastic belief but he cannot shake it. In Othello syndrome, the patient is convinced of the infidelity of the spouse, and no amount of evidence to the contrary (often presented by a despairing family) will shake the belief. McNamara and Durso (1991) showed that the delusional belief system in one patient with Othello's syndrome was associated with catecholaminergic dysfunction in the frontal lobe. In folie à deux, two closely related persons—usually a mother and child or an adult couple—hold a delusional belief about their environment despite overwhelming evidence to the contrary. Theorists of these syndromes usually suggest a disconnect between frontal and temporal lobes such that mnemonic information from temporal sites cannot be integrated with control processes in the frontal lobe. In order to persist, beliefs must be protected from the effects of interference or countervailing evidence. This protection probably depends on insulating the belief from evaluation by insight systems (anteriorly located cortical systems). These syndromes illustrate both the overwhelming need for individuals to create and maintain a sense of meaning despite great obstacles to this creation and maintenance and the dependence of this meaning creation and maintenance on neural functioning.

OVERLAP OF BRAIN NETWORKS MEDIATING MEANING AND RELIGION

We have elsewhere (McNamara, 2000, 2001; McNamara, Durso, & Brown, 2003) reviewed the evidence for participation of the frontal lobes in religiosity and in functions likely to be related to religiosity. Recent neuroimaging studies (Newberg et al., 2001; Newberg, Pourdehnad, Alavi, & d'Aquili, 2003) confirm participation of frontal lobes in prayer and meditation. This should not be surprising when one considers what is required to pray to a God conceived as a personal being with paradoxical properties. To communicate with such a being, we would employ all those capacities we have developed to communicate with persons we interact with on a daily basis. The frontal lobes, for example, mediate processes of agency, theory of mind, prosocial behaviors of empathy and moral insight, belief fixation, self-awareness, and emotional processing (Damasio, 2005). The right frontal cortex, in particular, appears to mediate the sense of self, crucial mind-reading abilities, inferences about social interactions, discourse, autobiographical recall, and delusional belief fixation (see review of right frontal functions in Edwards-Lee & Saul, 1999). Thus, it is clear that the frontal lobes must be critically involved in fundamental aspects of religious cognition.

We have seen that neural networks that mediate meaning construction are widely distributed across brain regions but crucially involve the right frontal cortex. Our earlier reviews of religion-related cognitive functions also implicated the right frontal cortex. We make no claims about the significance of this overlap, but merely note it for future investigation.

EVOLUTIONARY FORCES

The above discussion has focused on the question of *how* religion (in contrast to the brain) produces meaning. At a minimum, religion appears to rely heavily on production and comprehension of messages in ritual contexts (self-referential, performative, indexical, and canonical in Rappaport's scheme) to make a multitude of meanings available to recipients of the messages. The brain, on the other hand, appears to rely on various types of memories to provide conceptual frameworks with which to evaluate or appraise all kinds of events and experiences. From the point of view of survival, it is not clear why people would need a system such as the messages encoded in religious rituals to produce meanings when the system based on memories seems more than adequate.

In this final section, we attempt to address *why* humans want to produce meanings via religious rituals. We argue that religious ritual might have functional components linked to its capacity to produce meaning. Several of the chapters in this volume advance a costly signaling theory (CST) of religious ritual (see chapters by Sosis [Vol. 1, chap. 4], Alcorta [Vol. 2, chap. 4], & Bubulia [Vol. 1, chap. 5] and the contributions of Sosis, 2005; Sosis & Alcorta, 2003). We therefore offer the following in the spirit of these other chapters. Our reading of the implications of CST for religion and meaning starts from the paradoxical observation that rituals seem nonsensical and empty of meaning rather than full of meanings as we argued above. CST is perfectly comfortable with apparently empty and meaningless practices and behaviors because these practices and behaviors can be considered "costly" to the individual who engages in them. CST likes costly practices because they can function as honest or hard-to-fake signals. The costlier the signal, the better it is (up to a point). Using these CST-related assumptions, religion and religious practices (including rituals) may be designed to signal commitment to the group with which the sender wants to cooperate. It is as though the person is saying, "I am willing to adopt all these crazy [costly] practices and participate in these meaningless rituals, and do all this consistently over time. Therefore,

I am not a fake or a free-rider. Costly signals are hard to fake; therefore you can conclude that I am truly committed to the group. No fake or free-rider would be willing to incur the costs of all of these practices and rituals and restrictions, so this proves I am trustworthy, so allow me to be a member in good standing and get all the benefits of cooperation with other group members." In other words, costly signals (or costly behaviors) function to identify the sender as honest and committed and not a free-rider (Fehr & Rockenbach, 2004). Humans, therefore, need to develop techniques to advertise their honesty, integrity, and non–free-rider status. They also need costly signals to advertise their "good genes"—analogous to the peacock's tail, wherein the more wasteful and flamboyant the tail, the better the prospects for attracting the attention of the peahen. The peacock's message is, "Look at my elaborate and wasteful tail. This tail proves that my genes are good enough to sustain wasteful metabolic gambits. Even though I have this useless tail I can still function perfectly well; therefore I must have great genes." Examples of these types of advertisements in humans might be the wealthy men in traditional societies who exhibit conspicuous consumption.

How does all this apply to the meaning-making capacities of religion? In the context of religion, how can one send a signal that he or she is truly committed to the religious group? The answer is to become a "true believer" and passionately convince oneself that the doctrines are true. The best example is the professional religionist, such as a clergy person or theologian. Who else can afford to spend so much time on arcane religious doctrines? Therefore, the ability to derive meaning from apparently meaningless rituals and practices may be an indicator of true commitment or "good genes," because it is a costly, hard-to-fake signal of commitment to the religion. Also the willingness to spend a lifetime on arcane rituals and doctrinal study signals someone who can extract meaning from the most obscure or seemingly meaningless texts and rituals. In a chaotic world, we need people who are proficient at finding meaning and patterns where no such patterns appear to exist. People who are professional pattern-detectors or meaning-extractors are likely better able to survive under adverse circumstances than those who are unable to find patterns in apparent chaos (or, to put it negatively, to delude themselves). The victims in the concentration camps who were able to maintain a belief in a good god despite the overwhelming evidence to the contrary were, indeed, the ones who survived.

CONCLUDING COMMENTS

This chapter provides a broad and brief overview of the convergence of religion, meaning, and the mind/brain processes that underlie them both. Researchers have been busy defining and exploring the making of meaning and its implications for psychological and physical well-being. Further, researchers have been paying increasing attention to the roles of religion in this meaning making (e.g., Park, 2005). Meanwhile, neuroscience work proliferates, and scientists are working to link religious phenomena with the brain (d'Aquili & Newberg, 1999; McNamara, 2001; Newberg & Newberg, 2005; and see other chapters in these volumes). However, bringing together religion, meaning, and the brain is relatively uncharted territory. This chapter summarized the meaning of *meaning* and reviewed the reasons that religion may be a particularly potent source of meanings. We also examined the ways in which the mind/brain integrates and creates new meanings on a day-to-day basis, relying particularly on memory, and illustrated the critical nature of these meanings by highlighting what happens when the meaning system breaks down due to brain damage. In pulling these notions together, we are frustrated with the lack of integrative theories or empirical findings, but we also feel quite optimistic that, as this field advances, the religious involvements in making meaning will receive increasing emphasis and that brain scientists will find it worthwhile to map these meaning-making processes onto brain systems.

REFERENCES

Aldwin, C. M. (in press). *Stress, coping, and development* (2nd ed.). New York: Guilford Press.

Atran, S., & Norenzayan, A. (2004). Religion's evolutionary landscape: Counterintuition, commitment, compassion, communion. *Behavioral and Brain Sciences, 27*(6), 713–770.

Baumeister, R. F. (1991). *Meanings of life.* New York: Guilford Press.

Berridge, C. W., Espana, R. A., & Stalnaker, T. A. (2003). Stress and coping: Asymmetry of dopamine efferents within the prefrontal cortex. In B. K. Hugdahl & R. J. Davidson (Eds.), *The asymmetrical* (pp. 69–104). Cambridge, MA: MIT Press.

Boyatzis, C. J. (2005). Religious and spiritual development in childhood. In R. F. Paloutzian & C. L. Park (Eds.), *Handbook of the psychology of religion and spirituality* (pp. 123–143). New York: Guilford Press.

Bruder, G. E. (2003). Frontal and parietotemporal asymmetries in depressive disorders: Behavioral electrophysiologic and neuroimaging findings. In B. K. Hugdahl & R. J. Davidson (Eds.), *The asymmetrical* (pp. 719–742). Cambridge, MA: MIT Press.

Buzsaki, G. (1996). The hippocampo-neocortical dialogue. *Cerebral Cortex, 6*(2), 81–92.

Chaiken, S., & Trope, Y. (1999). *Dual-process theories in social psychology.* New York: Guilford Press.

Christodoulou, G. N. (1986). The delusional misidentification syndromes. *Basel: Biblioteca Psychiatrica, 164,* 143–148.

Churchland, P. S. (2002). Self-representation in nervous systems. *Science, 296,* 308–310.

Craik, F. I. M., Moroz, T. M., & Moscovitch, M. (1999). In search of the self: A positron emission tomography study. *Psychological Science, 10,* 129–178.

Damasio, A. (2005). The frontal lobes. In K. Heilman & E. Valenstein (Eds.), *Clinical neuropsychology* (4th ed., pp. 404–446). Cambridge, England: Cambridge University Press.

d'Aquili, E. G., & Newberg, A. B. (1999). *The mystical mind: Probing the biology of religious experience.* Minneapolis: Augsburg Fortress Press.

Edwards-Lee, T. A., & Saul, R. (1999). Neuropsychiatry of the right frontal lobe. In B. L. Miller & J. L. Cummings (Eds.), *The human frontal lobes: Functions and disorder* (pp. 304–320). New York: Guilford Press.

Emmons, R. A. (1999). *The psychology of ultimate concerns.* New York: Guilford Press.

Fehr, E., & Rockenbach, B. (2004). Human altruism: Economic, neural and evolutionary perspectives. *Current Opinion in Neurobiology, 14,* 784–790.

Fink, G. R., Markowitsch, H. J., Reinkemeier, M., Bruckbauer, T., Kessler, J., & Heiss, W. D. (1996). Cerebral representation of one's own past: Neural networks involved in autobiographical memory. *Journal of Neuroscience, 16*(13), 4275–4282.

Gallagher, S. (2000). Philosophical conceptions of the self: Implications for cognitive science. *Trends in Cognitive Science, 4,* 14–21.

Hairston, I. S., & Knight, R. T. (2004). Neurobiology: Sleep on it. *Nature, 430*(6995), 27–28.

Hartmann, E. (1998). *Dreams and nightmares: The new theory on the origin and meaning of dreams.* New York: Plenum Press.

Hobson, J. A., & Pace-Schott, E. F. (2002). The cognitive neuroscience of sleep: Neuronal systems, consciousness and learning. *Nature Reviews Neuroscience, 3*(9), 679–693.

Keenan, J. P., Nelson, A., O'Connor, M., & Pascual-Leone, A. (2001). Self-recognition and the right hemisphere. *Nature, 409,* 305.

Kelley, W. M., Macrae, C. N., Wyland, C. L., Caglar, S., Inati, S., & Heatherton, T. F. (2002). Finding the self? An event-related fMRI study. *Journal of Cognitive Neuroscience, 14,* 785–794.

Kertesz, A. (1999). Language and the frontal lobes. In B. L. Miller & J. L. Cummings (Eds.), *The human frontal lobes: Functions and disorders* (pp. 261–276). New York: Guilford Press.

Laughlin, C. D., & Throop, C. J. (2001). Imagination and reality: On the relations between myth, consciousness, and the quantum sea. *Zygon, 36,* 709–736.

Laureys, S., Peigneux, P., Phillips, C., Fuchs, S., Degueldre, C., Aerts, J.,et al. (2001). Experience-dependent changes in cerebral functioning connectivity during human rapid eye movement sleep. *Neuroscience, 105,* 521–525.

Lazarus, R. S., & Folkman, S. (1984). *Stress, coping, and appraisal.* New York: Springer.

LeDoux, J. E. (2002). *Synaptic self: How our brains become who we are.* New York: Viking Press.

Lezak, N. D. (1995). *Neuropsychological assessment* (3rd ed.). New York: Oxford University Press.

Loevinger, J. (1976). *Ego development: [Conceptions and theories].* San Francisco: Jossey-Bass.

Loevinger, J., Wessler, R., & Redmore, B. (1970). *Measuring ego development.* San Francisco: Jossey-Bass.

Maier, S. F., & Watkins, L. R. (2002). Cytokines for psychologists: Implications of bidirectional immune to brain communication for understanding behavior mood and cognition. In J. T. Caciopo, G. G. Bernstrom, R. Adolphs, C. Carter, R. Davidson,

M. McClintock, B. McEwen, M. Meaney, D. Shachter, E. Sternberg, S. Suomi, & S. Taylor (Eds.), *Foundations in social neuroscience* (pp. 1141–1182). Cambridge, MA: MIT Press.

Maquet, P., Smith, C., & Stickgold, R. (2003). *Sleep and brain plasticity.* Oxford, England: Oxford University Press.

Maruta, T., Colligan, R. C., Malinchoc, M., & Offord, K. P. (2000). Optimists vs. pessimists: Survival rate among medical patients over a 30-year period. *Mayo Clinic Proceedings, 75*(2), 140–143.

McNamara, P. (2000). The frontal lobes, social intelligence, and religious worship. Ideas for creative research in neurobiology. John Templeton Foundation. http://www.templeton.org/pdf/creative_research.pdf, pp. 50–60.

McNamara, P. (2001). Frontal lobes and religion. In J. Andresen (Ed.), *Religion in mind* (pp. 237–256). Cambridge, England: Cambridge University Press.

McNamara, P., & Durso, R. (1991). Reversible Othello syndrome in a man with Parkinson's disease. *American Journal of Geriatric Neurology and Psychiatry, 4*(3), 157–159.

McNamara, P., Durso, R., & Brown, A. (2003). Relation of "sense of self" to executive function in Parkinson's disease. *Cognitive and Behavioral Neurology, 14*, 139–148.

McNamara, P., von Harscher, H., Scioli, T., Krueger, M., Lawson, D., & Durso, R. (1995). The sense of self after brain damage: Evidence from aphasics and individuals with Parkinson's disease. *Journal of Cognitive Rehabilitation, November/December*, 16–23.

Metzinger, T. (2003). *Being no one: The self-model theory of subjectivity.* Cambridge, MA: MIT Press.

Miller, B., Seeley, W. W., Mychack, P., Rosen, H. J., Mena, I., & Boone, K. (2001). Neuroanatomy of the self: Evidence from patients with frontotemporal dementia. *Neurology, 57*(1), 817–821.

Newberg, A., Alavi, A., Baime, M., Pourdehnad, M., Santanna, J., & d'Aquili, E. (2001). The measurement of regional cerebral blood flow during the complex cognitive task of meditation: A preliminary SPECT study. *Psychiatry Research: Neuroimaging, 106*, 113–122.

Newberg, A. B., & Newberg, S. K. (2005). The neuropsychology of religious and spiritual experience. In R. F. Paloutzian & C. L. Park (Eds.), *Handbook of the psychology of religion and spirituality* (pp. 199–215). New York: Guilford Press.

Newberg, A., Pourdehnad, M., Alavi, A., & d'Aquili, E. (2003). Cerebral blood flow during meditative prayer: Preliminary findings and methodological issues. *Perceptual and Motor Skills, 97*, 625–630.

Northoff, G., & Bermpohl, F. (2004). Cortical midline structures and the self. *Trends in Cognitive Sciences, 8*(3), 102–107.

Nyberg, L., McIntosh, A. R., Cabeza, R., Nilsson, L. G., Houle, S., Habib, R., et al. (1996). Network analysis of positron emission tomography regional cerebral blood flow data: Ensemble inhibition during episodic memory retrieval. *Journal of Neuroscience, 16*(11), 3753–3759.

Ongur, D., & Price, J. L. (2000). The organization of networks within the orbital and medial prefrontal cortex of rats, monkeys and humans. *Cerebral Cortex, 10*, 206–219.

Pargament, K. I., Ano, G. G., & Wachholtz, A. B. (2005). The religious dimension of coping: Advances in theory, research, and practice. In R. F. Paloutzian & C. L. Park

(Eds.), *Handbook of the psychology of religion and spirituality* (pp. 479–495). New York: Guilford Press.

Park, C.L. (2005). Religion and meaning. In R.F. Paloutzian & C.L. Park (Eds.), *Handbook of the psychology of religion and spirituality* (pp. 295–314). New York: Guilford Press.

Park, C.L., & Folkman, S. (1997). Meaning in the context of stress and coping. *General Review of Psychology, 1,* 115–144.

Plihal, W., & Born, J. (1997). Effects of early and late nocturnal sleep on declarative and procedural memory. *Journal of Cognitive Neuroscience, 9*(4), 534–547.

Rappaport, R. (1999). *Ritual and religion in the making of humanity.* Cambridge, England: Cambridge University Press.

Reite, M., Kaemingk, K., & Boccia, M.L. (1989). Maternal separation in bonnet monkey infants: Altered attachment and social support. *Child Development, 60*(2), 473–480.

Reite, M., Seiler, C., & Short, R. (1978). Loss of your mother is more than loss of a mother. *American Journal of Psychiatry, 135*(3), 370–371.

Sauro, M.D., & Greenberg, R.P. (2005). Endogenous opiates and the placebo effect: A meta-analytic review. *Journal of Psychosomatic Research, 58*(2), 115–120.

Schnider, A., & Gutbrod, K. (1999). Traumatic brain injury. In B.L. Miller & J.L. Cummings (Eds.), *The human frontal lobes: Functions and disorders* (pp. 487–508). New York: Guilford Press.

Schulz, R., Bookwala, J., Knapp, J.E., Scheier, M., & Williamson, G.M. (1996). Pessimism, age, and cancer mortality. *Psychology and Aging, 11*(2), 304–309.

Silberman, I. (in press). Religion as a meaning system: Implications for the new millennium. *Journal of Social Issues.*

Smith, C. (1995). Sleep states and memory processes. *Behavioural Brain Research, 69*(1–2), 137–145.

Spilka, B., Hood, R.W., Jr., Hunsberger, B., & Gorsuch, R. (2003). *The psychology of religion: An empirical approach* (3rd ed.). New York: Guilford Press.

Spilka, B., Shaver, P.P., & Kirkpatrick, L.A. (1997). A general attribution theory for the psychology of religion. In B. Spilka & D.N. McIntosh (Eds.), *The psychology of religion: Theoretical approaches* (pp. 153–170). Boulder, CO: Westview Press.

Sosis, R. (2005). Does religion promote trust? The role of signaling, reputation, and punishment. *Interdisciplinary Journal of Research on Religion, 1,* 1–30.

Sosis, R., & Alcorta, C. (2003). Signaling, solidarity, and the sacred: The evolution of religious behavior. *Evolutionary Anthropology, 12,* 264–274.

Stickgold, R., Scott, L., Fosse, R., & Hobson, J.A. (2001). Brain-mind states: I. Longitudinal field study of wake-sleep factors influencing mentation report length. *Sleep, 24*(2), 171–179.

Vogeley, K., & Fink, G.R. (2003). Neural correlates of the first-person perspective. *Trends in Cognitive Sciences, 7,* 38–42.

Vogeley, K., Kurthen, M., Falkai, P., & Maier, W. (1999). Essential functions of the human self model are implemented in the prefrontal cortex. *Consciousness and Cognition, 8*(3), 343–363.

Walker, M.P., Brakefield, T., Hobson, J.A., & Stickgold, R. (2003). Dissociable stages of human memory consolidation and reconsolidation. *Nature, 425*(6958), 616–620.

Weingarten, S. M. (1999). Psychosurgery. In B. L. Miller & J. L. Cummings (Eds.), *The human frontal lobes: Functions and disorders* (pp. 446–460). New York: Guilford Press.

Wheeler, M. A., Stuss, D. T., & Tulving, E. (1997). Toward a theory of episodic memory: The frontal lobes and autonoetic consciousness. *Psychological Bulletin, 121*(3), 331–354.

Wilson, M. A., & McNaughton, B. L. (1994). Reactivation of hippocampal ensemble memories during sleep. *Science, 265,* 676–679.

Wong, P. T. P., & Fry, P. S. (1998). *The human quest for meaning.* Mahwah, NJ: Erlbaum.

CHAPTER 4

THE DARKER SIDE OF RELIGION: RISK FACTORS FOR POORER HEALTH AND WELL-BEING

Gina Magyar-Russell and Kenneth Pargament

INTRODUCTION

Although the founders of psychology believed that religion represented a critical topic of interest for the newly emerging field, empirical studies of religion lost favor for much of the twentieth century, perhaps because psychodynamic theories cast it in a negative light or perhaps because behaviorally oriented psychologists were eager to establish the discipline as a hard science and had little interest in a phenomenon as "soft" as religion. In the latter part of the century, this picture changed. An upsurge of religious study occurred within the health and social sciences, and, in contrast to critical depictions of religion within some major theoretical traditions, the mass of evidence from these empirical studies suggested that religion is generally linked to better health and well-being (e.g., Koenig, McCullough, & Larson, 2001).

Much of this research, however, has relied on global indicators of religiousness. Operationally, religion is defined by how often an individual attends religious services, how often he or she prays or meditates, whether the person belongs to a particular religious denomination, and how the individual rates him- or herself on a scale of religiousness. As a whole, these studies indicate that a greater degree of religious involvement among people in the United States is generally beneficial. Yet, because religion has been measured in such global ways, these studies provide little information about the specifics of religious life. In particular, this broad approach to religious study obscures the possibility that certain specific forms of religiousness have different, even deleterious, implications for health and well-being.

In fact, there are theoretical reasons to suggest that some religious expressions may be harmful rather than helpful. Consistent with this theory, a small but growing body of empirical study has begun to identify "religious risk factors" for poorer health. In this chapter, we review theory and evidence relevant to these religious risk factors, consider some of the factors that may help explain the links between these risk factors and poorer health, and conclude with a discussion of the clinical and empirical implications of this emerging line of study. Before beginning, however, we would like to emphasize that, in focusing on religious risk factors, we are not suggesting that religion is on-the-whole harmful or more destructive than constructive. To the contrary, we believe the weight of evidence underscores the generally positive value of religiousness for health and well-being. Nevertheless, it is important to move from the general to the specific. In the interest of a balanced and complete understanding of religious life, it is incumbent on researchers and health professionals to learn about religion in all of its forms, the harmful as well as the helpful. We begin with a definition of religion.

DEFINING RELIGION

Elsewhere, Pargament (1997) has defined religion as a search for significance in ways related to the sacred. Three terms are critical to this definition: significance, search, and sacred. First, this definition rests on the assumption that people are goal-directed beings, motivated to attain value or significance in life (Klinger, 1998). Objects of significance vary from person to person; they may be material (e.g., money, possessions), physical (e.g., appearance, health), psychological (e.g., self-esteem, meaning and purpose), or social (e.g., intimacy, friendship). People can be defined, in part, by the distinctive configuration of significant objects that provide motivation and direction to their lives.

Second, this definition assumes that people are involved in a search for significance. Every search refers to an ultimate destination, "significance," and a pathway to reach that destination. Pathways consist of thoughts, feelings, practices, and relationships that are designed to serve three interrelated purposes: to discover significance; to conserve or hold on to significance once it has been found; and to transform significance when required by internal or external changes and transitions.

The sacred element of religion includes concepts of God and the divine. The sacred also encompasses other aspects of life that take on transcendent character and significance by virtue of their association with, or representation of, divinity (Pargament & Mahoney, 2002). Through this process of sanctication, many seemingly secular parts of life can be perceived as sacred: time and space (the Sabbath, churches); events and transitions (birth, death); materials (wine, crucifix); cultural products (music, literature); people (saints, cult leaders); psychological attributes (self, meaning); social attributes (compassion, community); and, roles (marriage, parenting, work).

People can pursue the sacred as one class of significant destinations in life. For example, they may seek to know God, build a holy marital bond, experience the transcendent, or bring the world into greater alignment with a divine vision. People can also integrate the sacred in the pathways they take to significance, through religious study, religious practice, religious experience, and involvement in religious community. But regardless of its particular expression, the involvement of the sacred in the search for significance is what distinguishes religion from other phenomenon.

Religion, from this perspective, is not a static set of beliefs or practices. It is instead a process by which the sacred becomes a part of the pathways people take in search of whatever they hold significant, including the sacred itself. This process is complex, multiform, and individualized. Why? Because there are innumerable pathways, because pathways shift and change over life, because people seek out many different destinations in living, and because the sacred can take so many different forms in people's pathways and destinations.

With this definition in mind, we consider some of the theoretical reasons that certain forms of religiousness may pose risks to health and well-being, and we review empirical studies that have begun to test these theories. We focus on four theories: motivational theory, attachment theory, process theory, and coping theory. Because much of the evidence for religious risk factors comes from coping theory, we pay particular attention to this area of research. The list below summarizes the religious risk factors that have been generated from these areas of theory and research.

RELIGIOUS RISK FACTORS FOR POORER HEALTH

Motivation Theory

    Idolatry

    Extrinsic Religious Motivation

    Religious Introjection (i.e., Guilt-Based, Externally Based Motivation)

Attachment Theory

    Avoidant Attachment to God

    Anxious Attachment to God

Process Theory

    Poor Fit between Religion and the Situation

    Religious Rigidity

    Lack of Religious Breadth and Depth

MOTIVATIONAL THEORY AND RESEARCH

According to motivational theory, it matters "both what you pursue and why you pursue it" (Sheldon, Ryan, Deci, & Kasser, 2004). This point applies well to the religious realm. Initial empirical research suggests that people who devote more of their energy to the pursuit of spiritual ends experience emotional benefits. Emmons, Cheung, and Tehrani (1998) asked samples of college and community-based adults to generate their personal strivings and found that those who reported more spiritual strivings (e.g., seeking God's will; seeking to deepen a relationship with God; attempting to live by one's spiritual beliefs in daily life) manifested greater purpose in life and marital and overall life satisfaction. Furthermore, the correlations between these spiritual strivings and measures of subjective well-being were stronger than the correlations between all other strivings and well-being. On the other hand, people can sanctify destructive as well as constructive spiritual ends, and, as Parker Palmer (1998) wrote, "There are real dangers involved when the sacred gets attached to the wrong things" (p. 25). Drugs, alcohol, consumerism, and self-worship are a few of the ways in which people attempt to fill a spiritual vacuum. Consider how one man confused his thirst for God with a thirst for alcohol:

> As my alcoholism progressed my thirst for God increasingly became transmuted into a thirst for the seemingly godlike experiences that alcohol induced. Alcohol gave me a sense of well-being and connectedness—and wasn't that an experience of God? Alcohol released me from the nagging sense that I was never good or competent enough—and wasn't that God's grace? (Nelson, 2004, p. 31)

Unfortunately, there is little research on false gods. Yet there is no shortage of dramatic cases that point to the destructive implications of idolatry for health and well-being, from those who devote themselves to abusive spouses or despotic authority figures to those who center their lives around food, drugs, and alcohol. For example, commenting on the prevalence of self-worship among Nazis in World War II, Carl Jung (1945/1964) wrote:

> "God-almightiness" does not make man divine, it merely fills him with arrogance and arouses everything evil in him. It produces a diabolical

caricature of man, and this inhuman mask is so unendurable, such a torture to wear, that he tortures others. He is split in himself, a prey to inexplicable contradictions. (p. 215)

Motivational theory also underscores the importance of why people involve themselves in religion. In a classic work, Gordon Allport compared intrinsically motivated religious individuals, those who approach their religion as an end in itself, favorably to extrinsically motivated people, those who "use their religion" for personal or social ends (Allport & Ross, 1967). Higher levels of extrinsic religiousness have been linked to poorer mental health in a number of studies (e.g., Donahue, 1985). Similarly, Ryan, Rigby, and King (1993) distinguished between religious motivation based on personal choice (i.e., "identification") from religious motivation based on guilt, anxiety, and external pressures (i.e., "introjection"). In an empirical study of several Christian samples, they found that religious introjection was associated with poorer mental health, while religious identification was related to better mental health. These studies suggest that people may be at greater risk for problems when religiousness is pursued for reasons other than personal conviction.

ATTACHMENT THEORY AND RESEARCH

In his efforts to explain why institutionalized children often failed to thrive, psychiatrist John Bowlby (1969) developed a theory of attachment that has important implications for the psychology of religion. Bowlby proposed that an attachment system evolved in humans and other primates to protect helpless infants from internal and external dangers. He noted that infants and young children engage in a variety of attachment behaviors (e.g., crying, outstretched arms, clinging) to gain closer proximity to the caregiver in times of stress. Infants who develop a secure attachment to their parents achieve a safe haven from dangers and a secure base for exploration at other times. Not all children, however, attain secure attachments to their parents. Through observational studies of infant and parents, Ainsworth and her colleagues identified two types of insecure attachments: avoidant infants who appeared to be indifferent to separation and reunion with their parents, and anxious/ambivalent infants who showed a great deal of distress when separated from their parents and fearfulness in exploring the environment (Ainsworth, Blehar, Waters, & Wall, 1978). A large body of empirical evidence indicates that a person's attachment system has important implications for his or her health and well-being (Maunder & Hunter, 2001).

Lee Kirkpatrick (2005) has argued persuasively that God can also be understood as an attachment figure. The parallels with parents are

numerous and striking, he concludes from his review of a diverse literature. First, as they do with parents, people often seek proximity to God in
stressful situations. Second, like a parent, God can provide a haven of safety
in dangerous times and a secure base from which to explore the world
with confidence in safer conditions. In some sense, God may be the most
ideal of attachment figures because, unlike parents, God can be perceived
as immune to danger and continually available regardless of time or situation. Third, people who report that they have been separated from God
often react with distress similar to children separated from their parents.
Fourth, as with their parents, people can form insecure as well as secure
attachments to God. In fact, Kirkpatrick (2005) cites a number of studies
that show a correspondence between the nature of a child's attachment
to his or her parents and the child's attachment to God. Finally, like the
attachment to parents, an individual's attachment to God is tied to his or
her health and well-being.

In support of this latter assertion, a growing body of literature suggests that people with insecure attachments to God experience poorer
health and well-being (see Kirkpatrick, 2005, for a review). For example,
Rowatt and Kirkpatrick (2002) found that college students with more
anxious attachments to God reported greater neuroticism and negative affect, and less positive affect. Similarly, working with a community
sample responding to a newspaper survey, Kirkpatrick and Shaver (1992)
found that individuals with avoidant attachments to God (e.g., perceiving
that God is distant and uncaring) manifested greater depression, psychosomatic symptoms, loneliness, and less life satisfaction than respondents
who described secure or anxious attachments to God. Consistent with
these findings, higher levels of religious strain and conflict (e.g., feeling
distant from God, difficulty trusting God, feelings one's sins are too big
to be forgiven, feeling guilt for wavering faith) have been associated with
depression and suicidality (Exline, Yali, & Sanderson, 2000) and greater
likelihood of panic disorder (Trenholm, Trent, & Compton, 1998) in
samples of adult psychotherapy outpatients. Overall, this literature suggests that an insecure religious attachment represents a risk factor for
the individual's well-being.

PROCESS THEORY AND RESEARCH

For the most part, theorists and researchers have attempted to identify
specific forms of religiousness that might be helpful or harmful, such as
church attendance, prayer, meditation, fundamentalism, and so on. In contrast, several theorists suggest that the efficacy of religion may depend not
on specific types of religious beliefs and practices, but rather on the degree
to which the individual's religion is well integrated or poorly integrated

(Allport, 1950; Pargament, 1997). Integration is not easy to describe, for it has to do with the workings of the whole rather than its parts. Perhaps for that reason, writers have often turned to metaphors to capture the meaning of a well-integrated religion. For example, writing about religion at its best, Allport (1950) put it this way: "It is a rich pudding, smooth and simple in its blend, but intricate in ingredients. Or to dignify the metaphor, it is a white light in personality which, though luminous and simple, is in reality multi-colored in composition" (p. 9). In contrast, a poorly integrated religion has been described as a system that "loses its balance, its synchrony. The fault here lies not with any one element of the process, but with the system itself" (Pargament, 1997, p. 316).

Mental health professionals and clergy appear to attend to integration in their evaluations of the efficacy of religion. In one study, Butter and Pargament (2003) presented these groups with vignettes that varied in their degree of religious integration. For example, one well-integrated vignette described the case of one man with an incurable physical ill-ness who defers the responsibility for his health to God. A second poorly integrated vignette described the case of another man with a treatable illness who engages in the exact same form of religious deferral. While religious deferral is a reasonable response to an uncontrollable illness, it fits less well with an illness that calls for an active response on the part of the patient. Both clergy and mental health professionals rated reli-gion as more harmful in the poorly integrated vignettes than in the well-integrated vignettes. It is important to stress that the religious behavior of the individuals was identical in these vignettes; what varied was the degree of integration of religion with other dimensions of life, in this case, the fit between the religious approach to problem solving and the control-lability of the situation.

Theorists and researchers have examined other elements of religious integration and dis-integration, including religious rigidity and inflexibility, the lack of religious breadth and depth, and religious extremism. Mature faith, Allport (1950) asserted, is heuristic, a "working hypothesis . . . it can act whole-heartedly even without absolute certainty. It can be sure without being cocksure" (p. 81). In contrast, poorly integrated religion is rigid and inflexible, unable to respond to changing individual needs, times, and circum-stances. Although rigid systems of belief can provide people with a sense of absolute certainty and conviction, they may also lead people to take extreme steps when they feel their beliefs are threatened. In this vein, Altemeyer and Hunsberger (1992) found that people who reported a less flexible religious faith demonstrated greater prejudice toward homosexuals as well as other minority groups. For example, religious inflexibility was linked to more agreement with the belief that "the AIDS disease currently killing homo-sexuals is just what they deserve" (p. 123).

Theorists have also generally agreed that mature systems of religious belief and practice have breadth and depth. They are capable of providing overarching frameworks of meaning that help people come to terms with the full range of life experiences. In contrast, poorly integrated religious systems lack comprehensiveness. Perhaps the most common example involves religious systems of belief that account for the positive dimensions of life but founder when confronted with suffering, pain, and injustice. The notion that there is a higher power who ensures that good things will happen to good people can be of great comfort in stress-free times of life. More difficult periods, however, can throw individuals into a crisis of meaning in which they must face serious questions about their own goodness or the goodness and power of God. William James (1902) described this kind of faith as "healthy-minded religion" but criticized it for its narrowness:

> There is no doubt that healthy-mindedness is inadequate as a philosophical doctrine, because the evil facts which it refutes positively to account for are a genuine portion of reality; and they may after all be the best key to life's significance, and possibly the only openers of our eyes to the deepest levels of truth. (p. 160)

Conversely, some systems of religious belief focus on the dark side of life and allow no place for atonement or redemption, as we hear in John Bunyan's account of his religious melancholy:

> I was more loathsome in my own eyes than was a toad; and I thought I was so in God's eyes too. Sin and corruption, I said, would as naturally bubble out of my heart as water would bubble out of a fountain. . . . I thought none but the Devil himself could equal me for inward wickedness and pollution of mind. (cited in James, 1902, p. 155)

In a study that speaks to the negative implications of narrow systems of religious belief, Watson, Morris, and Hood (1988) found that Christian college students who reported higher levels of religious guilt experienced more depression and anxiety. However, these effects were reduced when a measure of grace (e.g., "My sins are forgiven") was entered into the equation.

Finally, theorists have spoken of the dangers of religious extremism, the problem that arises when religious means become disproportionate to religious ends. Religious extremism can take the form of violence in the name of the sacred, self-degradation in the pursuit of sacred goals, or scrupulosity that interferes with the attainment of religious ends. For example, Greenberg, Witztum, and Pisante (1987) recounted the case of one scrupulous, orthodox Jewish man who was tremendously fearful of violating the religious injunction to be "clean at all orifices." To avoid the risk of this transgression, he would spend 20 minutes cleaning and checking his anal area before each of his three daily periods of prayer. As a result of the scrupulous attention to his cleanliness, however, he was often late to prayer and failed to fulfill a religious obligation of greater importance than the cleanliness of orifices. Unfortunately, even though it is a central topic of concern today, religious extremism has received little research attention.

COPING THEORY AND RESEARCH

Few people, if any, go through their lives without being impacted by significant life stressors. And yet, empirical studies have shown that the relationship between exposure to major life stressors and subsequent physical and mental health is relatively modest (Rabkin & Streuning, 1976). Coping theorists, such as Richard Lazarus and Susan Folkman, explain these modest links by noting that people do not simply react to critical life events; they appraise these events in terms of their implications for well-being, and they cope with these events in ways to maximize the sense of significance in life (Hopfoll, 1988; Lazarus & Folkman, 1984). It follows that the impact of life stressors on health and well-being depends at least in part on how people appraise and cope with critical events. A considerable body of research has supported this assertion (e.g., Aldwin, 1994; Mullen & Suls, 1982). Depending on how events are understood and handled, the effects of major life stressors may be mitigated or exacerbated.

Religion also can be involved in how people understand and deal with life events. This is, by no means, unusual. In fact, a number of studies have shown that many people turn to religion for help in their most difficult moments (e.g., Conway, 1985–1986; McCrae, 1984). Pargament (1997) has described how religion can be a critical part of both appraisals and coping. Life events, he points out, affect people not only psychologically, socially, and physically, but spiritually as well. Take, for example, the crisis of clergy sexual abuse. For many survivors, the trauma is first and foremost spiritual in nature. One survivor put it bluntly: "I don't think I'll ever step foot in a church again. . . . I lost my religion, faith, and ability to trust adults and institutions" (Matchan, 1992, p. 8). People appraise life events according to their implications for their spirituality as well as their other aspects of well-being. To put it another way, events are evaluated with an eye to whatever people hold sacred.

Religion is also part and parcel of the ways many people choose to cope with critical life events (Pargament, 1997). The major religious traditions of the world provide their adherents with a variety of coping resources that can be accessed in stressful times. They take the form of religious rituals (e.g., rites of passage, purification), religious beliefs (e.g., life after death, a loving God), religious experiences (e.g., prayer, meditation), and religious relationships (e.g., support from congregation and clergy). Not all forms of religious coping are necessarily positive, however. In some instances, life stressors may threaten or destabilize the individual's orientation of religious beliefs and practices. A religious struggle may follow in which the individual attempts to conserve a religious framework or, if necessary, transform it (Pargament, Murray-Swank, Magyar, & Ano, 2005).

Although empirical studies have shown that religious involvement in coping is, by and large, beneficial (Ano & Vasconcelles, 2005; Pargament, 1997), a growing body of studies identifies religious risk factors on the coping process. We focus on two of these risk factors: appraisals of life events as losses or violations of the sacred and religious struggles.

Appraisals of Sacred Loss and Desecration

Recently, researchers have begun to investigate explicit spiritual appraisals of negative events that may relate to poor health outcomes (Magyar, Pargament, & Mahoney, 2000; Magyar-Russell, 2005; Pargament, Magyar, Benore, & Mahoney, 2005). Two spiritual appraisals in particular appear to be problematic: the perception that a sanctified object has been lost (sacred loss) and the perception that a sanctified object has been violated (desecration).

In an initial study of desecration, Magyar et al. (2000) examined the psychological, physical, and spiritual implications of perceiving that a past or current romantic relationship had been spiritually violated (i.e., desecrated). Working with a sample of college men and women ($n = 344$) from a mid-sized Midwestern university, the researchers found that desecration was associated with more negative affect (e.g., feeling distressed, nervous, scared, irritable, upset), more negative physical health symptoms (e.g., nausea or upset stomach, headaches, loss of appetite), and more symptoms of intrusive and avoidant thoughts and behaviors related to the desecration event(s). Importantly, the links between desecration and outcomes were not reduced by controlling for traditional religious variables, the number of offenses committed in the desecration event, and the negativity of the impact of the betrayals. Thus, perceptions that a violation of a spiritual nature had taken place impacted the participants on emotional, physical, and psychological levels.

In a second study of spiritual appraisals of negative life events, Pargament, Magyar, Benore, and Mahoney (2005) examined perceptions of sacred loss and desecration in a community sample in northwest Ohio. Participants recounted the most significant negative life event that took place in their lives in the past two years. Hierarchical regression analyses were conducted that controlled for traditional religious variables, the belief that another person caused the negative event, and the number of objects perceived as lost or violated by the event. Sacred loss was uniquely predictive of intrusive thoughts, avoidant behaviors, and feelings of depression linked to the event. Desecration was uniquely predictive of more avoidant behaviors related to the desecration event, greater feelings of anger related to the event, and less post-traumatic growth from experiencing the event.

Another study explored the spiritual appraisals of desecration following the September 11, 2001, terrorist attacks. In samples of college students in New York City and a Midwest town, Mahoney et al. (2002) found that greater perceptions of desecration were linked to higher levels of post-traumatic stress and depressive symptoms following the attacks, as well as more days of missed work or school.

A final longitudinal study of spiritual appraisals was conducted by Magyar-Russell (2005) with medical rehabilitation inpatients who had experienced stroke, spinal cord injury, lower-limb amputations, and other unexpected physical traumas. Participants who experienced their accident, illness, or injury as a sacred loss reported greater depression and anxiety, after controlling for age, impact of the event, the number of objects viewed as lost or violated, and global religiosity. Additionally, appraisals of sacred loss at admission significantly predicted depression at discharge and six weeks after discharge from inpatient rehabilitation. Greater appraisals of desecration at admission were predictive of higher levels of anxiety at admission and greater depressive symptoms six weeks after discharge. At the six-week follow-up period, greater perception of both sacred loss and desecration were significant predictors of decreased spiritual well-being. The findings from this study demonstrate that appraisals of sacred loss and desecration are relevant in situations of personal physical health challenges and that these spiritual appraisals continue to exert a negative emotional, psychological, and spiritual impact over time.

Two additional points are important to stress. First, appraisals of sacred loss and desecration are common. For example, 80 percent of the students in the college sample reported a desecration in a romantic relationship. In the adult community sample, 72 percent appraised their negative life event as a sacred loss, and 50 percent appraised it as a desecration. Among medical rehabilitation patients, 69 percent reported a sacred loss, and 43 percent reported a desecration. Furthermore, these appraisals were common among both men and women of all ages. Second, appraisals of sacred loss and desecration should not be confused with indicators of general religiousness. Indeed, Magyar-Russell (2005) noted that indices of global religiousness were not significantly correlated with appraisals of sacred loss or desecration at any of three assessment periods in her work with rehabilitation patients. One participant in this study was a 21-year-old African American woman who suffered an unexpected and inexplicable stroke. Her global religiousness score was a standard deviation below the sample mean, and her sacred loss and desecration scores were well over one standard deviation above the sample means. During a research interview, this participant supplemented her responses to the psychological and spiritual questionnaires by emphatically remarking, "Damn it, I had a stroke and I'm only 21! Why did God let

this happen to me?" Her story illustrates how assessing the spiritual appraisals linked to a specific life event may lead to a better understanding of the
intimate connections between religion and health. Her story also illustrates
how particular types of spiritual appraisal can contribute to adverse mental, physical, and spiritual health following unexpected and distressing life
events.

Religious Struggles

Researchers have shown that individuals are vulnerable to spiritual
challenges that overwhelm their spiritual resources in times of stress
(Fitchett, Rybarczyk, DeMarco, & Nicholas, 1999; Koenig, Pargament, &
Nielson, 1998; Pargament, 1997; Pargament, Koenig, Tarakeshwar, & Hahn,
2001; Pargament, Smith, Koenig, & Perez, 1998). Unexpected negative life
events, loss, and trauma often shatter previously held assumptions about the
benevolence, fairness, and meaningfulness of the world (Janoff-Bulman, 1992).
For many, this shattering of assumptions extends to the spiritual dimension of their lives. In response to this "spiritual upheaval," they may experience religious struggles, including struggles with the divine, intrapsychic
struggles, and interpersonal struggles. These struggles are not unusual. For
example, in a survey of over 5,000 college students, 25 percent reported considerable distress related to their religious and spiritual concerns (Johnson &
Hayes, 2003). In a study of patients with diabetes mellitus, congestive heart
failure outpatients, and oncology inpatients, 15 percent of the total sample
reported moderate to high levels of spiritual struggle (Fitchett et al., 2004).

Divine Struggles

Major life stressors can challenge an individual's understanding of the
divine, triggering fundamental questions about the benevolence of God, the
limits of God's powers, and feelings of divine abandonment, anger toward
God, and demonic forces at large in the world. In a series of studies, Pargament
and his colleagues examined the impact of these divine struggles on physical
health and mental health among people coping with a variety of stressors.
Divine struggles were measured by the negative religious coping subscale
of the RCOPE (Pargament et al., 1998; Pargament, Koenig, & Perez, 2000).
The findings have been consistent. Negative religious coping has been linked
through cross-sectional studies to a variety of indicators of poorer health,
including poorer physical health, poorer quality of life, and greater depression (Koenig et al., 1998); greater psychological distress among victims of the
1993 Midwest floods (Smith, Pargament, Brant, & Oliver, 2000); and more
symptoms of PTSD among members of churches near the Oklahoma City
bombing (Pargament et al., 1998). Other researchers have generated similar

findings. For example, in a large sample of racially diverse female trauma survivors, Fallot & Heckman (2005) reported that negative religious coping was linked to more symptoms of post-traumatic stress and overall severity of mental health problems. Exline and her colleagues (2000) found that both college students and adults in outpatient psychotherapy who reported higher levels of alienation from God also indicated higher levels of depression. College students who expressed difficulty forgiving God reported higher levels of depression, anxiety, trait anger, and difficult forgiving oneself and others (Exline, Yali, & Lobel, 1999).

Physical health problems that threaten ones' sense of mortality can create especially powerful conditions for spiritual vulnerability, conflict, and questions of meaning and purpose. For example, Sherman, Simonton, Latif, Spohn, and Tricot (2005) studied 213 multiple myeloma patients and found that negative religious coping was associated with a variety of indices of poorer health: fatigue, pain, clinician and self-rated depression, distress, and mental health. Interestingly, measures of general religious involvement and positive religious coping were unrelated to these outcomes. Manning-Walsh (2005) reported that spiritual struggle, as measured by the negative religious coping subscale of the Brief RCOPE, was significantly linked to lower quality of emotional and spiritual life and lower life satisfaction in a sample of women who had recently undergone surgical intervention for breast cancer. In a sample of men diagnosed with prostate cancer, Gall (2004a, 2004b) found that religious discontent and attributing the cause of the cancer to God's anger contributed unique variance in the prediction of greater role limitation and decreased emotional functioning after controlling for age, illness characteristics, and general coping resources. Rippentrop, Altmaier, Chen, Found, and Keffala (2005) reported similar adverse health effects in a sample of chronic musculoskeletal pain patients. These researchers found that negative religious coping was linked to greater pain intensity, poorer mental health status, and greater use of disability compensation programs (e.g., social security disability, disability insurance, worker's compensation).

A few longitudinal studies have shown negative religious coping to be a significant predictor of declines in health. For example, working with 96 medical rehabilitation inpatients, Fitchett (1999) found that negative spiritual coping was predictive of poorer physical recovery (limited recovery in activities of daily living such as walking, cooking, bathing) over a four-month follow-up period, even after controlling for demographic factors, social support, depression, and level of independent functioning at admission. One type of negative spiritual coping, feeling anger toward God, was a particularly powerful predictor of compromised physical recovery in this patient sample. Similarly, in the longitudinal study of rehabilitation patients, Magyar-Russell (2005) found that negative religious coping was significantly linked to anxiety, depression, and less spiritual well-being at admission, discharge, and six weeks after discharge from inpatient hospitalization. In a longitudinal study of religious struggles among 596 medically ill patients age 55 and over, negative religious coping at baseline predicted increases in depressed mood and declines in physical functional status and quality of life over a two-year period after controlling for selective attrition, mortality, demographic factors, and baseline physical and mental health (Pargament, Koenig, Tarakeshwar, & Hahn, 2004). Further analyses revealed that elders who demonstrated high levels of negative religious coping at both baseline and follow-up periods (i.e., chronic religious strugglers) were at greatest risk for declines in health. Negative religious coping also held significant implications for mortality. After accounting for selective attrition, demographic variables, and physical and mental health variables in this sample, higher religious struggle scores at baseline were predictive of 22–33 percent greater risk of dying over the two-year follow-up period (Pargament, Koenig, Tarakeshwar, & Hahn, 2001). Religious struggles in this study included patients wondering whether God had abandoned them, questioning God's love for them, feeling that the devil played a role in their illness, and feeling punished by God. Thus, these types of struggles not only heightened health problems, but also increased the risk of death.

Intrapsychic Struggles

Other struggles center on questions and doubt about religion and matters of faith. As one adolescent described her struggles:

> Is Christianity a big sham, a cult? If an organization were to evolve in society, it would have to excite people emotionally, it would have to be self-perpetuating, it would need a source of income, etc. Christianity fits all of these. How do I know that I haven't been sucked into a giant perpetual motion machine? (Kooistra, 1990, p. 95)

Religious doubts such as these have been associated with psychological distress, including greater anxiety and negative affect among adolescents and church members (Kooistra & Pargament, 1999; Pargament et al., 1998), higher levels of depression and less positive affect among Presbyterian leaders and members (Krause, Ingersoll-Dayton, Ellison, & Wulff, 1999), and less life satisfaction and happiness in a national sample of adults (Ellison, 1991).

Interpersonal Struggles

Another class of struggles focuses on religious conflicts and tensions with family, friends, congregation, or community. Krause, Chatters, Meltzer, and Morgan (2000) conducted focus groups with older adults and identified several types of negative interactions among the members of the church, such as gossiping, cliquishness, and hypocrisy. One church member complained:

> They get off in a corner and talk about you and you're the one that's there on Saturday working with their children and ironing the priest's vestments and doing all that kind of thing and washing the dishes on Sunday afternoon after church. But they don't have the Christian spirit. (p. 519)

Perhaps because these types of experiences violate expectations about how religious people should enact their spiritual values with each other, they are especially painful. Interpersonal religious conflicts have been associated with psychological distress in several studies. For example, interpersonal religious conflicts among church members and college students were associated with greater anxiety, more negative mood, and lower self-esteem (Pargament et al., 1998). Similarly, negative church interactions among clergy and leaders in the Presbyterian Church were associated with higher levels of psychological distress (Krause, Ellison, & Wulff, 1998). Sorenson, Grindstaff, and Turner (1995) studied a sample of young adolescent mothers who varied in their level of involvement in their religious institutions. Unlike the married mothers, religious involvement among unmarried mothers was associated with higher levels of depression. The authors suggest that out-of-wedlock pregnancy creates conflicts with the church that can induce emotional distress among unmarried adolescents. In a longitudinal study, medically ill elderly patients who reported more religious conflicts with family, congregation members, and clergy were more likely to become depressed over a two-year period (Pargament, Koenig, Tarakeshwar, & Hahn, 2001). Finally, in a meta-analysis of marital research, Mahoney and her colleagues found an indicator of interpersonal struggle, religious heterogamy (i.e., different religious beliefs, affiliations, and practices) was linked to higher rates of divorce, more frequent disagreements, and lower marital satisfaction (Mahoney, Pargament, Tarakeshwar, & Swank, 2001).

Overall, the associations between religious struggles and poorer health appear to be robust. Recent meta-analyses of empirical studies pointing to significant relationships between indicators of religious struggle, depression, and other indicators of health and well-being lend further support to this conclusion (Ano & Vasconcelles, 2005; Smith, McCullough, & Poll, 2003).

HOW MIGHT RELIGION HARM HEALTH?

Identifying the mechanisms through which religion and spirituality exert their impact on health and well-being is one of the most critical areas of inquiry for social scientists who study associations between religion and health. Although evidence is limited, especially with regard to the manner in which specific forms of religiousness lead to negative health effects, recent empirical and theoretical work has begun to shed some light on these fundamental questions.

A number of researchers suggest that social and psychological variables may act as mediators between religion and health (Ellison & Levin, 1998; George, Ellison, & Larson, 2002). Religious and spiritual communities have generally been shown to provide positive social resources for their members (Bradley, 1995; Ellison & George, 1994). Nevertheless, in some cases, the relation between religious involvement and adverse health may be due to members feeling judged or castigated when their actions and attitudes place them at odds with church teachings and ideals. Similarly, members may experience profound anger toward and disappointment in the behavior of other members of their religious or spiritual communities who fail to live up to sacred ideals. It is equally plausible that the religious risk factors lead to fundamental cognitive and emotional disorientation that leads, in turn, to poorer health outcomes. For example, certain forms of religious involvement could result in low self-confidence and self-worth; lack of meaning in life; hopelessness; and feelings of guilt, shame, and fear. Some evidence suggests that personality traits may act as mediators as well. For instance, in their study with college students, Exline et al. (1999) found that trait anger linked difficulty forgiving God with negative emotion.

A number of studies have yielded evidence that suggests that proximal religious variables may be strong mediators of the relationships between more general measures of religiousness and health outcomes (Pargament, 1997; Pargament, Magyar, & Murray-Swank, in press). Some of this evidence is indirect. As noted above, several studies have shown that the relationships between various religious risk factors and poorer health are not eliminated when controls for potentially mediating psychological and social variables are introduced. For example, Trenholm et al. (1998) found that religious conflict was a unique predictor of panic disorder, even after taking into account state anxiety, hypochondriacal beliefs and abnormal illness behavior, and irrational thinking. Indirect as they are, findings such as these suggest that religion may have some direct links to poorer health. A few studies offer stronger empirical evidence proximal religious variables mediate the relationship between religious risk factors and health. For instance, in their studies of spiritual appraisals, Pargament and colleagues (Magyar et al., 2000; Magyar-Russell, 2005; Pargament, Magyar, Benore, et al., 2005) consistently found that the method of religious coping used in response to appraisals of sacred loss and desecration partially mediated the relation between outcomes. More specifically, perceptions of sacred loss and desecration were more likely to predict negative mental and physical health when negative religious coping strategies were used. Conversely, participants were more likely to report personal and spiritual growth and positive affect when they engaged in positive religious coping strategies in response to appraisals of sacred loss and desecration.

In keeping with theory and research that points to the key roles appraisals and coping play in affecting the outcomes of negative life events (Lazarus & Folkman, 1984; Pargament, 1997), the manner in which individuals respond to matters of a sacred nature may be predictive of outcomes. Pargament et al. (in press) reviewed literature supportive of the notion that religion and spirituality can add unique benefits, as well as unique forms of distress, to the coping process. Negative religious reframing and coping efforts may link more gross measures of religion to decreased health and well-being by exacerbating the effects of stressful experiences in ways that lead to more adverse mental and physical health problems, more negative affect, more spiritual discontent, and less positive personal and spiritual growth from the experience. In other words, one of the pathways through which religion may lead to negative health is by interacting with stressors to magnify their harmful effects. For instance, religious involvement intensified the effects of family stressors on depression among community dwelling adults (Strawbridge, Shema, Cohen, Roberts, & Kaplan, 1998), and poorly integrated personal spirituality among college students increased the effects of stressors on low levels of life satisfaction (Fabricatore, Handel, & Fenzel, 2000). Additionally, self-directed religious coping style exacerbated the effects of high levels of stress on depressive affect in a sample of Presbyterian church members (Bickel et al., 1998), and the use of deferring religious coping methods among college students intensified the detrimental effects of high stress on affect and life satisfaction (Fabricatore, Handel, Rubio, & Gilner, 2004).

Religion has also been found to exert its impact on health through physiological and biological mechanisms. Improvements in technology and the sophistication of measurement of physiological parameters in the past decade have allowed for studies that demonstrate a positive relation between religious functioning and the immune system, blood pressure, neuroendocrine functioning, and regional brain activity (see Koenig & Cohen, 2002, and Seeman, Dubin, & Seeman, 2003, for reviews). Virtually all of the research carried out in this area has indicated that religion is associated with physiology and biology in health-promoting ways (Ironson et al., 2002; Koenig et al., 1998; Koenig & Cohen, 2002; Sephton, Koopman, Schaal, Thoresen, & Spiegel, 2001; Woods, Antoni, Ironson, & Kling, 1999). Illustrative studies include Ironson and colleagues' (2002) finding that the relation between religion and long-term survival in AIDS patients was mediated by lower urinary cortisol concentrations and Lazar et al.'s (2000) finding that neural structures in the brain involved in attention and control of the autonomic nervous system were activated in individuals versed in meditation. Just as researchers have begun to uncover adverse effects of certain types of religious involvement in other domains, it is likely that negative physiological and health consequences can result from religious engagement. Internal religious conflict, distressing interpersonal interactions, and struggles with the divine may increase psychological and physiological stress, thereby stimulating the autonomic nervous system and the production of stress hormones, which, over time, may lead to decreased immune functioning and increased susceptibility to disease (Koenig et al., 2001). Future research that examines the physiological, biological, and neurological mechanisms of action between specific forms of religiousness and adverse health outcomes will undoubtedly advance the pursuit of greater scientific understanding of the religion-health connection.

IMPLICATIONS, CONCLUSIONS, AND FUTURE DIRECTIONS

Much of the research in the scientific study of religion and health has relied on global measures of religiousness. Most of these studies demonstrate that religious involvement is largely beneficial, enhancing health and promoting well-being. Yet when assessed more closely, in some forms, in some situations, and in some people, a darker side of religion and spirituality can be identified. In this chapter, we have focused on religious risk factors for poorer health and well-being. Our objective in is not to challenge the positive role of religion and spirituality. Indeed, we believe religion is largely helpful. Instead, our intent is to identify aspects of religiousness that may be problematic. Researchers and clinicians must first be aware of the potential for negative implications stemming from religiousness in order to appreciate its power; continue to study it in innovative and useful ways; and work effectively with people who express the full range of religious thought, feeling, and behavior.

Working from different theoretical frameworks, we have articulated a variety of religious risk factors for reduced health. Empirical studies provide increasing support for the assertion that religion can heighten risks for psychological, physical, and spiritual distress. The methodological quality, strength of associations, and types of religiousness assessed among the studies reviewed varies. The strongest support comes from studies of religious struggle (e.g., negative religious coping) and religious motivation, though there have been no empirical investigations on the health consequences of idolatry. Studies of religious attachment and process theory are still emerging and represent promising areas for further investigation.

Least clear at this point are the explanatory mechanisms that might account for the links between these religious risk factors and poorer health. This is an area ripe for innovative and exciting programs of research. Studying the impact of religious risk factors on measures of psychological and social functioning that have already been linked to poorer health (e.g., pessimism; hopelessness;

and low levels of control, meaning, self-esteem, coherence, and social support); conducting brain imaging studies of individuals in the midst of spiritual conflict; assessing and comparing the immune functioning of individuals who do, and do not, engage in negative religious coping following a negative life event; and continuing to develop more proximal measures of religiousness and spirituality are imperative to the progression of knowledge in this area of study. It will also be important to learn more about predictors of religious risk that increases the vulnerability of people to religious struggles during times of stress. These predictors include personality variables (Ano & Pargament, 2003; Exline et al., 1999), family-related problems (Kooistra & Pargament, 1999), stage of life (Fitchett et al., 2004; Magyar-Russell, 2005; Manning-Walsh, 2005), childhood abuse (Fallot & Heckman, 2005), and psychopathology (Fallot & Heckman, 2005; Trenholm et al., 1998).

Even though it remains unclear why religion may pose threats to health and well-being, there are a number of important practical implications of these findings. First, risky forms of religiousness appear to occur at relatively high rates in the populations studied (approximately 10% to 20%). Recalling that chronic religious strugglers appear to be at greatest risk for declines in health status (Pargament et al., 2001), these findings underscore the need for early identification of religious risk factors before they become chronic and contribute to poorer health. It cannot be assumed that this group will seek resources on their own to address their religious concerns. Fitchett (1999) studied 200 newly admitted medical and surgery patients and found that those who were high in need of spiritual intervention and had few spiritual resources were less likely to request spiritual assistance in comparison to those with less need and greater spiritual resources. Thus, active screening of people for "spiritual risk" is needed in health care settings and religious congregations. Unfortunately, this is a seldom-implemented strategy for identifying individuals who are more vulnerable to poor health outcomes as a result of "underdeveloped, conflicted, overwhelmed, or negative spirituality" (Fitchett, 1999, p. 4). Fitchett and colleagues (1999, 2004) recommend brief and direct screening questions that address anger at God, fear of punishment by God, disappointments in faith or religious institutions, and lifetime changes in the importance of spiritual or religious faith to determine whether an in-depth spiritual assessment may be warranted (see Fitchett, 1999, for a discussion of spiritual screening versus spiritual assessment). Clinicians who have not received training in assessing or addressing religious and spiritual issues, or who feel uncomfortable doing so, should consider referring patients with spiritual needs to a chaplain or pastoral counselor.

The empirical studies reviewed in this chapter suggest that religion, even potentially destructive forms, plays a significant role in lives of many people. Mental health professionals may be able to intervene effectively at the level of cognitive and spiritual appraisals, as well as assist patients in modifying potentially maladaptive religious coping strategies in response to adversity. For instance, several widely practiced cognitive techniques could be successfully applied to spiritual appraisals, such as gaining an understanding of patients' idiosyncratic religious and spiritual meaning systems through guided association, helping patients identify the origin of their religious assumptions and automatic thoughts, and challenging absolute or dichotomous thinking when appropriate (Nielsen, Johnson, & Ellis, 2001; Richards & Bergin, 1997; Shafranske, 1996; Worthington, Kurusu, McCullough, & Sandage, 1996). Behavioral strategies could also be effectively adapted to assist patients in their religious coping process (Miller & Martin, 1988; Propst, 1988, 1996). Techniques such as activity scheduling may be used to plan times for contemplation, meditation, or prayer, and relaxation and breathing exercises could be integrated into these religious and spiritual activities as well. Bibliotherapy with religious works, as well as "behavioral experiments" in which patients practice asking for spiritual support from loved ones or clergy (e.g., prayers; requests for religious rituals or sacraments; engage in discussions about God, spirituality, or meaning), may also be options in clinical interventions aimed at modifying maladaptive religious and spiritual coping methods (Miller, 1999; Miller & Martin, 1988).

Spiritually integrated interventions (see Pargament et al., 2005; Pargament, Murray-Swank, & Tarakeshwar, 2005, for reviews) in which religious issues and concerns are the focus of clinical attention have just begun to be scientifically developed, empirically tested, and practiced in applied settings. One intervention that addresses intrapsychic religious conflict is interreligious encounter groups in which members express, listen to, and discuss their internal religious struggles in a format that is open to and inclusive of various faith traditions (Genia, 1990). This group intervention focuses on enhancing religious development through the exploration of religious conflict, the resolution of internal distress, solidification of a spiritual sense of identity and meaning, and the development of personal spiritual goals. The majority of interventions for religious struggles with the divine have been developed with particular life experiences in mind. For instance, Cole and Pargament (1999) implemented an intervention to address feelings of spiritual disconnection and conflict with God for cancer survivors. Pargament and colleagues (2004) carried out an eight-week psychospiritual intervention designed to help women draw on their spiritual resources in coping with the challenges of HIV, including spiritual struggles. Similarly, Murray-Swank and Pargament (2005) developed a spiritually integrated intervention to help survivors of sexual abuse come to terms with the psychological, social, and spiritual concerns raised by their trauma. The development of interventions for interpersonal religious conflict represents an important area for future research. Forgiveness interventions may be especially promising for helping people deal with the profound distress and disillusionment that is triggered by religious and spiritual violations occurring within faith communities (e.g., abuse of privileges, power, and money and clergy sexual abuse; McCullough, Pargament, & Thoresen, 2000). Continued basic and applied research in this area is necessary to further the development of effective and appropriate interventions for people of various religious faiths and spiritually oriented belief systems.

Finally, no discussion of the darker side of religion would be complete without noting that, according to most traditions, a period of intense religious struggle is often a prelude to growth and transformation. Virtually every tradition presents its adherents with great religious exemplars—from Moses and Buddha to Jesus and Muhammed—who experienced their own "dark nights of the soul," only to come through the process strengthened and steeled. Likewise, people may grow through their own periods of religious conflict and turmoil. In a few of the empirical studies cited above, religious risk factors were linked not only to indices of physical and psychological distress, but also to measures of stress-related growth (e.g., Magyar et al., 2000; Pargament et al., 1998). Reviewing this line of study, Exline and Rose (2005) conclude: "Perhaps then, the opportunity for struggle is actually one of the greatest gifts that religion and spirituality have to offer" (p. 325). Thus, it is important to recognize that religious stress and turmoil offers the possibility of growth. Nevertheless, even though some studies suggest positive links between religious struggles and growth, the weight of the evidence is clear and leads to a straightforward conclusion: certain forms of religion can pose a significant risk to health and well-being. We leave researchers and practitioners with some intriguing questions. Are periods of religiously related decline followed by periods of religious growth? If so, what factors determine whether religion will lead to decline followed by growth, decline without growth, or growth without decline? And how best do we facilitate growth rather than decline among people in their encounters with the darker side of religion?

REFERENCES

Ainsworth, M. D. S., Blehar, M. C., Waters, E., & Wall, S. (1978). *Patterns of attachment: A psychological study of the Strange Situation.* Hillsdale, NJ: Erlbaum.

Aldwin, C. M. (1994). *Stress, coping, and development: An integrative perspective.* New York: Guilford Press.

Allport, G. W. (1950). *The individual and his religion: A psychological interpretation.* New York: Macmillan.

Allport, G. W., & Ross, J. M. (1967). Personal religious orientation and prejudice. *Journal of Personality and Social Psychology, 5,* 432–443.

Altemeyer, B., & Hunsberger, B. (1992). Authoritarianism, religious fundamentalism, quest, and prejudice. *International Journal for the Psychology of Religion, 2,* 113–133.

Ano, G. G., & Pargament, K. I. (2003). *Correlates of religious struggles: An exploratory study.* Unpublished master's thesis, Bowling Green State University.

Ano, G. G., & Vasconcelles, E. B. (2005). Religious coping and psychological adjustment to stress: A meta-analysis. *Journal of Clinical Psychology, 61,* 461–480.

Bickel, C. O., Ciarrocchi, J. W., Sheers, N. J., Estadt, B. K., Powell, D. A., & Pargament, K. I. (1998). Perceived stress, religious coping styles, and depressive affect. *Journal of Psychology and Christianity, 17*(1), 33–42.

Bowlby, J. (1969). *Attachment and loss: Vol. 1. Attachment.* New York: Basic Books.

Bradley, D. E. (1995). Religious involvement and social resources: Evidence from the data set "Americans Changing Lives." *Journal for the Scientific Study of Religion, 34,* 259–267.

Butter, E. A., & Pargament, K. I. (2003). Development of a model for clinical assessment of religious coping: Initial validation of the Process Evaluation Model. *Mental Health, Religion, and Culture, 6,* 175–194.

Cole, B., & Pargament, K. I. (1999). Re-creating your life: A spiritual/psychotherapeutic intervention for people diagnosed with cancer. *Psycho-Oncology, 8,* 395–407.

Conway, K. (1985–1986). Coping with the stress of medical problems among black and white elderly. *International Journal of Aging and Human Development, 21,* 39–48.

Donahue, M. J. (1985). Intrinsic and extrinsic religiousness: Review and meta-analysis. *Journal of Personality and Social Psychology, 48,* 400–419.

Ellison, C. G. (1991). Religious involvement and subjective well-being. *Journal of Health and Social Behavior, 32,* 80–99.

Ellison, C. G., & George, L. K. (1994). Religious involvement, social ties, and social support in a Southeastern community. *Journal for the Scientific Study of Religion, 33,* 4–61.

Ellison, C. G., & Levin, J. S. (1998). The religion-health connection: Evidence, theory, and future directions. *Health Education and Behavior, 25*(6), 700–720.

Emmons, R. A., Cheung, C., & Tehrani, K. (1998). Assessing spirituality through personal goals: Implications for research on religion and subjective well-being. *Social Indicators Research, 45,* 391–422.

Exline, J. J., & Rose, E. (2005). Religious and spiritual struggles. In R. Paloutzian & C. Park (Eds.), *Handbook of the psychology of religion and spirituality* (pp. 295–314). New York: Guilford Press.

Exline, J. J., Yali, A. M., & Lobel, M. (1999). When God disappoints: Difficulty forgiving God and its role in negative emotion. *Journal of Health Psychology, 4,* 365–380.

Exline, J. J., Yali, A. M., & Sanderson, W. C. (2000). Guilt, discord, and alienation: The role of religious strain in depression and suicidality. *Journal of Clinical Psychology, 56,* 1481–1496.

Fabricatore, A. N., Handel, P. J., & Fenzel, L. M. (2000). Personal spirituality as a moderator of the relationship between stressors and subjective well-being. *Journal of Psychology and Theology, 28*(3), 221–228.

Fabricatore, A. N., Handel, P. J., Rubio, D. M., & Gilner, F. H. (2004). Stress, religion, and mental health: Religious coping in mediating and moderating roles. *International Journal for the Psychology of Religion, 14*(2), 91–108.

Fallot, R.D., & Heckman, J.P. (2005). Religious/spiritual coping among women trauma survivors with mental health and substance use disorders. *Journal of Behavioral Health Services and Research, 32*(2), 214–226.

Fitchett, G. (1999). Screening for spiritual risk. *Chaplaincy Today, 15*(1), 2–12.

Fitchett, G., Murphy, P.E., Kim, J., Gibbons, J., Cameron, J.R., & Davis, J.A. (2004). Religious struggle: Prevalence, correlates and mental health risks in diabetic, congestive heart failure, and oncology patients. *International Journal of Psychiatry in Medicine, 34*(2), 179–196.

Fitchett, G., Rybarczyk, B.D., DeMarco, G.A., & Nicholas, J.J. (1999). The role of religion in medical rehabilitation outcomes: A longitudinal study. *Rehabilitation Psychology, 44*, 1–22.

Gall, T.L. (2004a). The role of religious coping in adjustment to prostate cancer. *Cancer Nursing, 27*(6), 454–461.

Gall, T.L. (2004b). Relationship with God and the quality of life of prostate cancer survivors. *Quality of Life Research, 13*, 1357–1368.

Genia, V. (1990). Interreligious encounter groups: A psychospiritual experience for faith development. *Counseling and Values, 35*, 39–51.

George, L.K., Ellison, C.G., & Larson, D.B. (2002). Explaining the relationships between religious involvement and health. *Psychological Inquiry, 13*(3), 190–200.

Greenberg, D., Witztum, E., & Pisante, J. (1987). Scrupulosity: Religious attitudes and clinical presentations. *British Journal of Medical Psychology, 60*, 29–37.

Hopfoll, S.E. (1988). *The ecology of stress.* New York: Hemisphere.

Ironson, G., Solomon, G.F., Balbin, E.G., O'Cleirigh, C., George, A., Kumar, M., et al. (2002). The Ironson-Woods Spirituality/Religiousness Index is associated with long survival, health behaviors, less distress, and low cortisol in people with HIV/AIDS. *Annals of Behavioral Medicine, 24*(1), 34–48.

James, W. (1902). *The varieties of religious experience: A study in human nature.* New York: Modern Library.

Janoff-Bulman, R. (1992). Shattered assumptions: Towards a new psychology of trauma. New York: Free Press.

Johnson, C.V., & Hayes, J.A. (2003). Troubled spirits: Prevalence and predictors of religious and spiritual concerns among university students and counseling center clients. *Journal of Counseling Psychology, 50*, 409–419.

Jung, C.G. (1964). *After the catastrophe.* In C. Jung (Ed.), *Collected works* (Vol. 10, pp. 194–217). Princeton, NJ: Princeton University Press. (Original work published 1945)

Kirkpatrick, L.A. (2005). *Attachment, evolution, and the psychology of religion.* New York: Guilford Press.

Kirkpatrick, L.A., & Shaver, P.R. (1992). An attachment-theoretical approach to romantic love and religious belief. *Personality and Social Psychology Bulletin, 18*, 266–275.

Klinger, E. (1998). The search for meaning in evolutionary perspective and its clinical implications. In P.T.P. Wong & P.S. Fry (Eds.), *The human quest for meaning* (pp. 27–50). Mahwah, NJ: Erlbaum.

Koenig, H.G., & Cohen, H.J. (2002). *The link between religion and health: Psychoneuroimmunology and the faith factor.* New York: Oxford University Press.

Koenig, H.G., George, L.K., Hays, J.C., Larson, D.B., Cohen, H.J., & Blazer, D.G. (1998). The relationship between religious activities and blood pressure in older adults. *International Journal of Psychiatry in Medicine, 28,* 189–213.

Koenig, H.G., McCullough, M.E., & Larson, D.B. (2001). *Handbook of religion and health.* New York: Oxford University Press.

Koenig, H.G., Pargament, K.I., & Nielsen, J. (1998). Religious coping and health status in medically ill hospitalized older adults. *Journal of Nervous and Mental Disease, 186,* 513–521.

Kooistra, W.P. (1990). *The process of religious doubting in adolescents raised in religious environments.* Unpublished doctoral dissertation, Bowling Green State University.

Kooistra, W.P., & Pargament, K.I. (1999). Predictors of religious doubting among Roman Catholic and Dutch Reformed high school students. *Journal of Psychology and Theology, 27,* 33–42.

Krause, N., Chatters, L.M., Meltzer, T., & Morgan, D.L. (2000). Negative interaction in the church: Insights from focus groups with older adults. *Review of Religious Research, 41,* 510–533.

Krause, N., Ellison, C.G., & Wulff, K.M. (1998). Church-based support, negative interaction, and psychological well-being: Findings from a national sample of Presbyterians. *Journal for the Scientific Study of Religion, 37,* 725–741.

Krause, N., Ingersoll-Dayton, B., Ellison, C.G., & Wulff, K.M. (1999). Aging, religious doubt and psychological well-being. *The Gerontologist, 39,* 525–533.

Lazar, S.W., Bush, G., Gollub, R.L., Fricchione, G.L., Khalsa, G., & Benson, H. (2000). Functional brain mapping of the relaxation response and meditation. *NeuroReport, 11,* 1581–1585.

Lazarus, R.S., & Folkman, S. (1984). *Stress, appraisal, and coping.* New York: Springer.

Magyar, G.M., Pargament, K.I., & Mahoney, A. (2000). Violating the sacred: A study of desecration among college students. Paper presented at the 108th Annual Convention of the American Psychological Association, Washington, DC.

Magyar-Russell, G.M. (2005). *Sacred loss and desecration: A longitudinal study of spiritual appraisals among patients in rehabilitation hospitals.* Unpublished doctoral dissertation, Bowling Green State University.

Mahoney, A., Pargament, K.I., Ano, G., Lynn, Q., Magyar, G.M., McCarthy, S., et al. (2002). *The devil made them do it: Desecration and demonization and the 9/11 attacks.* Paper presented at the annual meeting of the American Psychological Association, Chicago, Illinois.

Mahoney, A., Pargament, K., Tarakeshwar, N., & Swank, A.B. (2001). Religion in the home in the 1980's and 90's: A review and conceptual integration of empirical links between religion, marriage, and parenting. *Journal of Family Psychology, 15,* 559–596.

Manning-Walsh, J. (2005). Spiritual struggle: Effect on quality of life and life satisfaction in women with breast cancer. *Journal of Holistic Nursing, 23*(2), 120–140.

Matchan, L. (1992, 8 June). Ex-priest's accusers tell of the damage. *Boston Globe,* 1–8.

Maunder, R.G., & Hunter, J.J. (2001). Attachment and psychosomatic medicine: Developmental contributions to stress and disease. *Psychosomatic Medicine, 63,* 556–567.

McCrae, R. R. (1984). Situational determinants of coping response: Loss, threat, and challenge. *Journal of Personality and Social Psychology, 46,* 919–928.

McCullough, M. E., Pargament, K. I., & Thoresen, C. E. (Eds.). (2000). *Forgiveness: Theory, research, and practice.* New York: Guilford Press.

Miller, W. R. (Ed.). (1999). *Integrating spirituality into treatment: Resources for practitioners.* Washington, DC: American Psychological Association.

Miller, W. R., & Martin, J. E. (Eds.). (1988). *Behavior therapy and religion: Integrating spiritual and behavioral approaches to change.* Newbury Park, CA: Sage.

Mullen, B., & Suls, J. (1982). The effectiveness of attention and retention as coping styles: A meta-analysis of temporal differences. *Journal of Psychosomatic Research, 26,* 43–49.

Murray-Swank, N. A., & Pargament, K. I. (2005). God, where are you?: Evaluating a spiritually-integrated intervention for sexual abuse. *Mental Health, Religion, and Culture, 8*(3), 191–203.

Nelson, J. B. (2004). *Thirst: God and the alcoholic experience.* Louisville, KY: Westminster John Knox Press.

Nielsen, S. L., Johnson, W. B., & Ellis, A. (2001). *Counseling and psychotherapy with religious persons: A rational emotive behavior therapy approach.* Mahwah, NJ: Erlbaum.

Palmer, P. J. (1998, September). The grace of great things: Reclaiming the sacred in knowing, teaching, and learning. *The Sun,* 24–28.

Pargament, K. I. (1997). *The psychology of religion and coping: Theory, research, practice.* New York: Guilford Press.

Pargament, K. I., Koenig, H. G., & Perez, L. M. (2000). The many methods of religious coping: Initial development and validation of the RCOPE. *Journal of Clinical Psychology, 56,* 519–543.

Pargament, K. I., Koenig, H. G., Tarakeshwar, N., & Hahn, J. (2001). Religious struggle as a predictor of mortality among medically ill elderly patients: A two-year longitudinal study. *Archives of Internal Medicine, 161,* 1881–1885.

Pargament, K. I., Koenig, H. G., Tarakeshwar, N., & Hahn, J. (2004). Religious coping methods as predictors of psychological, physical, and spiritual outcomes among medically ill elderly patients: A two-year longitudinal study. *Journal of Health Psychology, 9,* 713–730.

Pargament, K. I., Magyar, G. M., Benore, E., & Mahoney, A. (2005). Sacrilege: A study of sacred loss and desecration and their implications for health and well-being in a community sample. *Journal for the Scientific Study of Religion, 44*(1), 59–78.

Pargament, K. I., Magyar, G. M., & Murray-Swank, N. (in press). The sacred and the search for significance: Religion as a unique process. *Journal of Social Issues.*

Pargament, K. I., & Mahoney, A. (2002). Spirituality: Discovering and conserving the sacred. In C. R. Snyder & S. J. Lopez (Eds.), *Handbook of positive psychology* (pp. 646–659). Oxford, England: Oxford University Press.

Pargament, K. I., Murray-Swank, N., Magyar, G. M., & Ano, G. (2005). Spiritual struggle: A phenomenon of interest to psychology and religion. In W. R. Miller & H. D. Delaney (Eds.), *Judeo-Christian perspectives on psychology.* Washington, DC: American Psychological Association.

Pargament, K. I., Murray-Swank, N., & Tarakeshwar, N. (Eds.). (2005). Spiritually-integrated psychotherapy. *Mental Health, Religion, and Culture, 8,* 155–238.

Pargament, K. I., Smith, B. W., Koenig, H. G., & Perez, L. (1998). Patterns of positive and negative religious coping with major life stressors. *Journal for the Scientific Study of Religion, 37*, 710–724.

Pargament, K. I., Zinnbauer, B. J., Scott, A. B., Butter, E. M., Zerowin, J., & Stanik, P. (1998). Red flags and religious coping: Identifying some religious warning signs among people in crisis. *Journal of Clinical Psychology, 54*, 77–89.

Propst, L. R. (1988). *Psychotherapy in a religious framework: Spirituality in the emotional healing process.* New York: Human Sciences Press.

Propst, L. R. (1996). Cognitive-behavioral therapy and the religious person. In E. P. Shafranske (Ed.), *Religion and the clinical practice of psychology* (pp. 391–407). Washington, DC: American Psychological Association.

Rabkin, J. G., & Streuning, E. L. (1976). Life events, stress, and illness. *Science, 194*, 1013–1020.

Richards, P. S., & Bergin, A. E. (1997). *A spiritual strategy for counseling and psychotherapy.* Washington, DC: American Psychological Association.

Rippentrop, A. E., Altmaier, E. M., Chen, J. J., Found, E. M., & Keffala, V. J. (2005). The relationship between religion/spirituality and physical health, mental health, and pain in a chronic pain population. *Pain, 116*, 311–321.

Rowatt, W. C., & Kirkpatrick, L. A. (2002). Dimensions of attachment to God and their relation to affect, religiosity, and personality constructs. *Journal for the Scientific Study of Religion, 41*, 637–651.

Ryan, R. M., Rigby, S., & King, K. (1993). Two types of religious internalization and their relations to religious orientation and mental health. *Journal of Personality and Social Psychology, 65*, 586–596.

Seeman, T. E., Dubin, L. F., & Seeman, M. (2003). Religiosity/spirituality and health: A critical review of the evidence for biological pathways. *American Psychologist, 58*(1), 53–63.

Sephton, S. E., Koopman, C., Schaal, M., Thoresen, C., & Spiegel, D. (2001). Spiritual expression and immune status in women with metastatic breast cancer: An exploratory study. *Breast Journal, 7*(5), 345–353.

Shafranske, E. P. (Ed.). (1996). *Religion and the clinical practice of psychology.* Washington, DC: American Psychological Association.

Sheldon, K. M., Ryan, R. M., Deci, E. L., & Kasser, T. (2004). The independent effects of goal contents and motives on well-being: It's both what you pursue and why you pursue it. *Personality and Social Psychology Bulletin, 30*, 475–486.

Sherman, A. C., Simonton, S., Latif, U., Spohn, R., & Tricot, G. (2005). Religious struggle and religious comfort in response to illness: Health outcomes among stem cell transplant patients. *Journal of Behavioral Medicine, 28*, 1–9.

Smith, B. W., Pargament, K. I., Brant, C., & Oliver, J. M. (2000). Noah revisited: Religious coping by church members and the impact of the 1993 midwest flood. *Journal of Community Psychology, 28*, 169–186.

Smith, T. B., McCullough, M. E., & Poll, J. (2003). Religiousness and depression: Evidence for a main effect and the moderating influence of stressful life events. *Psychological Bulletin, 129*, 614–636.

Sorenson, A. M., Grindstaff, C. F., & Turner, R. J. (1995). Religious involvement among unmarried adolescent mothers: A source of emotional support? *Sociology of Religion, 56*, 71–81.

Strawbridge, W.J., Shema, S.J., Cohen, R.D., Roberts, R.E., & Kaplan, G.A. (1998). Religiosity buffers effects of some stressors on depression but exacerbates others. *Journal of Gerontology Series B: Social Sciences, 53*(3), S118–S126.

Trenholm, P., Trent, J., & Compton, W.C. (1998). Negative religious conflict as a predictor of panic disorder. *Journal of Clinical Psychology, 54,* 59–65.

Watson, P.J., Morris, R.J., & Hood, R.W., Jr. (1988). Sin and self-functioning: Part 3. The psychology and ideology of irrational beliefs. *Journal of Psychology and Theology, 16,* 348–361.

Woods, T.E., Antoni, M.H., Ironson, G.H., & Kling, D.W. (1999). Religiosity is associated with affective and immune status in symptomatic HIV-infected gay men. *Journal of Psychosomatic Research, 46,* 165–176.

Worthington, E.L., Kurusu, T.A., McCullough, M.E., & Sandage, S.J. (1996). Empirical research on religion and psychotherapeutic processes and outcomes: A 10-year review and research prospectus. *Psychological Bulletin, 119,* 448–487.

CHAPTER 5

THE COMMON CORE THESIS IN THE STUDY OF MYSTICISM

Ralph W. Hood, Jr.

Two extreme poles have defined the psychology of religion since its inception. On one extreme are psychologists convinced of the falsity of religious beliefs and committed to a naturalistic reductive interpretation of religious phenomena. Perhaps most illustrative of this view is Freud's assertion that religion is not only an illusion (motivated by desire) but ultimately a *delusion*, fated to be abandoned as humankind progresses in its scientific understanding of the natural world, the only one there is (Hood, 1992, 1997b). On the other extreme are psychologists committed to a religious worldview who seek to defend the ontological claims of religion in what Beit-Hallahmi (1985) has identified as essentially a religious apologetics disguised as scientific psychology. In Beit-Hallahmi's terms, the former psychologists perform a legitimate function in developing a psychology of religion that is necessarily reductive, and the later distort the science of psychology, cloaking it in a religious psychology that cannot ultimately be valid as a scientific psychology.

Although the extremes are worthy of note, a well-established middle ground is open to a dialogue between various psychological and religious claims. It was best defined by William James, who is most noted to psychologists of religion for his *Varieties of Religious Experience* (1902/1985) continuously in print since its initial publication and universally acclaimed as the one true classic in the psychology of religion. However, few psychologists of religion make reference to James's first and also classic text, *The Principles of Psychology* (1890/1981). Over a decade in the writing and published at the turn of the previous century, it made the case for a psychology bound by no other metaphysics than those that support a natural science framework. Yet struggle as James did to reject the necessity of religious concepts in that text (for instance, the soul), he eventually concluded that psychology was far from an established science; nor did he think it could become one in purely naturalistic terms. Thus, as I have argued elsewhere, the *Varieties* can be read as a sequel to the *Principles* (Hood, 1995, 2002). The *Varieties* resolves issues left hanging in the *Principles* insofar as religious experience was ignored in that text (as it still is in most general psychological texts unconcerned with religion). We learn from the *Varieties* that when religious experience is taken seriously, the methods and scope of psychology must be extended (Hood, 2002). In the first section of this chapter, I note several assumptions that define the range and scope of this extension in order to form the basis for my defense of the common core thesis in the study of mysticism. These assumptions leave open the ontological issue of the reality of what is experienced in mysticism. Thus, the assumptions are neither a priori apologetic nor reductionistic. These six assumptions do, however, lay the foundation for my defense of what is the common core thesis in mysticism.

BASIC ASSUMPTIONS

In what many identify as a postmodern world, claims to foundational realities can be perpetually problematic. Hence, I will not debate these assumptions but simply identify them explicitly as foundational to the frame of my discussion of the common core thesis. These six assumptions can be the focus of philosophical debate that is not without merit, yet on a purely cognitive level can be interminable. Yet this applies to any other set of assumptions and so, in a postmodern sense, does not differentially apply to our own view (Rosenau, 1992).

The first assumption is that in James's language, personal religious experience has "its root and centre in mystical states" (1902, p. 301). The claim is that, within all religious traditions, a mystical stream flows. Further, it is that stream that gives life and, for many, is an essential sustenance to faith traditions. As Katz (1983) and others have noted, those for whom religion is a powerful life-sustaining presence have had a troubled but passionate commitment to the particulars of their religious faith. We must explore the basis for the troublesome presence of mysticism *within* faith traditions and note as well the emergence of mysticism *outside* of faith traditions. The irony, as James knew well, is that faith traditions draw their strength from the very presence of those whose experience troubles what James referred to as secondhand believers—those for whom mystical experience is foundational to their faith but lurks as a threat to the dogmatic defense of the particulars of the tradition. James's words are worth quoting here, for they imply a theory of religious development that is not unrelated to the emergence of mysticism independent of faith traditions—something that is of recent historical development. Here James waxes poetic as he provides both a description and a theory of mystical development from what he terms a "genuine first hand experience," which, he claims,

> is bound to be heterodoxy to its witness, the prophet appearing as a mere lonely madman. If his doctrine prove contagious enough to spread to any others, it becomes a definite and labeled heresy. But, if it then still prove contagious enough to triumph over persecution, it becomes itself an orthodoxy, and when a religion has become an orthodoxy its day of inwardness is over: the spring is dry; the faithful live at second hand exclusively and stone prophets in their turn. The new church, in spite of whatever goodness it may foster, can be henceforth counted on as a staunch ally in every attempt to stifle the spontaneous religious spirit, and to stop all later bubblings of the fountain from which in purer days it drew its own supply of inspiration. (1902/1985, p. 270)

The second assumption follows from the first and is sympathetic to James's lack of concern with religious orthodoxy. James does not go quite as far as Scharfstein (1973) does in dismissing the noetic claims based on mystical experience as "ontological fairy-tales" (p. 45), but his dismissal of them as "over beliefs" (James, 1902/1985, p. 402) comes close. It is the priests, not the prophets, who defend orthodoxies. Orthodoxies are fashioned second-hand and weight the interpretation of experience more than the experience itself. To defend the common core thesis, I too focus on the inwardness of religious experience and not its outward expression in interpretation and belief that tends to reify into orthodoxy. I recognize this is a controversial issue, especially among those who assert that some form of construction-ist thesis has trumped all other options. By constructionism is meant the crucial, even definitive, role interpretation is claimed to play in constructing experience, and not simply its interpretation. This dominant and dominat-ing view (e.g., Katz, 1978b, 1992; Proudfoot, 1985) essentially takes a neo-Kantian turn and argues that experience is always mediated (phenomena) and that unmediated experience of whatever is ultimate (noumena) is neither possible nor describable. However, as Parsons (1999) has noted, to make this claim is simply to assert what many mystics deny based on their own experience and to take a curiously Western neo-Kantian perspective that is not accepted as nonproblematic in Eastern modes of thought. Eastern philosophies have long accepted that unmediated experiences of reality are possible. However, part of the persuasion is in the level of illumination of those who make the claim. As Huxley (1944) rightly noted long ago, "Kant was right only as regards minds that have not yet come to enlightenment and deliverance. . . . The thing in itself *can* be perceived—but only by one, who, in himself, is no-thing" (pp. 223–224, emphasis in original).

A caveat is that we acknowledge that any claim to experience is partly an interpretation. To identify anything as if it could be pulled from the stream of consciousness in bucketfuls (to paraphrase James) is to confuse the water in the bucket with the stream from which it came. It is interpretation that is the bucket that pulls water from the stream that continues on. It is not merely metaphor when mystics fumble to describe their experience as if a river flowing into the sea or as a drop of water from the ocean of life. The ability to discount the description of experience in favor of experience itself is essential to any under-standing of mysticism and to our support of the common core thesis. Thus, there is no description of experience that involves no interpretation whatsoever (Stace, 1960, p. 203). Even if mystical experiences are unmediated, neither their recollection nor their description can be. This is the basis for Stace's (1960) claim that mystical experiences are "allegedly ineffable" (p. 79).

A third assumption follows closely. Mystical experiences are ineffable. The experience itself is ineffable, and absolutely so. Royce, James's great friend and adversary to whom the *Varieties* was largely addressed, once quipped something to the effect that mystics have experiences that are ineffable, and that is all they should say. However, the irony is that mystics write volumes. Among religious studies scholars, an almost exclusive emphasis on mystical texts accentuates the influence of language on mystical experience (Katz, 1978, 1992; McGinn, 1994). However, rather than a study of mystical texts, left as skins shed by serpents who have moved on, we seek the experience ref-erenced by such texts, available to everyone disciplined or fortunate enough to be graced with experiences that, although ineffable, can be referenced in language and used to evoke what it cannot describe. The language of the mystics is many faceted, often used to evoke experience in the reader rather than describe the experience of the author (Katz, 1978a, 1992, pp. 5–15; Scholem, 1941, pp. 59–60). The language of the mystics is not to be taken as literally descriptive of an experience for which language is ill equipped by its very nature of subject/object distinctions to describe. In the tradition of the Sufi mystics, those who say do not know; those who know do not say.

A fourth assumption is that mystical experiences are neither simply emo-tive states nor are they simply cognitive recollections of truths available to the discursive intellect (to paraphrase James again). Yet they are noetic. The noetic claim of the mystic is to have known reality, often elevated to Reality or God. Both in personal (God) and impersonal (Godhead; Reality; One) terms, mystics provide us with hypotheses that must be explored as possible ontological claims regarding the nature of God or Reality. The knowledge is not as much *about* reality as *of* reality, in which the unity of the subject and the object is noesis. In James's (1902/1985, p. 332) succinct phrasing, "In mystic states we both become one with the Absolute and we become aware of our oneness." It is this that Stace (1960) refers to as the "dissolution of individuality" (pp. 111–113) actually experienced by mystics and by its very nature ineffable.

The fifth assumption is that, in order to adequately explore mystical experience, one must include phenomenological methods. As Staal (1975) has persuasively argued, if one wants to know what it is like to experience reality as the mystics do, one must experience it directly. Likewise, as James says in the *Principles* (1981/1890), "*Introspective observation is what we have to rely on first and foremost and always*" (p. 185, emphasis in original). If modern psychology has denied this proposition, it is, in the words of Stace (1960), "their loss and their folly" (p. 58). The mystical claim to unmediated experience of reality can with only little profit be studied from the outside. Investigators who do explore mysticism from the "outside" can at best produce correlational or causal claims to phenomena that remain obscure to those who have not had the experience (Hood, 1994; Staal, 1975). Again from the Sufi tradition we are reminded that only those who taste know. Likewise, as noted above, the assertion that all experience is mediated experience can be directly refuted by those whose experience of reality is unmediated. The skeptic can attempt to experience the same or to simply rest assured with the dogmatic assertion that "*There are* NO *pure (i.e. unmediated) experiences*" (Katz, 1978a, p. 26, emphasis and italics in original). In this sense, Wulff (2000) is more than merely suggestive when he states that the study of mysticism may be best acknowledged as leading to a change in the methods by which such experiences are investigated.

A sixth and final assumption is what Stace (1960) has referred to as "causal indifference" (pp. 29–31). This phrase is meant to include any and all mystical experiences regardless of the proximate context or conditions that precede the experience. Most controversial is the possibility that entheogens (formerly called psychedelics) can facilitate mystical experience. One cannot discount the reality of the experience as genuinely mystical because it was facilitated by a chemical or any other proximate cause. As James long ago noted, one cannot dismiss an experience because one can identify the physiological conditions that may accompany it. James's (1902) discussion of "medical materialism" (pp. 11–29) reminds us that, even if experience is both embodied and contextualized, neither condition can be used to dismiss the validity of the experience nor determine its existential value. Furthermore, identifying triggers of an experience cannot be used to reduce the experience to a causal claim that it was the trigger that caused the experience. Triggers may allow one to move beyond mediation to unmediated experience of reality, the lasting claim of the mystics of all faith traditions. It may be that entheogens are one such set of triggers (see Spilka, Hood, Hunsberger, & Gorsuch, 2003, pp. 283–288).

EXAMPLES OF MYSTICISM: INTROVERTIVE AND EXTROVERTIVE

Having stated our assumptions explicitly, we can now identify what is meant by mysticism. The term is of recent coinage, and for the vast majority

of recorded history it is unlikely that anyone would identify him- or herself as a "mystic" (McGinn, 1994; Troeltsch, 1931). However, within and
eventually outside of the great faith traditions, mysticism has flourished.
A common assumption of many social scientists is that mysticism is like
suicide: difficult to study because of its rarity and the limited ability of social
scientists to identify the presuicidal person. Social scientists are not able to
predict with any accuracy who will report mystical experiences, but survey
studies of the report of mystical experiences reveal that as much as one-
third of British and American people report having had such experiences
(see Spilka et al., 2003, pp. 300–314). Scharfstein (1973) notes that social
scientists have likely grossly underestimated the frequency of mystical
experiences and goes so far as to talk of a common everyday mysticism—
so common that the reader of this chapter has likely had such an experience.
An easy way to "measure" this is simply to record the mystical experiences
of others and to ask people to rate themselves on the degree to which they
have had a similar experience.

Because the focus of this chapter is on the empirical study of mysticism,
it will be helpful to give an example what is being measured. A widely cited
mystical experience from the English poet John Symonds is one of three
examples chosen by David Wulff (2000, pp. 399–400) and is favorably cited
by Stace as well (1960, pp. 91–93). Both identify the original description in
James's *Varieties* (1902/1985, p. 306) in which James took the description from
a biography of Symonds. My example is taken from the Religious Episodes
Measure, which is composed of descriptions of religious experiences culled
from James's *Varieties:*

> I would suddenly feel the mood coming when I was at church, or with people
> or reading, but only when my muscles were relaxed. It would irresistibly
> take over my mind and will, last what seemed like forever, and disappear in
> a way resembling waking up from anesthesia. One reason that I disliked this
> kind of trance was that I could not describe it to myself; even now I can't
> find the right words. It involved the disappearance of space, time, feeling,
> and all the things I call my self. As ordinary consciousness disappeared, the
> sense of underlying or essential consciousness grew stronger. At last nothing
> remained but a pure, absolute, abstract self. (in Burris, 1999b, p. 224)

This description of a mystical experience contains the essentials of what
Stace called introvertive mysticism. Here, an experience of union timeless
and spaceless and devoid of any content defines what mystics claim to be an
unmediated union with reality. A dissolution of individuality into a universal
consciousness identified as God, Reality, One, or Pure Consciousness. In a
phrase not quoted above, but part of Symond's original description, Symonds
concludes what is the essential introvertive mystical claim: "*The universe*

became without form and void of content. But self persisted" (Stace, 1960, p. 91; emphasis in original).

It is important to note that this claim violates neo-Kantian assumptions and is not argued for as much as it is declared to be an unmediated experience of reality. At this point, rather than argue the case for or against mediated realities, I simply note that the report of such unmediated claims can be reliably measured. Of course, the measurement is of the reports of such experiences and not of the experiences themselves. However, before explicitly discussing this thesis, I will cite another example of a mystical experience— one that Stace refers to as extrovertive mysticism. Here the experience is more like sense perception and looks "outward" rather than "inward."

In extrovertive mysticism, the experience of unity is perceived through the multiplicity of the objects of perception. A common phrase that describes this type of experience is "all is one." An example cited by Stace has both beauty and simplicity. Stace took it from Otto's *Mysticism East and West* (1932). The quote is from Meister Eckhart: "All that a man has here externally is intrinsically One. Here all blades of grass, wood, and stone, all things are One" (in Stace, 1960, p. 63). Likewise, from Abulafia's *Book on Untying Knots* from the thirteenth century, we have:

> All the inner forces and the hidden souls in man are distributed and differentiated in the bodies. It is, however, in the nature of all of them that when their knots are untied they return to their origin, which is one without any duality and which comprises the multiplicity. (in Scholem, 1961, p. 131)

Both Eckhart's and Abulafia's quotes are presented as declarations but are obviously based on personal experiences. The unity that is One also suggests the same described in Symond's introvertive experience noted above. The claim that there are two unities (Stace, 1960, p. 133) is logically refuted on the simple basis that with an undifferentiated experience of unity there is no *principium individuatonis* (Stace, 1960, pp. 133, 153).

Having established the nature of these two experiences at the purely descriptive level, it is time to consider the claim to a common core that can be found within various faith traditions. The common core is quite simply mysticism, whether introvertive or extrovertive.

MYSTICAL EXPERIENCE: THE COMMON CORE

Scholem's (1961, p. 5) claim that there is no such thing as mysticism in the abstract reminds us that mysticism has historically been found *within* the great faith traditions. However, his claim that "There is no mysticism as such, there is only the mysticism of a particular religious system" (p. 6) goes too far, as we will see in the discussion of the emergence of mysticism as an independent type. Further, neither does Scholem's claim mean that one cannot identify mysticisms that share a common unity in the particulars of various faith traditions. It is this unity that forms the common core thesis. Although expressed within various faith traditions, this common core simultaneously transcends them. James (1902/1985) expressed the thesis directly:

> In Hinduism, in Neoplatonism, in Sufism, in Christian Mysticism, in Whitmanism, we find the same recurring note, so that there is about mystical utterances and eternal unanimity which ought to make a critic stop and think and which brings about that the mystical classics have as has been said, neither birthday nor native land. (p. 332)

James's "essential unanimity" does not entail a common set of higher-order beliefs and practices shared by all religious traditions. It is decidedly not a perennial philosophy (Huxley, 1944) nor a perennial psychology (Forman, 1998). What is does entail is the claim that, *at the experiential level,* there is a common experience of unity (either extrovertive or introvertive) that is the firsthand basis on which mystics of diverse faith traditions provided the basic experiential fodder that different religious dogmas, rituals, and practices both protect and give expression to. Religions move far beyond what experience alone provides. However, we can ignore much of religion since our focus is on the nature of mystical experience that transcends any particular interpretation. Even if Scharfstein (1973) is correct in claiming that most interpretations of mystical experience are "ontological fairy-tales" (p. 45), the experience remains what it is, in itself (Kant not withstanding)

Although James is often cited favorably in defense of the common core thesis, it is Stace (1960) who has been most often the target of criticism in the conceptual literature (Gimello, 1978, p. 195). Much of this criticism is contained in two texts edited by Katz (1978a, 1992). The claim to unmediated experience noted above has been declared invalid, as if the authority Western philosophy has granted Kant was absolute. Yet, as noted above, the claim to unmediated contact with reality is commonplace enough in mysticism to be its central defining feature. The issue to be engaged is why scholars deny the possibility of unmediated experience that is the essence of the experience of the dissolution of individuality reported in mystical experience. As Parsons (1999, p. 121) notes, it is an open possibility that one could develop a post-Kantian epistemology congruent with the mystical noesis. And to this I add that one could develop a post-Kantian psychology that is congruent with this noesis as well. To do this, I reaffirm my assumptions stated at the beginning of this chapter by noting my opposition to a too-strongly constructionist position insofar as constructionism demands that all experience be mediated experience.

First, it is an open question as to whether a post-Kantian epistemology and a psychology derived from it can be developed that supports the mystic claim to unmediated experience. Although I agree with James that the authority of mystical experience is only absolute for those who have the experience, it also must be accepted that the report of mystical experience is a valid source of hypothesis-testing for researchers. One hypothesis to be tested is whether there are unmediated experiences, and suggestions have been made on how to do this (Almond, 1982). My position leaves the ontological issues open and accepts that mystics may be correct in the report of their experiences as simple empirical fact, introspectively or phenomenologically revealed.

Second, I accept that both mystical texts and their contexts must be respected. The claim to a common core is not simply a reductive assertion of identity that ignores differences in reports of experience. It is not a perennial philosophy or psychology that claims a higher-order interpretation common to all faith traditions. Mystics have supported a wide range of interpretations of their experience, from monism to dualism and from theism to pantheism and even atheism. But the brute phenomenological fact remains that an experience of undifferentiated unity is just that. Matilal (1992) has rightly noted that a salient feature of mysticism, however interpreted, is that it "promotes a special type of human experience that is at once unitive and nondiscursive, at once self-fulfilling and self-effacing" (p. 143). Why this particular experience is so often reported within various faith traditions must be explored as well as its emergence independent and outside of faith traditions.

If Katz has marshaled authors critical of Stace, others have begun to marshal authors to support the common core thesis. In two edited works, Forman (1990, 1998) has essentially argued that introversive mysticism, which he identifies as pure consciousness experience (PCE) necessarily lacks content and as such is independent of both culture and person. The fact that PCEs are variously interpreted after the fact can account for much of the diversity that is only apparent across mystical traditions. Again, the differences in mystical experience are at the interpretative, not experiential, level.

While the debate about whether mystical experiences share a common core is largely based on texts in the conceptual literature, it has become apparent that there are four significant literatures on mysticism, each unfortunately isolated from the other. McGinn (1994) refers to an "unrealized conversation" (p. 343) between three literatures that he has identified: the theological, the philosophical, and the comparative-psychological. Like Katz, McGinn focuses on texts and their interpretation for his illumination of mysticism. However, to these largely textually based literatures, I add a fourth: the empirical study of mysticism. Particularly useful is the empirical study of mysticism that links the phenomenological investigation of mysticism with measurement-based studies of contemporary persons reporting these experiences (Hood, 1997b). It is the fourth area that has lent considerable support to the common core thesis and to which we now turn.

PSYCHOMETRIC SUPPORT FOR THE COMMON CORE THESIS

The most common measurement scale for the study of mysticism is the Mysticism scale or M-Scale (Burris, 1999a). For purposes of this chapter, it is important to note that the 32 items of the M-scale were specifically derived from Stace's delineation of the common core that he derived phenomenologically (Hood, 1997b, 2001, in press). Thus, the M-scale is directly linked to the phenomenological (and hence conceptual) literatures. However, what it adds to our understanding of mysticism is its ability to assess the report of mystical experience among contemporary persons.

The M-scale consists of 32 items, two positively worded and two negatively worded items, all but one (paradoxicality) of the original common core criteria of mysticism proposed by Stace. Independent investigators have supported Hood's original work, indicating that the M-scale contains at least two factors (Caird, 1988; Reinert & Stifler, 1993). For our purposes, it is important to note that Factor I consists of items assessing an experience of unity (introvertive or extrovertive), while Factor II consists of items referring both to religious and knowledge claims. This is compatible with Stace's claim that a common experience (mystical experience of unity) may be variously interpreted. Other factor analyses of the M-scale by Caird (1988) and Reinert and Stifler (1993) support the original two-factor solution to the M-scale. Reinert and Stifler also suggest the possibility that religious items and knowledge items emerge as separate factors. This splits the interceptive factor into religious and other modes of interpretation, a possibility not inconsistent with Stace's phenomenological classification. This would allow for an even greater range of interpretation of experience, a claim to knowledge that can be either religiously or nonreligiously based. This is consistent with the distinction between spirituality and religion discussed below. However, the factor analytic studies cited above are far from definitive and suffer from inadequate subject-to-items ratios. Overall, they are consistent in demonstrating two stable factors: one an experience factor associated with minimal interpretation, the other an interpretative factor, probably heavily religiously influenced. However, two-factor analyses collapse introvertive and extrovertive mysticisms and do not permit independent identification.

LANGUAGE AND THE M-SCALE

A persistent problem with the M-scale is that it attempts to be neutral with respect to religious language (Hood, 2001). For instance, the scale refers to experience with ultimate reality, not to experience of union with God. However, the language of neutrality is perplexing as emphasized by theorists that oppose the common core thesis (Katz, 1992). How do we know that union with God is the same experience as union with ultimate reality? Two issues are empirically relevant.

First, no language is neutral. Hence, an attempt to speak of union with "God" or "Christ" in language that references only "ultimate reality" suggests to some conservative religionists a "New Age" connotation. Likewise, to reference "God" or "Christ" is itself problematic for secularists. While the distinction between experience and interpretation acknowledges that language is an important interpretive issue, it also forces one to focus on the experiential basis from which genuine differences in interpretation can arise. Like texts, measurement scales use particular language and thus confound the distinction between interpretation and experience. However, empirical methods are available to suggest how this confound can be clarified. One method is to show similar factor structure despite different language use (Hood & Williamson, 2000).

Second, some individuals demand that profound experiences be interpreted. In Barnard's (1997) extended treatment of James's theory of mysticism, mystical experience is defined as one that is necessarily transformative with respect to contact with some transpersonal reality. Although I do not accept this definition of mysticism as properly Jamesean, it does indicate that intense, transformative experiences will be acknowledged in some language that identifies, defines, and expresses what the experienced transpersonal reality is. In Jamesean terms, this language is less constructionist of the experience than descriptive of it. Therefore, those who have experienced ultimate reality may not wish to claim it as God. Moreover, Christians may want that reality to be identified as Christ, something that non-Christian mystics may eschew. Thus, the claim of what is experienced is important as part of the social construction of the expression of experience. However, differently expressed experiences may have similar structures if confounds with language issues can be avoided.

Hood and Williamson (2000) created two additional versions of the M-scale. Each paralleled the original M-scale but, where appropriate, made reference to either God or Christ. Both the original M-scale and either the God-language version or the Christ-language version was given to relevant Christian committed samples. The scales were then factor-analyzed to see if similar structures emerged. Basically, whether the language of the M-scale referenced God, Christ, or simply reality, the factor structures were identical. Furthermore, the common factor structure for all three versions matched Stace's phenomenologically derived model quite well. For all versions of the scale, clear introvertive, extrovertive, and interpretation factors emerged. The exception is that, as anticipated, ineffability emerged as part of the introvertive factor in all samples and not part of the interpretation factor as suggested by Stace. However, as Hood and Williamson note, an experience devoid of content is inherently "ineffable," because there is no content to describe. This is also Stace's (1960) claim with respect to the introvertive experience in that he claims the experience itself is ineffable but the recollection of it is not (pp. 297–298).

In additional studies directly testing Hood's modification of Stace's phenomenological classification, confirmatory factor analysis was used. Hood and his colleagues translated the M-scale into Persian and administered this scale to a sample of Iranian Muslims (Hood et al., 2001). The scale in its original English version was also administered to a sample of Americans. Confirmatory factor analysis was then used to directly test Hood's model of mysticism in both samples (with ineffability as part of introvertive mysticism) to other possible models, including Stace's (where ineffability was part of the interpretative factor). Results showed that, overall, both Stace's and Hood's models were better than any other models and that, overall, Hood's model of mysticism was better than Stace's. Thus, empirically, there is strong support for the claim that, as operationalized from Stace's criteria, mystical experience is identical as measured across diverse samples, whether expressed in "neutral language" in either English or Persian or in specific religious language uses "God" or "Christ" references with appropriate samples. Furthermore, three factor solutions that do not collapse introvertive and extrovertive experiences

Table 5.1 Phenomenologically Derived (Stace) and Empirically Derived (Hood) Models of Mystical Experience

Phenomenologically Derived Model of the Common Core

Introvertive mysticism	Extrovertive mysticism
A Undifferentiated pure consciousness	A. The perception of unity in diversity
B. Timeless/spaceless	B. Inner subjectivity to all

Interpretation
A. Noetic
B. Religious
C. Positive affect
D. Paradoxicality (not measured in M-scale)
E. Ineffability (alleged)

Empirically Derived Model of the Factor Structure of the M-Scale

Introvertive mysticism (12 items)	Extrovertive mysticism (8 items)
A. Pure consciousness items	A. Unity in diversity items
B. Time/space items	B. Inner subjectivity items
C. Ineffability items	

Interpretation (12 items)
A. Noetic items
B. Religious items
C. Positive affect items

of unity fit well with Stace's model (Hood, Morris, & Watson, 1993; Hood & Williamson, 2000; Hood et al., 2001). The basic structure of mysticism that emerges from empirically based measurement studies is directly compared to Stace's phenomenological classification shown in Table 5.1.

Three factor solutions to the M-scale are not simply the most adequate overall measure of mysticism in psychometric terms, but they offer strong empirical support for Stace's common core thesis. Both introvertive and extrovertive mysticism can be clearly identified with ineffability as a defining component of the actual experience of introvertive mysticism. Likewise, regardless of the language of the M-scale, the basic structure of the experience remains constant across diverse samples and cultures. This is a way of stating Stace's common core thesis in measurement-based terms. It also allows us to return to the issue raised by James's view of religious experience. The possibility that mysticism emerges within religious traditions which then come to oppose this primary source from which they derive their existence can be explored empirically. The common core thesis, supported by measurement studies, makes clear that the interpretation of mystical experience can be religious but it need not be.

MYSTICISM WITHIN AND OUTSIDE RELIGION: TROELTSCH'S MODEL

The unfortunate fact of an unrealized conversation between literatures noted by McGinn can partly account for the fact that psychological studies of mysticism have ignored a powerful theory of mysticism embedded in the work of Troeltsch (1931), usually referenced only in the sociological literature (Hood, 2003).

Troeltsch, like Bouyer (1980), saw mysticism as an inherent tendency to seek personal piety and an emotional realization that serves to intensify commitment to a religious tradition. This is mysticism that is inherent and foundational to any and all faith traditions. It is a religion infused with spirituality. Troeltsch classified the traditions into ideal types. The church type is open to all who profess belief, while the sect type is more exclusive as it seeks to purify a church tradition that has been perceived to have strayed from the rigors and pure demands of the faith tradition. The sect thus demands firmer criteria for membership and opposes a strict exclusiveness to the universality and openness of the church type. Both churches and sects are defined as much by their beliefs and rituals that, as noted above, are not directly derivable from mystical experiences. Here is the essence of James's claim that the faithful live by criteria that are far removed from and only indirectly related to firsthand religious experiences, including mystical ones. If churches or sects cannot keep this inward spirituality alive, some seek it elsewhere. Likewise, if either the church or sect closes off the possibility of such experiences, some will seek their spiritual nourishment from other sources.

Only when mysticism emerges as an independent religious principle as a reaction to the church and the sect type does it become a new social force and seeks an independent philosophical or psychological justification. This is mysticism as a third ideal type. This justification can be outside of the faith tradition, and indeed, as noted above, mystical experiences need not be religiously justified at all. Thus, there are two forms of mysticism: one integral to any and all faith traditions and another that can emerge out of and be independent of any faith tradition. These two forms of the mystical type must be clearly distinguished; something social scientists have failed to do. Garrett simply identifies these as M1 and M2 (Garrett, 1975; Troeltsch, 1931, pp. 214–215).

In the widest sense, mysticism is simply a demand for an inward appropriation of a direct inward and present religious experience (Bouyer, 1980; Troeltsch, 1931, p. 730). It takes the objective characteristics of its tradition for granted and either supplements them with a profound inwardness or reacts against them as it demands to bring them back "into the living process" (Troeltsch, 1931, p. 731). This is Garrett's M_1, or Troelstch's "wider mysticism." We identify this as *religious mysticism* because it is a mysticism that Troeltsch (1931, p. 732) and Bouyer (1980, p. 51) assert is found within all religious systems as a universal phenomena. Thus, as an empirical fact, it entered Christianity partly from *within* insofar as Christianity entails the same logical form as all traditions relative to this type and partly from *without* from other sources that were "eagerly accepted" by Christianity (Troeltsch, 1931, p. 732). Concentrating among the purely interior and emotional side of religious experience, it creates a spiritual interpretation of every objective side of religion such that mystics typically stay within their tradition (Katz, 1983). However, Troeltsch (1931) also identifies a "narrower, technically concentrated sense" of mysticism (p. 734). This is Garrett's M2. It is a mysticism that has become independent in principle and contrasted with religion. It gives rise to persons who identify themselves as "spiritual but not religious." It claims to be the true inner principle of all religious faith but is not contained within any particular tradition. This we refer to as *spiritual mysticism*, but the term "spiritual" is redundant. Mysticism now breaks away from religion which it disdains. It accepts no constraint or community other then self-selected and realized. It is a spiritual religion with the term "religion" as redundant here as "mysticism" was above. It is what many today profess to be spirituality as opposed to religion. It is a mysticism not linked to the interpretative mandates of any one faith tradition.

EMPIRICAL EXAMPLES OF RELIGIOUS AND SPIRITUAL MYSTICISM

Pargament and his students have taken the lead in descriptive and correlational work identifying distinctions between religious and spiritual self-identification (Zinnbauer et al., 1997). I focus on one study to illustrate the conceptual distinction between the two mysticisms noted above. One motivation for this study was to paraphrase part of the title of the article in which these data are presented—to "unfuzzy the fuzzy" (a phrase first coined by Spilka). If critics of religion find it too constraining, critics of spirituality find it is not constrained enough. Using an essentially forced-choice procedure, participants were asked to endorse one of the following five options: (1) Religiousness and spirituality overlap, but they are not the same concept. (2) Spirituality is a broader concept than religiousness, and includes religiousness. (3) Religiousness is a broader concept than spirituality and includes spirituality. (4) Religiousness and spirituality are the same concept and overlap completely. (5) Religiousness and spirituality are different and do not overlap. In addition, participants rated themselves on spirituality and religion on a five-point scale. Participants also identified themselves as either *religious, spiritual, both,* or *neither,* in a forced-choice context. Finally, a content analysis was performed on the participant's personal definitions of religiousness and spirituality.

Data were solicited from 11 small convenience samples, ranging from "conservative Christian college students" to "New Age groups." Most of the 364 participants were either college students or members of some religious group. Exceptions included small samples of residents of a nursing home ($n = 20$) and of mental health workers ($n = 27$). Overall, 78 percent of participants identified themselves as religious, while 93 percent identified themselves as spiritual. Most religious persons considered themselves to be spiritual (74%). Overall, few persons thought religiousness and spirituality to be identical concepts (2.6%) or entirely nonoverlapping concepts (6.7%). Thus, for most, religiousness and spirituality are somehow and variously intertwined. Nearly identical percentages identify themselves as religious but not spiritual (4%) or as neither (3%). Very few people consider themselves religious but not spiritual. Hence, for most, religion is inherently involved with spirituality.

Content analysis for personal definitions of spirituality and religiousness revealed a fact consistent with our discussion of the interview data above: the most common categories for spirituality were *experiential* while those for religion were *belief.* For all groups, self-rated spirituality equals or exceeds self-rated religiousness. Not surprisingly, the greatest differences between self-ratings are among participants who are members of religious groups distant from traditional expressions of faith, such as New Age groups and Unitarians. While members of more traditional faith groups differ in levels of self-rated religiousness and spirituality, within specific groups (such as Roman Catholics) there is no significant difference. Among New Age groups, self-rated spirituality greatly exceeds self-rated religiousness. Furthermore, conservative religious groups make less distinction between spirituality and religiousness (Zinnbauer et al., 1997, pp. 554–567).

These data are congruent with previous empirical work. In particular, the finding that mental health workers are more spiritual than religious replicates previous work on mental health professionals. Shafranske (1996) reviewed the empirical research on the religious beliefs, associations, and practices of mental health professionals. Focusing primarily on samples of clinical and counseling psychologist who are members of the American Psychological Association, Shafranske noted that psychologists are less likely to believe in a personal God or to affiliate with religious groups than other professionals or the general population. In addition, while the majority of psychologists report that spirituality is important to them, a minority report that religion is important to them (p. 153). Shafranske summarizes his own data and the work of others to emphasize that psychologists are more like the general population than previously assumed. However what Shafranske lumps together by various indices as the "religious dimension" (p. 154) can be misleading. Psychologists are not like the general population. In fact, psychologists neither believe, practice, nor associate with the institutional aspects of faith ("religion") as much as they endorse what Shafranske properly notes are "noninstitutional forms of spirituality" (p. 154). One could predict that, in forced-choice contexts, they are most likely to be "spiritual but not religious." Empirically, three facts about religious and spiritual self-identification ought to be clear.

First, most persons identify themselves as both religious and spiritual. These are largely person's sampled from within faith traditions for which it is reasonable to assume that spirituality is at least one expression of and motivation for their religion (e.g., institutional participation). Hence, many measures of spirituality simply operate like measures of religion (Gorsuch & Miller, 1999). Here is a mysticism that is comfortable within the bounds of a specific faith tradition. This is religious mysticism.

Second, a significant minority of individuals use spirituality as a means of rejecting religion. However, what is rejected is religious belief and claims to exclusiveness, not the mysticism contained within the tradition This is particularly obvious in qualitative studies in which individuals identify their spirituality in defiant opposition to religion. They oppose various aspects of the institution of religion such as its authority, its more specific ("closed") articulation of beliefs ("dogma") and practices ("ritual"), and they seek to move away from religion to be "more developed" spiritually. The move is from belief to experience, as Day (1994) has perceptively noted. To this I add that experience need not seek explicit interpretation. The common core of mysticism can break free of any interpretative bounds.

Third, religiousness and spirituality overlap considerably, at least in American populations. The majority of the population is religious *and* spiritual, both in terms of self-identification and in terms of self-representations. Exceptions are easy to identify, but one ought not to lose sight of the fact that they are *exceptions.* Significantly, they include not only scientists in general but psychologists in particular (Beit-Hallahmi, 1977; Shafranske, 1996). Among these people, a hostility to religion as thwarting or even falsifying spirituality is evident. This hostility is readily revealed in qualitative studies in which there is some degree of rapport between interviewer and respondents (see Hood, for review). These persons report mystical experiences without the need for faith-bound interpretations. Indeed, persons within and outside religious traditions who report mystical experiences seldom refute the experiential claims of one another. As Stace (1960) has perhaps overstated the case, "There is no instance of a person who has been illumined denying or disputing the teachings of another who has passed through the same experience" (p. 33). Neither are they bound by each other's interpretation of what the experience might mean. There emerges no perennial philosophy from the common experiential core.

SUMMARY AND CONCLUSION

This allows us to come full circle with the common core thesis. Religions are much more than efforts to confront mystical experience. However, there is little doubt that mystical experiences, whether introvertive or extrovertive, share a common core. They can elicit a sense of the scared that demands some form of religious interpretation. Most mystics struggle within their faith tradition to give expression to this primary experience. Huxley (1944, p. 132) reminds us that mystics both make theology and are made by it. However, as religions emerge with some hostility toward these experiences or demand a too-constrictive dogmatic interpretation, mystics can break away from churches and sects, become indifferent or hostile to religion, and identify themselves as simply "spiritual" or indeed as simply "mystics." They may seek secular interpretations of their experience or be satisfied with the experience itself. This dynamic process can be found throughout mystical traditions in all cultures. The tension is always between an experience that is ineffable and the claims to describe it. Stace (1960) noted this as well. His common core thesis led him to conclude, as did Huxley (1944), that the link between mysticism and religion exists only insofar as each claim to acknowledge a transcendence that is both sacred and holy. However, as noted above, mysticism may be both a self-fulfilling and a self-effacing experience of oneness—or perhaps, as the common core thesis suggests, it is also self-authenticating. While the fascination with the issue of unity and diversity, the one and the many, has largely been linked in the history of thought with a religious sensitivity (Copleston, 1982), mysticism has emerged independent of religion and can exist without it. Whether mysticism persists depends much on how the issues of religion and spirituality play out. Regardless, mystical experience remains what it is, self-authenticating for the mystic in all its ineffability.

REFERENCES

Almond, P. (1982). *Mystical experience and religious doctrine.* Berlin: Mouton.

Barnard, G.W. (1997). *Exploring unseen worlds: William James and the philosophy of mysticism.* Albany: State University of New York Press.

Beit-Hallahmi, B. (1977). Curiosity, doubt and devotion: The beliefs of psychologists and the psychology of religion. In H.N. Malony (Ed.), *Current perspectives in the psychology of religion* (pp. 381–391). Grand Rapids, MI: Eerdmans.

Beit-Hallahmi, B. (1985). Object relations theory and religious experience. In R.W. Hood, Jr. (Ed.), *Handbook of religious experience* (pp. 254–268). Birmingham, AL: Religious Education Press.

Bouyer, L. (1980). Mysticism: An essay in the history of the word. In R. Woods (Ed.), *Understanding mysticism* (pp. 42–55). Garden City, NY: Image.

Burris, C.T. (1999a). The Mysticism scale: Research form D (M-scale). In P.C. Hill & R.W. Hood, Jr. (Eds.), *Measures of religiosity* (pp. 363–367). Birmingham, AL: Religious Education Press.

Burris, C.T. (1999b). The Religious Experience Episodes Measure (REEM). In P.C. Hill & R.W. Hood, Jr. (Eds.), *Measures of religiosity* (pp. 220–224). Birmingham, AL: Religious Education Press.

Caird, D. (1988). The structure of Hood's Mysticism scale: A factor analytic study. *Journal for the Scientific Study of Religion, 27,* 122–127.

Copleston, F. (1982). *Religions and the one.* New York: Crossroad.

Day, J.M. (1994). Moral development, belief and unbelief: Young adult accounts of religion in the process of moral growth. In J. Corveleyn & D. Hutsebaut (Eds.), *Belief and unbelief* (pp. 155–173). Amsterdam: Rodopi.

Forman, R.K.C. (Ed.). (1990). *The problem of pure consciousness.* New York: Oxford University Press.

Forman, R.K.C. (Ed.). (1998). *The innate capacity.* New York: Oxford University Press.

Garrett, W.R. (1975). Maligned mysticism: The maledicted career of Troeltsch's third type. *Sociological Analysis, 36,* 205–223.

Gimello, R.M. (1978). Mysticism and mediation. In S. Katz (Ed.), *Mysticism and philosophical analysis* (pp. 170–199). New York: Oxford University Press.

Gorsuch, R.L., & Miller, W.R. (1999). Assessing spirituality. In W.R. Miller (Ed.), *Integrating spirituality into treatment* (pp. 47–64). Washington, DC: American Psychological Association.

Hood, R.W., Jr. (1992). Mysticism, reality, illusion and the Freudian critique of religion. *International Journal for the Psychology of Religion, 2,* 141–159.

Hood, R.W., Jr. (1994). Self and self-loss in mystical experience. In T.M. Briunthauptm & R.P. Likas (Eds.), *Changing the self* (pp. 279–303). Albany: State University of New York Press.

Hood, R.W., Jr. (1995). The soulful self of William James. In D. Capps & J.L. Jacobs (Eds.), *The struggle for life: A companion to William James' the varieties of religious experience* (pp. 209–219). Newton, KS: Mennonite Press.

Hood, R.W., Jr. (1997a). The empirical study of mysticism. In B. Spilka & D.N. McIntosh (Eds.), *The psychology of religion* (pp. 222–232). Boulder, CO: Westview Press.

Hood, R. W., Jr. (1997b). Psychoanalysis and fundamentalism: Lessons from a feminist critique of Freud. In J. L. Jacobs & D. Capps (Eds.), *Religion, psychoanalysis and society* (pp. 42–67). Boulder, CO: Westview Press.

Hood, R. W., Jr. (2001). *Dimensions of mystical experience: Empirical studies and psychological links.* Amsterdam: Rodopi.

Hood, R. W., Jr. (2002). The mystical self: Lost and found. *International Journal for the Psychology of Religion, 1,* 1–24.

Hood, R. W., Jr. (2003). Spirituality and religion. In A. L. Griel & D. Bromley (Eds.), *Defining religion: Investigating the boundaries between sacred and secular* (Vol.10 of *Religion and the social order,* pp. 241–262). Oxford, England: Elsevier.

Hood, R. W., Jr. (in press). The empirical study of mysticism. In D. Wulff (Ed.), *Handbook of the psychology of religion.* New York: Oxford University Press.

Hood, R. W., Jr., Ghorbani, N., Watson, P. J., Ghramaleki, A. F., Bing, M. B., Davison, H. R., et al. (2001). Dimensions of the mysticism M-scale: Confirming the three factor structure in the United States and Iran. *Journal of the Scientific Study of Religion, 40*(4), 691–705.

Hood, R. W., Jr., Morris, R. J., & Watson, P. J. (1993). Further factor analysis of Hood's mysticism-scale. *Psychological Reports, 73,* 1176–1178.

Hood, R. W., Jr., Spilka, B., Hunsberger, B., & Gorsuch, R. (2003). *The psychology of religion: An empirical approach* (3rd ed.). New York: Guilford Press.

Hood, R. W., Jr., & Williamson, W. P. (2000). An empirical test of the unity thesis: The structure of mystical descriptors in various faith samples. *Journal of Christianity and Psychology, 19,* 222–244.

Huxley, A. (1944). *The perennial philosophy.* New York: Harper Colophon.

James, W. (1981). *The principles of psychology.* Cambridge, MA: Harvard University Press. (Original manuscript published 1890.)

James, W. (1985). *The varieties of religious experience.* Cambridge, MA: Harvard University Press. (Original manuscript published 1902.)

Katz, S. T. (1978a). Language, epistemology, and mysticism. In S. T. Katz (Ed.), *Mysticism and philosophical analysis* (pp. 22–74). New York: Oxford University Press.

Katz, S. T. (Ed.). (1978b). *Mysticism and philosophical analysis.* New York: Oxford University Press.

Katz, S. T. (Ed.). (1983). *Mysticism and religious traditions.* New York: Oxford University Press.

Katz, S. T. (Ed.). (1992). *Mysticism and language.* New York: Oxford University Press.

Matilal, B. K. (1992). Mysticism and ineffability: Some issues of logic and language. In S. T. Katz (Ed.), *Mysticism and language* (pp. 143–157). New York: Oxford University Press.

McGinn, B. (1994). The presence of God: A history of Christian mysticism. *The foundations of mysticism* (Vol. 1). New York: Crossroads.

Otto, R. (1932). *Mysticism east and west* (B. L. Bracey & R. C. Payne, Trans.). New York: Macmillan.

Parsons, W. B. (1999). *The enigma of the oceanic feeling: Revisioning the psychoanalytic theory of mysticism.* New York: Oxford University Press.

Proudfoot, W. (1985). *Religious experience.* Berkeley: University of California Press.

Reinert, D. F., & Stifler, K. R. (1993). Hood's Mysticism-scale revisited: A factor analytic replication. *Journal for the Scientific Study of Religion, 32,* 383–388.

Rosenau, P. M. (1992). *Postmodernism and the social sciences: Insights, inroads, and intrusions*. Princeton, NJ: Princeton University Press.

Scharfstein, B. A. (1973). *Mystical experience*. Indianapolis, IN: Bobbs-Merrill.

Scholem, G. G. (1941). *Major trends in Jewish mysticism*. New York: Schocken Books.

Shafranske, E. (1996). Religious beliefs, practices and affiliations of clinical psychologists. In E. Shafranske (Ed.), *Religion and the clinical practice of psychology* (pp.149–164). Washington, DC: American Psychological Association.

Spilka, B., Hood, R. W., Jr., Hunsberger, B., & Gorsuch, R. (2003). *The psychology of religion: An empirical approach* (3rd ed.). New York: Guilford Press.

Staal, F. (1975). *Exploring mysticism: A methodological essay*. Berkeley: University of California Press.

Stace, W. T. (1960). *Mysticism and philosophy*. Philadelphia: Lippincott.

Troeltsch, E. (1931). *The social teaching of the Christian churches* (2 vols., O. Wyon, Trans.). New York: Macmillan.

Wulff, D. M. (2000). Mystical experience. In E. Cãrdena, S. J. Lynn, & S. S. Krippner (Eds.), *Varieties of anomalous experience* (pp. 397–440). Washington DC: American Psychological Association.

Zinnbauer, B. J., Pargament, K. I., Cole, B., Rye, M. S., Butter, E. M., Belavich, T. G., et al. (1997). Religion and spirituality: Unfuzzying the fuzzy. *Journal for the Scientific Study of Religion, 36*, 549–584.

CHAPTER 6

CROSS-CULTURAL ASSESSMENTS OF SHAMANISM AS A BIOGENETIC FOUNDATION FOR RELIGION

Michael Winkelman

The concept of the shaman has been widely applied but remains problematic for a number of reasons. The underlying issues are whether the concept of the shaman is strictly emic, related to a particular culture; or whether shamanism constitutes an etic or universal phenomenon, with cross-cultural applicability and commonalities derived from underlying features of human biology. The central contentions include whether shamans are specific to particular cultures or areas (e.g., Paleosiberia), whether they constitute a human universal found in all societies, or whether they are a widely distributed phenomena found in specific kinds of societies (e.g., hunter-gatherer). Cross-cultural investigations are indispensable methods for empirically addressing these questions and for establishing the nature of shamanism. This article summarizes cross-cultural studies (Winkelman, 1985, 1986a, 1986b, 1990, 1992, 1996; Winkelman & White, 1987, Winkelman & Winkelman, 1991) establishing the cross-cultural nature of shamanism and the universal distribution of shamanistic healers who share biological roots with shamanism. These studies also differentiate shamans from shamanistic healers—practitioners who share similarities with shamans in their common biogenetic foundations involving the use of altered states of consciousness (ASCs) in community rituals involving interaction with spirits and as the basis for training and healing activities. The relationship of various types of shamanistic healers to subsistence, social, and political characteristics provides evidence of the evolutionary transformation of a hunter-gatherer shamanism into other types of religious practitioners. The principal universals of shamanistic healers are assessed to identify their biogenetic structural bases involving: integrative functions of consciousness; sociophysiological mechanisms involving the attachment and bonding mechanisms; and forms of metaphoric self and other reference allowing for development of personal and social identity.

DEFINITIONAL VERSUS CROSS-CULTURAL APPROACHES TO SHAMANISM

Questions regarding the nature of shamanism have been problematic because of the general lack of systematic cross-cultural empirical investigations by those who wish to generalize about shamans. The term "shaman" has been used to refer to many different magico-religious practitioners, generally with the presumption that, despite the apparent diversity of the practices referred to by the term, they are nonetheless in some sense essentially the same. Some researchers have specified what they viewed as the commonalities of shamans (e.g., Eliade, 1964; Hultkrantz, 1973), but many authors have failed to explicate the commonalities they presume and establish that they are, in fact, universals of shamanism. Those who purport that there are universals of shamanism have generally based this on a haphazard synthesis of data from select cultures. Most studies, however, have employed a definitional approach, specifying the particular characteristics they consider to define the shaman (e.g., see Jakobsen, 1999; Townsend, 1997). Some generalize shamans to any practitioners using trances (Peters & Price-Williams, 1981), while others wish to restrict the term regionally (e.g., Siikala, 1978).

Arbitrary definitional approaches do not establish the characteristics of shamans, nor explain cross-cultural similarities and differences in shamanistic practices. A cross-cultural or holocultural method (e.g., see Murdock & White, 1969) is required to answer these questions regarding the issue of the universality of shamans and their characteristics. An empirical approach needs to be based in culturally derived criteria for recognizing practitioners in order to derive a true etic structure rather than an arbitrarily imposed structure. This article reports on such cross-cultural studies that identify the features associated cross-culturally with shamanism, their characteristic and differences from other religious healing practitioners, and the biological bases underlying shamanic universals.

Cross-Cultural Studies of Magico-Religious Practitioners

An empirical determination of the cross-cultural status of shamans and other magico-religious practitioners and their characteristics is provided by a cross-cultural research project (Winkelman, 1985, 1986a, 1986b, 1990, 1992; see Winkelman & White, 1987, for data). This study was based on the Standard Cross-Cultural Sample (SCCS) (Murdock & White, 1969), which is representative of the geographic, social, and cultural regions of the world and a time span of approximately 4,000 years. Winkelman's study focused on the culturally recognized magico-religious practitioners in a stratified 47-society subset of the SCCS. Other studies of the SCCS provided the subsistence and social variables used to identify the associated conditions.

In each of these societies, all of the culturally recognized positions (statuses or roles) involving interaction with supernatural entities or power were individually assessed in terms of a large number of variables (see Winkelman, 1985). These culturally recognized magico-religious practitioners (see Winkelman, 1992; Winkelman & White, 1987) were assessed in terms of their characteristics and irrespective of their labels (i.e., shaman, priest, witch), using a common set of variables reflecting magico-religious activities that were developed from the descriptions of these practices as provided in the ethnographic literature. These variables included, but were not limited to, the practitioners': selection procedures; training conditions; "trance" (altered state of consciousness) induction techniques and procedures; sources of power; relationships to spirits; psychological, social, and economic characteristics; life cycle rituals; social context of and motives for professional activities; sociopolitical powers and activities; and healing, divination, malevolent, propitiation, seasonal, and other rituals. The coded variables for the characteristics of these magico-religious practitioners were submitted to coding reliability checks (Winkelman & White, 1987).

This empirically derived and independently validated cross-cultural data were submitted to statistical analysis to empirically determine the similarities in practitioners from diverse societies. These empirical similarities were used as the basis for deriving distinct groups or types of magico-religious practitioners that have cross-cultural validity. Cluster analyses procedures were used for mathematical assessments of the shared characteristics across practitioners and for determination of the different etic types of practitioners, which were subjected to independent validation (for methods and analysis, see Winkelman, 1986a, 1990, 1992; see Winkelman & White, 1987, for data). I have labeled these empirically derived groups with the terms shaman, shaman/healer, healer, and medium (collectively constituting shamanistic healers); priest; and sorcerer/witch (see Winkelman, 1992, for coverage of priests and sorcerers/witches).

This empirically derived typology provided a basis for establishing the etic status of shamans and other types of magico-religious practitioners and for determining their characteristics.[1] The findings show that some religious practitioners found in Eurasia, the Americas, and Africa are more similar to one another *across* these different regions than they are to other magico-religious practitioners found *within* the regions. Restated, practitioners from different societies and different regions of the world are more similar to each other, based on empirically shared characteristics, than they are to geographically more proximate practitioners, including other practitioners in their own culture. This empirical similarity is more relevant than geographical location or definitions. These findings include an empirically derived group of magico-religious healers that correspond closely to classic characteristics attributed to the shaman. This indicates that the term shaman should be used on the basis of empirically shared characteristics. It is noteworthy that some of the magico-religious practitioners that are labeled as shamans by ethnographers are significantly different from the characteristics of the empirically derived group that is labeled shamans. Instead, these practitioners may be empirically classified as mediums or other types of shamanistic healers, providing support for the contention that the term shaman is overextended in its applications.

These cross-cultural findings (Winkelman, 1986a, 1990, 1992) suggest the use of the term shaman to refer to healers of hunter-gatherer and other simple societies who are trained through ASC for healing and divination and share other characteristics (see below). These shamans are distinguished from other magico-religious healers (mediums, healers, and shaman/healers) found in more complex societies who also use ASC but have other characteristics that distinguish them from shamans. The universal features of shamanism reflect biogenetic foundations of human nature and structural principles of the organism and its brain. The foundations of these biological features are addressed in the final section of this chapter. Although the characteristics of shamanism are principally manifested in hunter-gatherer societies, some of the core features of the shaman—altered states of consciousness, community rituals, and spirit interactions—are a human universal. These characteristics are associated with other religious healing practitioners in advanced agricultural societies, particularly those with political integration and social stratification. This reflects the fundamental role of ecological and social factors as determinants in the form of religious practices, even those with a biogenetic structural basis. These social influences modify the original forms of shamanism, giving rise to a variety of other socially structured forms of shamanistic healers, practitioners who use the principles of shamanism in more complex societies. Shamanistic healers and their similarities and differences described in the subsequent section are based on Winkelman's research (1985, 1986a, 1986b, 1990, 1992; Winkelman & White, 1987).

Cross-Cultural Characteristics of Shamans

Cross-cultural research illustrates empirically similar magico-religious practitioners found in hunter-gatherer and simple agricultural and pastoral societies. Harner (1990) refers to this worldwide phenomenon as "core shamanism." These empirically derived shamans were found in societies in regions around the world, with the exception of the Circum-Mediterranean; this absence is related to the lack of hunter-gatherer societies from this region in the sample used (Winkelman, 1986a). Shamans are found worldwide in nomadic or semi-nomadic hunter-gather, horticultural, and pastoral societies, and are statistically associated with nomadism and a lack of political integration beyond the local community. These predictors maintain significance independent of controls for diffusion, indicating independent origins (Winkelman, 1986a, 1992).

The practitioners empirically clustered in the group labeled shaman included characteristics core to Eliade's description of shamans as individuals who use ecstasy to interact with the spirit world on behalf of the community. Shamans are also charismatic social leaders who engage in spirit-mediated healing and divination for the local community. Shamans' all-night ceremonies are the major religious activity, involving the entire local community in dancing, drumming, and chanting. Shamans also lead raiding parties, organize communal hunts, and direct group movement. Shamans engage in activities on behalf of a client, but generally with the entire local community (the band) participating. Shamans also may engage in malevolent magical acts designed to harm others.

Shamans tend to come from shaman families whose ancestors provided spirit powers. Shamans' selection may result from the desires of a deceased shaman relative who provides spirit allies, but in most shamanic cultures anyone may become a shaman if he or she is selected by the spirits, undergoes training, and is successful in practice. Shamans are selected through a variety of procedures, including involuntary visions, receiving signs from spirits, and serious illness. In most cultures, shamans are predominantly male; however, most cultures also allow females to become shamans, but typically limit their practice to before or after childbearing years. Shamans' developmental experiences might include an attack by spirits that results in death and rebirth. This dismemberment and reconstruction by the spirits provides shamans with powers, especially animal allies, that provide assistance in healing, divination, hunting, and the ability to use sorcery to harm others.

Shamanic training involves induction of an altered state of consciousness and seeking contact with the spirits, often an extension of vision quest experiences undertaken by the entire population (or all males) as a part of adult development. Shamans' ASCs are induced through a variety of procedures: auditory driving (e.g., drumming and chanting), fasting and water deprivation, exposure to temperature extremes, extensive exercise such as dancing, hallucinogens, painful austerities, sleep deprivation, and social and sensory deprivation. A central aspect of the shaman's experience involves the shaman's "soul journey" or "magical flight," during which an aspect of the shaman departs the body and travels to other places. Shamans' ASCs are generally labeled as involving soul flight, journeys to the underworld, and/or transformation into animals. Shamans are not normally possessed by spirits; rather they control spirits and are believed to accomplish their feats through the actions of their spirit allies. A characteristic feature of shamans' ASC is a visionary experience (Noll, 1983) during which they contact the spirit world; animal spirits are central to shamans' powers.

Shamans therapeutic processes involve removal of objects or spirits sent by other shamans through sorcery and soul journeys to recover lost souls and power animals—aspects of the patient's personal essence and powers. Shamanic soul recovery involves a soul journey to do battle with the spirits to rescue the patient's lost soul. Therapeutic processes involve community participation, healing through enhancing social bonding processes, restoring a sense of identity and emotional well-being, and restoring and transforming self (see Halifax, 1979; Ingerman, 1991).

Associated with shamans worldwide are:

community ritual with chanting, drumming, and dancing;

an ASC experience characterized as a soul journey or magical flight;

shamanic training with ASC to produce visionary experiences;

an initiatory crises involving a death and rebirth experience;

abilities of divination, diagnosis, and prophecy;

therapeutic processes focused on soul loss and recovery;

disease caused by spirits, sorcerers, and the intrusion of objects or entities;

animal relations, including control of animal spirits and transformation into animals;

malevolent acts or sorcery; and

hunting magic.

RELIGIOUS UNIVERSALS AND SOCIETAL SPECIFICS: SHAMANISTIC HEALERS

The hunter-gatherer shamans' utilization of ASC to communicate with the spirit world on behalf of the community and for divination and healing is found in all societies; these features constitute universals of religion with biological bases (Winkelman, 2000, 2004a, p. 231). These ASC, spirit relations, and community rituals are a human religious universal; however, these activities are associated with different types of practitioners in more complex societies. The term "shamanistic healers" has been proposed for these universally distributed practitioners who use ASC for training, healing, and divination (Winkelman, 1990). The different types of shamanistic healers share the following characteristics:

induction of ASC in training and professional activities;

providing divination, diagnosis, and healing;

physical treatments (e.g., massage, herbal preparations);

use of rituals and invocations; and

removal of detrimental effects of spirits and human agents (e.g., sorcerers) (Winkelman & Winkelman, 1991).

Shamanistic healers share other features, including providing relief by meeting needs for assurance and counteracting anxiety and its physiological effects. Their symbolic manipulations can change emotional responses and share commonalities in addressing emotional distress. The processes include eliciting community support and meeting needs for belonging, comfort, and bonding with others. Shamanistic healing practices can also heal emotional problems by eliciting repressed memories and restructuring them, providing opportunities for social confession and forgiveness, resolving intrapsychic and social conflicts, and providing processes for expression of unconscious concerns. Emotions and unconscious dynamics typically are manipulated by attributing these processes to external forces (spirits).

Shamanistic healing practices utilize universal aspects of symbolic healing (Dow, 1986). This involves placing the patient's circumstances within the broader context of cultural mythology and ritually manipulating these relationships to emotionally transform the patient's self and emotions. Ritual manipulation of unconscious psychological and physiological structures enables shamanistic healers to evoke cognitive and emotional responses that cause physiological changes. These are achieved by the manipulation of cultural symbols associated with autonomic responses and through activities that cause physiological changes (e.g., drumming, fasting).

There are differences in the emotional psychodynamics of shamans and other shamanistic healers, reflected in the psychodynamic differences in soul journey, possession, and meditation (Winkelman, 2000). Shamanistic healers also differ with respect to a variety of other characteristics, including the types of societies in which they are found, the processes involved in their training, the nature and source of their powers, and their relationships to social institutions. These differences in shamanistic healers are illustrated in the following discussion of shaman/healers, mediums, and healers.

Shaman/Healers

The empirically derived group of magico-religious practitioners labeled shaman/healers are associated with sedentary agricultural societies at all levels of social stratification and political integration. The adoption of agriculture and its associated consequences are the fundamental cause of the transformations of shamans into shaman/healers. The fundamental role of agriculture in the transformation of the original forms of shamanism into other types of shamanistic healers is further supported by the significant association of agricultural societies with the presence of another form of magico-religious practitioner, priests (Winkelman, 1992). Although the shaman/healers engage in healing and divination for the community, they differ from shamans on a number of key features. Shaman/healers are also engaged in agricultural rituals. Their training emphasizes the role of a professional group that provides instruction, ceremonial recognition of formal status, and group activities (Winkelman, 1992). Shaman/healers also have specialized roles: they may perform diagnosis or agricultural rituals but not healing, or they may heal specific kinds of illness. Shaman/healers enter ASC and have interactions with the spirit world, but these generally do not involve soul journey (not possession). Many are typified by meditative ASC (Winkelman, 1986b, 1992, 2000). Their powers include both spirits and impersonal sources, including rituals and techniques learned from other professionals.

Healers

Healers are found in agricultural societies with political integration beyond the level of the local community. Healers are almost exclusively male and generally hold high social and economic status that is reflected in political, legislative, and judicial powers and officiation at group ceremonial activities. Their professional organizations that provide costly training and certify initiates also wield considerable power, which enables healers to be full-time specialists. Healers also engage in specialized diagnosis and healing, but many seem to lack the ASC activities that are the defining characteristics of shamans. ASC may nonetheless be part of the clients' experience in the interaction with the healers. The cultural significance and structuring of interactions with healers has profound effects on consciousness. Healers' treatments emphasize rituals, spells, incantations, formulas, and sacrifices. Their divination procedures use material systems, which they interpret to make diagnoses. Exorcism is a significant activity; they also frequently use herbal medicines. Healers engage in life cycle activities such as naming ceremonies, marriage rituals, and funerals. Their differences from shamans emphasize the healers' lack of ASC and direct communication with spirits; the existence of powerful professional organizations and formal political power; their relations with superior spirits rather than animal spirits; the use of material and mechanical systems for divination; and their learning of spells, formulas, and ritual enactments for healing. Healers are found in societies with priests and generally work in collaboration with them. Healers also have the power to determine who is a sorcerer or witch and take actions against those individuals. The roles of healers are often complemented, especially in stratified societies, with the role of mediums, who more directly engage the ASC capacities associated with shamanism.

Mediums

The practitioners empirically classified as mediums are called diviners, healers, prophets, and shamans, but they have profiles distinct from the empirically derived characteristics of shamans. Mediums are found primarily in agricultural societies, and their presence in a society is significantly predicted by the presence of political integration beyond the local community. Mediums are predominantly women and are generally of low social and economic status. Mediums are generally not believed to engage in malevolent acts, but rather act against the influences of sorcerers, witches, and evil spirits. They engage in worship and propitiation of their possessing spirits and make sacrifices to them. Mediums' ASC generally begin as spontaneous possessions that occur in late adolescence or early adulthood and constitute both an illness and a call to the profession. Possession ASC episodes are interpreted as the personality and volition of the individual being taken over by a spirit entity. The ASCs are characterized by symptoms of lability in the central nervous system (e.g., compulsive motor behavior, tremors, convulsions, seizures, and amnesia)—symptoms of temporal lobe discharges not associated with shamans or other types of shamanistic healers (Winkelman, 1986b). The training of mediums involves deliberate induction of ASCs, which are also characterized as involving spirit possession and post-ASC amnesia, reflecting the belief that the medium's body is controlled by the spirits that make the utterances. This auditory revelation contrasts with the shaman's visions. Other significant contrasts of mediums and shamans, apart from the features of their respective societies, involve the medium's control by the spirits; the affliction and training occurring later in life (early adulthood); ASC characteristics of possession, amnesia, and convulsions; and agricultural rituals and propitiation.

Mediums and healers both specialize in treatment of possession (see Bourguignon, 1976). The psychodynamics of possession provide symbolic mechanisms for externalization of the control of emotions and attachments. The concept of possession involves outside forces that act upon the patient's body and consciousness. The possession ASC involves dramatic changes in emotions and self, with the possessing spirits providing opportunities to engage in alternate selves that express socially prohibited roles and emotions. The phenomena of possession allow the responsibility for feelings and behaviors to be displaced from the patient and instead attributed to a spirit entity that controls the body and mind. Possession manipulates self, emotions, and relations to others (Boddy, 1994). Possession may shift responsibility for illness and deviance from self to other, placing responsibility for emotions and behavior within the domains of the spiritual or social relations. Possession allows for indirect influences and subtly alters power relations, enabling transformative influences on one's own and others' sense of identity. Possession affects emotional dynamics by expanding self-expression and reconstructing identity and altering self and interpersonal relations through channeling expression of emotions of anxiety, fear, and desire.

The Socioeconomic Transformation of Shamans and Shamanistic Healers

Shamans formed the original basis of magico-religious practices in hunter-gatherer societies. These practices of core shamanism were transformed as a consequence of social evolution. The emergence of sedentary agricultural societies, political integration, and class structures had significant effects on the psychobiological foundations of shamanism, but their origin in innate brain structures and functions of consciousness assured the persistence ASC-based healing practices in more complex societies. The persistence of shamanic potentials was in the shamanistic healers (shaman/healers, mediums, and healers), who represent the universal manifestation of the core characteristics of shamanism postulated by Eliade (1964): the use of ASCs in training, healing, and divination activities; their enactment in a community context; and their relations with the spirit world. Differences among shamanistic healers reflect the adaptation of these psychobiological potentials to different subsistence practices and social and political conditions that transformed the manifestation of shamanic potentials in terms of types of ASC and spirit relations, selection and training practices, the sources and nature of their power, their socioeconomic and political status, illness ideologies, and the nature of their treatments and professional practices (Winkelman, 1990, 1992; Winkelman & Winkelman, 1991).

Cross-cultural data (Winkelman, 1986a, 1990, 1992, 1996) illustrate this evolution of the shamanic potentials in the systematic relationships of different types of shamanistic healers and other magico-religious practitioners (e.g., sorcerers/witches and priests) to socioeconomic conditions. The transformation of shamanic practices into other types of shamanistic healers and magico-religious practitioners is a function of: (1) agriculture replacing hunting and gathering; (2) transformation of nomadic life-style to fixed residence patterns; (3) political integration of local communities into hierarchical societies; and (4) social stratification—the creation of classes and castes and hereditary slavery. Relationships of practitioner types to socioeconomic conditions are illustrated in Table 6.1 (adapted from Winkelman, 1992). These practitioner-societal configurations also correspond to relationships between practitioner selection procedures and their professional functions (Winkelman, 1992), providing the basis for a model of the evolution of magico-religious functions. These involve three major dimensions: (1) the psychobiological basis in ASC (shamanistic healers); (2) the role of social-political and religious leadership (priests); and (3) the conflict of shamanistic healers and priests, manifested in the sorcerer/witch. Shamans were the original source of ASC traditions and provided the social leadership potentials at the basis of priesthoods. Shamanistic practitioners were eventually persecuted by priestly religious structures, giving rise to a phenomena recognized as witchcraft.

The general model of the relationship among magico-religious practitioner types and social conditions outlined in Table 6.1 was assessed with multiple linear regression and log linear analyses. The variables used were the number of types of magico-religious practitioners (1 to 4) and binary variables representing the socioeconomic conditions of the presence of agriculture, two or more levels of political integration beyond the local community, and the presence of classes. The multiple r (.82) was highly significant ($p < .001$), and all of the predictor variables were independently significant. In the log linear analyses, the interaction among the socioeconomic variables were not significant in the prediction of number of types of magico-religious practitioners. The model that specified independent effects of these variables (agriculture, political integration, and classes) on the magico-religious configurations was highly significant (.9796) and fit the data well (see Winkelman, 1986a, for details).

THE BIOLOGICAL BASES OF SHAMANIC UNIVERSALS

The universals of shamanism—the similarities in shamanistic healers across cultures—indicate underlying biogenetic foundations. Winkelman (2000, 2002a, 2002b, 2004a, 2004b) has identified aspects of these biological universals in the context of evolutionary psychology, implicating natural

Table 6.1 Magico-Religious Practitioner Types, Social Conditions, and Biosocial Functions

		Magico-religious practitioner types and societal configurations			Biosocial functions
		Priest	Priest Sorcerer/ witch	Priest Sorcerer/ witch	Social control Social conflict
			or medium	medium	Altered states of
	Shaman	Shaman/ healer	Healer	Healer	consciousness
Socioeconomic conditions	Hunter/ gatherer	Agriculture	Political integration	Social classes	

structures and processes of the human organism and in terms of the concepts of innate processing modules. Central aspects of these biological bases include:

1. the biogenetic roots and functions of ritual as a communication and social coordination system that enables community bonding rituals that manipulate the mammalian attachment processes, eliciting the opioid-attachment mechanisms
2. altered states of consciousness that produce an integrative mode of consciousness, an integration of the potentials of the triune brain through synchronized ascending brain discharges, which are manifested in the shamanic soul flight and visionary experiences
3. manipulation of innate representational modules or cognitive operators related to self-awareness and social identity formation, employing the concepts of spirits as personal and social representation systems
4. integrative forms of thought based in an analogical representation system produced through integration of innate cognitive modules related to animal, self, and other representations and information capacities operating in the somatic (bodily) and visual ("presentational symbolism" [Hunt, 1995]) modalities.

The Psychobiological Consequences of Community Rituals

Shamanic activity requires community participation. Community rituals produce both psychosocial (community cohesion, positive expectation, and social support) and psychobiological effects (eliciting attachment and opioid mechanisms). Frecska and Kulcsar (1989) describe how communal rituals elicit attachment bonds and other psychosociophysiological mechanisms that release endogenous opiates and produce psychobiological synchrony in the group. Shamanic rituals release endogenous opiates through a variety of mechanisms—for example, austerities, fasting, water restriction, strenuous exercise, hyperstress of emotions (Winkelman, 1997). Rituals use social attachment and conditioned cultural symbols to elicit brain opioid systems. Emotionally charged symbols elicit the opioid system and permit ritual manipulation of physiological responses in integrating psychic, mythological, and somatic spheres. One mechanism for community bonding involves chanting, music, dance, and imitative ritual—eliciting an ancient communicative system that Donald (1991) discusses as mimesis, an imitative communication channel that evolved to enhance social bonding and communication of internal states. Music, chanting, singing, and dancing have origins in mimetic modules that provide rhythm, affective semantics, and melody (also see Wallin, Merker, & Brown, 2000). Chanting and music not only provide a nonlinguistic channel for communication—promoting cohesion, coordination, and cooperation among the group—but they also induce healing and altered states of consciousness through engaging theta and alpha brain wave production.

Altered States of Consciousness: The Integrative Mode of Consciousness

The "ecstasy," or ASC, central to shamans' selection, training, and professional practice typically involves singing, chanting, drumming, and dancing, followed by collapse and apparent unconsciousness, but accompanied by intense visual experiences. This ASC involves a natural response of the brain that produces physiological, functional, and psychological integration. Mandell (1980) found that the overall physiological dynamics of ASC involve slow wave discharges from the serotonin circuits of the limbic brain (the "emotional brain" or paleomammalian brain) with lower brain structures, producing synchronized brain waves across levels of the brain. Auditory driving (singing, chanting, drumming, and music) is a primary mechanism for producing ASC and brain wave synchronization; dancing, fasting, and other austerities, most psychoactive drugs, and social and sensory isolation reinforce the response (Winkelman, 1997, 2000). Shamanic ASCs typically activate the autonomic nervous system to the point of exhaustion and collapse into a parasympathetic dominant state that evokes the relaxation response. The shaman's ASC elicits the "integrative mode of consciousness" (Winkelman, 2000), a normal brain response to many activities (e.g., chanting, drumming, fasting, meditation) with synchronized brain wave patterns in the theta and alpha range. These connections produce coherent theta brain wave discharges that synchronize the frontal areas of the brain, replacing the normal fast and desynchronized brain wave activity with slow wave activity representing preverbal behavioral and emotional information.

Shamanic ASCs involve intense visual imagery that Noll (1985) refers to as "mental imagery cultivation." These experiences reflect an innate representational system referred to as "presentational symbolism" by Hunt (1995). Visions provide analysis, analogic synthesis, diagnosis, and planning. Shamanic visions are natural brain phenomena resulting from release of suppression of the visual cortex and involve the same brain substrates for processing of perceptual information. Images are a form of psychobiological communication experienced in a preverbal symbol system. Imagery plays a fundamental role in cognition, providing a basis for relations between different levels of information processing, integrating unconscious information with emotions, linking somatic and cognitive experience. The shamanic ASC is typified by the soul-flight experiences, involving natural symbolic systems for self-representation that are found cross-culturally in out-of-body and near-death experiences. The homologies reflect their innate basis in psychophysiological structures as forms of self-representation that are a natural response of the human nervous system. Laughlin (1997) discusses the universality of body-based metaphor that is manifested in shamanic cosmology and a natural body-based epistemology (also see Laughlin, McManus, & d'Aquili, 1992). Soul flight involves "a view of self from the perspective of other," a form of "taking the role of the other" in presentational symbolism (Hunt, 1995). These self-representations provide forms of self-awareness referenced to the body, but apart from the body, producing shamans' altered consciousness and transcendence.

Spirits and Innate Processing Modules

Fundamental features of shamanism—animism, totemism, and animal spirits—are self, intrapsychic, and social representations produced through integration of specialized innate processing modules for natural history intelligence (recognition of animal species), self-conceptualization, and mental attributions regarding social "others" ("mind reading") (Winkelman, 2000, 2002a, 2004a, 2004b). The shamanic role in managing these modules is exemplified in shamans' characteristics: social intelligence—being group leader and mediator of intergroup relations; natural history knowledge—being master of animals; and self conceptualization—exemplified in identity shifts developed through animal familiars, soul flight, and death-and-rebirth experiences.

Perceptions of spirits are a natural phenomena of the human brain, the outcome of fundamental properties of the human brain and consciousness (Winkelman, 2004b). Spirits are "sacred others," the result of the integration of the spiritual and social worlds in cultural processes that Pandian (1997) characterizes as the production of the symbolic self. Spirit beliefs exemplify social norms and psychosocial relations, structuring individual psychodynamics and social behavior. Spirit beliefs protect from stress and anxiety through management of emotions and attachments. Spirits provide variable command-control agents for mediating conflict between the different instinctive agents and aspects of self, facilitating operation with respect to a hierarchy of goals.

These representations reflect preverbal structures of consciousness and thought processes of lower brain structures. These specialized forms of knowledge production are combined in metaphoric processes to produce shamanic features—animism, totemism, and animal spirits. The spirit world (animism) and anthropomorphism use innate representation modules for understanding self and social others, attributing human mental and social characteristics to animals, nature, and the unknown. Spirit concepts are based in social intelligence, the ability to infer the mental states of others. This intuitive psychology and "theory of mind" attributes mental states to others through the organism's use of its own mental states to model others' minds and behaviors. This attribution underlies the spirit world. Totemism and animal allies and powers involve the natural history intelligence, employing capacities for distinguishing animal species to understand and mold personal identity and produce differentiation of self and social groups. This universal analogical system for creation and extension of meaning uses natural history intelligence to differentiate personal and social identities (also see Winkelman, 2004a).

THE HOLISTIC IMPERATIVE AND SHAMANIC HEALING: INTEGRATING THE TRIUNE BRAIN

Shamanism integrates a mammalian caring heritage into community ritual practices; it provides healing and survival through: eliciting the visionary and psychosomatic capacities of hypnotic susceptibility; physiological effects of community rituals and ritually induced ASC, eliciting the parasympathetic response and the opioid and serotonergic neurotransmitter systems; bonding different groups in alliances for food and protection; social therapies engaging community participation and social symbol systems engaging self-development and the mammalian attachment dynamics; psychological and self-therapies engaging spirits as psychocultural systems and representations of innate psychological dynamics of the self represented in animal spirits; and symbolic-psychophysiological dynamics from ritual manipulation of emotions, self-structures, and the nervous system (see Winkelman, 2000, for details).

HYPNOSIS AS A RITUAL HEALING CAPACITY

McClenon (2002) describes how an inheritable quality manifested in hypnosis was a central factor in our evolved psychology and propensity for religious healing. Hypnotizability contributes to ritual healing through the induction of relaxation and ASC and the ability to engage attention and imagination. McClenon reviews evidence for the presence of the hypnotic capacities in other primates, illustrating that it is an ancient primate adaptation. Hypnotic behavior among other animals provides mechanisms for reducing social stress and engaging the relaxation response. Rituals among animals involve the kinds of repetitive movements that facilitate hypnotic induction in humans and produce relaxation, thereby reducing aggression. In humans, rituals' repetitive and stereotyped behaviors produce both an alteration of consciousness and a sense of intragroup cohesion experienced as "union" or "oneness," classic aspects of religious and mystical experiences. Hypnosis is part of the general physiological changes associated with ASC.

McClenon contends that the tendency to suggestibility, which is based in hypnotic capacities, contributes to a biological capacity for recovery from disease. This capacity of suggestibility enhances symbolically induced physiological changes, psychophysiological responses that facilitate healing. Hypnosis enhances placebo effects that have physiological consequences for healing. Shamanic practices are successful in treating the same kinds of conditions for which hypnosis has been shown to have significant clinical effects: somatization, mild psychiatric disorders, simple gynecological conditions, gastrointestinal and respiratory disorders, self-limiting diseases, chronic pain, neurotic and hysterical conditions, and interpersonal, psychosocial, and cultural problems (see McClenon, 2002, for review).

The hypnotic capacity provides enhanced innovation derived from access to the unconscious mind and its creative visions. Hypnotizability involves focused attention, reduced peripheral awareness, and an abeyance of critical mentation that facilitates a focus on internal imagetic representations and enhanced belief and expectation. Shamanism exploits the co-occurrence of hypnotizability, dissociation, fantasy proneness, temporal lobe lability, and thin cognitive boundaries. These share a common underlying dimension in a "transliminality factor" involving enhanced connections between the unconscious and conscious aspects of the mind. Highly hypnotizable people have thin cognitive boundaries that enable greater access to the unconscious and the flow of information from the unconscious to the conscious. The thin cognitive boundaries provide survival advantages by facilitating the development of creative strategies and facilitating the induction of altered states of consciousness.

INTEGRATING THE TRIUNE
AND MODULAR BRAINS

Human evolution produces a fragmentation of consciousness due to the modular structure of the brain (Mithen, 1996), the diversification of personal and social identities, and the automization of brain processes (Laughlin et al., 1992). This produces a need for integrative brain processes—what Laughlin et al. refer to as the holistic imperative, the drive toward expansion and integration of consciousness at higher levels. Shamanistic activities produce psychological, social, and cognitive integration, managing relationships among behavioral, emotional, and cognitive processes and between physiological and mental levels of the organism. Shamanistic activities use metaphors, ASC, visual symbols, and group rituals to integrate the operations of various brain systems and their functions.

One aspect of this shamanic integration involves linkages across the evolutionary strata of the brain. MacLean (1990, 1993) proposes the brain involves three anatomically distinct yet interconnected systems—the reptilian brain, paleomammalian brain, and neomammalian brain—which provide the basis for behavioral, emotional, and informational functions that MacLean (1993, p. 39) calls protomentation, emotiomentation, and ratiomentation, respectively. These communication systems have been referred to as "subsymbolic" (Ashbrook, 1993) and presentational symbolism (Hunt, 1995). Interactions across levels of the brain are not mediated primarily through verbal language, but through nonverbal forms of mentation that utilize social, affective, and presentational (visual symbolic) information.

The hierarchical management of behavior, emotions, and reason is mediated both physiologically and symbolically. The relationships among innate drives, social attachment, and cultural demands create many different kinds of health problems—chronic anxiety and fears, behavioral disorders, conflicts, excessive emotionality or desires, obsessions and compulsions, dissociations, repression, and so on. The paleomammalian brain mediates many of these processes to promote an integration of the self within the community. The paleomammalian brain's emotiomentation processes provide a major basis for shamanic healing, based on integrating its subjective evaluative influences and self-reference with the instinctual responses of the reptilian brain and the cognitive processes of the neomammalian brain.

These integrative processes are elicited by key aspects of shamanism—the ASC, the physiological and psychological effects of community rituals, and the representations of person and social processes in spirits. Shamanic traditions produce an integration of consciousness through rituals that stimulate physiologically based psychological integration, metaphoric cognitive processes, and community bonding rituals. Shamanic therapies involve a variety of mechanisms for the transformation of the patient's health, eliciting physiological responses and social support and enhancing symbolically mediated placebo and other psychosomatic effects (Winkelman, 2000). The physiological basis of shamanism involves ASCs that produce systemic brain integration, a coordination and increased coherence of the potentials of many parts of the brain. ASC imposes the paleomammalian brain's analogical processes and material of an emotional, social, and personal nature into the self-conscious processes of the frontal cortex. The diverse conditions and procedures that evoke this integrative brain condition indicate that it is a natural state of the human organism. The shaman engages transformative process through ASCs that entrain neurognostic structures and provoke restructuring of the self at levels below conceptual and operational thought, acting upon the psychological and cultural structures of consciousness. Physiological aspects of ASC—parasympathetic dominance, interhemispheric synchronization, and limbic-frontal integration—have inherent therapeutic effects. The relaxation response is elicited by parasympathetic dominance, which counteracts excessive activity of the sympathetic nervous system. This has preventive and therapeutic value in diseases characterized by increased sympathetic nervous system activity and a range of stress-related maladies.

Shamanistic rituals provide assurance; they counteract emotional distress and anxiety and their deleterious physiological effects. Symbolic manipulations are the most effective processes for intervention in stress mechanisms, reestablishing balance in the autonomic nervous system by changing cognitive and emotional responses. Precipitous stress-induced parasympathetic states can cause erasure of memories and previously conditioned responses, alterations in beliefs, increased suggestibility, and reversal of conditioned behavior.

ASC and ritual effects have the ability to elicit emotional memories and reduce the ego-centeredness that inhibits the experience of community connectedness and support that meets needs for belonging, comfort, and bonding with others. Shamanistic healing elicits and restructures repressed memories, providing processes for expression of unconscious concerns and resolving intrapsychic and social conflicts. Shamanic ritual management of behavior, emotions, and reason is mediated physiologically and symbolically within the paleomammalian brain, where social signaling and bonding provide subjective evaluations that play a vital role in integrating instinctual responses of the ancient brains with the cognitive processes of the neomammalian brain. Shamanic ritual evolved as a system for managing the relationships among innate drives and needs, social bonding processes, and cultural representational systems. It provides a system for managing health problems derived from anxiety, fears, conflicts, excessive emotionality, obsessions, and compulsions. Basic therapeutic mechanisms of shamanism link the individual to modal physiological patterns and social expectations.

CONCLUSIONS

Not all religions are based on shamanism and ASC. However, all societies have religious practices based in shamanistic healing, the biologically based roots of shamanism manifested in the use of ASC for community healing through contact with the spirit world. Human evolution selected for these potentials because they were adaptive in enhancing social cohesion, mediating stress responses, and producing psychophysiological integration. Shamanism's primordial, cross-cultural, and empirically derived status gives it a central role in the development of theories of human religiosity. The empirically derived nature of the shamanic paradigm makes it a natural epistemology of religiosity and an explanatory resources for a naturalistic approach to the nature, origins, development, and persistence of religious experiences. The shamanic paradigm identifies central issues for a biology of religion in the congruence of shamanic elements with aspects of an evolved psychology, revealing the biogenetic structuralist foundations of religious conceptions and practices.

NOTES

The findings here were first reported in a doctoral dissertation (Winkelman, 1985) and elaborated in a series of publications (Winkelman, 1986a, 1986b, 1990, 1992, 1996, 1997, 2000, 2002a, 2002b, 2004a).

1. Universals were inferred for a category of practitioners when the characteristics were reported for 75 percent or more of the group, and the presence of information was significantly predicted by data quality control measures assessing the ethnographers' extent of coverage and involvement with magico-religious practices. In essence, universality of a feature was inferred when most of the practitioners of a type had the characteristic in question, and its absence was a reflection of poor data available for the culture and its magico-religious practitioners.

REFERENCES

Ashbrook, J. (1993). The human brain and human destiny: A pattern for old brain empathy with the emergence of mind. In J. Ashbrook (Ed.), *Brain, culture and the human spirit: Essays from an emergent evolutionary perspective* (pp. 183–210). Lanham, MD: University Press of America.

Boddy, J. (1994). Spirit possession revisited: Beyond instrumentality. *Annual Review of Anthropology, 23,* 407–434.

Bourguignon, E. (1976). *Possession.* San Francisco: Chandler and Sharpe.

Donald, M. (1991). *Origins of the modern mind.* Cambridge, MA: Harvard University Press.

Dow, J.W. (1986). Universal aspects of symbolic healing: A theoretical synthesis. *American Anthropologist, 88,* 56–69.

Eliade, M. (1964). *Shamanism: Archaic techniques of ecstasy.* New York: Pantheon Books.

Frecska, E., & Kulcsar, Z. (1989). Social bonding in the modulation of the physiology of ritual trance. *Ethos, 17*(1), 70–87.

Halifax, J. (1979). *Shamanic voices.* New York: Dutton.

Harner, M. (1990). *The way of the Shaman.* San Francisco: Harper & Row.

Hultkrantz, A. (1973). A definition of shamanism. *Temenos, 9,* 25–37.

Hunt, H. (1995). *On the nature of consciousness.* New Haven, CT: Yale University Press.

Ingerman, S. (1991). *Soul retrieval.* San Francisco: Harper Collins.

Jakobsen, M. (1999). *Shamanism: Traditional and contemporary approaches to the mastery of spirits and healing.* New York: Berghahn Books.

Laughlin, C. (1997). Body, brain, and behavior: The neuroanthropology of the body image. *Anthropology of Consciousness, 8*(2–3), 49–68.

Laughlin, C., McManus, J., & d'Aquili, E. (1992). *Brain, symbol and experience toward a neurophenomenology of consciousness.* Boston: Shambhala.

MacLean, P. (1990). *The triune brain in evolution.* New York: Plenum.

MacLean, P. (1993). On the evolution of three mentalities. In J. Ashbrook (Ed.), *Brain, culture and the human spirit: Essays from an emergent evolutionary perspective* (pp. 15–44). Lanham, MD: University Press of America.

Mandell, A. (1980). Toward a psychobiology of transcendence: God in the brain. In D. Davidson & R. Davidson (Eds.), *The psychobiology of consciousness.* New York: Plenum.

McClenon, J. (2002). *Wondrous healing: Shamanism, human evolution and the origin of religion.* DeKalb: Northern Illinois University Press.

Mithen, S. (1996). *The prehistory of the mind: A search for the origins of art, religion and science.* London: Thames and Hudson.

Murdock, P., & White, D. (1969). Standard cross-cultural sample. *Ethnology, 8,* 329–369.

Noll, R. (1983). Shamanism and schizophrenia: A state-specific approach to the schizophrenia metaphor of shamanic states. *American Ethnologist, 10*(3), 443–459.

Noll, R. (1985). Mental imagery cultivation as a cultural phenomenon: The role of visions in shamanism. *Current Anthropology, 26,* 443–451.

Pandian, J. (1997). The sacred integration of the cultural self: An anthropological approach to the study of religion. In S. Glazier (Ed.), *Anthropology of religion: A handbook of method and theory* (pp. 505–519). Westport, CT: Greenwood Press.

Peters, L., & Price-Williams, D. (1981). Towards an experiential analysis of shamanism. *American Ethnologist, 7,* 398–418.

Siikala, A. (1978). *The rite technique of Siberian shaman* (Folklore fellows communication 220). Helsinki, Finland: Soumalainen Tiedeskaremia Academia.

Townsend, J. (1997). Shamanism. In S. Glazier (Ed.), *Anthropology of religion: A handbook of method and theory* (pp. 429–469). Westport, CT: Greenwood Press.

Wallin, N. L., Merker, B., & Brown, S. (Eds.). (2000). *The origins of music.* Cambridge, MA: MIT Press.

Winkelman, M. (1985). *A cross-cultural study of magico-religious practitioners.* Unpublished doctoral dissertation, University of California.

Winkelman, M. (1986a). Magico-religious practitioner types and socioeconomic analysis. *Behavior Science Research, 20*(1–4), 17–46.

Winkelman, M. (1986b). Trance states: A theoretical model and cross-cultural analysis. *Ethos, 14,* 76–105.

Winkelman, M. (1990). Shaman and other "magico-religious healers": A cross-cultural study of their origins, nature and social transformation. *Ethos, 18*(3), 308–352.

Winkelman, M. (1992). *Shamans, priests and witches. A cross-cultural study of magico-religious practitioners.* Anthropological research papers #44. Tempe: Arizona State University.

Winkelman, M. (1996). Religious practitioners. In D. Levinson & M. Ember (Eds.), *Encyclopedia of cultural anthropology* (pp. 1105–1109). New York: Henry Holt.

Winkelman, M. (1997). Altered states of consciousness and religious behavior. In S. Glazier (Ed.), *Anthropology of religion: A handbook of method and theory* (pp. 393–428). Westport, CT: Greenwood Press.

Winkelman, M. (2000). *Shamanism: The neural ecology of consciousness and healing.* Westport, CT: Bergin and Garvey.

Winkelman, M. (2002a). Shamanism and cognitive evolution. *Cambridge Archeological Journal, 12*(1), 71–101.

Winkelman, M. (2002b). Shamanic universals and evolutionary psychology. *Journal of Ritual Studies, 16*(2), 63–76.

Winkelman, M. (2004a). Shamanism as the original neuroethology. *Zygon, 39*(1), 193–217.

Winkelman, M. (2004b). Spirits as human nature and the fundamental structures of consciousness. In J. Houran (Ed.), *From shaman to scientist: Essays on humanity's search for spirits* (pp. 59–96). Lanham, MD: Scarecrow Press.

Winkelman, M., & White, D. (1987). A cross-cultural study of magico-religious practitioners and trance states: Data base. In D. Levinson & R. Wagner (Eds.), *Human relations area files research series in quantitative cross-cultural data* (Vol. 3D). New Haven, CT: HRAF Press.

Winkelman, M., & Winkelman, C. (1991). Shamanistic healers and their therapies. In W. Andritzky (Ed.), *Yearbook of cross-cultural medicine and psychotherapy 1990* (pp. 163–182). Berlin: Verlag Fur Wissenschaft Und Bildung.

CHAPTER 7

SCHIZOPHRENIA, NEUROLOGY, AND RELIGION: WHAT CAN PSYCHOSIS TEACH US ABOUT THE EVOLUTIONARY ROLE OF RELIGION?

Steven A. Rogers and Raymond F. Paloutzian

Religious ideation and delusion have long been part of the symptomatology of individuals with schizophrenia. Over the past several decades, the nature of this relationship has generally been considered disadvantageous, with religious delusions and hallucinations presupposed as the source of much of the social isolation and personal torment associated with schizophrenia. Some of this may be owing to the current reign of the disease model of psychopathology, where the symptoms of schizophrenia or other mental illness are perceived as vagaries to be rooted out and cured. This does not answer the question about what distinguishes the meaning of religious experiences of individuals with schizophrenia from the experiences of those without it. Granted, much public and personal harm can be laid at the feet of individuals responding to grandiose delusions and perceptual abnormalities, such as hearing voices commanding ego-dystonic violence. However, the process of decrying the negative consequences of the religious content of schizophrenic symptoms may overlook the personal or social contribution of individual symptoms. It may be that individuals with schizophrenia have an ability to tap into a spiritual realm and experience the divine via hallucination, delusion, and anomalous perceptual experiences. This ability may represent one of the unique societal contributions of schizophrenia that has led to its persistence across races, continents, and a common genetic ancestry. To the extent that we can understand the biological and neurological substrates of religious delusion and ideation in schizophrenia, we may develop unique insights into the biological and evolutionary nature of religion, including why humans developed the capabilities that enable them to have religious systems of meaning.

This chapter (a) highlights the biological, neurological, and clinical substrates of schizophrenia; (b) explores the relationship between schizophrenia and religion, including the role of the frontal and temporolimbic systems in religious delusions; and (c) discusses the implications of religious delusions and schizophrenia for the biology, evolutionary underpinnings, and psychology of religion.

THE BIOLOGY AND NEUROLOGY OF SCHIZOPHRENIA

The Syndrome of Schizophrenia

Schizophrenia represents a chronic and frequently debilitating group of illnesses that are characterized by cognitive, emotional, and behavioral symptoms. Considering the heterogeneous nature of its symptoms, schizophrenia is generally held to represent a syndrome rather than a single, identifiable disease (Puri, Lekh, Nijran, Bagary, & Richardson, 2001). It lacks a pattern of regularities or a unified body of symptoms that is manifested in every patient (Kemp, 2000), but the unique combination of these symptoms has led to a readily identifiable condition or syndrome. These symptoms can be grouped into three domains: positive, negative, and cognitive phenomenon (Kasai et al., 2002; Wong & Van Tol, 2003).

Positive symptoms refer to the presence of unusual phenomenon, such as hallucinations, delusions, positive thought disorders, and disorganized speech—the first three generally representing what clinicians understand as psychosis. Most of those with schizophrenia report that their hallucinations are auditory (i.e., hearing voices of family members, God, or angry others) and that their delusions involve persecution, grandiosity, external control, or ideas of reference. Negative symptoms refer to features of normal human behavior that are absent, such as emotional flattening, social withdrawal, apathy, and poverty of speech. Central to the cognitive symptoms of schizophrenia are deficits in executive function, attention, memory, and general intellectual function (Mohr & Huguelet, 2004).

Typically, the negative and cognitive symptoms are persistent and chronic, whereas the positive, psychotic symptoms are episodic in presentation (Wong & Van Tol, 2003). However, the positive symptoms are the most unsettling and noticeable clinical phenomenon, often leading to stigmatization and hospitalization. This is evident in the discomfort, perplexity, and fear of those who encounter individuals responding to internal voices or shouting their status as messengers of God.

Religious Meaning Systems

Many of these symptoms of schizophrenia may sound bizarre and unusual when compared to our own experiences. This makes it easy to assume that the religious experiences of such persons are also somehow essentially different from those of the rest of the population, as if the differences are in kind rather than amount. Perhaps the more acute question is whether the shared meaning system that religion provides is somehow different among those with schizophrenia or whether the elements of this meaning system are in disarray consistent with the symptoms of schizophrenia.

By using the concept of a meaning system, we are referring to a cognitive structure that allows for abstraction, generalization, and representation of a relationship or relatedness between two entities (Baumeister, 1991; Paloutzian, 2005; Park, 2005a, 2005b; Park & Folkman, 1997; Silberman, 2005). According to Park (2005a, 2005b; see also Paloutzian & Swenson, in press, and Park & McNamara, this volume), the two main elements of a meaning system are global meaning and an infinite array of specific daily meanings. Typically, the global meaning gets translated into smaller daily meanings for the comings and goings of daily life, such as everyday events and experiences. Religion provides one type of global meaning system that serves as an overarching umbrella subsuming beliefs about the divine-human relationship, global goals and values, and a subjective sense of meaningfulness—a sense that, at the end of it all, there is continuity and the self and community are included in it. This system enables individuals to evaluate everyday events, such as whether a behavior is consistent with one's beliefs, if a communication or event can be attributed to God, or if an event that follows a prayer constitutes God's divine answer.

This is particularly relevant during times of stress and coping. When distressing information confronts the individual or community, an appraisal process is set in motion to determine whether the information is relatively consistent or inconsistent with the expectations of the religious meaning system. New information that is congruent with this meaning system is incorporated and strengthens it, whereas new information that is incongruent with the religious meaning system may represent a form of distress that invokes a process of meaning assessment, reappraisal, and perhaps reconstruction. In other words, information that is discrepant from the global meaning system is either rejected or used to modify the global meaning system and its effects on the daily meanings. For example, difficult events may be interpreted as part of a divine plan, new attitudes or behaviors may be adopted toward the stressor, or new meaning may be given toward the stressor and those exposed to it. In this way, new meaning is made out of the confluence of the old and the stressors that confront it, and this new meaning is then carried forward to face new life circumstances.

This is how meaning systems operate in the mind of the normative population, but it remains unclear how these elements relate in the mind of those with schizophrenia. It may be that the particular pattern of these elements is adaptive in the mind of those with schizophrenia and once played an essential role that contributed to the survival of early human societies. To answer these questions, however, requires understanding the structural underpinnings of schizophrenia and the processes that are involved in making meaning.

Structural Underpinnings

Despite the heterogeneity in the religious and nonreligious symptoms of schizophrenia, it has remained clear that schizophrenia represents a chronic brain condition with identifiable neurological and biological substrates. There is heterogeneity in the structural and neurophysiological abnormalities that comprise the substrates of schizophrenia, which is consistent with the variety of symptoms inherent to schizophrenia. However, research has consistently shown that the brains of individuals with schizophrenia are generally differentiated by diffuse enlargement of the ventricles and decreased cortical volume, with particular reductions in the gray matter of the medial temporal and frontal lobes, as well as their thalamic relays (Clinton & Meador-Woodruff, 2004; Crow, 1995; Halliday, 2001; Kasai et al., 2002; Wong & Van Tol, 2003).

This is evident in a review of 193 peer-reviewed studies that conducted MRI on patients with schizophrenia (Shenton, Dickey, Frumin, & McCarley, 2001). Central to the findings of this study were that the brains of individuals with schizophrenia had ventricular enlargement and significant reductions in the size of the medial temporal lobe (amygdala, hippocampus, parahippocampal gyrus), superior temporal gyrus, and the prefrontal gray matter and orbitofrontal regions of the frontal lobe. Similarly, brain SPECT imaging has shown hypofrontality and temporal lobe hypoperfusion among those with schizophrenia (Camargo, 2001), with the medial temporal lobe being a particularly crucial and principal site for abnormality, largely owing to its connections with prefrontal cortices (Arnold, 1997).

These structural abnormalities are consistent with the cognitive impairments that often accompany schizophrenia. Ventricular enlargement has been associated with deficits in abstraction, attention, and language, all of which are central to meaning system processes. Medial temporal dysfunction corresponds to deficits in verbal and visual memory; abnormalities in superior temporal gyrus may account for disordered thinking and memory; and frontal lobe deficits are correlated with impaired working memory, attention, cognitive inflexibility, and set shifting (Antonova, Sharma, Morris, & Kumari, 2004; Arnold, 1997; Levin, Yurgelun-Todd, & Craft, 1989; Shenton et al., 2001). Although environmental factors invariably play a role in the development of schizophrenia, these neural and structural abnormalities have led most to conclude that schizophrenia represents a biological brain disorder.

To the extent that clinical phenomena are tied to these structural abnormalities, one would expect that positive and negative symptoms, including religious delusions, should also be largely determined by neuropathological substrates. Indeed, many of the negative symptoms of schizophrenia, such as flattened affect and apathy, are associated with reductions in the gray matter of the ventromedial frontal regions and the white and gray matter of the prefrontal regions (Kurachi, 2003; Wong & Van Tol, 2003). The presence of positive symptoms of delusions implicates frontal and temporolimbic systems (Kurachi, 2003; Saver & Rabin, 1997), whereas thought disorders have been inversely correlated with activity and gray matter volume in the bilateral inferior frontal, left superior temporal, and middle temporal regions (Kasai et al., 2002; Puri et al., 2001). Similarly, those experiencing auditory hallucinations have significant volume reductions in the superior temporal gyrus and the medial temporal lobe, especially in the left hemisphere (Heckers et al., 1998; Kurachi, 2003; Stephane, Barton, & Boutros, 2001). Neuroimaging on those experiencing auditory hallucinations revealed decreased metabolism in lateral temporal language regions and increased cerebral blood flow from the inferior frontal lobe to Broca's area (Wong & Van Tol, 2003).

Schizophrenia as a Disruption of Normal Brain Activity

Interestingly, the substrates for the positive and negative symptoms of schizophrenia are not separate, additive, or unique processes, but instead represent disruptions of normal brain activity. For example, each of the cortical regions implicated during auditory hallucinations is related to normal speech perception and auditory processing. These normal processes involve interconnections between frontotemporal cortices, limbic and paralimbic regions, and the thalamus, but the disruption of these interconnections appears to result in the secondary activation of Wernicke's areas (speech perception) and Broca's area (expression). The disruption of the first leads to the experience of hallucinations and the second induces subvocal speech activity that accompanies the hallucinations (Stephane et al., 2001). In other words, the experience of auditory hallucinations appears to partially stem from the activation of those areas responsible for subvocal speech generation and speech perception, but there is a biological failure to differentiate external and internal speech, so that inner speech is perceived as external to the self. Similar deficits in frontal and temporolimbic systems likely account for the perceptual distortions, defects in formal reasoning, and failed search for disconfirming evidence that characterize thought disorders (Saver & Rabin, 1997). Hence, the symptoms of psychosis, such as auditory hallucinations and delusions, are deeply rooted in normal brain activity for speech, perception, and thought.

In a sense, the symptoms of psychosis are deeply rooted in what it means to be human. This is particularly striking when we realize how they are fundamentally connected to many of the ways we distinguish ourselves as human, including the way we make meaning or sense of our internal and external worlds. Many of the areas compromised in schizophrenia, including the superior temporal gyrus, frontal lobes, and gray matter connectivity, are intimately involved in abstraction, relating, and the construction of meaning and the perception of coherence. When these areas are compromised through reduced cortical volume and pressure from ventricular enlargement, it becomes difficult to make judgments, engage in abstract thinking, and formulate conceptual relationships. In a sense, the areas responsible for how we make meaning and patterns out of chaos are dysregulated in schizophrenia. This may explain some of the disintegrated thinking, incoherence, and unusual ways for constructing new meaning that are experienced by those with schizophrenia (see Park & McNamara, this volume, for additional discussion of meaning and neurology). Not only does this raise interesting questions about the biological basis by which we construct meaning, but it also suggests that the symptoms of psychosis disrupt normal neural channels to create existential differences between those with schizophrenia and those without it. These differences include the ways they construct meaning, purpose, and coherence, which intimates the possibility of a unique existential role for those with schizophrenia.

Neurochemical Changes

The symptoms of schizophrenia are not only supported by structural abnormalities that impact what it means to be human, but also by neurochemical pathology. Most likely, changes in neurotransmitter levels contribute to and mediate the larger changes in brain structure. The two primary systems that have been implicated are the dopaminergic and glutamatergic systems. The results of both PET imaging and the effectiveness of medications that target dopamine receptors have intimated that overactivity of the dopamine system may be partially responsible for the emergence of psychosis (Lewis & Lieberman, 2000; Wong & Van Tol, 2003). In particular, abnormalities in the metabolic mechanisms, presynaptic storage and release, vesicular transport, and postsynaptic reuptake of dopamine in the meso-limbic systems may foster hallucinations, delusions, and other psychotic symptoms (Carlsson, Waters, Waters, & Carlsson, 2000; Lewis & Lieberman, 2000).

The symptoms of psychosis may also be related to hypofunction of the N-methyl-D-asparate (NMDA) receptors in the glutamatergic system. This is intimated by the ability of NMDA antagonists to induce psychotic symptomatology. Although the exact mechanisms of the glutamatergic system are uncertain, its impact on psychosis may be related to excitotoxic damage to hippocampal neurons or interactions with the dopamine system, such as fostering dopamine release in the mesolimbic system (Lewis & Lieberman, 2000; Wong & Van Tol, 2003). In particular, glutamatergic neurons appear to regulate dopamine neurons, so hyperglutamertergica may cause an increase or decrease in dopamine function, which in turn influences the emergence of psychotic symptomatology (Carlsson et al., 2000). In fact, it may be that the interplay between the dopaminergic and glutamatergic pathways acts on striatothalamic pathways in a way that fosters psychosis. These two pathways are largely antagonistic, with dopamine being inhibitory and glutamate being stimulating, so one possibility for psychosis is that the hyperactivity of dopamine or hypofunction of glutamate overstimulates the thalamus, leading to sensory overload and hyperarousal (Carlsson et al., 2000).

It is most likely, however, that schizophrenia cannot be simply reduced to dopamine-receptor blocking or glutamatergic intervention. In order for neurochemical changes to mediate the progressive structural abnormalities that give rise to schizophrenia, it seems likely that multiple neurochemical system changes are involved. This is evident in the recent effectiveness of medications with a high affinity for serotonin receptors (Ban, 2004).

Nevertheless, these neurochemical, structural, and functional departures from normal development suggest that the specific positive and negative symptoms of schizophrenia may be artifacts of a disruption in the neural regions that regulate or control those symptoms. This is not to dismiss the influence of biology or psychosocial pressures on the symptoms of schizophrenia, nor to suggest that schizophrenia occurs in a biological vacuum. Quite the contrary, research has consistently demonstrated that environmental insults, such as exposure to infectious diseases and stress during gestation or childhood, may contribute to the pathogenesis of schizophrenia (Lewis & Lieberman, 2000). These events may act as stressors on susceptible neural circuits and compound deficits in maturational processes of apoptosis, synaptic pruning, and myelination (Shenton et al., 2001).

However, the close association between the symptoms of schizophrenia and underlying neural substrates suggests that even the influence of environmental and psychosocial factors may be mediated by neurological sequaelae. In fact, schizophrenia is most accurately conceived as a neurodevelopmental syndrome, or an encephalopathy, where subtle, nonclinical abnormalities are present early in life and later expressed as the full syndrome. The emergence of the full syndrome may be related to developmental alterations in the temporal lobe that interrupt connections between temporolimbic and prefrontal regions (Kasai et al., 2002; Shenton et al., 2001). Therefore, schizophrenia and its corresponding symptoms are intimately tied to a common biology. This removes some of the comfort of saying that schizophrenia is external or outside, and instead forces us to see it within and internal to a shared humanity. By understanding the neural and biological substrates for the religious character of schizophrenia, including religious delusions and hallucinations, we may be able to better understand the biological etiology and persistence of religious symptoms. Ultimately, we may also be able to better shape our understanding of religious meaning systems in general, how they differ from the nonschizophrenic population, and how the religious symptoms of psychosis may perpetuate the cross-cultural constancy of schizophrenia.

SCHIZOPHRENIA AND RELIGION

The Importance of Religion for Those with Schizophrenia

There is much contemporary debate surrounding the relationship between schizophrenia and religion. Some of this debate may be occurring because this relationship crosses the boundaries between science and faith, the political and the individual, and the personal and the institutional. Those adhering to the views of Sigmund Freud or Albert Ellis may contend that religious beliefs are unnecessary at best for mental health and detrimental at worst. Others, such as the *Diagnostic and Statistical Manual for Mental Disorders* (American Psychiatric Association, 1994), may embrace political correctness and simply avoid any discussion of the religious content of psychosis (Pierre, 2001).

However, these often represent artificial distinctions, particularly for individuals with schizophrenia who see religion and spirituality as salient aspects of their everyday functioning and coping. Over one-third of those with schizophrenia are highly interested in religious practices, and two-thirds perceive spirituality as having a significant meaning in their lives (Mohr & Huguelet, 2004). Among psychiatric inpatients in particular, 95 percent believe in God and 53 percent pray or consult the Bible (Kroll & Sheehan, 1989).

For many with schizophrenia, religion also represents an important resource for coping. In London, 61 percent of psychotic patients use religion as a significant coping strategy (Kirov, Kemp, Kirov, & David, 1998), much like the majority of Saudi Arabian patients with schizophrenia use religious forms of coping to combat their auditory hallucinations (Wahass & Kent, 1997). In North America, 80 percent of individuals with severe mental illness use religious forms of coping to deal with their symptoms and daily difficulties, with nearly half indicating that religion becomes more important when their symptoms are exacerbated (Rogers, Poey, Reger, Tepper, & Coleman, 2002). Consequently, religion is not only personally meaningful and important in the lives of individuals with schizophrenia, but it also represents a resource that they have found to be particularly effective in dealing with the symptoms of their illness. It may, therefore, represent a disservice to remove our understanding of religion from our understanding of schizophrenia. On the contrary, our knowledge of both religion and schizophrenia may be enhanced by respecting their relationship and acknowledging that what seems foreign to us may not be the religious experiences themselves but the meanings that individuals with schizophrenia attribute to them.

Considering the high importance placed on religion, it is not surprising that many of the symptoms of schizophrenia, particularly hallucinations and delusions, are infused with religious content and meaning. Up to 70 percent of those with schizophrenia experience auditory visual hallucinations (Stephane et al., 2001), and 90 percent experience delusions at some point during their illness (Saver & Rabin, 1997). Among patients with auditory hallucinations, it is not uncommon for them to describe their hallucinations as the voice of God or the taunting of demons. Similarly, many patients with psychosis or schizophrenia experience grandiose delusions with religious themes or content (Getz, Fleck, & Strakowski, 2001).

The prevalence of these religious delusions may vary by culture and prior religious affiliation. Among individuals with schizophrenia in Britain, 24 percent had religious delusions (Siddle, Haddock, Tarrier, & Faragher, 2002), and 36 percent of American inpatients had religious delusions (Appelbaum, Robbins, & Roth, 1999). In contrast, only 7 percent of Japanese inpatients and 6 percent of Pakistani inpatients with schizophrenia had religious delusions (Stompe et al., 1999; Tateyama et al., 1993). These differences may reflect the relative emphasis placed on religion in the larger culture. Both the British and American cultures have higher rates of belief in God than the Japanese and Pakistani cultures. Moreover, the frequency and severity of religious delusions appears to depend on the level of patients' religious activity, with a greater likelihood and severity of religious delusions among those who are more religiously active (Getz et al., 2001). This may be because they have greater access to religious language and content, as well as a religious meaning system to shape the attributional style for their hallucinations and delusions. In contrast, those with less religious activity may have auditory hallucinations expressed as the voices of family members or delusions manifested as persecution by the government. Nevertheless, religious themes are intrinsic to the hallucinations and delusions of many individuals with schizophrenia.

Biological and Neurological Correlates

Religious Delusions

Research has revealed that the religious delusions of people with schizophrenia also have neural substrates and can be tied to specific biological correlates. SPECT neuroimaging on individuals with schizophrenia who are actively experiencing religious delusions revealed increased uptake in the frontal and left temporal regions, as well as reduced occipital uptake (Puri et al., 2001). This may reflect the overactivation and dysfunction of the left temporal region, as well as the potential inhibition of visuosensory processing in the occipital regions.

Temporal Lobe Epilepsy

Similar profiles are evident in the religious experiences and psychotic symptoms of individuals with other brain conditions, such as temporal lobe epilepsy. There has long been a relationship between religious experiences and temporal lobe epilepsy across the ictal, post-ictal, and inter-ictal stages. In the ictal phase, religious or spiritual experiences frequently occur as components of psychic auras that involve depersonalization, derealization, ecstasy, and visual and auditory hallucinations, similar to schizophrenia. For some, these psychic auras are accompanied by "ecstatic seizures," or ictal sensations of intense pleasure, joy, and contentment that provide insight into the unity, harmony, and divinity of all reality (Saver & Rabin, 1997). Neuroimaging research has discovered that these ictal events of spiritual or mystical experiences may have a temporolimbic origin and become evoked by transient, electrical microseizures within deep structures of the temporal lobe (Hansen & Brodtkorb, 2003). The positive and affective nature of these experiences may be the result of electrical stimulation of the limbic system, which adds an affective dimension to perceptual data processed by the temporal neocortex. Interestingly, these experiences are frequently resolved with anterior temporal lobectomy, which raises strong implications for the biological mediation of religious experiences.

Moreover, the post-ictal and inter-ictal phases of temporal lobe epilepsy have been associated with high levels of religious behaviors or ideation. Similar to the psychotic process in schizophrenia, the state of post-ictal psychosis is accompanied by religious experiences in 27 percent of individuals with temporal lobe epilepsy (Arnold, 1997; Ogata & Miyakawa, 1998). This state of post-ictal psychosis is usually incurred by increased spike discharges in the subcortex and limbic system of the temporal lobe (Ogata & Miyakawa, 1998), but the content of the psychoses is often religious and accompanied by grandiosity and elevated mood. Due to inter-ictal spiking in the temporal lobe, a sort of sensory-limbic hyperconnection syndrome is created, leading to inter-ictal hyperreligiosity (Persinger & Makarec, 2002). It is thought that this hyperconnection leads to a heightened emotional responsiveness to stimuli, with religion being a frequent response or schema for ordering these stimuli due to its personal meaningfulness and explanatory power. This hyperreligiosity occurs at a level similar to schizophrenia (Saver & Rabin, 1997), which suggests the possibility that religious experience, interest, and expression have a common neurological underpinning that is expressed in the context of organic brain conditions such as epilepsy and schizophrenia.

This strong connection between epileptic events and religious intensity has led to recent conclusions that a substantial number of founders of major religions, prophets, and leading religious figures have been documented as having epilepsy. The auras of Paul and Dostoevsky may have been triggered by simple partial seizures, and the spiritual lives of leaders like Joan of Arc and Soren Kierkegaard may have been influenced by afflictions with epilepsy (Hansen & Brodtkorb, 2003). However, it is evident that one does not have to suffer from an organic brain condition to be religious. If the religious delusions and ideations of those with schizophrenia or temporal lobe epilepsy are rooted in temporolimbic hyperconnectionism, it is likely that there is a continuum of temporolimbic lability that may account for religious, mystical, or paranormal experiences across cultures and ages. This is supported by the high level of mystical and religious experiences, as well as the strong sense of a presence of a sentient being, that occurs among individuals who do not have epilepsy, but who score high on measures of complex partial epilepsy (Persinger & Makarec, 2002).

Schizotypy

Similar research has been conducted on individuals with schizotypal traits. Schizotypy exists on a continuum with schizophrenia, somewhere between normal and the full syndrome of schizophrenia. Similar to those with schizophrenia, these individuals tend to have strong religious proclivities and abnormal perceptual or cognitive experiences, including religious experiences (Maltby & Day, 2002). Interestingly, they also share decreased gray matter in the frontal and medial temporal lobes, although they do not have the changes in the medial and dorsolateral frontal regions that are associated with the full expression of schizophrenia (Kurachi, 2003).

If taken at face value, these findings suggest that the perceived differences between the religious experiences of nonpsychotic adults and the religious delusions and hallucinations of individuals with schizophrenia may be slim when examined from a neurological perspective. It may be more appropriate to say that all individuals exist on a continuum of temporal lobe sensitivity, where certain stimuli, such as grief, loss, and crisis, enhance the lability of the temporal lobe and thereby elevate the likelihood of religious experience. Hence, religion appears to be biologically linked to the continuum of schizophrenia-related symptoms.

THE EVOLUTION OF SCHIZOPHRENIA AND RELIGION

The Schizophrenia Paradox

One of the consequences of this evidence for the biological substrates of schizophrenia and religious experience is that they are likely to be highly shaped by evolutionary and genetic processes. Contemporary research has consistently documented that schizophrenia occurs with 1 percent incidence across time and place (Ban, 2004; Burns, 2004; Lewis & Lieberman, 2000). This incidence rate has come to represent a cross-cultural constant because it persists with equal levels across races, continents, and societies that have gross differences in climatic, physical, industrial, and cultural environments (Crow, 1995). This stable and resilient incidence rate is especially telling because it exceeds known mutation rates and persists despite the early mortality rates and 50 percent reduction in fecundity that are associated with schizophrenia (Brune, 2004; Burns, 2004). In fact, the persistence of schizophrenia despite its reproductive disadvantages has come to be called the *schizophrenia paradox*. It begs the question why a condition that confers personal torment and societal suffering, and that frequently leads to early death and low reproductive rates, prevails and persists with such consistency in the general population. This paradox suggests that environmental influences, such as prenatal insults and viral infections, cannot fully explain the ubiquity and emergence of this condition. The persistence of schizophrenia must therefore be related to genetics and the evolution of the human brain.

Genetic Studies

Consistent with a genetic explanation for schizophrenia, family studies on twins and adoptees have established that over 80 percent of the risk for developing schizophrenia is accounted for by genetic mechanisms (Wong & Van Tol, 2003). Family studies have consistently demonstrated highest risk (5–17%) in first-degree relatives with schizophrenia, which gradually diminishes in second-degree (2–6%) and third-degree (2%) relatives, although these rates are still higher than the general population (Kirov, Donovan, & Owen, 2005; Lewis & Lieberman, 2000; Wong & Van Tol, 2003). In fact, the risk for developing schizophrenia among children who have one parent with schizophrenia is nearly 15 times higher than the general population (Ban, 2004). In twin studies, monozygotic twins shared a concordance rate of 30–69 percent for schizophrenia, whereas dizygotic twins have a concordance rate of 10–26 percent (Ban, 2004; Kirov et al., 2005; Lewis & Lieberman, 2000; Wong & Van Tol, 2003). Similarly, adoption studies have consistently demonstrated greater risk for schizophrenia in biological parents than adoptive parents. These results confirm that there is a significant genetic and inherited quality to schizophrenia, where susceptibility is inherited and transmitted through genetic processes. In fact, strong research suggests that schizophrenia is a cross-cultural and genetic constant, predating the formation of the oldest genetically isolated racial enclaves and persisting through ancient Mesopotamia, Grecian and Roman history, and modern time (Burns, 2004; Jeste, del Carmen, Lohr, & Wyatt, 1985; Polimeni & Reiss, 2003). Considering this strong genetic inheritance, the persistence of schizophrenia despite formidable societal and reproductive resistance seems mostly likely linked to evolutionary processes.

The Evolutionary Advantage of Schizophrenia

From an evolutionary perspective, and perhaps from the mindset of contemporary medicine, natural selection should have eliminated the susceptibility genes of schizophrenia. Few can argue against the economic, personal, and societal costs incurred by schizophrenia. However, one of the reasons why it might not have been eliminated is because its disadvantages were offset by certain advantages for the individual, kin, or group. Schizophrenia may be an ancient phenomenon because it has an advantageous phenotypic quality, such as a distinct contribution that satiates one of the needs of society, thereby enabling it to persist.

Creativity

Throughout our present understanding of schizophrenia, there has been little disagreement that this neurological condition is associated with high levels of achievement. For many people with schizophrenia, the gifts of creativity, charisma, and leadership occur alongside personal torment and societal disruption. Studies of families in Iceland, which has a small, stable, and isolated gene pool, have consistently revealed exceptional creative potential and achievement in adopted children with at least one biological parent with schizophrenia (Brune, 2004; Horrobin, 1998), which was not demonstrated among adopted children of normal biological parents. Cases of schizophrenia in famous individuals like Henry VI of England, Felix Platter, Isaac Newton, and John Nash all provide evidence that genius may occasionally be the bedfellow of psychosis (Heinrichs, 2003; Jeste et al., 1985). This high level of achievement and creative capacity is similar to the strong levels of creativity and the high number of musicians, writers, and artists who score high on inventories of temporal lobe sensitivity (Persinger, 2001). This is not surprising considering that the major neurological correlate of creativity is the temporal lobe (Persinger, 2001), so that the shared creativity and accomplishment between schizophrenia and epilepsy may follow from shared temporal lobe abnormalities. If the price of achievement is madness, then the persistence of schizophrenia across time and culture may be partially rooted in the leadership, charisma, and creativity it brings.

Religious Attunement

The persistence of schizophrenia may also be related to a unique level of attunement to religious experiences. Individuals with schizophrenia may have a unique ability to tap into a possible spiritual realm and to experience the divine via hallucination, delusion, and anomalous perceptual experiences in a way that may have contributed to its endurance. The adopted children of biological parents with schizophrenia are not only more creative and achievement-oriented than those with normal parents, but they are also significantly more religious, with almost a quarter expressing strong religious sentiments (Horrobin, 1998). Similarly, individuals with schizophrenia not only find religion to be particularly meaningful and salient to their lives, but it represents a significant source of coping and often infuses the content of their hallucination and delusions. Therefore, the boundaries between the human and the divine may be significantly more blurred for those with schizophrenia, perhaps in a way that provided a historical advantage. In their own way, people with schizophrenia may function like mediums, or intermediaries, between the spiritual and the corporeal, the human and divine.

Shamanism

In traditional or tribal communities, shamans are believed to possess spiritual powers and to commune with the supernatural world. Interestingly, shamanism shares a similar epidemiology with schizophrenia, such as an adolescent onset and a similar incidence rate. It also frequently involves psychotic-like behaviors, such as abnormal perceptual experiences, profound emotional upheavals, bizarre mannerisms, and religious ideation (Kripper, 2002; Polimeni & Reiss, 2002). The symptoms of social isolation, bizarre mentation, spiritual hallucinations, and religious grandiosity that characterize schizophrenia may parallel the societal retreat, prophecy, divine communion, and spiritual unity of the shaman. Both share moments of dissociation between reality and unreality, and both share trance-like states in which profound visual and auditory phenomena are experienced.

Considering these strong similarities, it is highly likely that those with schizophrenia historically played a shamanistic role. Religion has been with humans as long as there have been humans (Albright & Ashbrook, 2001), so it has been necessary for certain members of society to construct new religious meaning systems or maintain preexisting ones that would lead to values, goals, and a sense of identity that fosters the survival of the group. In a sense, the role of the shaman, and perhaps the role of religious symptoms in schizophrenia, is to be responsive to the society's needs for religiousness and mediate a shared meaning system. In fulfilling this shamanistic role, it seems likely that the symptoms of psychosis would be highly advantageous, especially when spearheading religious rituals (Polimeni & Reiss, 2003). To the extent that shamans have abnormal perceptual experiences, bizarre mannerisms, and religious ideation, they may be able to commune with a perceived transcendent in a way that dispenses divine meaning for the experiences of a society. This is particularly true prior to the past few thousand years, when humanity largely existed within hunting and gathering societies that were shaped and influenced by some form of shamanism. In these societies, the religious symptoms of individuals with schizophrenia would be meaningful to understanding changes in the weather, animal behavior, and ways of successfully surviving within and between communities. This suggests that part of the reason why religious symptoms of individuals with schizophrenia may have survived is because they subserved this adaptive shamanistic role when human nature as we know it emerged. They were able to see something in a new way and construct religious or spiritual meaning out of it. In modern society, the religious delusions and hallucinations of schizophrenia may seem nonsensical, perhaps because we are less dependent on religion and more dependent on reason and intellect to provide a meaning system, but these experiences may have been especially meaningful to human societies at one time.

Granted, there are differences between shamans and individuals with schizophrenia (Stephen & Suryani, 2000), including documented differences in personality traits (Kripper, 2002) and the tendency for the former to have visual hallucinations rather than auditory hallucinations (Polimeni & Reiss, 2002). Some of these differences may be shaped by culture and language, but it does not negate the historical probability that individuals with schizophrenia subserved an important societal role of mediating the human and the divine. In other words, maybe schizophrenia persisted because it performed certain essential religious functions for society. Maybe it did not persist due to a distinct reproductive advantage, but rather because of group selection and behavioral specialization in a shamanistic role.

The Test of Culture

One test for this theory is to determine whether schizophrenia is particularly adaptive in contemporary contexts that have increased sensitivity to religious issues and experiences. For much of human history, the symptoms of schizophrenia were not considered the domain of medicine, but rather the realm of religion and the supernatural (Jeste et al., 1985). This is largely because the high value placed on the attunement of schizophrenia with the divine resulted in little distinction between the religious and the psychotic. However, over the past several decades, the prevalence of religious hallucinations and delusions has pivoted on a cultural axis, with higher frequencies in cultures in which religion exerts a more powerful influence. In Okinawa, where spiritual specialists called *yuta* actively provide spiritual intervention, hallucinations are highly valued as a marker of genuine spiritual intervention. In fact, many *yutas* have been diagnosed with schizophrenia and are treated in mental hospitals, but they are still actively sought for religious, spiritual, and other counseling by other patients in the hospital (Allen, Naka, & Ishizu, 2004). Similarly, many of the yogis in India exhibit beliefs and behaviors that are akin to psychosis and that would be considered delusions in Western culture (Castillo, 2003). These include positive symptoms such as grandiose beliefs and religious auditory and visual hallucinations, as well as negative psychotic symptoms, such as affective flattening, alogia, and avolition. Furthermore, religious delusions occur with significantly greater frequency in Seoul and Taipei when compared to Shanghai (Kim et al., 2001). Interestingly, the major religious orientations of Seoul and Taipei are shamanistic in nature, whereas religion has been predominantly oppressed in China. This suggests that there is little separation between schizophrenia and shamanistic roles in those cultures that place a high premium on religious experiences. It also suggests that the elements of psychosis in one culture may be holy in another.

In fact, when compared to modern Western cultures, the incidence of nonaffective psychoses with acute onset was 10 times higher in traditional cultures with strong religious sentiments (Castillo, 2003). Even more profound is the better course and outcome of functional psychoses in traditional cultures, possibly because these cultures place higher value on psychotic experiences and respond with greater sympathy and social support than might be offered in Western settings (Castillo, 2003).

Together, these findings suggest that, although the rate of schizophrenia is independent of culture and era, the content of schizophrenic delusions and hallucinations appears to be sensitive to sociocultural and political situations. There may be a gradual fading of religious delusions within cultures that have a reduced emphasis on religion, largely because there is a reduced evolutionary need for the shamanistic role of schizophrenia. Clinicians in Western societies most likely discourage the religious content of psychosis because it has been associated with poorer treatment outcomes, reduced adherence to treatment, and literal interpretations of commands in the Bible (i.e., "cutting out one's eye"; Siddle et al., 2002). However, this approach may discount the possibility that poorer outcomes and treatment adherence may reflect the loss of a meaningful role for those with schizophrenia. The loss of this role may represent the loss of identity and the elevation of fragmentation. In traditional, non-Western societies in which this role is preserved, schizophrenia and religious psychoses may have a better home.

IMPLICATIONS FOR RELIGION

The current picture that has emerged thus far is that schizophrenia and the religious content of psychosis are subserved by biological and neurological substrates. When these biological and genetic underpinnings are paired with the cross-cultural persistence of schizophrenia and religiously oriented psychosis, schizophrenia appears to have a distinct evolutionary advantage. Considering the strong parallels between shamanistic tendencies and psychotic behavior, this advantage may be rooted in the mediation of a spiritual realm (or rooted in the neural substrates of a religious meaning system that defines global meaning via religious hallucination, delusion, and anomalous perceptual experiences). In a sense, the continuum of psychoticism may be fundamental to religiousness, particularly when the contradictions and tragedies of life raise existential questions and crises of meaning (Joseph, Smith, & Diduca, 2002). It is the need for mediation between the human and divine during these occasions that may have fostered the biological emergence of the religious symptoms of psychosis. This understanding of the biological basis for schizophrenia and religious delusions, as well as the specialized role of schizophrenia for religion, raises some necessary questions and may lead to some unique insights, particularly for religion.

Implications from the Neurology of Schizophrenia and Religion

A Physicalist View of the Person

Among these implications is the notion that phenomena on the far end of the continuum of religious experiences, such as delusions and hallucinations, are biologically mediated. Not only is schizophrenia a neurodevelopmental and biological brain disorder, but all of its clinical phenomena, including religious delusions and hallucinations, are also mediated by neurological substrates and neurochemical changes. This argues for a monistic or physicalist view of the person, where religion represents an aspect of a unitary, corporeal self, rather than a separate entity within the person that is imposed from without in a Platonic dualism between spirit and body. Such a monistic view may be more respectful to those with schizophrenia because it does not differentiate between the neurological and the religious. It is this sense of differentiation, or a fragmented sense of self, that is central to the clinical phenomenon of schizophrenia, where the individual has a skewed sense of ego boundaries between the self and other, the real and the unreal. Any attempt to separate the biological from the religious may exacerbate this dissociated sense of self. In contrast, and similar to many therapeutic approaches to schizophrenia, a physicalist or monistic conception of the self integrates the symptoms and experiences of schizophrenia into a holistic view of the person.

At first glance, the contention for a physicalist view of the person may seem like it reduces all religious experience to biology and precludes the intervention of a higher power. Quite the contrary, it could foster humbleness at the foresight of a higher power to biologically construct humans in a way that enables them to experience the divine (Saver & Rabin, 1997). It also retains the possibility of supervenient properties, where the biological substrates of religious experience create religious phenomena that are not reducible to the sum of the individual, neurological parts (Murphy, 1999).

Perhaps it is helpful to distinguish between mediation and generation. To suggest that religious delusions and experiences have neural substrates in temporolimbic abnormalities or deficiencies in the dopaminergic and glutamatergic systems says nothing of the origin or source of these abnormalities. Much about the development and action of these neurological mechanisms remains a hypothesis, which renders it more appropriate to say that the religious experiences and psychotic content of individuals with schizophrenia are *mediated* rather than *caused* by empirical and biological substrates. This leaves significant room for emphasizing the operation of supervenient processes, the possibility of emergent properties greater than the starting parameters, and the remarkable intervention of a higher power in creating the neurological capacity for experiencing the divine. In other words, the neurological substrates of religious experience, psychotic or otherwise, retains room for special grace while reducing the gap between the biological and the miraculous.

A Monistic View of Religion?

Regardless of how individuals retain the mystery of faith, the physicalist nature of schizophrenia and religious psychoses forces a blurring of the experiential boundaries between the religious experiences of nonpsychotic and psychotic individuals. It may be tempting to argue that the bizarre religious experiences associated with schizophrenia are clearly reducible to biology because of their aberrancy, whereas the religious experiences of normal adults are somehow more genuine or external to the corporeal self. However, the frontotemporal quality of religious experiences suggests that these are inaccurate distinctions. Religion itself may be monistic, similar to the monistic nature of the person. To the extent that the religious experiences of individuals with schizophrenia, schizotypal traits, and temporal lobe epilepsy are subserved by common neurological abnormalities that are shared with normal church attendees, it may be more appropriate to adopt an integrated view of religion and religious experiences. Many religions share common themes and stories, and the biological mediation of religious experience, as evidenced in the religious delusions and hallucinations of those with schizophrenia, may unify these religions under a common neurological umbrella. To this end, different religions may be similar in theme as well as broad biological origin.

This invariably raises questions about what accounts for differences between religions. One possibility is that the differences reflect the operation of disparate sociocultural factors on shared neural substrates, similar to the way cultural and environmental factors shape the specific religious content of schizophrenic delusions and hallucinations. Nevertheless, it may not be appropriate to separate religious experiences into distinct categories, such as those experiences that are "genuine" versus those that are "unreal." Rather, the common neurology behind all religions suggests a continuum of religious experiences, with schizophrenia or temporal lobe epilepsy at a far end and the religious experiences of nonafflicted individuals at the other.

Can Religion Be Biologically Altered?

The neurological mediation of religious psychosis also raises questions about the appropriateness of biological intervention for religious experience. Knowing that many of the intense religious experiences associated with temporal lobe epilepsy can be mitigated with anterior temporal lobectomy, it seems plausible that the intensity of religious delusion and hallucination can be similarly attenuated through surgical intervention, providing that anatomical locations or pathways can be identified with microscopic precision. In converse fashion, it seems equally tenable that religious experiences can be biologically stimulated. Research shows that even those without identifiable features of psychopathology can experience a sensed presence of something larger by applying complex magnetic fields over the right hemisphere and bilaterally stimulating the temporal lobes (Persinger, 2001). Moreover, the ingestion of hallucinogenic agents, including LSD and mescaline, can induce visual illusions and hallucinations with religious themes in a way that closely parallels religious or mystical experiences. Might this suggest that biological intervention can be used for those psychotic and nonpsychotic individuals who feel spiritually dry and long for the voice of the divine? Alternatively, should biological resection be implemented in cases in which individuals are disturbed by religious content, such as possession, feelings of conviction, or fearful spiritual encounters? These are politically and emotionally laden questions that are unearthed by the biological underpinnings of religion and may need to be answered in the near future.

Schizophrenia and Religious Institutions

One relatively certain implication is that religious institutions may need to more readily embrace people with schizophrenia. Despite the finding that over 80 percent of individuals with mental illness use religious coping, only 15 percent feel comfortable enough to meet with a religious leader (Tepper, Rogers, Coleman, & Malony, 2001). Although the exact reasons for this are unknown, it may be partially related to the uncertainty of religious institutions about how to incorporate bizarre behaviors and religious delusions into their theological schema. Religious leaders and laypersons seldom receive training in mental illness, and when they encounter schizophrenia on their doorstep, they may be paralyzed about how to reconcile religious delusions and hallucinations with their own faith.

However, the common and shared biological ancestry of religion warrants greater inclusion of those with schizophrenia. This is particularly true in light of the historical tendencies of individuals with schizophrenia to serve shamanistic roles and to tap into the divine. Invariably, there are religious truths embedded in the context of religious delusions and hallucinations, but this truth can only be revealed by coming alongside and listening to those with schizophrenia. In doing so, religion may learn something about itself from schizophrenia. To the extent that schizophrenia is either ignored or bypassed by religious communities, the door to this truth is closed, and the shared religious ancestry is dismissed.

Implications from the Evolution of Schizophrenia and Religion

By virtue of their religious delusions and hallucinations, individuals with schizophrenia may also have a substantial and necessary biological and societal role. They may have a distinct social function, if only allowed to perform it. Not only are they more likely to demonstrate creative capacity and extraordinary achievements, but they are also prone to hyperreligosity, leadership, and to serving intermediary roles between the spiritual and earthly. Rather than seeing this condition as an accident or the result of mutation, maybe it would be helpful to occasionally see it as an adaptation sustained for a specific cultural need. Put differently, maybe the aberration of schizophrenia was not always a curse, but the result of the capability to construct divine meaning mediated through evolutionary processes.

This is not an attempt to glamorize schizophrenia; in fact, many individuals can testify to the personal and public harm caused by the symptoms of schizophrenia. It is to say, however, that one of the possible benefits or contributions of madness is its closeness to religion, its creation of intermediaries to a possible spiritual realm, and its provision of a religious system of meaning. It might be fearful to embrace the proximity between religion and psychosis, almost as if it risks losing the potency of religion. But maybe there is a potentially valuable role for those who blur madness and religion in their lives.

This raises questions about what would happen if we treated those with schizophrenia as cultural or religious sages. If lessons are learned from traditional, non-Western cultures, then the symptoms of psychosis would more quickly resolve and the outcome of treatment would be more favorable. In a sense, this would appropriate afflicted individuals with the evolutionary role that has been selected for them for centuries. With the waning of religious sentiment in many Western cultures, however, those with schizophrenia may be experiencing a loss of identity and greater fragmentation of the self. It is uncertain whether it is universally appropriate to recapture the shamanistic role of schizophrenia. The process of doing so might integrate the fragmented selves of those with schizophrenia and return to them an important religious role. Alternatively, the growth of Western culture and its changes in religious trends may be foretelling the evolutionary deselection of religious delusions and psychosis. These are questions that have yet to be answered, but in the meantime, society may still have much it can learn about religion from schizophrenia.

CONCLUSION

It appears that schizophrenia and religion are both deeply mediated by neurological substrates, and these substrates may have contributed to an evolutionary advantage for schizophrenia. This advantage may be rooted in the service of a distinct intermediary role for relating to the divine via religious delusion and hallucination. This is not to suggest that all the clinical phenomena of schizophrenia are positive qualities or that individuals with schizophrenia should uniformly embrace their religious delusions or hallucinations. In fact, it may be that the genes for schizophrenia do not have any distinct advantage in themselves but persist by virtue of their fortuitous association with other adaptive genes (Burns, 2004). However, there may be potential value in certain features of schizophrenia, including the larger, shamanistic role that they once may have played.

In particular, those who are symptomatic and asymptomatic for schizophrenia both have similar needs that are served by religion. Central to these is the need to develop a global meaning system that constructs new meanings in a way that fosters group survival. The shamanistic ability of the individual with schizophrenia to see human interaction in a new way and to imagine global values that increase interpersonal care and reduce greed and violence means that there was a perpetual role for these individuals in human culture. The fact that the religious symptoms of schizophrenia have survived so long is surprising considering that many segments of society can easily react and rebel against this shamanistic role of schizophrenia, primarily because it requires that those in power change or give up some of what they have. It would be tempting for those in power to subdue the shaman and suppress the new way of seeing the world proposed by the shaman. However, if the cross-cultural constant holds, then it is reasonable to conclude that approximately one person per hundred had an imagination and vision for the good of society that was strong enough to let it survive. Some might ask where the shamans or visionaries are in Western society today. Perhaps the artifacts of shamanism still reside with those afflicted with schizophrenia.

ACKNOWLEDGEMENTS

The authors wish to thank Erica Swenson for her help in the preparation of this chapter and the Catlin Foundation whose grant supported her research assistantship.

REFERENCES

Albright, C. R., & Ashbrook, J. B. (2001). *Where God lives in the human brain.* Naperville, IL: Sourcebooks.

Allen, M., Naka, K., & Ishizu, H. (2004). Attacked by gods or by mental illness? Hybridizing mental and spiritual health in Okinawa. *Mental Health, Religion, and Culture, 7,* 83–107.

American Psychiatric Association. (1994). *Diagnostic and statistical manual of mental disorders* (4th ed.). Washington, DC: American Psychiatric Association.

Antonova, E., Sharma, T., Morris, R., & Kumari, V. (2004). The relationship between brain structure and neurocognition in schizophrenia: A selective review. *Schizophrenia Research, 70,* 117–145.

Appelbaum, P. S., Robbins, P. C., & Roth, L. H. (1999). Dimensional approach to delusions: Comparison across types and diagnoses. *American Journal of Psychiatry, 156,* 1938–1943.

Arnold, S. E. (1997). The medial temporal lobe in schizophrenia. *Journal of Neuropsychiatry and Clinical Neurosciences, 9,* 460–470.

Ban, T. A. (2004). Neuropsychopharmacology and the genetics of schizophrenia: A history of the diagnosis of schizophrenia. *Progress in Neuro-Psychopharmacology and Biological Psychiatry, 28,* 753–762.

Baumeister, R. F. (1991). *Meanings of life.* New York: Guilford Press.

Brune, M. (2004). Schizophrenia—An evolutionary enigma? *Neuroscience and Biobehavioral Reviews, 28,* 41–53.

Burns, J. K. (2004). An evolutionary theory of schizophrenia: Cortical connectivity, metarepresentation, and the social brain. *Behavioral and Brain Sciences, 27*(6), 831–855.

Camargo, E. E. (2001). Brain SPECT in neurology and psychiatry. *Journal of Nuclear Medicine, 42*(4), 611–623.

Carlsson, A., Waters, N., Waters, S., & Carlsson, M. L. (2000). Network interactions in schizophrenia—therapeutic implications. *Brain Research Reviews, 31,* 342–349.

Castillo, R. J. (2003). Trance, functional psychosis, and culture. *Psychiatry, 66,* 9–21.

Clinton, S. M., & Meador-Woodruff, J. H. (2004). Thalamic dysfunction in schizophrenia: Neurochemical, neuropathological, and in vivo imaging abnormalities. *Schizophrenia Research, 69,* 237–253.

Crow, T. J. (1995). A theory of the evolutionary origins of psychosis. *European Neuropsychopharmacology Supplement,* 59–63.

Getz, G. E., Fleck, D. E., & Strakowski, S. M. (2001). Frequency and severity of religious delusions in Christian patients with psychosis. *Psychiatry Research, 103,* 87–91.

Halliday, G. M. (2001). A review of the neuropathology of schizophrenia. *Clinical & Experimental Pharmacology and Physiology, 28,* 64–65.

Hansen, B. A., & Brodtkorb, E. (2003). Partial epilepsy with "ecstatic" seizures. *Epilepsy and Behavior, 4,* 667–673.

Heckers, S., Rauch, S. L., Goff, D., Savage, C. R., Schacter, D. L., Fischman, A. J., et al. (1998). Impaired recruitment of the hippocampus during conscious recollection in schizophrenia. *Neuroscience, 1*(4), 318–323.

Heinrichs, R. W. (2003). Historical origins of schizophrenia: Two early madmen and their illness. *Journal of the History of the Behavioral Sciences, 39*(4), 349–363.

Horrobin, D. F. (1998). Schizophrenia: The illness that made us human. *Medical Hypotheses, 50*, 269–288.

Jeste, D. V., del Carmen, R., Lohr, J. B., & Wyatt, R. J. (1985). Did schizophrenia exist before the eighteenth century? *Comprehensive Psychiatry, 26*, 493–503.

Joseph, S., Smith, D., & Diduca, D. (2002). Religious orientation and its association with personality, schizotypal traits, and manic-depressive experiences. *Mental Health, Religion, and Culture, 5*, 73–81.

Kasai, K., Iwanami, A., Yamasue, H., Kuroki, N., Nakagome, K., & Fukuda, M. (2002). Neuroanatomy and neurophysiology in schizophrenia. *Neuroscience Research, 43*, 93–110.

Kemp, D. (2000). A Platonic delusion: The identification of psychosis and mysticism. *Mental Health, Religion, and Culture, 3*, 157–172.

Kim, K., Hwu, H., Zhang, L. D., Lu, M. K., Park, K. K., Hwang, T. J., et al. (2001). Schizophrenic delusions in Seoul, Shanghai, and Taipei: A transcultural study. *Journal of Korean Medical Sciences, 16*, 88–94.

Kirov, G., Donovan, M. C., & Owen, M. J. (2005). Finding schizophrenia genes. *Journal of Clinical Investigation, 115*, 1440–1448.

Kirov, G., Kemp, R., Kirov, K., & David, A. A. (1998). Religious faith after psychotic illness. *Psychopathology, 31*, 234–245.

Kripper, S. C. (2002). Conflicting perspectives on shamans and shamanism: Points and counterpoints. *American Psychologist*, 963–977.

Kroll, J., & Sheehan, W. (1989). Religious beliefs and practices among 52 psychiatric inpatients. *American Journal of Psychiatry, 146*, 67–72.

Kurachi, M. (2003). Pathogenesis of schizophrenia: Part I. Symptomatology, cognitive characteristics, and brain morphology. *Psychiatry and Clinical Neurosciences, 57*, 3–8.

Levin, S., Yurgelun-Todd, D., & Craft, S. (1989). Contributions of clinical neuro-psychology to the study of schizophrenia. *Journal of Abnormal Psychology, 98*(4), 341–356.

Lewis, D. A., & Lieberman, J. A. (2000). Catching up on schizophrenia: Natural history and neurobiology. *Neuron, 28*, 325–334.

Maltby, J., & Day, L. (2002). Religious experience, religious orientation, and schizotypy. *Mental Health, Religion, and Culture, 5*, 163–174.

Mohr, S., & Huguelet, P. (2004). The relationship between schizophrenia and religion and its implications for care. *Swiss Medical Weekly, 134*, 369–376.

Murphy, N. (1999). Supervenience and the downward efficacy of the mental: A non-reductive physicalist account of human action. In R. J. Russell, N. Murphy, T. O. Meyering, & M. A. Arbib (Eds.), *Neuroscience and the person: Scientific perspectives on divine action* (pp. 147–164). Berkeley, CA: Center for Theology and the Natural Sciences.

Ogata, A., & Miyakawa, T. (1998). Religious experiences in epileptic patients with a focus on ictus-related episodes. *Psychiatry and Clinical Neurosciences, 52*, 321–325.

Paloutzian, R. F. (2005). Religious conversion and spiritual transformation: A meaning-system analysis. In R. F. Paloutzian & C. L. Park (Eds.), *Handbook of the psychology of religion and spirituality* (pp. 341–347). New York: Guilford Press.

Paloutzian, R. F., & Swenson, E. L. (in press). Spiritual experiences, neurology, and the making of meaning. In C. Jäger (Ed.), *Brain-religion-experience: Multidiscipline encounters.* New York: Springer.

Park, C. L. (2005a). Religion and meaning. In R. F. Paloutzian & C. L. Park (Eds.), *Handbook of the psychology of religion and spirituality* (pp. 295–314). New York: Guilford Press.

Park, C. L. (2005b). Religion as a meaning making framework in coping with life stress. *Journal of Social Issues, 61*(4), 707–730.

Park, C. L., & Folkman, S. (1997). Meaning in the context of stress and coping. *Review of General Psychology, 1*, 115–144.

Persinger, M. A. (2001). The neuropsychiatry of paranormal experiences. *Journal of Neuropsychiatry and Clinical Neurosciences, 13*, 515–524.

Persinger, M. A., & Makarec, K. (2002). Temporal lobe epileptic signs and correlative behaviors displayed by normal populations. *Journal of General Psychology, 114*, 179–195.

Pierre, J. M. (2001). Faith or delusion? At the crossroads of religion and psychosis. *Journal of Psychiatric Practice, 7*, 163–172.

Polimeni, J., & Reiss, J. P. (2002). How shamanism and group selection may reveal the origins of schizophrenia. *Medical Hypotheses, 58*, 244–248.

Polimeni, J., & Reiss, J. P. (2003). Evolutionary perspectives on schizophrenia. *Canadian Journal of Psychiatry, 48*, 34–39.

Puri, B. K., Lekh, S. K., Nijran, K. S., Bagary, M. S., & Richardson, A. J. (2001). SPECT neuroimaging in schizophrenia with religious delusions. *International Journal of Psychophysiology, 40*, 143–148.

Rogers, S. A., Poey, E. L., Reger, G. M., Tepper, L., & Coleman, E. M. (2002). Religious coping among those with mental illness. *International Journal for the Psychology of Religion, 12*, 161–175.

Saver, J. L., & Rabin, J. (1997). The neural substrates of religious experience. *Journal of Neuropsychiatry and Clinical Neurosciences, 9*, 498–510.

Shenton, M. E., Dickey, C. C., Frumin, M., & McCarley, R. W. (2001). A review of MRI findings in schizophrenia. *Schizophrenia Research, 49*, 1–52.

Siddle, R., Haddock, G., Tarrier, N., & Faragher, E. B. (2002). Religious delusions in patients admitted to hospital with schizophrenia. *Social Psychiatry and Psychiatric Epidemiology, 37*, 130–138.

Silberman, I. (2005). Religion as a meaning-system: Implications for the new millennium. *Journal of Social Issues, 61*(4), 641–664.

Stephane, M., Barton, S., & Boutros, N. N. (2001). Auditory verbal hallucinations and dysfunction of the neural substrates of speech. *Schizophrenia Research, 50*, 61–78.

Stephen, M., & Suryani, L. K. (2000). Shamanism, psychosis, and autonomous imagination. *Culture, Medicine, and Psychiatry, 24*, 5–40.

Stompe, T., Friedman, A., Ortwein, G., Strobl, R., Chaudhry, H. R., Najam, N., et al. (1999). Comparisons of delusions among schizophrenics in Austria and in Pakistan. *Psychopathology, 32*, 225–234.

Tateyama, M., Asai, M., Kamisada, M., Hashimoto, M., Bartels, M., & Heimann, H. (1993). Comparison of schizophrenic delusions between Japan and Germany. *Psychopathology, 26*, 151–158.

Tepper, L., Rogers, S. A., Coleman, E. M., & Malony, H. N. (2001). The prevalence of religious coping among persons with persistent mental illnesss. *Psychiatric Services, 52*, 660–665.

Wahass, S., & Kent, G. (1997). Coping with auditory hallucinations: A cross-cultural comparison between Western (British) and non-Western (Saudi Arabian) patients. *Journal of Nervous and Mental Disease, 185*, 664–668.

Wong, A.H.C., & Van Tol, H.H.M. (2003). Schizophrenia: From phenomenology to neurobiology. *Neuroscience and Biobehavioral Reviews, 27*, 269–306.

CHAPTER 8

BETWEEN YANG AND YIN AND HEAVEN AND HELL: UNTANGLING THE COMPLEX RELATIONSHIP BETWEEN RELIGION AND INTOLERANCE

Ian Hansen and Ara Norenzayan

Religious faith deserves a chapter to itself in the annals of war technology, on an even footing with the longbow, the warhorse, the tank, and the hydrogen bomb. (Richard Dawkins, 1989, pp. 330–331)

The baseness so commonly charged to religion's account are thus, almost all of them, not chargeable to religion proper, but rather to religion's wicked practical partner, the spirit of corporate dominion. And the bigotries are most of them in their turn chargeable to religion's wicked intellectual partner, the spirit of dogmatic dominion. (William James, 1982/1902, p. 337)

Religion's relationship to intolerance, conflict, and mass violence is well known but controversial and poorly understood. Although religion has waxed and waned in perceived importance as a driver of conflict in human history, the rising share of worldwide violence attributed to extremists of one religion or another appears symptomatic of a worldwide resurgence in religion-related conflict and religiously motivated intolerance and violence (Atran, 2002, 2003). This rise has brought renewed interest to the role of religion and culture in motivating intolerance and violence (Appleby, 2000; Juergensmeyer, 2003; Kimball, 2002; Nelson-Pallmeyer, 2003). Because religion is often named a human universal in a species with tremendous cultural variation, its association with intolerance and support for violence, and potential explanations for these relationships, are of utmost importance.

In this chapter, we explore different components of the construct "religion," especially for predicting socially relevant psychological phenomena like prejudice, intolerance, scapegoating, and support for religious violence. Anthropologists, psychologists, philosophers, theologians, and even religious figures have often proposed distinctions between two different kinds of religion or religiosity, morally elevating one kind of religiosity at the expense of the other. This dual understanding of religion is remarkably recurrent, and the joints at which religion is carved often appear to be similar across perspectives, temperaments, and life callings. Specifically, those who divide religiosity generally divide it between subjectively centered natural-organic religiosity (e.g., inward revelation, personal religious experience), and socially transmitted cultural religiosity (e.g., learned doctrines, practices, and social identities; what one dogmatically believes to be true and false). We dispute the notion that subjective-natural and objective-cultural religiosity are inversely related or even orthogonal, instead proposing that they are best understood as bound together, sometimes quite tightly bound together. With regard to predicting religious intolerance and support for religious violence, we argue against carving religion into empirically inverse or unrelated elements, arguing specifically against the utility of the intrinsic/extrinsic religiosity dichotomy commonly employed in the religion and prejudice literature and in the psychology of religion generally (Allport & Ross, 1967). We find that the aspect of religion that involves devotion to the supernatural or to a specific supernaturally grounded faith and practice (devotional religiosity) indeed goes along with the aspect that involves adopting one religious community's epistemic and moral vision as true, and treating all deviations from that moral vision as false, dangerous, alien, or degenerate (coalitional religiosity).

As empirically related as these aspects of religion are, our research has found that they have opposite relationships to religious intolerance: coalitional religiosity independently predicts intolerance and scapegoating, and devotional religiosity independently predicts tolerance and rejection of scapegoating. With an eye to developments in the cognitive sciences, evolutionary psychology, and cultural psychology, we explore why these distinct aspects of religiosity might be so tightly bound together and yet be associated with opposite social attitudes toward outgroups.

GROUNDING RELIGION IN AN EVOLUTIONARY FRAMEWORK

An evolutionary approach to religion attempts to explain most religious phenomena as arising from adaptive group selection (Wilson, 2002), adaptive individual selection (e.g., Landau, Greenberg, & Solomon, 2004; Sosis & Alcorta, 2003), or some invocation of individual selection that at best sees religion as an exaptation, spandrel, or by-product of other adaptive psychological tendencies (Atran & Norenzayan, 2004; Boyer, 2003; Guthrie, 1993).

Whether invoking notions of group selection or individual selection, adaptation, exaptation, or spandrel, however, scientific researchers of religion increasingly consider religion "natural" or organic, in the sense that religion is rooted in ordinary human cognition and transmitted via social interactions among individuals (see Atran, 2002; Barrett, 2000; Boyer, 2001; Lawson & McCauley, 1990; Pyysiäinen & Anttonen, 2002). This emphasis on the natural or organic aspect of religion as being paramount is a departure from the previously reigning paradigm in the social sciences that treated religions and cultures as primarily superorganic—that is, brought about, maintained, and developed through processes that are irreducible to individual mind/brain mechanisms. The most radical examples of such a seemingly superorganic process is Durkheim's (1915/1965) view of religion as an organizer of social life that supersedes individual psychology and Dawkins's (1989) famously hypothesized "meme"—a faithfully self-replicating unit of information, analogous to yet fully independent from the gene. Indeed, religious and cultural changes (perhaps including the apparent genesis of culture and religion itself) appear to have some degree of independence from genetic changes, yet the afore-mentioned research into the natural origins of religion is accumulating evidence that religious thought and behavior are shaped by psychological inclinations rooted in natural selection.

Generally, those of us who take naturalized approaches to religion do not dispute, and in fact take great interest in, the processes of cultural transmission that shape religious thought and behavior. However, a natural science of religion ought to take as its starting point the psychological building blocks of religion—those elements, possibly rooted in human evolution, that tend to reoccur across time and place and may canalize the cultural transmission of religion into predictably convergent yet culturally distinct pathways. Anthropologically speaking, there is a near universality of (1) belief in supernatural agents who (2) relieve existential anxieties such as death and deception but (3) demand passionate and self-sacrificing social commitments, which are (4) validated through emotional ritual (Atran & Norenzayan, 2004). There are salient similarities to be found between even the most radically divergent cultures and religions (Norenzayan & Heine, 2005). There are even traces of ritual, cooperative, and self-sacrificing behavior in the animal kingdom (Burkert, 1996). All this suggests that religion, for all its variation, may contain a common framework ultimately based in the slow processes of evolution by natural selection. If we are to go beyond proximal explanations of the relationship of religion to prejudice, intolerance, and war, an evolutionary paradigm can be immensely helpful.

THE MULTIPLICITY OF THE CONSTRUCT "RELIGION"

Before seeking to explain religion's relationship to intolerance, it helps to adopt an understanding of religion that is neither too monolithic to be credible nor too pluralistic to be coherent. Because the phenomena of religion are so many and varied—or at least because "religion" as a word can be used to refer to so many different kinds of thought and behavior—it makes sense to try to organize religious phenomena according to a minimal set of psychologically plausible tendencies. For centuries, those who have attempted to explain religion (and even those who have propagated certain religions) have often distinguished two aspects of religion, treating them not only as distinct but also as opposites. For predicting religious intolerance, a dual understanding may reflect a relatively reliable and practical differentiation of one broad group of religious phenomena from another.

Dual understandings of religion generally consider a sense of the omnipresence of the divine (whether sensed directly and spontaneously or with the aid of prayer, meditation, or drug ingestion) more subjective/natural than it is socially transmitted/cultural. It would require a separate chapter to review the intellectual history of attributing the experience of divinity to something inward, personal, and subjective, in contrast to the absorbing of collective religious identity and religious creed and dogma as outward, cultural, and objective. Some illustrative examples are: James's (1982/1902) distinction between the "babbling brook" from which all religions originate (p. 337) and the "dull habit" of "second hand" religion "communicated . . . by tradition" (p. 6) as well as that between "religion proper" and corporate and dogmatic dominion (p. 337); Freud's (1930/1961) distinction between the "oceanic feeling" as an unconscious memory of the mother's womb and "religion" as acceptance of religious authority and morality as a projection of the father; Weber's (1947, 1978) distinction between religious charisma in its basic and "routinized" forms; Adorno's distinction between "personally experienced belief" and "neutralized religion" (Adorno, Frenkel-Brunswick, Levinson, & Sanford, 1950); Rappaport's (1979) distinction between the "numinous"—the experience of pure being—and the "sacred" or doctrinal; and, more recently, Sperber's (1996) cognitive distinction between "intuitive" beliefs—"the product of spontaneous and unconscious perceptual and inferential process" (p. 89), and "reflective" beliefs "believed in virtue of other second-order beliefs about them." It is not only modern twentieth- and twenty-first-century philosophers and social scientists who have made this distinction. Even the Christian Apostle Paul elevated "the Spirit" of the new Christian convent over "the letter" (2 Corinthians 3:6), a distinction he equated with that between giving life and killing. The text that inspired the Daoist religious and philosophical movements, the Dao De Jing, parallels this distinction between the revelatory and the culturally transmitted by warning against the decline from intuitive knowledge of the Way to an attachment to the trappings of ritual:

> When Tao is lost, there is goodness. When goodness is lost, there is kindness. When kindness is lost, there is justice. When justice is lost, there is ritual. Now ritual is the husk of faith and loyalty, the beginning of confusion. (Feng & English trans., 1972)

In all of these dual understandings, the subjective/natural is named and discussed in a more positive light than the cultural/socially transmitted and they are sometimes treated as mutually exclusive orientations. Assigning opposite moral valence to subjective-natural and objective-cultural religion makes them seem more like dichotomies than distinctions, bitter rivals that cannot easily cooperate toward a common end any more than good and evil should cooperate to a common end. With a more dialectical perspective, however, one could view these dichotomies not as rivals but as complementary elements that harmonize with each other as the dark and light droplets of the Daoist yin-yang symbol are thought to complement and harmonize with each other. With a dialectical understanding of religion, we may see subjective-natural and objective-cultural religion not as incompatible competitors, but as complementarily skilled partners, each containing an element of the other, each reinforcing each other's existence. There may still be a place for a heaven-hell understanding of devotional and coalitional religiosity, however, where one droplet deserves moral praise and the other moral blame, and harmonious coexistence between the droplets, even if empirically demonstrable, reflects a mere interlude before the inevitable divorce.

Interestingly, the model that best reflects this nuanced understanding of religion may have been that of William James, quoted at beginning of this chapter. James spoke in excoriating terms of "corporate dominion" and "dogmatic dominion" and yet admitted that each may be a "practical . . . and . . . intellectual partner" of religion respectively. James generally admired "religion proper" and was somewhat defensive about its pollution by its "wicked" partners. Even if corporate and dogmatic dominion rarely, if ever, divorced themselves from "religion proper," James might have had good moral reasons to wish for such a divorce. Specifically, if corporate and dogmatic dominion predicted prejudice, intolerance, and war, while "religion proper" predicted openness, tolerance, and peace, then wishing for a divorce was quite reasonable for someone who morally preferred openness to prejudice, tolerance to intolerance, and peace to war. Was James right to perceive such different moral natures among such close partners? In the following sections, we illustrate how our studies of religion and religious intolerance offer support to James's paradoxical assessment.

HOW TO ISOLATE "RELIGION PROPER" FROM ITS "WICKED" PARTNERS

One way to see how religious devotion relates to tolerance independent of anything like corporate and dogmatic dominion is to isolate the different constructs with different measures and see whether the different measures make different predictions. The measures we are most concerned with are those tapping religious devotion, rooted in supernatural belief, and coalitional religiosity, rooted in the costly commitment to a community of believers—a community that is morally and epistemically elevated above other communities. Religious devotion centers on the awareness of and attention to God or the "divine" broadly conceived. Typical religious devotion scale items would be "My religion involves all my life" or "In my life I feel the presence of God" (both from Hoge's [1972] Intrinsic Religious Motivation Scale).

Coalitional religiosity, on the other hand, should be approximated by validated scales measuring what social psychologists consider coalitional boundary-setting social tendencies, such as authoritarianism, fundamentalism, dogmatism, and related constructs (e.g., Kirkpatrick, 1999), These constructs all unquestioningly exalt one way of living and understanding as morally and epistemically superior to others, thus conveying unswerving loyal commitment to a specific identity and ideology. Typical coalitional items would be "The things I believe in are so completely true, I could never doubt them" (from Altemeyer's [1996] Dogmatism Scale) or "When our government leaders condemn the dangerous elements in our society, it is the duty of every patriotic citizen to help stomp out the rot that is poisoning our country from within" (from Altemeyer's [1999] Authoritarianism Scale) or "There is a complete, unfailing guide to Divine happiness and salvation, which must be totally followed" (from Altemeyer & Hunsberger's [1992] religious Fundamentalism Scale). We call these items "coalitional religiosity" not because they always explicitly convey a concern with membership in a coalition but because they reflect an absolute and exclusive attachment to one particular epistemic and moral understanding. It is theoretically possible to be rigidly committed to one's own personal and privately developed understanding, but we assume such rigid stances generally derive from half-understood dogmas and moral prescriptions of one's group or its leadership. That is to say, it is generally from groups that we derive our rigid ideological attachments.

A statistical procedure called multiple regression makes it possible to see how coalitional and devotional variables independently predict intolerance. When religious devotion variables and coalitional variables are analyzed in a multiple regression for their relationship to religious tolerance, the regression procedure essentially freezes the empirical "partners" of religious devotion and looks at the independent part of religious devotion that still varies from less devoted to more devoted even as all of its partners are held in place (equal levels of authoritarianism, fundamentalism, etc. across varying levels of religious devotion). This makes it possible to investigate the independent relationship between religious devotion and intolerance while holding coalitional variables constant. A few studies in the literature have found that if authoritarianism or fundamentalism is held constant, then a religious devotion measure such as Christian orthodoxy[1] can have a *negative* relationship to prejudice, even a religiously sanctioned prejudice such as anti-gay prejudice (Kirkpatrick, 1993; Laythe, Finkel, & Kirkpatrick, 2001; Rowatt & Franklin, 2004). This is despite the fact that the Christian orthodoxy scale is positively correlated with every item on Altemeyer's authoritarianism scale (Altemeyer, 1988), which we consider a coalitional variable and is a robust predictor of many different kinds of prejudice (Altemeyer, 1981, 1988, 1996). Our research also shows tolerant potential in religious devotion even when the dependent variable is religious intolerance instead of race prejudice or anti-gay prejudice. Whether measured by Hoge's (1972) intrinsic religiosity scale (a measure of devotional religiosity) or by a related scale (devotion to the divine) adapted from Fiorito & Ryan (1998) or by self-reported prayer frequency, religious devotion is often negatively related to religious intolerance when measures of coalitional attitude are controlled for—even if devotion is positively related to intolerance when coalitional attitude is not controlled for.

In statistics, when a certain relationship emerges between variables only when controlling for other variables, the variable with the hidden independent relationship is called a suppressor variable (Cohen & Cohen, 1975; Conger, 1974). Suppressor variables are difficult phenomena to understand when described abstractly, but in one of our studies we luckily had data that allowed us to illustrate it visually and intuitively. A procedure called "median split" was used on a sample of 194 Canadian students who were divided into two groups of 97 according to their scores on religious devotion (the average of two devotion scales)—the higher scorers comprised one group (devoted), and the lower scorers comprised the other group (not devoted). This sample was taken from Study 2 in Hansen and Norenzayan (2005). As shown in Figure 8.1, authoritarianism, dogmatism, fundamentalism, and exclusivity covaried with devotion, so the more devoted group was also more authoritarian, dogmatic, fundamentalist, and exclusivist. As for intolerance (see Figure 8.2), the more devoted group was more intolerant than the nondevoted group on one measure (civil intolerance, or willingness to violate the civil and political rights of religious others), more tolerant on another (religious/moral violence—specifically support for "killing the wicked"), but not different on the other measures. This pattern of religious devotion predicting some kinds of tolerance and other kinds of intolerance but being generally orthogonal to tolerance is consistent with the many contradictory and null

Figure 8.1   Means on Religiosity Variables for a Canadian Sample (Simple Median Split on Religious Devotion)

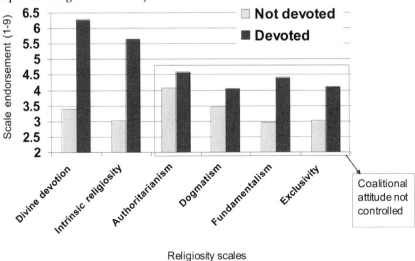

Religiosity scales

Figure 8.2   Means on Intolerance Variables for a Canadian Sample (Simple Median Split on Religious Devotion)

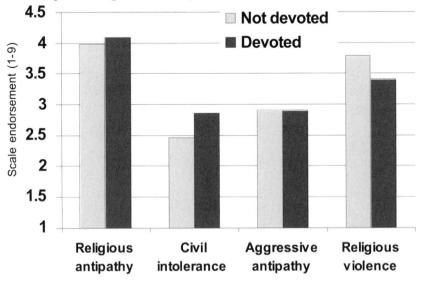

Religious intolerance scales

findings in the religion and prejudice literature (Donahue, 1985; Kirkpatrick & Hood, 1990).

Figures 8.3 and 8.4 illustrate how this uninteresting finding becomes interesting. Again we split the sample in half, but in order to hold coalitional attitude constant, we divided the sample not simply with a median split based on religious devotion scores, but based on a "more devoted than coalitional" score. We created this score by subtracting the average of the four coalitional variables from the average of the two devotional variables, or

$$(\text{divine devotion} + \text{religious devotion})/2 - (\text{authoritarianism} + \text{fundamentalism} + \text{dogmatism} + \text{exclusivity})/4.$$

While this formula bears no resemblance to the formulas used in multiple regressions, splitting the sample by this formula luckily accomplished what a multiple regression effectively does: holding some variables constant while allowing other variables to vary. As shown in Figure 8.3, authoritarianism, fundamentalism, dogmatism, and exclusivity are a lot less different between the two groups than they were in Figure 8.1: These coalitional attitude variables are more or less held constant between the devoted group and the not devoted group. Even with this more controlled division of the devoted from the nondevoted, the devoted group is above the mean of the scale (5), and the nondevoted group is below it. Figure 8.4 shows that with this more controlled division of the sample between the devoted and nondevoted, the devoted group was *less* intolerant on all measures, even on civil intolerance (recall that the devoted group was *more* intolerant on this measure when coalitional variables were not controlled).

To summarize, when not controlling for coalitional attitude (Figures 8.1 and 8.2), the religiously devoted showed a generally orthogonal (zero) relationship to tolerance; but when coalitional attitude was controlled for (Figures 8.3 and 8.4), they showed less intolerance on all measures. These figures mirror the pattern found with multiple regression. In multiple regression, the independent effect of religious devotion positively predicted religious tolerance when controlling for coalitional attitude (as well as for religious affiliation, ethnicity, and nation of birth). The independent core of religious devotion appears to be related to tolerance.

THE ROLE OF DEVOTIONAL AND COALITIONAL RELIGIOSITY IN SUPPORT FOR VIOLENCE

Even in the face of this evidence one may still argue that this independent core of religious devotion is only related to tolerance when there is something tolerant to be found in a specific religious or cultural milieu: Figures 8.1 through 8.4 describe a Canadian sample composed mostly of the religiously unaffiliated, Christian, and Buddhist college students. College students have

Figure 8.3   Means on Religiosity Variables for a Canadian Sample (Controlled Median Split: Religious Devotion Minus Coalitional Attitude)

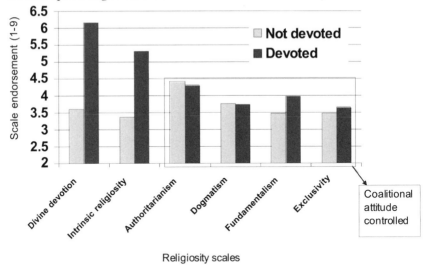

Figure 8.4   Means on Intolerance Variables for a Canadian Sample (Controlled Median Split: Religious Devotion Minus Coalitional Attitude)

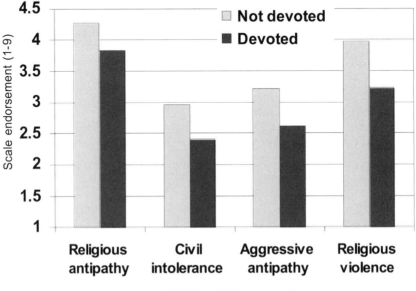

a reputation for tolerance. Canada has a reputation for tolerance. The unaffiliated are thought to be more tolerant than the affiliated. Buddhism has a reputation for tolerance as a religion, and the plurality Christian West has a reputation for tolerance as a culture. Both halves of the sample had coalitional scores below the midpoint of the scale. Perhaps this sample provided unusually ample opportunities for religiosity to be expressed in a tolerant way. But we found similar results in a non-Western Malaysian sample, with religious devotion predicting intolerance when not controlling for coalitional attitude and predicting tolerance when coalitional attitude was controlled for (Hansen & Norenzayan, 2005). In Malaysia, coalitional feeling ran considerably higher, yet the pattern of relationships was the same.

In an effort to investigate this phenomenon with a broader cross-cultural sample, we examined an international sample of 10,069 people in 10 nations: the United States, the United Kingdom, Israel, South Korea, India, Indonesia, Lebanon, Russia, Mexico, and Nigeria (Ginges, Hansen & Norenzayan, 2005; Hansen & Norenzayan, 2005). Representative samples were drawn in each of the 10 countries. Participants in these nations had completed a survey about religious attitudes carried out under the auspices of the British Broadcasting Corporation (BBC) in 2004. As an indicator of religious devotion we chose frequency of prayer. As indicators of coalitional attitude and behavior we chose frequency of attendance at organized religious services and a statement of religious exclusivity: "My God (beliefs) is the only true God (beliefs)." We call this "exclusivity" because it asserts the truth of one's own beliefs to the exclusion of all other beliefs. As with all of our studies, devotional and coalitional measures were positively and strongly related to one another, all $rs > .3$. One measure of intolerance was a statement scapegoating other religions: "I blame people of other religions for much of the trouble in this world." Again, we used regressions to analyze how each aspect of religiosity independently predicted scapegoating. Again, we found that exclusivity was a positive independent predictor of scapegoating, while prayer was a negative independent predictor. Attending religious services was not an independent predictor when other predictors were controlled for. Religious affiliation, nation surveyed, work type, gender, and age were all controlled for.

To illustrate the results of the regressions more intuitively, we divided the 10,069 participants into eight subsamples based on the different aspects of religious engagement to determine how adding prayer, adding exclusivity, and adding religious attendance are associated with different levels of scapegoating. It is possible to compare two groups that are otherwise similar, but differ only on one aspect of religiosity—for example, looking at those who attend services but do not pray as compared with those who attend services and pray to see what prayer contributes to scapegoating among attenders.

Although we only report data for the full sample in this chapter, if the sample is divided by religion (Christians, Jews, Muslims, Hindus) and each religion divided into the eight subcategories, the results are remarkably similar to the full sample, especially with regard to the effect of prayer. In this case, however, some of the eight categories have very few people in them, so differences in the means are difficult to interpret by themselves. These are the eight categories into which we divided the sample.

1. PRAY ONLY: Those who pray regularly (but are not regular attenders or exclusivists) [$n = 493$]
2. ATTEND ONLY: Those who are regular attenders (but are not regular prayers or exclusivists) [$n = 160$]
3. EXCLUSIVIST ONLY: Those who are exclusivists; say their God is the only true God (but are not regular prayers or attenders) [$n = 1,411$]
4. PRAY + ATTEND: Those who are prayers and attenders only (not exclusivists) [$n = 543$]
5. PRAY + EXCLUSIVIST: Those who are prayers and exclusivists only (not attenders) [$n = 1,344$]
6. ATTEND + EXCLUSIVIST: Those who are attenders and exclusivists only (not prayers) [$n = 420$]
7. ALL THREE: Those who are prayers, attenders, and exclusivists [$n = 3,497$]
8. NONE: Those who are not regular prayers, attenders, or exclusivists [$n = 2,200$]

Thus, to examine what prayer contributes to scapegoating, we compared:

1. NONE with PRAY ONLY
2. ATTEND ONLY with PRAY + ATTEND
3. EXCLUSIVIST ONLY with PRAY + EXCLUSIVIST
4. ATTEND + EXCLUSIVIST with ALL THREE

These comparisons are graphed in Figure 8.5. Note that the group that prays is always less scapegoating than the comparable group that does not. The scapegoating difference between the praying and the not praying is not confined to the mostly secular (not attending and not exclusive) but also is evident among the most coalitionally religious (both exclusivist and attending organized services). This suggests that a decline in prayer (or subjectively experienced faith generally) among the fundamentalist (coalitionally religious) may be associated with greater intolerance rather than greater tolerance. This finding is in contrast to the widely held belief that secularization is the surest path to religious tolerance. Since prayer's independent association with decreased scapegoating is true across religious groups (as mentioned previously, Jews, Christians, Hindus, and Muslims examined separately all show the pattern of Figure 8.5), this also challenges the idea that devotional processes yield tolerance in some religions and intolerance in others. There are discernible group differences between religions in coalitional religiosity, devotional religiosity, and intolerance. Yet prayer is associated with tolerance regardless of the relative intolerance of the prayer's religion. By this analysis, many religions appear to contain potential for tolerance, and that potential may lie in part in prayer, or perhaps more generally in subjectively experienced religious devotion, of which regular prayer would be one manifestation. It is interesting to note that prayer is a stronger independent predictor of belief in God and importance of religion in one's life than religious attendance and exclusivity (Ginges et al., 2005). In fact, we also found that multi-item measures of religious devotion (intrinsic religiosity, devotion to the divine) also predict belief in God better than coalitional religiosity (authoritarianism, exclusivity) (Hansen & Norenzayan, 2003). Because what best predicts belief in God also best predicts tolerance, these results are especially challenging to any secularization-promotes-tolerance hypothesis.

Regular prayer correlates substantially with belief that one's God or beliefs is the only true God or beliefs, $r\,(10,069) = .40$. Yet it is possible

Figure 8.5   Proportion of Participants Endorsing the Statement, "I Blame People of Other Religions for Much of the Trouble in this World"

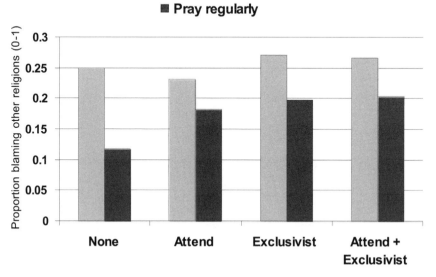

Note: Contrasting those who pray regularly vs. those who do not among those who neither attend services nor are exclusivist, those who attend only, those who are exclusivist only, and those for whom both are true.

that the independent contribution of exclusivity to scapegoating is the opposite of prayer's independent contribution to scapegoating. To examine what exclusivity contributes to scapegoating, we compared:

1. NONE with EXCLUSIVIST ONLY
2. ATTEND ONLY with ATTEND + EXCLUSIVIST
3. PRAY ONLY with PRAY + EXCLUSIVIST
4. PRAY + ATTEND with ALL THREE

These comparisons are graphed in Figure 8.6. Note that the group that is exclusive is always more scapegoating than the comparable group that is not. This is in stark contrast to the effect of prayer.

To examine what regular attendance at religious services contributes to scapegoating, we can compare:

1. NONE with ATTEND ONLY
2. EXCLUSIVIST ONLY with ATTEND + EXCLUSIVIST
3. PRAY ONLY with PRAY + ATTEND
4. PRAY + EXCLUSIVIST with ALL THREE

Figure 8.6   Proportion of Participants Endorsing the Statement, "I Blame People of Other Religions for Much of the Trouble in this World"

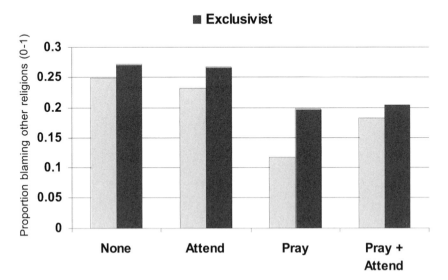

Note: Contrasting those who are exclusivist vs. those who are not among those who neither attend services nor pray, those who attend only, those who pray only, and those who do both.

These comparisons are graphed in Figure 8.7. In this case, attendance adds surprisingly little or nothing to scapegoating—increasing scapegoating only when compared with a prayer only condition. As mentioned earlier, these results essentially mirror the findings of the multiple regressions: Exclusivity is a positive predictor of scapegoating, prayer is a negative predictor, and attendance is not an independent predictor.

Although religious attendance did not independently predict blame, in other studies (Ginges et al., 2005) religious attendance showed more evidence of being a potentially coalitional variable relative to prayer. In a representative sample of Muslim West Bank Palestinians, frequency of religious attendance predicted support for suicide attacks on Israelis (more mosque attendance was related to more support), but frequency of prayer was unrelated to support for such attacks. Similar results were obtained in an experimental study among religious Jewish settlers in the occupied territories; in this case, reminders of synagogue attendance produced substantial support for Baruch Goldstein's historic suicide attack on Palestinian worshippers at the Machpela Cave mosque in 1994, whereas reminders of prayer did not.

Figure 8.7   Proportion of Participants Endorsing the Statement, "I Blame People of Other Religions for Much of the Trouble in this World"

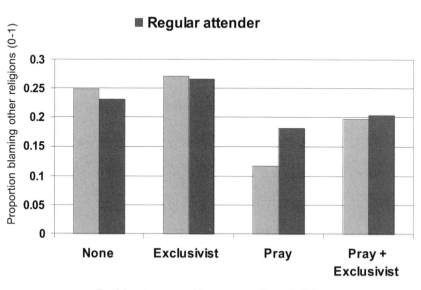

Note: Contrasting those who attend regularly vs. those who do not among those who neither pray nor are exclusivist, those who are exclusivist only, those who pray only, and those for whom both are true.

In Study 3 of Ginges et al. (2005), we amended our measure of scapegoating in the BBC study to count only scapegoaters of other religions who were also willing to die for their God or beliefs (thus creating a more stringent two-variable measure of support for combative martyrdom). Using this measure, our findings supported those of Ginges et al. (2005). In the six different faiths that we examined (comprising the majority faiths of six different nations: Protestants in the United Kingdom, Catholics in Mexico, Russian Orthodox in Russia, Jews in Israel, Muslims in Indonesia, and Hindus in India), regular attendance was a greater positive predictor of combative martyrdom than regular prayer (which was, in some cases, a nominally negative predictor of combative martyrdom). When all six samples were combined, regular prayer was unrelated to combative martyrdom, while regular religious attendance was a significant positive predictor of combative martyrdom. Those who attended services regularly were more than twice as likely to endorse combative martyrdom (Ginges et al., 2005).

In contrast to predicting scapegoating alone, prayer was not a reliably negative predictor of combative martyrdom in the BBC study or in the West Bank study. Perhaps this is because these studies did not measure enough coalitional variables to partial out the coalitional variance in prayer—in our studies in Malaysia and Canada, failing to control for any two of the four coalitional variables left religious devotion with a null rather than negative relationship to intolerance. It may also have been because prayer was quite strongly correlated with martyrdom generally. In the BBC study, even when exclusivity and attendance were controlled for, prayer was still strongly related to willingness to die for one's God and beliefs (though prayer was less strongly associated with martyrdom than exclusivity). Willingness to die for God, however, is not on its face a prejudiced, intolerant, or violent attitude, though it certainly is a potentially self-sacrificing one. But when the self-sacrifice begins to take on a dimension of scapegoating, blaming, or hostility to others, then religious devotion becomes unrelated to such tainted sacrifice, while coalitional religiosity maintains its positive relationship.

REEXAMINING THE RELIGION AND PREJUDICE LITERATURE

Our seemingly paradoxical paradigm of religion and intolerance rests on the premise that the intolerance-predicting aspect of religion (coalitional attitude) is strongly correlated with the tolerance-predicting aspect (religious devotion). This marks a departure from the religion and prejudice literature, which has generally attempted to force a dichotomous understanding onto the aspects of religion to match a dichotomous understanding of prejudice. Dichotomous understandings of religion, however, have yielded messy, inconclusive, and contradictory findings on how religion relates to prejudice, an issue to which we now turn.

Gordon Allport (1950) is widely credited with beginning empirical investigations of religion and prejudice and of religion generally. Allport arguably got empirical investigations of religion and prejudice off on the wrong foot by speaking of "mature" and "immature" religion, hypothesizing that "mature" or intrinsic religiosity was about directly experiencing one's religious faith while "immature" or extrinsic religiosity was geared toward seeing religion as little more than a source of community or conventional moral values, friends, financial opportunities, etc. In this regard, Allport's constructs map conceptually onto the widely noted subjective/natural versus objective/cultural distinction, but Allport, whose Protestant heritage likely inclined him to value the intrinsic as morally superior to the extrinsic (Cohen, Hall, & Koenig, 2005), was disappointed to find that intrinsic and extrinsic religiosity, which were supposed to be mutually incompatible, were unrelated rather than inversely related (Allport and Ross, 1967). Even as unrelated measures, however, intrinsic and extrinsic religiosity were less than satisfactory tools for investigating how different aspects of religion predict prejudice. In the first couple of decades of research using Allport's scales, extrinsic religiosity predicted racial prejudice and some other undesirable outcomes (Donahue, 1985). Intrinsic religiosity, while only occasionally predicting lack of prejudice, was generally orthogonal to prejudice, at least to racial prejudice (Donahue, 1985). Since early investigations, however, measures of intrinsic religiosity have produced a whole spectrum of relationships with different kinds of prejudice under different circumstances, ranging from negative (Duck & Hunsberger, 1999; Fisher, Derison, & Polley, 1994; Ponton & Gorsuch, 1988) to orthogonal (Donahue, 1985) to positive (Duck & Hunsberger, 1999; Fisher et al., 1994; Herek, 1987; McFarland 1989)—with the prediction of prejudice often depending on the kind of prejudice explored.

Moreover, extrinsic religiosity has also shown inconsistent relationships with prejudice, predicting prejudice in Allport and Ross's (1967) research and in many occasions afterward (see Donahue, 1985, for a review), but occasionally manifesting no relationship to prejudice (e.g., Griffin, Gorsuch, & Davis, 1987) or a negative relationship (Duck & Hunsberger, 1999; Strickland & Weddell, 1972). Further, extrinsic religiosity when measured as orthogonal to intrinsic has been found to have inadequate reliability (Trimble, 1997). When Hoge (1972) produced a psychometrically viable intrinsic religiosity scale with extrinsic reversed items, the three extrinsic items that fit in the scale were more indicative of a wholesale lack of religious devotion than an alternative socially driven understanding of it (Batson, Schoenrade, & Ventis, 1993). Generally, the body of literature on intrinsic and extrinsic religiosity has failed to reach empirically satisfying conclusions with regard to prejudice and intolerance (Kirkpatrick & Hood, 1990). These scales may still be useful for other pursuits, however—for example, distinguishing the relative importance of socially mediated and personally felt religiosity in different religious faiths (Cohen, Siegal, & Rozin, 2003).

Several researchers (e.g., Altemeyer, 1996; Batson et al., 1993; Kirkpatrick & Hood, 1990) have suggested that part of the problem may be that intrinsic religiosity scales are not the ideal measure of nonprejudiced "mature" religiosity. Rather, these scales indicate religious devotion or commitment, a psychological inclination that is widespread but logically (and often empirically) orthogonal to prejudice as generally conceived and may be as easily held by "immature" as by "mature" religious people.

We hold that, although the construct of intrinsic religiosity fails to capture "mature" or "intrinsic" religiosity (and thus is misnamed), it may nevertheless capture a kind of generalized subjectively rich devotion. As a measure of devotion, intrinsic religiosity may yield the odd relationships with prejudice recorded in the literature because religious devotion tends to be linked with coalitional attitudes. This relationship between intrinsic religiosity and coalitional variables was not a novel finding in our research but is documented in numerous studies (Duck & Hunsberger, 1999; Kahoe, 1975; Leak & Randall, 1995; Moghaddam & Vuksanovic, 1990; Watson, Sawyers, & Morris, 2003). This fits with William James's assertion that corporate and dogmatic dominion are partners of religion proper.

In fact, when evolution-minded social scientists propose any possible utility or value in religion to survival and procreation, that utility is often described in terms of religion's value to coalition-building (Kirkpatrick, 1999; Sosis & Alcorta, 2003; Wilson, 2002). Because all our measures of coalitional attitude are empirically related to some kind of prejudice, coalitional attitude appears to be a kind of intermediary between religious devotion and prejudice or intolerance. When this intermediary is statistically held out of the picture, religious devotion appears, at the least, unrelated to intolerance, and in many cases, inversely related to it.

Coalitional religiosity is likely rooted in the costly sacrifice to the community of believers that is the hallmark of religion. As evolutionary theorists have noted, sacrificial displays can be selected for if carriers of honest signals of group membership are more likely to be reciprocated by a community of cooperators. Even in rights-oriented "individualist" cultures, one is expected to sacrifice all selfish gains that might accrue from being on the benefiting end of injustice toward others. Atran (2002) and others (Atran & Norenzayan, 2004; Sosis & Alcorta, 2003) note that sincere expressions of willingness to make any kind of sacrifice (including the potential ultimate sacrifice of one's own life) only occasionally necessitate actually following through on that sacrifice in a way that has long-term costs to the potential for survival and reproduction of the genes carried by that individual. However, the material and social support benefits that can accrue to those who sincerely express or demonstrate such willingness are both more likely to occur and are of more obvious value to the long-term survival of one's genes—unless one is among the unlucky individuals whose sincere demonstration involves actually dying before reproductive potential is maximized (and even then, socially given benefits to close kin may offset the genetic loss of one individual). This "adaptive sacrifice display" explanation for religious devotion is related to the evolutionary concept of "costly signaling," a process that explains many forms of sacrificial displays in the animal kingdom—for example, why peacocks who burden themselves with more costly plumage may nevertheless be more likely to pass on their genes by increasing their chances of mating with a receptive peahen. Costly signaling theory offers an explanation of why humans engage in altruistic displays such as sacrifice and ritual without treating the group as a unit of selection (Sosis & Alcorta, 2003).

Does Religious Devotion Foster Empathy and Self-Boundary Transcendence?

That coalitional religiosity encourages intolerance toward outgroups seems obvious. But it is less clear why devotional religiosity can, under some conditions, foster tolerance. Some evidence from neuroscience provides a novel speculation as to the process by which devotional experience may lead to transcendence of group boundaries. Neuroscience investigations of religion[2] tend to focus exclusively on the spiritual, meditative, or ecstatic aspects of religious experience (d'Aquili & Newberg, 1999) and almost never with the coalitional aspects. Some investigations (e.g., d'Aquili & Newberg, 1998, 1999; Holmes, 2001; Newberg, d'Aquili, & Rause, 2001) have found that when people are subjectively experiencing a transcendent or supernatural-oriented state, there is often decreased activity in the parietal lobe or other object association areas, where perceptions that distinguish self from non-self are processed. The frontal lobes known to be associated with sense of self (Edwards-Lee & Saul, 1999) and theory of mind (Brune, 2005) are also implicated in religious practices (McNamara, 2001; McNamara, Andresen, & Gellard, 2003), including meditation (Newberg et al., 2001) and religious recitation (Azari et al., 2001), both of which are common in prayer. These areas may play a role in any relationship prayer might have to greater tolerance, empathy or other-concern, since they all seem potentially relevant to whether sense of self is experienced in a more limited or more expansive way. Perhaps commonplace empathic experiences of seeing oneself in another or caring for another as one would care for oneself have some family relationship to rarer mystical experiences of "oneness" and even to more extreme cases where the self-other boundary completely dissolves.[3]

It is reasonable, though admittedly speculative, to propose that any area of the brain generally involved in breaking down distinctions should have some relevance to breaking down distinctions between oneself and other closely related individuals. This breakdown may well be involved in enabling identification with a group as extended social self—an identification of obvious relevance to coalitional religiosity. Coalitional concerns are not central to typical religious experience, however. This breakdown of the distinction between self and other appears more directly bound up in feeling emotionally and even viscerally related to something far greater than both oneself and any finite group: God or some other supernatural being or reality. It is plausible that this feeling of connection with this numinous realm may often stop at or recede after time to a more limited sense of connection with an identifiable human group, perhaps because human groups are easier to integrate into understanding and decision-making than are numinous mystical deities. Nevertheless, numinously oriented beliefs and practices may potentially lead in some cases, to a much greater openness, even an expansion of one's moral circle to include humanity at large, with all of its different nations, races, religions, and ways of living.

This sort of broad transcendent manifestation of religion may express itself infrequently, however, as evidenced by religious devotion's unclear relationship to tolerance when coalitional religiosity is not controlled. Coalitional religiosity arguably reflects a limited kind of self-transcendence that simply upgrades individual selfishness to group selfishness, sometimes with dramatically violent consequences. Yet religious devotion's independent relationship to tolerance suggests that religion has the potential to transcend group selfishness as well. It is almost as if a more limited religious transcendence is in tension with a more thoroughgoing transcendence. What lies beyond group selfishness we may dub "God-selfishness," a focus of oneself on a God or divine being or principle that is transcendent of all individuals and groups, including oneself and one's own groups. God-selfishness would appear to be what religious devotion measures tap into when the variance of coalitional religiosity is controlled for. To the extent that this broader transcendence of self often manifests itself as a tolerant sense of kinship with all, then it would appear to render Dawkins's pessimism about religion unwarranted.

Whether or not pessimism is warranted, circumspection certainly is. Religious devotion is a tenuously broad expansion of selfishness, one that might often revert to a strain of group selfishness or individual selfishness enhanced by religious self-deception and narcissism, as observers of religious persecution and hypocrisy will readily attest. Nevertheless, our findings suggest that religious devotion is more than a hypocritical disguise for individual selfishness and group selfishness. Such devotion also appears to coexist with a genuine concern for all people, and perhaps even for all beings. Moreover, the God-selfishness of religious devotion appears potentially more attuned to this all-embracing concern than individual selfishness or group selfishness stripped of supernatural understanding.

In English, the word "religion" is related to the Latin word *religio, religere* meaning to bind together. The individuals that religion binds together may form groups that do as much or more violence to each other than the individuals might have done on their own out of unaligned selfishness. Yet, to the extent that people experience some degree of self-transcendence in prayer and other acts of devotion, a broad feeling of connectedness with others may result. This connectedness may make intolerance and violence less appealing for that moment of devotion and perhaps, over time, as a chronic habit of mind and behavior. Transcendent moments pass, and the many forces that generate human conflict will likely continue to be a part of the human drama. But when religious transcendence is broad rather than narrow, it has the potential to contribute to a world where the bloody rivalries of nation, race, and religion are known only as shadowy memories of fading history.

ACKNOWLEDGMENTS

The writing of this chapter was supported by a Social Sciences and Humanities Research Council of Canada grant to the second author (410-2004-0197) and by a University of British Columbia Killam Predoctoral Fellowship to the first author. We thank Eleanor Chow for helpful comments on an earlier version of this chapter.

NOTES

1. A scale that, as named, sounds like a measure of credal fundamentalism, but in its actual content (see cite) is more of a positive statement of faith in Christianity than an epistemic and moral elevation of Christianity above other faiths.

2. In citing neurotheological investigations, we are neither endorsing nor critiquing the scientific merit of this research. Regardless of whether the conclusions of neurotheological investigations follow from the evidence, we find these conclusions illustrative of a widespread and, we think, plausible intuition that religious experience is at least in part about self-transcendance, specifically transcendence of the boundary between self and other.

3. Holmes (2001) notes that persons whose parietal superior lobes were damaged or destroyed suffer an agonizing disability, in that they experience great difficulty in distinguishing between themselves and the rest of the world. This condition makes it difficult, for example, for the patient to walk, because he's unsure of where the floor ends and his foot begins, or even to sit down, because she doesn't know where her body ends and the chair begins. This is not unlike the mystical experience that is reported by deep meditators of being "at one" with the universe. For these patients, being "at one" with the universe is such a constant experience, performing tasks that require the simple differentiation between "self" and "world" become extraordinarily difficult.

REFERENCES

Adorno, T. W., Frenkel-Brunswick, E., Levinson, D. J., & Sanford, R. N. (1950). *The authoritarian personality.* New York: Norton.

Allport, G. (1950). *The individual and his religion.* New York: Macmillan.

Allport, G. W., & Ross, J. M. (1967). Personal religious orientation and prejudice. *Journal of Personality and Social Psychology, 5,* 432–443.

Altemeyer, R. A. (1981). *Right-wing authoritarianism.* Winnipeg, Canada: University of Manitoba Press.

Altemeyer, R. A. (1988). *Enemies of freedom: Understanding right-wing authoritarianism.* San Francisco: Jossey-Bass.

Altemeyer, R. A. (1996). *The authoritarian specter.* Cambridge, MA: Harvard University Press.

Altemeyer, R. A. (1999). Right-wing authoritarianism (1990 version). In J. P. Robinson, P. R. Shaver, & L. S. Wrightsman (Eds.), *Measures of political attitudes* (Vol. 2, pp. 104–106). Toronto: Academic Press.

Altemeyer, R. A., & Hunsberger, B. (1992). Authoritarianism, religious fundamentalism, quest, and prejudice. *International Journal for the Psychology of Religion, 2,* 113–133.

Appleby, R. S. (2000). *The ambivalence of the sacred: Religion, violence and reconciliation.* Lanham, MD: Rowman & Littlefield.

Atran, S. (2002). *In Gods we trust: The evolutionary landscape of religion.* Oxford, England: Oxford University Press.

Atran, S. (2003). Genesis of suicide terrorism. *Science, 299,* 1534–1539.

Atran, S., & Norenzayan, A. (2004). Religion's evolutionary landscape: Cognition, commitment, compassion, communion. *Behavioral and Brain Sciences, 27,* 713–770.

Azari, N. P., Nickel, J., Wunderlich, G., Niedeggen, M., Hefter, H., Tellmann, L., et al. (2001). Neural correlates of religious experience. *European Journal of Neuroscience, 13,* 1649–1652.

Barrett, J. (2000). Exploring the natural foundations of religion. *Trends in Cognitive Science, 4,* 29–34.

Batson, C. D., Schoenrade, P., & Ventis, L. (1993). *Religion and the individual.* New York: Oxford University Press.

Boyer, P. (2001). *Religion explained: The evolutionary origins of religious thought.* New York: Basic Books.

Boyer, P. (2003). Religious thought and behaviour as by-products of brain function. *Trends in Cognitive Sciences, 7,* 119–124.

Brüne, M. (2005). Emotion recognition, "theory of mind," and social behavior in schizophrenia. *Psychiatry Research, 133,* 135–147.

Burkert, W. (1996). *Creation of the sacred: Tracks of biology in early religions.* Cambridge, MA: Harvard University Press.

Cohen, A. B., Hall, D. E., & Koenig, H. G. (2005). Social versus individual motivation: Implications for normative definitions of religious orientation. *Personality and Social Psychology Review, 9,* 48–61.

Cohen, A. B., Siegel, J. I., & Rozin, P. (2003). Faith versus practice: Different bases for religiosity judgments by Jews and Protestants. *European Journal of Social Psychology, 33,* 287–295.

Cohen, J., & Cohen, P. (1975). *Applied multiple regression/correlation analysts for the behavioral sciences.* New York: Wiley.

Conger, A.J. (1974). A revised definition for suppressor variables: A guide to their identification and interpretation. *Educational and Psychological Measurement, 34,* 35–46.

d'Aquili, E., & Newberg, A.B. (1998). The neuropsychological basis of religions, or why God won't go away. *Zygon, 33,* 187–201.

d'Aquili, E., & Newberg, A.B. (1999). *The mystical mind: Probing the biology of religious experience.* Minneapolis, MN: Augsburg Fortress.

Dawkins, R. (1989). *The selfish gene.* Oxford, England: Oxford University Press.

Donahue, M.J. (1985). Intrinsic and extrinsic religiousness: Review and meta-analysis. *Journal of Personality and Social Psychology, 48,* 400–419.

Duck R., & Hunsberger, B. (1999). Religious orientation and prejudice: The role of religious proscription, right-wing authoritarianism and social desirability. *International Journal for the Psychology of Religion, 9,* 157–179.

Durkheim, E. (1915/1965). *The elementary forms of the religious life.* New York: Free Press.

Edwards-Lee, T.A., & Saul, R.E. (1999). Neuropsychiatry of the right frontal lobe. In B.L. Miller & J.L. Cummings (Eds.), *The human frontal lobes: Functions and disorders* (pp. 304–320). New York: Guilford Press.

Feng, G.F., & English, J. (Trans.). (1972). *The tao te ching.* New York: Vintage.

Fiorito, B., & Ryan, K. (1998, August). *Development and preliminary reliability of a new measure of religiosity: Religiousness and spirituality questionnaires.* Poster session presented at the annual meeting of the American Psychological Association, San Francisco, CA.

Fisher, R.D., Derison, D., & Polley, C.F. (1994). Religiousness, religious orientation, and attitudes towards gays and lesbians. *Journal of Applied Social Psychology, 24,* 614–630.

Freud, S. (1961). *Civilization and its discontents* (J. Strachcy, Trans.). New York: Norton. (Original manuscript published 1930)

Ginges, J., Hansen, I., & Norenzayan, A. (2005). *Religion and combative martyrdom.* Unpublished manuscript, University of Michigan.

Griffin, G.A., Gorsuch, R.L., & Davis, A.L. (1987). A cross-cultural investigation of religious orientation, social norms, and prejudice. *Journal for the Scientific Study of Religion, 26,* 358–365.

Guthrie, S. (1993). *Faces in the clouds: A new theory of religion.* New York: Oxford University Press.

Hansen, I.G., & Norenzayan, A. (2003). Devotional religiosity, coalitional religiosity and belief in the supernatural. Unpublished raw data.

Hansen, I.G., & Norenzayan, A. (2005). *Coalitional vs. devotional religiosity: Explaining cultural differences between Christians and Buddhists in religious intolerance.* Unpublished manuscript, University of British Columbia.

Herek, G.M. (1987). Religious orientation and prejudice: A compilation of racial and sexual attitudes. *Personality and Social Psychology Bulletin, 13,* 34–44.

Hoge, D.R. (1972). A validated intrinsic religious motivation scale. *Journal for the Scientific Study of Religion, 11,* 369–376.

Holmes, B. (April 21, 2001). In search of God. *New Scientist,* 25–27.

James, W. (1982). *The varieties of religious experience.* New York: Penguin Books. (Original manuscript published 1902.)

Juergensmeyer, M. (2003). *Terror in the mind of God: The global rise of religious violence.* Berkeley: University of California Press.

Kahoe, R. D. (1975). Authoritarianism and religion: Relationships of F-scale items to intrinsic and extrinsic religious orientations. *JSAS Catalog of Selected Documents in Psychology, 5,* 284–285.

Kimball, C. (2002). *When religion becomes evil.* San Francisco: Harper San Francisco.

Kirkpatrick, L. (1993). Fundamentalism, Christian orthodoxy, and intrinsic religious orientation as predictors of discriminatory attitudes. *Journal for the Scientific Study of Religion, 32,* 256–268.

Kirkpatrick, L. A. (1999). Toward an evolutionary psychology of religion and personality. *Journal of Personality, 67,* 921–951.

Kirkpatrick, L. A., & Hood, R. W. (1990). Intrinsic-extrinsic religious orientation: The boon or bane of contemporary psychology of religion? *Journal for the Scientific Study of Religion, 29,* 442–462.

Landau, M. J., Solomon, S., & Greenberg, J. (2004). Deliver us from evil: The effects of mortality salience and reminders of 9/11 on support for President George W. Bush. *Personality and Social Psychology Bulletin, 30,* 1136–1150.

Lawson, E. T., & McCauley, R. (1990). *Rethinking religion.* Cambridge, England: Cambridge University Press.

Laythe, B., Finkel, D., & Kirkpatrick, L. A. (2001). Predicting prejudice from religious fundamentalism and right-wing authoritarianism: A multiple-regression approach. *Journal for the Scientific Study of Religion, 40,* 1–10.

Leak, G. K., & Randall, B. A. (1995). Clarification of the link between right-wing authoritarianism and religiousness: The role of religious maturity. *Journal for the Scientific Study of Religion, 34,* 245–252.

McFarland, S. (1989). Religious orientations and the targets of discrimination. *Journal for the Scientific Study of Religion, 28,* 324–336.

McNamara, P. (2001). Religion and the frontal lobes. In J. Andresen (Ed.), *Religion in mind: Cognitive perspectives on religious belief, ritual, and experience* (pp. 237–256). New York: Cambridge University Press.

McNamara, P., Andresen, J., & Gellard, J. (2003). Relation of religiosity and scores on fluency tests to subjective reports of health in older individuals. *International Journal for the Psychology of Religion, 13,* 259–271.

Moghaddam, F. M., & Vuksanovic, V. (1990). Attitudes and behavior toward human rights across different contexts: The role of right-wing authoritarianism, political ideology, and religiosity. *International Journal of Psychology, 25,* 455–474.

Nelson-Pallmeyer, J. (2003). *Is religion killing us? Violence in the Bible and the Quran.* Harrisburg, PA: Trinity Press International.

Newberg, A., Alavi, A., Baime, M., Pourdehnad, M., Santanna, J., & d'Aquili, E. (2001). The measurement of regional cerebral blood flow during the complex cognitive task of meditation: A preliminary SPECT study. *Psychiatry Research, 106,* 113–122.

Newberg, A., d'Aquili, E., & Rause, V. (2001). *Why God won't go away.* New York: Ballantine Books.

Norenzayan, A., & Heine, S. (2005). Psychological universals: What are they and how can we know? *Psychological Bulletin, 13,* 763–784.

Ponton, M. O., & Gorsuch, R. L. (1988). Prejudice and religion revisited: A cross-cultural investigation with a Venezuelan sample. *Journal for the Scientific Study of Religion, 27,* 260–271.

Pyysiäinen, I., & Anttonen, V. (Eds.). (2002). *Current approaches in the cognitive science of religion.* London: Continuum.

Rappaport, R. (1979). *Ecology, meaning and religion.* Berkeley, CA: North Atlantic Books.

Rowatt, W. C., & Franklin, L. M. (2004). Christian orthodoxy, religious fundamentalism, and right-wing authoritarianism as predictors of implicit racial prejudice. *International Journal for the Psychology of Religion, 14,* 125–138.

Sosis, R., & Alcorta, C. (2003). Signaling, solidarity, and the sacred: The evolution of religious behavior. *Evolutionary Anthropology, 12,* 264–274.

Sperber, D. (1996). *Explaining culture: A naturalistic approach.* London: Blackwell.

Strickland, B. R., & Weddell, S. C. (1972). Religious orientation, racial prejudice, and dogmatism: A study of Baptists and Unitarians. *Journal for the Scientific Study of Religion, 11,* 395–399.

Trimble, D. E. (1997). The Religious Orientation Scale: Review and meta-analysis of social desirability effects. *Educational and Psychological Measurement, 57,* 970–986.

Watson P., Sawyers P., & Morris, R. J. (2003). Reanalysis within a Christian ideological surround: Relationships of intrinsic religious orientation with fundamentalism and right-wing authoritarianism. *Journal of Psychology and Theology, 31,* 315–328.

Weber, M. (1947). *The theory of social and economic organization.* Glencloe, IL: Free Press.

Weber, M. (1978). *Economy and society.* (G. Roth & C. Wittich, Eds.). Berkeley: University of California Press.

Wilson, D. S. (2002). *Darwin's cathedral: Evolution, religion, and the nature of society.* Chicago: University of Chicago Press.

CHAPTER 9

THE ORIGINS OF DREAMING

Kelly Bulkeley

The search for origins is one of the great themes of myth and legend. Every religion and cultural tradition has its story about how humans, the world, the heavens, and life itself began. These are more than just stories. What we believe happened at the beginning, *in illo tempore*, matters right now, in the present. To take the most contentious example in the contemporary United States, the different views of human origins proposed by the Bible and evolutionary science have led people to adopt highly divergent approaches to the politics of sexuality, marriage, and reproduction. Likewise, religious traditions and scientific researchers hold quite different views of the origins of dreaming, which naturally color their approaches to the nature, function(s), and meaning of dreams. If you believe dreams originate in the disembodied wandering of one's spirit or soul, your general attitude toward dreaming will likely differ from someone who believes that dreams originate in the random firing of neurons in the brain during sleep. Stories of origins *matter.*

The opposition between religious and scientific views of the origin of dreaming may seem absolute, with no possibility of reconciliation or meaningful integration. What common ground can be found between the mystic's revelatory vision of the night and the sleep laboratory subject's brief, disjointed post-awakening report? What do neurons have to do with God?

In this chapter I argue that the religion-science opposition on dreams may be bridged by connecting important but unappreciated facts from each realm. A strong case can be made that dreaming is a primal, *originating* source of both religious experience and brain-mind growth. In ways that are inextricably religious *and* neuropsychological, human dreaming has the effect of provoking greater consciousness of self, others, world, and cosmos. My aim is to develop that case by integrating key findings from contemporary brain-mind science with current work in religious studies. Looking first at brain-mind science, I review the last century of research on the phenomenology of highly memorable dreams (what Carl Jung [1974] called "big dreams") and establish some basic facts about prototypical human dream experience. Then I turn to religious studies and look at the special role of dreaming in people's experiences of religious, spiritual, and existential origins, with an eye to the recurrence of those same oneirological patterns identified by contemporary science. This dual focus, on highly memorable dreams and on stories of religious origins, reveals the ways in which a strong, autonomous, creative, and iconoclastic force is at work in human dreaming. It is not necessarily a confession of religious faith, nor should it be regarded as an exhaustive scientific explanation. It is rather a reasonable conclusion that comes from considering, critically and creatively, the latest evidence from several branches of scholarship.

CURRENT SCIENTIFIC EVIDENCE ON HIGHLY MEMORABLE TYPES OF DREAMS

For the past one hundred years, the main goal of Western scientific dream research has been to explain the form and content of dreams in terms of sleep physiology. Sigmund Freud developed the psychoanalytic model by which dreams were explained as "guardians of sleep" whose manifest content (i.e., the dream as remembered) is actually a deceptive mask enabling the secret, hallucinatory fulfillment of repressed instinctual desires (Freud, 1965). Beginning in the 1950s, Freud's model was displaced by the discovery of rapid eye movement (REM) sleep and its connection to dreaming (Aserinsky & Kleitman, 1953, 1955). Researchers found that human sleep (and indeed all mammalian sleep) is structured by automatic cycles of greater and lesser brain activation (for summaries, see Cartwright & Lamberg, 1992; Dement, 1972; Shafton, 1995). This led to numerous investigations to identify correlations between the physiology of REM sleep and the psychological elements of dreams. Initial efforts focused on eye movements (Roffwarg, Dement, Muzio, & Fisher, 1962), penile erections (Fisher, 1966), and various kinds of pre-sleep stimuli (Witkin & Lewis, 1967). Disappointingly, the results of later studies did not fulfill the initial expectations. The movements of the eyes during REM sleep do not directly match or track what people are seeing in their dreams (Aserinsky, Lynch, Mack, Tzankoff, & Hurn, 1985; Jacobs, Feldman, & Bender, 1970, 1972; Moskowitz & Berger, 1969). Penile erections (and clitoral swelling) are automatic physiological accompaniments of sleep and do not always correspond to dreams of sexual imagery or arousal (Hursch, Karacan, & Williams, 1972). No particular pre-sleep stimulus, whether a memory task, a physical activity, or watching a movie, has been shown to have a simple, direct impact on what people dream the subsequent night. More fundamentally, subsequent research demonstrated that dreams are not exclusively the province of REM sleep but are also reported with some frequency from NREM sleep (Foulkes, 1962; Kahan, 2000). The more closely researchers looked at actual dreams, the more they realized that REM physiology does not account for their basic features.

If nothing else, these findings indicate that pursuing a simplistic REM-dreaming isomorphism is a dead end for future scientific dream research. REM sleep may be a kind of triggering mechanism for most dreams, but the process of dreaming itself emerges from a complex, widely distributed system of brain-mind activities that are functionally independent of REM physiology. More evidence on this subject is presented later in the chapter, but for now the point is that the origins of dreaming are very clearly *not* in REM sleep. As sleep and dream researcher James Pagel notes, "Dreaming and REM sleep are complex states for which the Dreaming = REMS model has become excessively simple and limited" (Pagel, 2000, p. 988). A new scientific story of origins is needed, one that better accounts for current knowledge about the actual patterns of dreaming form and content.

Such a story will need to include an understanding of sleep physiology across REM and NREM stages. Indeed, there is no reason to believe that the artificial categories of REM and NREM are eternally valid, and we may hope that future researchers will find a better way to account for the complex, multidimensional sleep cycles of humans and other creatures. In the meantime, our stories of the origins of dreaming must include recognition of the strong and steady (if not absolute) relationship between the neurophysiology of REM sleep and the frequency and intensity of dreaming, while also acknowledging that genuine dreaming occurs outside of REM sleep. Our understanding of dreaming will always depend on our understanding of sleep in general, and future dream research will be most prosperous if it grounds itself in a more sophisticated foundation of knowledge about what's happening in the approximately one-third of our lives we pass in slumber.

With this preliminary background in sleep physiology, the next step is to look more closely at the form and content of dreaming. I focus not on dreams in general, but on those relatively rare types of dreams that make a strong and lasting impact on the dreamer's waking consciousness. If there is any function or value to dreaming, it is most likely to appear in those dreams that are remembered with greatest intensity, by the widest variety of people, from many different historical eras. The frequency of such dreams is increasingly well documented, and the Western psychological tradition has developed several important insights regarding their prototypical features. Drawing these insights together will provide a new basis for correlating dream psychology and sleep physiology, and this in turn will enable us to reassess the relation-ship between scientific and religious stories of the origins of dreaming.

Freud

The modern psychological study of dreams began with Sigmund Freud and the publication in 1899 (postdated to 1900) of his monumental *The Interpretation of Dreams* (Freud, 1965). Freud's psychoanalytic theory was cre-ated in large part through a probing investigation of his own dreams in the years following the death of his father. The central claim of his theory is that *dreams are the disguised fulfillment of repressed wishes.* To maintain healthy func-tioning of the mind, dreams serve as a kind of pressure valve, releasing pent-up instinctual energies in a safe and harmless fashion. The instinctual wishes that emerge in dreams are primarily egotistical and antisocial in nature, har-kening back to infantile pleasure-seeking. Freud says an agency within the mind called "the dream-work" employs symbolic imagery and metaphorical language to fulfill the instinctual wishes without arousing moral anxiety, thereby allowing the individual's sleep to continue undisturbed.

The psychoanalytic theory of dreams has attracted tremendous controversy over the past 100 years, and fortunately for our purposes we do not need to worry about the ongoing battles between Freud's friends and foes. Taken as a comprehensive explanation of all features of all dreams, Freud's wish-fulfillment theory is certainly wrong. However, taken as an insight into vital (but not all-encompassing) features of human dream experience, Freud's theory is certainly right: dreams frequently express instinctual wishes of an egotistical (especially sexual) nature, they do so by using a culturally saturated language of symbol and metaphor, and they contribute to the healthy functioning of mind and body. Freud had very little to say about highly memorable dreams per se. Indeed, he believed dreams were meant to be forgotten, the better to hide their disturbing instinctual core, and so he was not inclined to pay much attention to those rare dreams that for some reason or other can't be forgotten. But these three points—the role of instinctual desires, the language of symbol and metaphor, and the positive psychological function—are directly relevant to our contemporary understanding of prototypical human dreaming.

Jung

Carl Jung dates his fascination with dreaming to the earliest remembered dream from his childhood, in which he descends to an underground throne room and confronts a massive phallus on a throne (Jung, 1965, pp. 11–13). Jung was one of Freud's earliest and most enthusiastic followers, but after the angry break-up of their relationship Jung withdrew into professional and personal isolation, surrendering to an upsurge of fantasy material from his unconscious. Building on these numinous, life-altering experiences, Jung developed a theoretical synthesis of clinical psychiatry and comparative mythology that explained dreams as natural (i.e., undisguised) expressions of the psyche whose function, even in the case of intensely frightening nightmares, is to promote the ultimate goal of individuation (Jung, 1965, 1968, 1980). Dreaming, Jung says, has the beneficial functions of compensating for the imbalances of the conscious mind and anticipating future challenges and developments in life. The classic themes, motifs, and symbols of world mythology provide the inherited mental language for oneirological expression. For Jung, dreaming is not simply a matter of animal instinct but also of spiritual enlightenment. This is especially true with what he calls "big dreams," intensely vivid and memorable dreams that "are often remembered for a lifetime, and not infrequently prove to be the richest jewel in the treasure-house of psychic experience" (Jung, 1974, p. 36).

As with Freudian psychoanalysis, Jung's theory is questionable if taken in absolute terms. Whether we accept the entirety of his psychological system, several of his key points remain legitimate and important: the "naturalness" of remembered dreaming, the potential psychological value of nightmares, the symbolic interplay between dreaming and mythology, and, most crucially for our purposes, the recognition of various types of extraordinary "big dreams." Jung realized, in a way Freud never did, that certain dreams are different from other dreams, with recurrent images, themes, and feelings that deserve careful investigation in their own right (maybe in Freud's comments on Descartes's dreams as "dreams from above"). Jung's case studies may be open to debate as sources of evidence, but his key insight into the significance of highly memorable dreams has been strongly supported by subsequent research.

Content Analysis

The quantitative dream research of Calvin Hall, Robert Van de Castle, and G. William Domhoff was originally developed to measure dream content in such a way that the claims of Freudian, Jungian, and other dream theories could be empirically tested (Domhoff, 1996, 2003; Hall, 1966, 1984; Hall & Van de Castle, 1966; Van de Castle, 1994). Using a content analysis method by which dreams are scored according to several discrete categories (e.g., characters, social interactions, misfortunes and good fortunes, emotions, settings, descriptive modifiers), these researchers identified a central feature of dream experience, which Domhoff (2003) calls "the continuity principle" (p. 26). On average, humans tend to dream about the same people, places, and activities that are most prominent in their waking lives. How we feel, think, and behave in our dreams is by and large continuous with our waking personalities. The findings of content analysis may not seem relevant to the study of highly memorable dreams, especially when we note that the dream reports used by these researchers are either from most recent dream surveys, brief dream journals, or sleep laboratory awakenings—all of which are likely to under-represent the occurrence of relatively rare types of intensified, highly memorably dreaming. But this is precisely the value of the Hall, Van de Castle, and Domhoff findings: they provide background information on "ordinary" dreaming that enables us to see more clearly what makes "extraordinary" dreams so distinctive. Understanding the continuities between dreaming and waking gives a better insight into the *dis*continuities that emerge in dreaming—for example, the fantastic metamorphoses of time, space, character, and consciousness that are especially prominent in highly memorable dreams.

Hunt

Harry Hunt's *The Multiplicity of Dreams* (Hunt, 1989) makes the case for a more sophisticated qualitative study of the recurrent patterns of highly memorable dreams. He says,

> dream psychology, in its haste for its own Darwin, has bypassed the necessary foundations of a Linnaeus. The various available systems of quantitative content analysis are complex and reliable, and they correlate to a degree with cognitive, physiological, and personality variables, but they are still reminiscent of attempting to classify the natural order of species by first, ever so precisely, measuring length of limb, size of tooth, body weight, and so on— disregarding whether the animal is a reptile, fish, bird, or mammal. (p. 97)

For Hunt, the essential starting point for dream psychology is the development of a full, detailed phenomenology of dreaming in all its varied manifestations, from the ordinary to the extraordinary. Once we have such a phenomenology, then we can determine which theoretical perspectives are most helpful in understanding the data. Hunt's creative synthesis of cognitive psychology with anthropological and historical information allows him to offer a portrait of "a natural order of dream forms" (p. 90), with each type of dream involving a distinctively patterned interaction of visual-spatial and conceptual-verbal processes. The main ones he describes are *personal-mnemonic* dreams, regarding common matters in the dreamer's waking life; *medical somatic dreams*, relating to physiological processes in the dreamer's body; *prophetic dreams*, presenting omens or images of the future; and *archetypal-spiritual dreams*, with vivid, subjectively powerful encounters with numinous forces, often also including extremely strong physical or "titanic" sensations. Hunt's analysis of these types of dreams elaborates on Jung's initial distinction between "big" and "little" dreams, providing a more detailed account of the complex psychological processes at work in their generation.

Lucid Dreaming

One type of unusual dream experience that has received considerable research attention is lucid dreaming—that is, becoming aware within the dream state that you are dreaming (although, strangely, neither Freud nor Jung paid much attention to lucid dreaming). There is much to be said about these dreams, but for our purposes the findings of three researchers are especially significant. First, Jayne Gackenbach's research on relations between lucid awareness in dreaming and alterations of consciousness in transcendental meditation shows how sustained attention practices (whether in a religious context or not) can produce striking physiological and psychological changes of a positive nature (Gackenbach, 1991; Gackenbach & LaBerge, 1988). It appears that what makes lucid dreams so memorable is the momentary realization of a kind of conscious state that various disciplines of meditation and prayer actively seek to achieve. Second, Tracy Kahan's work on dreams that involve various degrees of intentional volition and metacognition (thinking about thinking) indicates that dreaming is not mentally "deficient," but rather uses the same cognitive abilities we use in our waking lives (Kahan, 2001; Kahan & LaBerge, 1994; Kahan, LaBerge, Levitan, & Zimbardo, 1997). In lucid dreams, what we consider the "highest" forms of cognition (self-awareness, selective attention, short-term memory) are fully operational, and this raises interesting questions about the cross-state flexibility of the human psyche. And third, Fariba Bogzaran's efforts to integrate research on lucidity, consciousness, and artistic creativity highlight the recurrent patterns of entoptic phenomena that spontaneously emerge in many lucid dreams (Bogzaran & Deslauriers, 2004; Krippner, Bogzaran, & de Carvalho, 2002). One way to follow her insights will be comparing visual patterns in lucid dreams with the ancient cave paintings found in several regions around the world, where similar entoptic images are portrayed and where dream incubation rituals likely took place (Lewis-Williams, 2002).

Kuiken

Don Kuiken's work with Sikora (Kuiken & Sikora, 1993) and Busink (Busink & Kuiken, 1995) on highly impactful dreams is directly relevant to our concerns. His motivating interest was to push beyond the idea that dreaming has a single, universal function:

> Perhaps dreaming *is* a sufficiently uniform phenomenon to consistently serve some function or integrated set of functions. On the other hand, perhaps dreaming is only *apparently* uniform because differences among kinds of dreaming—and among the functions of different kinds of dreaming—have not received sufficient research attention. (Kuiken & Sikora, 1993, p. 424)

Kuiken's research initially identified four types of dreaming with distinct clusters of content: *existential dreams* (distressing, concerned with separation and personal integrity); *anxiety dreams* (frightening, concerned with threats to physical well-being); *transcendent dreams* (ecstatic, concerned with magical accomplishments); and *mundane dreams* (little emotion, unimpactful). His later study added a fifth class of moderately impactful dreams, *alienation dreams*, which express emotional agitation and concerns about interpersonal efficacy. Kuiken's findings raise further questions about the best ways to conceptualize the most prominent and recurrent patterns in these dreams. He points out that anxiety and existential dreams both have negative emotions but are very different in form and content, which means that the simple term "nightmare" is too general to use for both types. He further cautions against conflating transcendent and archetypal dreams ("the term 'archetypal' suggests questionable aspects of Jungian theory rather than reflecting these dreams' phenomenology" (Kuiken & Sikora, 1993, p. 116), and against using the presence of specific religious characters or images as a defining typological feature:

> For instance, the presence of a spiritual figure in an existential dream and the presence of a spiritual figure in a transcendent dream would force these dreams into the same category even though they differ dramatically in almost all other respects. (Kuiken & Sikora, 1993, p. 116)

Solms

Mark Solms has done pioneering work in the neuroanatomy of dreaming (Solms, 1997, 2000), which he has used as a foundation for a reconstructed psychoanalytic theory of the mind (Kaplan-Solms & Solms, 2000). Whatever the merits of his effort to revive Freud, Solms's work bears on our subject in at least three ways. First, he has provided additional evidence that REM neurophysiology is a mostly sufficient but not necessary trigger for the psychological experience of dreaming. His findings support a distributed, nonmodular view of brain-mind functioning:

> [C]omplex mental faculties such as reading and writing (and, we might add, dreaming) are not localized within circumscribed cortical centers. . . . [They] are subserved by complex functional systems or networks, which consist of constellations of cortical and subcortical structures working together in a concerted fashion. (Solms, 1997, pp. 47–48)

Second, he has identified a double dissociation between primary visual system and dreaming. The patients in his study with visual problems had normal dreaming, and the patients with nonvisual dreaming had normal visual abilities. Specifically, he found that brain areas V1 and V2, which are crucial for the processing of external visual signals, are not necessary for the generation and maintenance of normal dream imagery. Dreaming thus expresses an autonomous capacity for visionary experience that is independent of ordinary eyesight. Third, Solms has developed a clinical definition of "excessive dreaming" (anoneirognosis), a syndrome by which people experience intensely emotional and hyperrealistic dreams, often with unusual characters and other content features. Although Solms takes no interest in dream content, his clinical descriptions of the 10 patients who had this syndrome include reports of meeting deceased loved ones (pp. 185–186), visiting the "pearly gates" (p. 178), visiting a very beautiful place (p. 183), and having a black snake crawl into the dreamer's vagina (p. 192). Both in form and content, these anoneirognostic dreams are quite similar to historical and cross-cultural reports of big dreams. If Solms is right that frontal limbic lesions are the cause of this syndrome, this may be a key region of the brain to study in connection with the religiously oriented experience of big dreams.

Nielsen

From his earliest writings, Tore Nielsen (1991) has been investigating highly impactful dreams, and in his recent neuroscientific work on the relationship between REM and NREM he coined the term "apex dreaming," which he describes as follows:

> The term "apex" dreaming is adopted to refer to a subcategory of dreaming that is distinguished by exceptional vividness, intensity, or complexity. . . . Apex dreaming [is] the most vivid, intense, and complex forms of dreaming: e.g., nightmare, sexual, archetypal, transcendental, titanic, existential, lucid. (Nielsen, 2000, p. 853)

Nielsen calls for recognition of the potential of the dreaming process to achieve a special degree of intensity, cohesiveness, and impact. Related to that, he has studied cross-cultural frequencies of typical dreams (Nielsen et al., 2003) and found, for example, that 81 percent of 1,181 participants reported a chasing dream, 76.5 percent a dream of sexual experience, 48.3 percent a dream of flying, 48.3 percent a dream of vividly sensing a presence in the room, 38.4 percent a dream of someone dead becoming alive, 24.4 percent a dream of having superior knowledge or mental ability, 23.8 percent a dream of seeing oneself as dead, 12.3 percent a dream of traveling to another planet or universe, and 11.2 percent a dream of encountering God in some form. These findings add substance to Hunt's notion of the multiplicity of dreams, filling out our knowledge of recurrent patterns of dream content across differences of age, gender, and cultural background. What begins to take shape in Nielsen's research are the recurrent, pan-human patterns that naturally emerge in apex dreaming.

Knudson

Roger Knudson's work has focused on the dynamics of beauty, aesthetics, and narrative integrity in what he calls "highly significant dreams" (Knudson, 2001; Knudson & Minier, 1999). He has explored, using elegantly detailed case studies, the specific ways in which extraordinary dreams have shaped individuals' subsequent lives. Inspired in large part by James Hillman's focus on imagery and imagination in dreams, Knudson's case studies show that the *aesthetic power* of particularly vivid dream images often enables such long-lasting effects on waking consciousness: the "image, its life never pinned down, never literalized into a fixed concept or 'meaning,' remains an animating, enlivening presence in the psychic life of the dreamer" (Knudson & Minier, 1999, p. 244). Contrary to the common presumption that dreaming is inherently bizarre, disordered, and meaningless, Knudson illuminates the extraordinary aesthetic qualities of rare but impactful types of dreams. This reminds us that, among its many other capacities, the dreaming psyche has the ability to generate images of astonishing beauty, complexity, and creativity, and this has to be acknowledged in any study of highly memorable dreams.

Revonsuo

Antti Revonsuo's threat simulation theory (Revonsuo, 2000) takes its point of departure from the "story of origins" of the human mind proposed by contemporary evolutionary psychology. The basic mental abilities humans have today originally evolved approximately 200,000 years ago on the African savannah. To understand dreams, Revonsuo says, it is necessary to ask what adaptive function they might have served in the early ancestral environment of the human species. How did dreaming contribute to the survival of our ancestors? Revonsuo argues that dreams, particularly nightmarish chasing dreams, improved the ability of early humans to escape their predators. By simulating what it would feel like to be attacked, the dreams gave the individual an opportunity to envision, prepare, and rehearse an effective response should a similar attack occur in waking life. The early humans who experienced such dreams had a better chance of survival than those who didn't, and thus the threat-simulating propensity of dreaming was incorporated by natural selection into the innate mental machinery of our species.

Given the high incidence of intensely frightening chasing dreams documented by the research of Nielsen, Domhoff, Kuiken, and others, Revonsuo is right to focus special attention on this dream type. He is also right to seek an understanding of highly memorable dreams in relation to evolution and biology, and future research will hopefully look beyond threat-simulating dreams to other types of dreams simulating other evolutionarily significant dimensions of human experience. Revonsuo has plenty of critics (Pace-Schott,

Solms, Blagrove, & Harnad, 2003), but the basic phenomenon he describes is a central fact of human dream experience: we are, as a species, predisposed (particularly in childhood) to have recurrent, frighteningly realistic dreams of being attacked, most often by animals and male strangers. The tangible impact of dreaming on a person's waking consciousness is nowhere clearer than with this type of dream.

Summary

So what can we say, based on the best available psychological evidence, about the nature of dreams? At least this much: Dreams are highly variable in form and content, perhaps infinitely so, ranging from chaotically disordered and nonsensical to elegantly structured and meaning-rich (the chaotic dimensions of dreaming have been explored by Kahn & Hobson, 1993, and Kahn, Krippner, & Combs, 2000). For the most part, dreams are continuous with waking-life emotional concerns—we dream about the major worries, hopes, and desires of everyday life. The full range of emotions is experienced in dreams, though not every dream involves emotion, and most dreams include strong visual sensations. Some dreams generate sensations so intense and vivid that they feel indistinguishable from waking reality. Occasionally there are dramatic carry-over effects in body and emotion—people may wake up gasping, crying, laughing, or sexually climaxing. Some dreams involve "higher" mental functions such as metacognition, and some dreams include dramatic alterations of self-awareness, memory, and volition.

Several mappings of dream phenomenology have been offered, not all of them compatible with one another. In other writings I have discussed several elements that should be included in any such mapping: an appreciation for the metaphorical expressiveness of dreaming (Bulkeley, 1994, 1999); the earliest remembered dreams of childhood (Bulkeley, Broughton, Sanchez, & Stiller, 2005; Siegel & Bulkeley, 1998); the frequency of good fortunes in the content analysis of dreams (Bulkeley, in press); and the themes of reassurance, sexuality, evil, death, and "titanic" experience (Bulkeley, 2000). It is still too early to settle on one particular mapping of dream phenomenology, especially given the wealth of new information coming from both scientific psychology and religious studies. For now, the most we can say with confidence is that Jung's basic typological distinction between "little" and "big" dreams is valid (even if we prefer to use different terms, like "personal" and "intensified" or "mundane" and "impactful"). Most dreams portray ordinary daily concerns and activities, make little impact on waking consciousness, and are usually forgotten immediately. A minority of dreams involves a combination of vivid imagery, intense sensations, metacognition, and/or extraordinary occurrences; these dreams make a big impact on waking consciousness and are usually remembered for a long time afterward.

At this point we turn to religious studies research on dreams, with a special focus on the various roles dreams play in religious *origins*. The primary goal is to show that contemporary psychological research on "big" dreams is confirming what most religious and spiritual traditions through history have taught regarding the powerful potentials of dreaming. Although Western scientific psychology and the world's religious traditions use very different concepts and methods of investigation, their discoveries are converging on a vital truth about human nature.

RELIGIOUS STUDIES EVIDENCE ON DREAMING OF ORIGINS

A great deal of research has been done in recent years on the dream beliefs, practices, and experiences of various people around the world and in different periods of history (Covitz, 1990; Ewing, 1989; Gregor, 1981; Hermansen, 2001; Irwin, 1994, 2001; Jedrej & Shaw, 1992; Kelsey, 1991; Lama, 1997; Lamoreaux, 2002; Lohmann, 2003; Mageo, 2003; Miller, 1994; O'Flaherty, 1984; Ong, 1985; Patton, 2004; Shulman & Stroumsa, 1999; Stephen, 1979; Szpakowska, 2003; Tedlock, 1987; Young, 1999). This body of research is a crucial testing ground for psychological theories about the origins of dreaming. If the claims of contemporary researchers are accurate representations of universal human mental functioning, then evidence for their claims should be clearly evident in different historical eras and cultural contexts. Because religion is the primary language in which human communities have discussed their dreams, dream scientists have no choice but to engage in a serious, sustained dialogue with the history of religions.

This chapter can only offer a foretaste of that historical exploration. What follows are brief descriptions of a few major themes that are especially significant for future conversations between scientific and religious approaches to dreaming.

Shamanic Initiation and Vision Questing

Researchers working in widely varied contexts have found a close connection between dream experience and the visionary practices of shamans (ritual and healing specialists of hunter-gatherer communities) (Benedict, 1922; Eliade, 1964; Irwin, 1994; Lewis-Williams, 2002; Radin, 1936; Tedlock, 2005; Toffelmeir & Luomala, 1936; Wallace, 1958). Shamanic initiations are often prompted by unusual dream experiences, and the initiation process usually involves nightmarish torments that "kill" the old self and give birth to the new shamanic identity. David Lewis-Williams (2002) argues in *The Mind in the Cave* that shamanic dreaming and vision questing is a key to understanding the origins of the cultural and religious imagination of homo sapiens in the Upper Paleolithic period, as illustrated by the remarkable cave paintings of modern-day France and Spain. The shaman's abilities to interact with supernatural powers, journey to otherworldly realms, heal illness, and prophesize the future are all rooted in experiences of intensified dreaming. If it is fair to regard shamanism as one of the earliest religious practices of known human history, then dreaming has been intertwined with religion from the very beginning.

Dreaming the Origins of the World

Some traditions have creation myths in which the world was created in and through a process of dreaming. The best-known of these traditions is the "Dreamtime" of the Aboriginal Australians. They believe their ancestors dreamed the land into being. "Dreaming" in this context is equivalent to "creating," meaning a power to generate life, reality, and truth. Later generations of Australian Aborigines have believed they could reconnect with those spiritually powerful creative ancestors by means of their own dream experiences (not *all* dreams are believed to have spiritual significance, just a relatively rare few of them; Lohmann, 2003; Stephen, 1979; Tonkinson, 1970; Trompf, 1990). Another myth of dreaming and cosmogenesis comes from the Hindu tradition. A popular myth from the *Matsya Purana* features a sage who briefly realizes the world is actually a dream of a sleeping god:

> After Visnu had burnt the universe to ashes at doomsday and then flooded it with water, he slept in the midst of the cosmic ocean. The sage Markandeya had been swallowed by the god, and he roamed inside his belly for many thousands of years, visiting the sacred places on earth. One day he slipped out of the god's mouth and saw the world and the ocean shrouded in darkness. He did not recognize himself there, because of God's illusion, and he became terrified. Then he saw the sleeping god, and he was amazed, wondering, "Am I crazy, or dreaming? I must be imagining that the world has disappeared, for such a calamity could never really happen." Then he was swallowed again, and, as soon as he was back in the belly of the god, he thought his vision had been a dream. (O'Flaherty, 1984, p. 111)

The idea that the world is born of divine illusion is too frightening and bizarre for the sage to accept, and he reasonably concludes that he merely imagined the whole thing. This myth reflects a cultural familiarity with upsetting, disturbing, nightmarish types of dreaming, and it highlights the way such dreams can force waking consciousness to face tough questions and unsettling truths. (It also shows how waking consciousness has a tendency to *resist* those questions and truths.)

Dreaming of Divine Births

Many other traditions tell stories of divine births heralded by dreams. In the Book of Matthew in the Christian New Testament, it is revealed to Joseph in a dream that his soon-to-be wife Mary will give birth to God's own child:

> An angel of the Lord appeared to him in a dream, saying, "Joseph, son of David, do not fear to take Mary your wife, for that which is conceived in her is of the Holy Spirit; she will bear a son, and you shall call his name Jesus, for he will save his people from their sins." (Matt. 2: 20–21)

After the baby's birth, Joseph has several additional dreams in which God guides his family away from the dangerous King Herod and ultimately to the safety of the town of Nazareth. These passages in the Book of Matthew presuppose a cultural familiarity with the ideas that (1) dreaming is a legitimate source of divine revelation, particularly in regard to births and origins, and (2) dreaming can be a source of warning and guidance in times of danger. Whether Joseph actually had these dreams, the Gospel story reflects a widely shared understanding of these potentials of dreaming. Likewise, Buddhist traditions have long taught that the Buddha was conceived in a dream experienced by his mother, Queen Maya, in which she is touched on her stomach by the trunk of a white elephant (Young, 1999). A fascination with dreams and birth is also evident in Korean culture, where *tae mong* dreams are avidly sought and interpreted for indications of the future character, personality, and fortunes of an unborn child (Kang, 2003). All of this indicates that the widespread connection between birth and dreaming reflects, in a more personal and human sphere, the same insight that is expressed in the cosmogonic myths: a creative power is at work in dreaming that fundamentally animates our existence.

New Religious Movements

According to anthropologists and ethnographers, remarkable dream experiences have been at the center of various new religions and revitalization movements over the past few centuries. During this time, many indigenous populations have been rapidly conquered and colonized by Western powers, provoking severe crises for these people's religious and cultural traditions. In this context of conflict and disruption, certain people experience powerful dreams that become the emotional and imagistic touchstones for a new spiritual response to the present crisis. This basic process is evident among the "cargo cults" of Melanesia (Burridge, 1960; Lohmann, 2003), the spread of African Independent Churches through Africa (Charsley, 1973, 1987; Jedrej & Shaw, 1992), the dreamer religions of Native American groups

(Irwin, 1994; Trafzer & Beach, 1985; Wallace, 1969), the charismatic voodoo-Christian cults of the Caribbean (Bourguignon, 1954; Lanternari, 1975), and perhaps even the Taliban movement of contemporary Afghanistan (Edgar, 2004). In each case, a painful clash with the forces of modernization (i.e., capitalism, Christianity, Euro-American military dominance) becomes the occasion for an eruption of visionary power in dreams. How that visionary power is *used*, whether for peaceful or violent ends, is another matter (and one deserving more analysis than is possible here). For our limited purposes, the main point is that, again, dreaming is found at the origins—when old cultural traditions crumble in the face of severe external threats and dangers, new religious inspiration regularly strikes people in the form of highly memorable dreams.

Philosophical Wonder

The world's religious and cultural traditions have also looked to dreaming as the origin of what I call "philosophical wonder." In Plato's (1961) dialogue *Theaetetus*, the young man of that name is brought before Socrates, whose playfully skeptical questioning leads the youth to realize how little certainty he has in knowing whether he is awake or dreaming. Theaetetus says, "It is extraordinary how they [such epistemological puzzles] set me wondering whatever they can mean. Sometimes I get quite dizzy with thinking of them." Socrates replies, "This sense of wonder is the mark of a philosopher. Philosophy indeed has no other origin" (p. 860). To become a philosopher, one must *experience* the dizzying, decentering wonder that comes from contemplating the vivid alternative reality of dreaming. The classic Chinese version of this comes in Chuang Tzu's philosophical text *Ch'i-wu lun (Discussion on Making All Things Equal)*, in which he tells of Chuang Chou's butterfly dream:

> Once Chuang Chou dreamed he was a butterfly, a butterfly flitting and fluttering around, happy with himself and doing as he pleased. He didn't know he was Chuang Chou. Suddenly he woke up and there he was, solid and unmistakable Chuang Chou. But he didn't know if he was Chuang Chou who had dreamed he was a butterfly, or a butterfly dreaming he was Chuang Chou. (Ong, 1985, p. 78)

It is significant that Chuang Chou's dream self is a butterfly—a creature who flies, is beautiful, and experiences radical transformations of identity (from caterpillar through chrysalis to butterfly). These are hallmark qualities of highly significant dreams, in addition to the intense feeling of complete immersion in the dream world. And, as an example with direct consequences for modern Western civilization, this vivid sensation of the *realness* of dreaming prompted a philosophical awakening for René Descartes, who had a series of three extraordinary dreams early in his life that he interpreted as divine revelations showing him the future path he must follow in his life. These dreams represented a kind of secret origin to his philosophy, a well-hidden shamanic inspiration for "the father of modern thought" and his rationalist vision of the world. (One of Descartes's mottoes was, "He has lived well who has hidden well"; Rodis-Lewis, 1998, p. 216; see also Bulkeley, 2004).

Summary

These are only brief snapshots of religious beliefs and practices related to dreams, and much more detailed information is available in the texts by area experts cited. The findings of all these researchers, taken as a whole, reveal to us the outline of several basic patterns in human dreaming that correspond almost exactly to the findings of contemporary psychological science. First and foremost, *all* humans are capable of dreaming, and people of all varieties—men and women, children and adults, rich and poor, powerful and weak—have experienced highly memorable types of dreams. Every culture makes distinctions among different types of dreams: some dreams are attributed to bodily processes; others to residual thoughts and feelings from the day; and still others to the influence of spiritual beings, powers, and realities. Two dream qualities are especially prominent—the visual and the emotional. Most cultures emphasize the sense of sight in dreams; they speak of "seeing" dreams, and they connect dreaming at night to "visions" seen during the day. The strong emotional qualities of dreaming are also widely acknowledged, particularly the way dreams bring forth vibrant passions and desires, often of a taboo nature. Many religious functions have been attributed to dreams, such as anticipating the future, warning of danger, heralding new births, mourning deaths and other losses, envisioning sexual pleasure, healing illness, giving moral guidance, and providing divine reassurance in times of distress. Most religious, mythological, and philosophical theories of dreaming revolve around the paradox that dreaming is both passive and active, something people receive and create, something coming from outside and inside at the same time, something that is both intimately personal and awesomely transcendent. And most traditions have developed ritual practices to elicit positive, power-inducing dreams, part of a general effort to cultivate the natural potentials of dreaming according to conscious intentions.

CONCLUSION

With the findings of both scientific psychology and the history of religions, we gain a new perspective on the origins of dreaming and its significance in human life. From the former, we learn that dreaming emerges from a substrate of neural activity in the brain-mind system. From the latter, we learn that factors of religion, philosophy, and existential self-awareness always come into play in dreaming, wherever and whenever humans have lived. Physiological forces are definitely at work in dreaming, hard-wired into us by evolution, operating independently of conscious attention or volition. And just as definitely, spontaneous psychospiritual processes emerge in dreaming that stimulate, challenge, and expand people's self-awareness.

So what *is* the origin of dreaming? *Why do we dream?* The simple scientific answer is, we dream because we are creatures with brains that have naturally evolved to sleep on a regular, instinctively patterned basis. A more religiously inclined answer is we dream because we are spiritual beings whose imaginations allow us to roam far beyond the confines of the present world, envisioning alternative realities and future possibilities.

Science says we dream because we are human. It is our nature to dream. Religions say we are human because we dream. Dreaming is our nature.

Drawing on both of these perspectives, dreaming is best seen as *originating activity*. Dreaming is perhaps the most primordial of our creative abilities and a vital factor in both neurophysiological and spiritual development. Especially in its intensified, "apex" types of expression, dreaming has the effect of provoking greater consciousness by means of free imaginative play and heightened emotional sensitivity. The evidence from both science and religion clearly shows the long-lasting impact such dreams can have on people's waking lives.

This chapter began with the question, "what is the origin of dreaming?" In the conclusion, the answer is reflected back: *dreaming is about origins.*

I would go so far as to say dreaming is a kind of autochthonic process that shares a family resemblance to other chaotic, self-organizing phenomena, from neurogenesis to weather patterns to star formation. The mysterious origin of the universe in the Big Bang, the mysterious origin of life on Earth, the mysterious origin of the random genetic mutations that propel evolution, the mysterious origin of consciousness in an otherwise undistinguished species of primates, the mysterious origin of dreaming in each of our minds every night—these are all kindred phenomena, all processes that spontaneously generate new clusters of emergent order.

REFERENCES

Aserinsky, E., & Kleitman, N. (1953). Regularly occurring periods of eye motility, and concomitant phenomena, during sleep. *Science, 118,* 273–274.

Aserinsky, E., & Kleitman, N. (1955). Two types of ocular motility occurring in sleep. *Journal of Applied Physiology, 8,* 1–10.

Aserinsky, E., Lynch, J. A., Mack, M., Tzankoff, S. P., & Hurn, E. (1985). Comparison of eye motion in wakefulness and REM sleep. *Psychophysiology, 22*(1), 1–10.

Benedict, R. (1922). The vision in plains culture. *American Anthropologist, 24*(1), 1–23.

Bogzaran, F., & Deslauriers, D. (2004). *Integral dreaming.* Paper presented at International Association for the Study of Dreams, Copenhagen, Denmark.

Bourguignon, E. E. (1954). Dreams and dream interpretation in Haiti. *American Anthropologist, 56*(2), 262–268.

Bulkeley, K. (1994). *The wilderness of dreams: Exploring the religious meanings of dreams in modern Western culture.* Albany: State University of New York Press.

Bulkeley, K. (1999). *Visions of the night: Dreams, religion, and psychology.* Albany: State University of New York Press.

Bulkeley, K. (2000). *Transforming dreams.* New York: Wiley.

Bulkeley, K. (2004). *The wondering brain: Thinking about religion with and beyond cognitive neuroscience.* New York: Routledge.

Bulkeley, K. (in press). Revision of the Good Fortune Scale: A new tool for the study of "big dreams." *Dreaming.*

Bulkeley, K., Broughton, B., Sanchez, A., & Stiller, J. (2005). Earliest remembered dreams. *Dreaming, 15*(3), 205–222.

Burridge, K. (1960). *Mambu: A Melanesian millenium.* London: Methuen.

Busink, R., & Kuiken, D. (1995). Identifying types of impactful dreams: A replication. *Dreaming, 6*(2), 97–119.

Cartwright, R., & Lamberg, L. (1992). *Crisis dreaming.* New York: Harper Collins.

Charsley, S. R. (1973). Dreams in an independent African church. *Africa: Journal of the International African Institute, 43*(3), 244–257.

Charsley, S. R. (1987). Dreams and purposes: An analysis of dream narratives in an independent African church. *Africa: Journal of the International African Institute, 57*(3), 281–296.

Covitz, J. (1990). *Visions of the night: A study of Jewish dream interpretation.* Boston: Shambhala.

Dement, W. (1972). *Some must watch while some must sleep: Exploring the world of sleep.* New York: Norton.

Domhoff, W. G. (1996). *Finding meaning in dreams: A quantitative approach.* New York: Plenum Press.

Domhoff, W. G. (2003). *The scientific study of dreams: Neural networks, cognitive development, and content analysis.* Washington, DC: American Psychological Association.

Edgar, I. R. (2004). The dream will tell: Militant Muslim dreaming in the context of traditional and contemporary Islamic dream theory and practice. *Dreaming, 14*(1), 21–29.

Eliade, M. (1964). *Shamanism: Archaic techniques of ecstasy* (W. R. Trask, Trans.). Princeton, NJ: Princeton University Press.

Ewing, K. (1989). The dream of spiritual initiation and the organization of self representations among Pakistani Sufis. *American Ethnologist, 16,* 56–74.

Fisher, C. (1966). Dreaming and sexuality. In R. Loewenstein, L. Newman, M. Schur, & A. Solnit (Eds.), *Psychoanalysis: A general psychology* (pp. 537–569). New York: International Universities Press.

Foulkes, D. (1962). Dream reports from different states of sleep. *Journal of Abnormal and Social Psychology, 65,* 14–25.

Freud, S. (1965). *The interpretation of dreams* (J. Strachey, Trans.). New York: Avon Books.

Gackenbach, J. (1991). Frameworks for understanding lucid dreaming: A review. *Dreaming, 1*(2), 109–128.

Gackenbach, J., & LaBerge, S. (Eds.). (1988). *Conscious mind, sleeping brain: Perspectives on lucid dreaming.* New York: Plenum Press.

Gregor, T. (1981). "Far, far away my shadow wandered. . . .": The dream symbolism and dream theories of the Mehinaku Indians of Brazil. *American Ethnologist, 8*(4), 709–729.

Hall, C. (1966). *The meaning of dreams.* New York: McGraw Hill.

Hall, C. (1984). A ubiquitous sex difference in dreams, revisited. *Journal of Personality and Social Psychology, 46,* 1109–1117.

Hall, C., & Van de Castle, R. (1966). *The content analysis of dreams.* New York: Appleton-Century-Crofts.

Hermansen, M. (2001). Dreams and dreaming in Islam. In K. Bulkeley (Ed.), *Dreams: A reader on the religious, cultural, and psychological dimensions of dreaming* (pp. 73–92). New York: Palgrave.

Hunt, H. (1989). *The multiplicity of dreams: Memory, imagination, and consciousness.* New Haven, CT: Yale University Press.

Hursch, C., Karacan, I., & Williams, R. (1972). Some characteristics of nocturnal penile tumescence in early middle-aged males. *Comprehensive Psychiatry, 13,* 539–548.

Irwin, L. (1994). *The dream seekers: Native American visionary traditions of the Great Plains.* Norman: University of Oklahoma Press.

Irwin, L. (2001). Sending a voice, seeking a place: Visionary traditions among native women of the Plains. In K. Bulkeley (Ed.), *Dreams: A reader on the religious, cultural, and psychological dimensions of dreaming* (pp. 93–110). New York: Palgrave.

Jacobs, L., Feldman, M., & Bender, M. (1970). The pattern of human eye movements during sleep. *Transactions of the American Neurological Association, 95,* 114–119.

Jacobs, J.L., Feldman, M., & Bender, M. (1972). Are the eye movements of dreaming sleep related to the visual images of dreams? *Psychophysiology, 9,* 393–401.

Jedrej, M.C., & Shaw, R. (Eds.). (1992). *Dreaming, religion, and society in Africa.* Leiden, The Netherlands: E.J. Brill.

Jung, C.G. (1965). *Memories, dreams, reflections* (R. Winston & C. Winston, Trans.). New York: Vintage Books.

Jung, C.G. (1968). *Man and his symbols.* New York: Dell.

Jung, C.G. (1974). On the nature of dreams. In *Dreams.* Princeton, NJ: Princeton University Press. (Original work published 1948)

Jung, C.G. (1980). *The archetypes and the collective unconscious* (R.F.C. Hull, Trans.). Princeton, NJ: Princeton University Press.

Kahan, T.L. (2000). The "problem" of dreaming in NREM sleep continues to challenge reductionist (2-Gen) models of dream generation (commentary). *Behavioral and Brain Sciences, 23*(6), 956–958.

Kahan, T.L. (2001). Consciousness in dreaming: A metacognitive approach. In K. Bulkeley (Ed.), *Dreams: A reader on the religious, cultural, and psychological dimensions of dreaming* (pp. 333–360). New York: Palgrave.

Kahan, T.L., & LaBerge, S. (1994). Lucid dreaming as metacognition: Implications for cognitive science. *Consciousness and Cognition, 3,* 246–264.

Kahan, T. L., LaBerge, S., Levitan, L., & Zimbardo, P. (1997). Similarities and differences between dreaming and waking cognition: An exploratory study. *Consciousness and Cognition, 6,* 132–147.

Kahn, D., & Hobson, J. A. (1993). Self-organization theory and dreaming. *Dreaming, 3*(3), 151–178.

Kahn, D., Krippner, S., & Combs, A. (2000). Dreaming and the self-organizing brain. *Journal of Consciousness Studies, 7*(7), 4–11.

Kang, H. (2003). *Taemong: Korean birth dreams.* Master's thesis, Graduate Theological Union, Berkeley, CA.

Kaplan-Solms, K., & Solms, M. (2000). *Clinical studies in neuro-psychoanalysis: Introduction to a depth neuropsychology.* Madison, CT: International Universities Press.

Kelsey, M. (1991). *God, dreams, and revelation: A Christian interpretation of dreams.* Minneapolis, MN: Augsburg.

Knudson, R. (2001). Significant dreams: Bizarre or beautiful? *Dreaming, 11*(4), 167–178.

Knudson, R., & Minier, S. (1999). The on-going significance of significant dreams: The case of the bodiless head. *Dreaming, 9*(4), 235–246.

Krippner, S., Bogzaran, F., & de Carvalho, A. P. (2002). *Extraordinary dreams and how to work with them.* Albany: State University of New York Press.

Kuiken, D., & Sikora, S. (1993). The impact of dreams on waking thoughts and feelings. In A. Moffitt, M. Kramer, & R. Hoffmann (Eds.), *The functions of dreaming* (pp. 419–476). Albany: State University of New York Press.

Lama, The Dalai. (1997). *Sleeping, dreaming, and dying.* Boston: Wisdom.

Lamoreaux, J. C. (2002). *The early Muslim tradition of dream interpretation.* Albany: State University of New York Press.

Lanternari, V. (1975). Dreams as charismatic significants: Their bearing on the rise of new religious movements. In T. R. Williams (Ed.), *Psychological anthropology* (pp. 221–235). Paris: Mouton.

Lewis-Williams, D. (2002). *The mind in the cave.* London: Thames and Hudson.

Lohmann, Roger (Ed.). (2003). *Dream travelers: Sleep experiences and culture in the South Pacific.* New York: Palgrave Macmillan.

Mageo, J. M. (Ed.). (2003). *Dreaming and the self: New perspectives on subjectivity, identity, and emotion.* Albany: State University of New York Press.

Miller, P. C. (1994). *Dreams in late antiquity: Studies in the imagination of a culture.* Princeton, NJ: Princeton University Press.

Moskowitz, E., & Berger, R. J. (1969). Rapid eye movements and dream imagery: Are they related? *Nature, 224,* 613–614.

Nielsen, T. A. (1991). Reality dreams and their effects on spiritual belief: A revision of animism theory. In J. Gackenbach & A. A. Sheikh (Eds.), *Dream images: A call to mental arms* (pp. 233–264). Amityville, NY: Baywood.

Nielsen, T. (2000). Cognition in REM and NREM sleep: A review and possible reconciliation of two models of sleep mentation. *Behavioral and Brain Sciences, 23*(6), 851–866.

Nielsen, T., Zadra, A., Simard, V., Saucier, S., Stenstrom, P., Smith, C., et al. (2003). The typical dreams of Canadian university students. *Dreaming, 13*(4), 211–235.

O'Flaherty, W. D. (1984). *Dreams, illusion, and other realities.* Chicago: University of Chicago Press.

Ong, R. K. (1985). *The interpretation of dreams in ancient China.* Bochum, Germany: Studienverlag Brockmeyer.

Pace-Schott, E., Solms, M., Blagrove, M., & Harnad, S. (Eds.). (2003). *Sleep and dreaming: Scientific advances and reconsiderations.* Cambridge, England: Cambridge University Press.

Pagel, J. F. (2000). Dreaming is *not* a non-conscious electrophysiological state. *Behavioral and Brain Sciences, 23*(6), 984–988.

Patton, K. (2004). Dream incubation: Theology and topography. *History of Religions, 43*(3), 194–223.

Plato. (1961). Theaetetus. In E. Hamilton & H. Cairns (Eds.), *Plato: Collected dialogues.* Princeton, NJ: Princeton University Press.

Radin, P. (1936). Ojibwa and Ottawa puberty dreams. In R. H. Lowie (Ed.), *Essays in anthropology presented to A. L. Kroeber* (pp. 233–264). Berkeley: University of California Press.

Revonsuo, A. (2000). The reinterpretation of dreams: An evolutionary hypothesis of the function of dreaming. *Behavioral and Brain Sciences, 23*(6), 877–901.

Rodis-Lewis, G. (1998). *Descartes: His life and thought* (J. M. Todd, Trans.). Ithaca, NY: Cornell University Press.

Roffwarg, H., Dement, W., Muzio, J., & Fisher, C. (1962). Dream imagery: Relationship to rapid eye movements of sleep. *Archives of General Psychiatry, 7,* 235–238.

Shafton, A. (1995). *Dream reader.* Albany: State University of New York Press.

Shulman, D., & Stroumsa, D. (Eds.). (1999). *Dream cultures: Explorations in the comparative history of dreaming.* New York: Oxford University Press.

Siegel, A., & Bulkeley, K. (1998). *Dreamingcatching: Every parent's guide to exploring and understanding children's dreams and nightmares.* New York: Three Rivers Press.

Solms, M. (1997). *The neuropsychology of dreams: A clinico-anatomical study.* Mahwah, NJ: Erlbaum.

Solms, M. (2000). Dreaming and REM sleep are controlled by different brain mechanisms. *Behavioral and Brain Sciences, 23*(6), 843–850.

Stephen, M. (1979). Dreams of change: The innovative role of altered states of consciousness in traditional Melanesian religion. *Oceania, 50*(1), 3–22.

Szpakowska, K. (2003). *Behind closed eyes: Dreams and nightmares in ancient Egypt.* Swansea, England: Classical Press of Wales.

Tedlock, B. (2005). *The woman in the shaman's body: Reclaiming the feminine in religion and medicine.* New York: Bantam Books.

Tedlock, B. (Ed.). (1987). *Dreaming: Anthropological and psychological interpretations.* New York: Cambridge University Press.

Toffelmeir, G., & Luomala, K. (1936). Dreams and dream interpretation of the Diegueno Indians of Southern California. *Psychoanalytic Quarterly, 5,* 195–225.

Tonkinson, R. (1970). Aboriginal dream-spirit beliefs in a contact situation: Jigalong, Western Australia. In R. M. Berndt (Ed.), *Australian Aboriginal anthropology* (pp. 277–291). Sydney: University of Western Australia Press.

Trafzer, C. E., & Beach, M. A. (1985). Smohalla, the Washani, and religion as a factor in Northwestern Indian history. *American Indian Quarterly, 9*(3), 309–324.

Trompf, G. W. (1990). *Melanesian religion.* Cambridge, England: Cambridge University Press.

Van de Castle, R. (1994). *Our dreaming mind.* New York: Ballantine Books.

Wallace, A. F. C. (1958). Dreams and wishes of the soul: A type of psychoanalytic theory among the seventeenth century Iroquois. *American Anthropologist, 60,* 234–248.

Wallace, A. F. C. (1969). *The death and rebirth of the Seneca.* New York: Vintage Books.

Witkin, H. A., & Lewis, H. B. (1967). Presleep experiences and dreams. In H. A. Witkin & H. B. Lewis (Eds.), *Experimental studies of dreaming* (pp. 148–201). New York: Random House.

Young, S. (1999). *Dreaming in the lotus: Buddhist dream narrative, imagery, and practice.* Boston: Wisdom.

CHAPTER 10

CHEMICAL INPUT, RELIGIOUS OUTPUT—ENTHEOGENS: A PHARMATHEOLOGY SAMPLER

Thomas B. Roberts

THE HIDDEN SPIRITUAL CONTINENT

Although she was writing in 1963, today we can apply Mary Barnard's comments on "drug plants" to religion and entheogens just as aptly as when she wrote her prescient words about mythologies and cults more than 40 years ago (1963/1966):

> [W]hich, after all, was more likely to happen first: the spontaneously generated idea of an afterlife in which the disembodied soul, liberated from the restrictions of time and space, experiences eternal bliss, or the accidental discovery of hallucinogenic plants that give a sense of euphoria, dislocate the center of consciousness, and distort time and space, making them balloon outward in greatly expanded vistas? . . . [T]he drug plants were there, waiting to give men a new idea based on a new experience. The experience might have had, I should think, an almost explosive effect on the largely dormant minds of men, causing them to think of things they had never thought of before. (pp. 21–22)

Today we would call Barnard's drug plants *entheogens* and name her field of study *pharmatheology.* Because the word *psychedelic* became encrusted with connotations of wild hippies, bright colors, visual distortion, and socially undesirable people and events, in 1979, Carl A. P. Ruck and others coined the word *entheogen* as a less negatively loaded substitute for *psychedelic.* With this change, the emphasis switched from "mind clearing, giving a clear view of the mind" to "generating the experience of god."

In 1995, the Right Rev. Aline Lucas-Caldwell coined and defined *entheology* (2001). I admire her definition so much, I adopt it as the definition of *pharmatheology* too; thus, they are synonyms:

> Entheology is that branch of theology which deals with the experience and/or knowledge of the divine, and of the revelation of the divine, through the agency of psychoactive substances (used as sacraments), be it a revelation of the divine within and/or without. (p. 147)

To this I would include the complementary influences of culture, language, beliefs, social context, and personality as they influence these experiences.

I prefer *pharmatheology* because it is a closer parallel to *neurotheology*, making it an easier fit into the existing idiom of medicine and biological sciences. Although the word *pharmacotheology* exists and is etymologically purer, the shorter *pharmatheology* is easier to say and sounds better to the ear. Like the *psychodelic* versus *psychedelic* tug-of-war between euphony and etymology, to me euphony wins. Others may have already coined *pharmatheology*, but this is the first published instance I know of. Whatever word is used, Bernard's point is well taken. In fact, it is stronger now that we have over 40 years of additional information to support her speculations.

The most accessible introductions to pharmatheology for general, educated nonscientific readers are *Entheogens and the Future of Religion* (Forte, 1997), *Cleansing the Doors of Perception* (Smith, 2000), *Psychoactive Sacramentals* (Roberts, 2001), Entheology.org (2005), and *Higher Wisdom* (Walsh & Grob, 2005). My syllabus designed for a possible course called *Entheogens—Sacramentals or Sacrilege?* (Roberts, 2005) lists over two dozen more books and numerous articles. The online reference *Religion and Psychoactive Sacraments* (Roberts & Hruby, 1995–2003) contains excerpts from over 550 books, dissertations, and topical issues of journals as well as extended bibliographic information.

This chapter collects some specimens of pharmatheology and considers the explosive effects entheogens are having on our ideas about religion, including—but not limited to—brain-religion studies. The chapter describes entheogen-derived ideas from some of the major scholars in the field and some of my own leanings on these topics. The expanding interest in entheogens is embedded in the larger intellectual context of multistate mind-body studies. Entheogens recast existing questions for churches and society while giving birth to entirely new ones. The chapter raises over 150 questions that deserve to become part of a program of sustained, systematic entheogenic inquiry into religion.

Most remarkably, entheogens make it possible to address both scientific and humanistic religious studies with experiments. I expect this experimentation will expand our knowledge of religion several fold, possibly even by several powers. On the face of it, this seems unlikely, a brash assertion, even absurd. How could entheogens promise this? This chapter explains some of entheogens' leads. And what are entheogens, anyway?

An entheogen is a psychoactive plant or chemical used in a spiritual context. The best known example is peyote as used by the Native American Church. Other examples are LSD, mescaline, psilocybin, marijuana, ecstasy, ayahuasca, and a host of other substances. Most of these plants and chemicals also have nonentheogenic uses such as medicine, psychotherapy, creativity, or problem solving, but this chapter focuses only on their entheogenic effects. Legal or illegal, accepted or taboo, it is the religious or spiritual context and/ or effect that qualifies something as an entheogen; not its chemical structure or governmental scheduling. It is common for someone to take a psychoactive without a spiritual intention but still have a spiritual experience, and these unintended spiritual encounters qualify as entheogenic too.

The chemical structure of many entheogens is similar to serotonin's. Serotonin is a neurotransmitter, one of the chemicals that nerve cells use to communicate with each other (and also found in the blood). As some of the earlier chapters in this series discuss, it is active in religious experiences. So experimenters could design religious experiments that use like-structured entheogens as close substitutes for serotonin. A whole research specialty might study the similarities and differences between entheogenic religious experiences and naturally occurring ones.

Sometimes, as with internationally renowned philosopher of religion Huston Smith's first mescaline experience, one's theological assumptions become manifest and confirmed (Smith, 2001). For others, the opposite happens; for the world's leading researcher on the clinical uses of psychedelics, Stanislav Grof (2001), his previous atheistic religious assumptions underwent a "180-degree turn" (p. 27). The idea of "god within"—more exactly, a subjective experience that might be interpreted as "god within"—often becomes more credible to entheogen questers and may occur to people who were previously unfamiliar with the idea.

In one of the hottest leads in neurotheology and pharmatheology, Grof (1975/1993) reports:

> In my experience, everyone who has reached these [perinatal] levels develops convincing insights into the utmost relevance of the spiritual and religious dimensions in the universal scheme of things. Even hard-core materialists, skeptics and cynics, and uncompromising atheists and antireligious crusaders such as Marxist philosophers suddenly became interested in a spiritual search after they confronted these levels in themselves. (pp. 95–96)

Grof is widely considered the world's leading expert on clinical psychedelic psychotherapy, and from a religious point of view his work is especially significant because the 5,400-plus sessions he has guided or whose clinical reports he has read have lead him to discover a transpersonal, or spiritual, part of our minds. Contrary to his philosophical and psychiatric expectations, while exploring the perinatal and transpersonal levels of their minds, his patients experienced basic religious phenomena such as the physiological process of being born again, religious symbols and concepts alien to their cultures, and ego transcendence. According to Grof, the birth process (perinatal level) includes an Edenic womb, Hellish entrapment, cosmic struggle, ego death, and rebirth. Do these presage parallel religious experiences? Must one experience ego death and rebirth to enter the kingdom of heaven? Mystical experiences include giving up the ego and being born into a new, fresher existence. Could we have stumbled onto a way to conduct entheogenic born-again experiments? The perinatal level is an almost untouched continent for brain-religion-psychology studies.

Are Grof's clinical findings replicable? What do they portend about universal and folk ideas about religion? Are cross-cultural similarities expressions of activated circuits in our brains? Do these circuits have their origin in the birth process? Do constants emerge across cultures and religions? More puzzling yet, what if they do? How are we to understand this? Are these questions now open to experimental confirmation or disconfirmation?

Might babies have genetic programs waiting to be activated by the stresses of the birth process, with a set of standard variations that show up as temperaments? Possibly related to this, two researchers at Vanderbilt University's Department of Pharmacology found that LSD influences gene expression in rat brains. Nichols and Sanders-Bush (2002) reported: "We have identified a number of genes that are predicted to be involved in the process of synaptic plasticity" (p. 635). Is this a clue to a mechanism involved when Grof's patients relived their birth traumas and recovered perinatal memories during deep, LSD-assisted psychotherapy? Is the religious phrase "born again" more psychophysiological than it is usually given credit for?

Michael Winkelman, a professor of anthropology at Arizona State University and a founder of the Society for the Anthropology of Consciousness (www.sacaaa.org), coined the word *psychointegrator* (2001) to draw attention to the fact that these substances integrate brain functions and help people through the psychotherapeutic process of integration. By integrating neural, sensory, and cognitive processes, psychointegrators (psychedelics) allow "the enhancement of access to deeper cognitive structures," and deeper cognitive structures may be at the root of religious cognition. His "neurophenomenological framework" (Winkelman, 2000, p. 27) links biology with subjective experience. He summarizes:

> The paleomammalian brain manages processes associated with self, identity, species survival, family and social relations, learning and memory, and sexual

and aggressive emotions as well as their behavioral integration. Entheogens (and [altered states of consciousness] in general) enhance systematic integration of the psyche by producing heightened arousal and awareness, and by interfering with habituated behavioral routines. The paleomammalian brain and limbic system provide the social and emotional mentation and behavior. These fundamental cognitive processes involve nonverbal communication and, forms of mental and social representation that manage the processes of emotional and social life. (Winkelman, 2002, pp. 56–57)

Marvelous neurotheological experiments could be done using as subjects people with various cultural, political, social, and religious backgrounds to see what changes, if any, would appear after having intense perinatal and/or mystical experiences. As Barnard implies in the epigraph to this chapter, entheogens may cause us to rethink our understandings of brain, religion, and psychology. Indeed, they are doing so now. And entheogens make it possible to examine these questions and assumptions experimentally.

Religion *Is* about Something

I find it helpful to distinguish two types of religious experiences. The first take place during egoic states, when we identify with our usual individual being (i.e., when I am Tom Roberts having an experience). A second type occurs when we have non-self experiences (i.e., when my identity as Tom Roberts is away on vacation, and I experience the transpersonal part of my mind). Barnard's "rethinking" happened for me as I came upon mystical experiences unexpectedly. Rather than a sudden conversion, my interest in entheogens and religion grew slowly from a blend of entheogen-derived mystical experiences over many years and reading about them over several decades. This chapter focuses on transpersonal entheogenic experiences.

The Mystical Door to Religion

To my surprise, I came to take religion seriously, not as a believer in one or another creed but when I realized: Religion *is* about something, and that something is mystical experiences. Like other experiences, mystical experiences are subjective events, but also ones that can be studied empirically. Given the experience, though, the real problem is what to make of them. And this is one place neurotheology studies can shed some light. This section briefly considers mystical experiences. The chapters in this series by Hood and by Azari discuss mystical experiences more thoroughly. After a quick scan of mystical experiences, I frame some questions for future neurotheological researchers under three categories: sciences, humanities, and church and polity.

First, why are mystical experiences so important, so overwhelmingly influential? Wilson Van Dusen (1961), who was chief clinical psychologist at Mendocino State Hospital in California at the time he wrote this, explains:

> There is a central human experience which alters all other experiences. It has been called satori in Japanese Zen, moksha in Hinduism, religious enlightenment or cosmic consciousness in the West. The experience is so central that men have spent their lives in search of it. Once found life is altered because the very root of human identity is deepened. I wish to draw attention to the fact that the still experimental drug . . . (LSD) appears to facilitate the discovery of this apparently ancient and universal experience. Many ways have been taken to enlightenment. Now I draw your attention to a relatively new way. (p. 11)

Imagine what it would mean for our understanding of this aspect of religion if these experiences could be more or less reliably stimulated (or simulated) in experimental conditions.

In 1994, I connected the Chicago Theological Seminary with the Council on Spiritual Practices (CSP), and in February of 1995 we co-sponsored a small invitational conference-retreat on entheogens. To help establish a common background for attendees and to satisfy my own curiosity, I compiled a bibliography of books, dissertations, and topical issues of journals about entheogens and included excerpts. The CSP collected my findings at its Web site *Religion and Psychoactive Sacraments: An Entheogen Chrestomathy* (www.csp.org/chrestomathy). A chrestomathy is a collection of short writings on a topic, similar to an anthology, but characteristically with brief excerpts rather than complete writings. The interdisciplinary nature of entheogenic studies lends itself not only to a common topic that a menagerie of disciplines can contribute to, but also to new avenues for scholarly and experimental studies. At the time, I naively thought it would be a simple job of collecting a couple dozen entries; in 2002, I stopped the chrestomathy project at over 550 entries, and I have a folder with about 100 more to add in that vague future of good intentions.

Thanks to entheogens, it is possible to design experiments that examine how various religious beliefs become more (or less) credible to people who have had entheogenic mystical experiences. Entheogens link chemicals, brain, and religious cognition in an experimental theology.

What are mystical experiences? What roles do they play in spiritual development, religion, and religious studies? What are entheogens, and how do they contribute to our understanding of these topics? What happens when entheogens, the brain sciences, and religious studies are hybridized? Since my first LSD-based mystical experiences about 35 years ago, these questions have guided me beyond seeing religion as a mere accretion of social and historical constructions to a rich collection of ideas across the spectrum of academic fields. As with most research, every finding generates more questions than it answers.

First, it is important to distinguish the way the word *mystical* is used in common language from the way it is used in religion. In common language, mystical connotes esoteric, occult, irrational, strange phenomena, and other odd, ghostly thoughts. In the psychology of religion, however, mystical denotes a specific kind of experience (or group of similar experiences), as Hood's chapters portray. Like many terms in philosophy, there are disagreements over mysticism's best definition but general agreement on the central family of experiences that compose it.

Primary Religious Experience

People who take an experience-based, mystical stance toward religion and spiritual development consider these experiences to be religion's foundation in two senses: foundation in the sense of founding or origin and foundation the sense of a building's solid foundation on which a structure is built. Thus, the phrase *primary religious experience* (PRE) is a synonym for *mystical experience*. To an increasing number of both religious mystics and secular skeptics, entheogens provide ways to experimentally study the links between the brain sciences, anthropology, psychology, and religious studies.

Several primary religious experiences are newly open to experimentation thanks to entheogens. Following the line of conceptual development from James (1902) through Stace (1961) to Pahnke (1963), Hood (1975), and Hood, Morris, and Watson (1993), Hruby (2001) lists nine typical subjective experiences that comprise mystical experiences. This list changes somewhat from instance to instance and is an ideal model, so any particular mystical experience will vary from this perfect specimen. The important point is, thanks to entheogens, we can study these experiences and the questions that stem from them experimentally. The nine experiences are unity, transcendence of time and space, deeply felt positive mood, sense of sacredness, objectivity and reality, paradoxicality, alleged ineffability, transience, and persisting positive changes in attitudes and behavior.

I had a hard time remembering the nine types of mystical experiences, so I gave my Psychedelic Mindview class in the honors program at Northern Illinois University the task of coming up with a mnemonic device. Keeping in mind that all the qualities need to be included but that their order is not important, they came up with POTT MUSIC:

Paradoxicality—opposites seem true

Objectivity—noetic quality

Transcendence—of time and/or space

Transience—limited duration

Mood—deeply felt positive mood

Unity—"All is one," egolessness

Sacredness—divine presence, holiness

Ineffability—impossible to explain

Change in behavior—serving humanity, cosmic values

These are subjective experiences seen through language and flavored by culture, so they may not imply an objective reality—although many people feel they do and have had their lives changed because of them. Depending on one's assumptions, qualities such as sacredness and unity are open to various interpretations, and this is where the exegetical fun begins.

Entheogenic approaches to religious studies build on the assumption (some would say observation) that mystical experiences were an experiential, historical origin of religion (as Barnard stated) and a constant though uncommon source of nourishment through the ages. Today, entheogens make PREs more accessible. As with other spiritual disciplines, entheogens can—but do not always—produce mystical experiences. By providing a useful mindset in the subjects and a supportive environment, researchers can increase the likelihood of such intense spiritual experiences.

Religions also have social, cultural, historical, philosophical, and theological input, but from a mystical perspective, primary religious experiences are the soil from which religion springs:

> Indeed, isn't religion, above all—before it is doctrine and morality, rites and institutions—*religious experience*. Under the influence of Protestant theologian Friedrich Schleiermacher in nineteenth century Europe and philosopher-psychologist William James in early twentieth-century America, many Westerners have come out in support of the priority of religious experience. And isn't religious experience in its highest form *mystical experience*, as in India, where it seems more at home than anywhere else? (Küng, Ess, von Stietencron, & Bechert, 1986, p. 168)

Entheogens provide a way to test this question experimentally. From this perspective, today's theology and beliefs, liturgy and rites, social concerns and moral action, and religious organizations all have some of their roots (not all of their roots) in primary religious experience (see Figure 10.1 for an illustration of this relationship).

Cultivating the Entheogenic Root

Beginning with the hypothesis that the core of religious experience is its mystical taproot, how do we cultivate this root? As the other volumes in this

Figure 10.1   Primary Religious Experience (PRE) as the Taproot of Religion

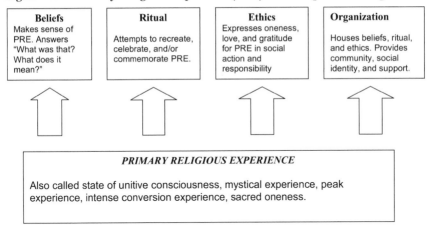

| **Beliefs**
Makes sense of PRE. Answers "What was that? What does it mean?" | **Ritual**
Attempts to recreate, celebrate, and/or commemorate PRE. | **Ethics**
Expresses oneness, love, and gratitude for PRE in social action and responsibility | **Organization**
Houses beliefs, ritual, and ethics. Provides community, social identity, and support. |

PRIMARY RELIGIOUS EXPERIENCE

Also called state of unitive consciousness, mystical experience, peak experience, intense conversion experience, sacred oneness.

series and the chapters in this book show, the brain sciences can contribute to our knowledge by documenting what entheogens and other mind-body psychotechnologies do to our nervous and hormonal systems. What are the brain, hormonal, and cognitive correlates of people who are having these experiences? Here is a rich vein to pursue, and many of the other chapters in this set of three books illustrate the inspiring indications and insightful nuggets leading to this vein. Largely missing, though, are studies that use entheogens to move from simple descriptions to experimental treatments. This lack is partly collateral damage from the war on drugs and partly because of theological disputes over whether entheogen-occasioned sacred experiences are genuine or misleading.

With natural, plant-derived entheogens and laboratory-synthesized entheogens, it is possible to develop what Smith (2000) called "empirical meta-physics" (pp. 9–13). These leads provide independent variables in the sciences and ways to develop experimental humanities. Most interestingly, entheogens can provide ways to bridge the mind-body gap experimentally by using these chemicals as independent treatments and humanistic variables as dependent ones. That is, it is possible to give an entheogen, map where it is active in the body, and chart changes in religious beliefs, values, and cognitions.

QUESTIONS AND TOPICS FOR THE SCIENCES

With the cautious acceptance of medical psychedelic research by the U.S. Food and Drug Administration (Kurtzweil, 1995), with exploratory medical research awakening (Horgan, 2005), and with scientific publications reviewing these leads (Nichols, 2004), we can look forward to updated information on mystical experiences, not yet as the major hypothesis, but as adjunct findings to medical and scientific research. After decades of prohibition, new studies using psychedelics' healing prospects have recommenced (Roberts and Winkelman, in press). It will probably be some time before the FDA and other government agencies permit religious entheogenic research, and correlations among the characteristics of entheogenic peak experiences, spontaneous remission, spiritual cognition, and our immune systems will likely draw them to it (Roberts, 2006; Roberts & Hruby, 1996). Other countries may scoop the United States in this area.

Before pointing to some good leads for future pharmatheological research, to the implications for the humanities (even for founding experimental humanities), and some implications for churches and polity, it is worth noting that psychedelics have—unbeknownst to most biologists—already greatly benefited the biological sciences. In his plenary address to the Serotonin Club, David E. Nichols, a professor of medicinal chemistry and molecular biology in the School of Pharmacy and Pharmacal Sciences at Purdue University, said: "Let me start off by suggesting that a significant number of the people in this room tonight and indeed a significant percentage of serotonin researchers worldwide first gained their interest in serotonin through some association with psychedelic agents" (Nichols, 1999–2000). Serotonin, LSD, and many psychedelics share the indole chemical structure: the so-called God spot (Connor, 1997) is also a serotonin spot.

In addition to lighting scientific curiosity about neurotransmitters and positing topics to study, psychedelics also have helped researchers learn valuable cognitive skills during sessions that they have transferred back to ordinary consciousness as aids to research. Kary Mullis, inventor of the polymerase chain reaction technique (a way of multiplying small biological samples so they will be large enough to study) attributes his Nobel Prize–winning insight to a visualization skill he learned with psychedelics. He says he was not under the influence of psychedelics at the time he had this idea, but that he owes his insight to his ability to visualize, and he owes his ability to visualize to LSD (Doblin, 1994).

Psychedelics have a third role in scientific thought, providing novel ways for thinking "outside the box" of our ordinary mind-body state. An analogy between computers and our brains helps describe this. When a new digital program (electronic information processing program) is installed on a computer, the computer can be used in new ways; similarly, when we change our brains' bioinformation processing routines with chemicals and botanicals, we use our brains in new ways. I predict that future historians of scientific thought will judge that inventing new mind-body psychotechnologies was the major intellectual advance of the late twentieth and early twenty-first centuries (Roberts, 2006).

Of course, many other-state ideas are useless, but the double helix is not. According to science journalist Alun Rees (2004), Francis Crick was on LSD when he thought of the double helix model of DNA. Crick did not deny Rees's suggestion but threatened to sue Rees if he published it, so Rees came public only after Crick's death.

It is credible that scientists of the future will use entheogens and other mind-body psychotechnologies to widen their array of professional cognitive skills and as ways to invent ideas. I hope this set of books will provide a responsible and accurate scientific and religious context for entheogenic ideas and promote the free and open discussion of entheogenic topics.

The Science-and-Religion Complex

Charles Tart's (1969) admonition for psychologists to include information on altered states in their theories and observations is equally apt for the researchers in pharmatheology: "The most important obligation of any science is that its descriptive and theoretical language embrace *all* the phenomena of its subject matter; the data from [altered states of consciousness] cannot be ignored if we are to have a comprehensive psychology" (p. 6). If scientists and theologians omit descriptive and theoretical language about entheogens, we can hardly have a comprehensive neurotheology or pharmatheology.

In the brain-religion studies, much (though not all) research is descriptive. Activities in the nervous system during religious experiences are described. Correlational studies look at relationships among religious activities, denominational membership, demographic variables, social values and morals, and political positions. Frequency of prayer and other religious activities are associated with health, mental adjustment, or other supposed outcomes. Researchers in the Department of Clinical Neuroscience at Stockholm's Karolinska Institute and Hospital hint at how correlational studies might advance to experimental ones:

> [W]e found the correlation of self-transcendence was shown to be fully dependent on the spiritual acceptance scale.... The spiritual acceptance scale measures a person's apprehension of phenomena that cannot be explained by objective demonstration. Subjects with high scores tend to endorse extrasensory perception and ideation, whether named deities or a commonly unifying force. Low scorers, by contract, tend to favor a reductionistic and empirical worldview.
>
> A role for the serotonin system in relation to spiritual experiences is supported by observations of drugs such as LSD, psilocybin [DPT] mescaline, and [MDMA] that are known to cause perturbations of the serotonin system in several brain regions.
>
> On a behavioral level, these drugs elicit perceptual distortions, illusions, a sense of insight, spiritual awareness, mystical experiences, and religious ecstasy. (Borg, Bengt, Soderstrom, & Farde, 2003, pp. 1967–1968)

The Good Friday Experiment

A trophy study for a future neurotheologian would be replicating the Good Friday Experiment including serotonin measures. This outstanding and classic example of experimental research using entheogens occurred in Marsh Chapel of Boston University on Good Friday 1962. Walter N. Pahnke, who was already a medical doctor and an ordained minister, conducted the most significant study to date on the entheogen-religion connection as the data for his doctoral dissertation in religion and society at Harvard. He gave psilocybin (the active ingredient in psychedelic mushrooms) to10 graduate students from a seminary, while another 10 received an active placebo. They met in the basement of Marsh Chapel and listened to the upstairs service over a sound system. Pahnke wanted to know whether the psilocybin subjects would experience mystical states and whether they would do so more than the 10 control subjects (Hruby, 2001; Pahnke, 1963; Pahnke & Richards, 1966; Smith, 2000). They did, and what has become legendary in the psychedelic community as "the Good Friday Experiment" remains a paradigmatic experiment for others to replicate when and where such research becomes legal again.

Although the experiment of giving an entheogen to seminarians in a religious setting is distinctive, that isn't what earns the Good Friday Experiment a nomination for the most remarkable experiment in the social sciences. In the social sciences, experimental studies are in short supply; those done outside controlled lab environments are scarce. Experiments in which the subjects are administered a treatment only once are infrequent. Single-treatment, ex-lab, experimental designs with measurable long-lasting effects are rare, but in a 25-year follow-up study of Pahnke's Good Friday subjects, Doblin (2001) found:

> This long-term follow-up, conducted twenty-four to twenty-seven years after the original experiment, provides further support to the findings of the original experiment. All seven psilocybin subjects participating in the long-term follow-up, but none of the controls, still considered their original experience to have had genuinely mystical elements and to have made a uniquely invaluable contribution to their spiritual lives. (p. 73)

An effect persisting 25 years from a single-treatment experimental study makes the Good Friday Experiment remarkable enough, but even that isn't what makes this experiment so amazing. "The positive changes described by the psilocybin subjects at six months, which in some cases involved basic vocational and value choices and spiritual understandings, had persisted over time and had deepened in some cases" (Doblin, 2001, p. 73). A deepened effect strengthened over a quarter of a century marks a permanent shift. Obtaining these results from a one-treatment, informal setting, experimental study makes the Good Friday Experiment unique in the social sciences: it speaks to the power of entheogens as experimental treatments.

Do humans have an innate spiritual nature? What parts do biology and culture play in this? Entheogens supply some leads to these questions, too. Smith (1976) reminds readers: "the goal, it cannot be stressed too often, is not religious experiences: it is the religious life" (p. 155). As a philosopher, Smith is interested in the implications of these experiences for our understanding of the human mind:

> In contradistinction to writings on the psychedelics which are occupied with experiences the mind can *have*, the concern here is with evidence they afford us as to what the mind *is*.... [J]udged both by the quantity of data encompassed and by the explanatory power of the hypotheses that make sense of this data, it is the most formidable evidence the psychedelics have thus far produced. The evidence to which we refer is that which has emerged through the work of Grof. (p. 156)

The title of Smith's 1976 book, *The Forgotten Truth: The Primordial Tradition,* echoes Barnard's speculation about the roles of drug plants in primitive mythologies and cults; now, entheogens give us a way to test her ideas in our times and based on our own experiences. Entheogens move us from conjectures to testing the credibility of ideas. If we suppose the human mind has an innate spiritual nature, can entheogens confirm or disconfirm that hypothesis by activating, describing, and/or developing it? Entheogens open up subjective experiences and beliefs to experimental investigation. This is no small trick.

Psychedelics (used in both entheogenic mode and secular mode) make two distinct contributions to health. The most obvious is in psychotherapy, and the broadest range of LSD-treated mental health diagnostic categories is reported in Grof's works (e.g., 1975, 1980, 2001). Passie's bibliography (1997) lists 687 studies and nine conferences. Of special interested to religion-based psychotherapy, states of unitive consciousness (peak or mystical experiences) are often the variable that determines whether a treatment was successful.

After decades of being in a deep freeze due to governmental restrictions and negative publicity, several pilot research projects are underway for psychosomatic conditions (Horgan, 2005): post-traumatic stress disorder (now including war-related trauma), HIV/AIDS, death anxiety with the terminally ill, alcoholism and addiction, and obsessive-compulsive disorder. Because psychedelics have bodily effects, mental effects, and spiritual effects, they may prove especially applicable to mind-body-spirit problems. Entheogens may be useful in pastoral counseling, say with alcoholics (Alcoholics Anonymous, 1984; Mangini, 1998) or in a hospice situation (Hansen, 2001).

Other studies are likely to be getting underway soon. The most up-to-date source is the Multidisciplinary Association for Psychedelic Studies (www.maps. org) and the *MAPS Bulletin* (1990+). A two-volume anthology of *Hallucinogens and Healing*, which collects these leads (Roberts and Winkelman, in press) will include a chapter on spiritual healing.

A second possible health benefit is linked more closely with psychedelics as entheogens. The characteristics of mystical experiences are similar to descriptions of spiritual healing and spontaneous remissions: overwhelmingly positive mood, transcendence of time and space, a sense of sacredness, being in the care of a powerful good force, unity, and so forth. With relationships well established between positive psychological mood, the immune system, and physical wellness, powerfully positive peak experiences might boost the immune system powerfully (Roberts, 1999). I speculate further on this connection in Roberts (2006).

Clearly, entheogens are not right for everyone. Who is most likely to benefit from entheogens? How should people be screened and prepared for their sessions, and what kinds of follow-up are best? Myron Stolaroff (1994), who headed a therapeutic-growth center in the 1960s where people could come for legal LSD sessions, recommends a gentle start:

> After a number of trials of MDMA with other people, it became apparent that this was the best substance with which to introduce people to psychoactive drugs. With other substances, we had always used great care to make sure that the subject was ready for an experience that would greatly alter his perceptions, understanding, and perhaps his view of himself and his behavior. MDMA is so generally euphoric and non-threatening that a much wider range of subjects can benefit from the experience without discomfort. (pp. 41–42)

Collecting his ideas on how best to design a religious session, Stolaroff (2001) addresses selecting candidates, preparation, conduct of the session, follow up, and the training guides. Roberts (2001, pp. 250–251) anticipates a time when it will be legally possible to be screened, prepared, take a known dose of guaranteed purity under the care of a qualified guide, and be debriefed.

The importance of entheogenic experiences goes beyond religious studies to broadening the data base cognitive scientists can draw on. Shanon (2002) bridges the cognition-entheogen gap:

> [T]he bringing together of Ayahuasca research and cognitive psychology defines a two-way interaction. Not only can a cognitive-psychological analysis make a crucial contribution to the study of Ayahuasca, the converse is also the case—the study of Ayahuasca may have implications of import to our general understanding of the workings of the human mind. Ayahuasca (along with other mind-altering substances) expands the horizons of psychology and reveals new, hitherto unknown territories of the

mind. Thus, the study of Ayahuasca presents new data pertaining to human consciousness, and thus new issues for investigation, new ways to look at things, new questions, and perhaps even new answers. (p. 37)

Scientific generalizations based on a wide range of observations are considered stronger than observations derived from a narrower scope. Broadening the sample observations that scientists and scholars can draw from, entheogens strengthen findings about cognition and religion. For example, with the help of ayahuasca, Shanon identified 11 cognitive parameters whose values depend on brain biochemistry, many with clear implications for religion: agenthood, personal identity, unity, inner/outer boundaries, individuation, calibration of one's size, locus of consciousness, time, self-consciousness, intentionality, and knowledge-noetic sense. Thus, ayahuasca makes it possible to experimentally unite biology, cognition, and philosophy. In this way, *Antipodes* could well become an inspiration and paradigmatic model for future generations of pharmatheologians and neurotheologians.

Inventing New Varieties of Religious Experience

Existing mind-body psychotechnologies (e.g., entheogens, meditation, chanting, contemplative prayer, ascetic practices, martial arts, or other mind-body spiritual practices) are usually used alone. Meanwhile, new psychotechnologies are being invented (e.g., biofeedback and neurotechnologies), while others are being imported into standard Western culture regularly (e.g., ayahuasca and peyote). Twenty-first-century mind-body inventors might sequence several of these in new ways. Just as new computer programs process electronic information new ways, we can invent new mind-body programs to process biological-cognitive information new ways. New recipes of these psychotechnologies might produce new, previously unknown, synthetic cognitive programs. As we learn to use our brains/minds in new ways, what will we learn about our minds? We may be on the verge of discovering (or constructing) novel mental states and resident capacities that haven't existed.

What religious experiences, thoughts, or qualia may emerge in those states (Roberts, 2006)? It seems logical to wonder whether future religious explorers and mind-body engineers will invent new kinds of spiritual experiences. Will they create new varieties of religious experience? A vast experimental unknown unfolds.

A strong bridge between science and religion cannot be built if we omit the entheogen girders. If we are to follow Tart's (1969) injunction to include all observations in our brain-and-mind disciplines, then neurotheology must be informed of pharmatheology. The most intellectually distinctive aspect of using entheogens experimentally is that they are chemicals and their effects go beyond biochemical reactions to influence philosophy, theology, beliefs, and cognition. With entheogens, "chemical input, religious output" links brain with cognition, the sciences with the humanities. Brain, cognition, and theology are one interacting process that is experimentally studiable.

TOWARD EXPERIMENTAL HUMANITIES

In today's humanities, religious and spiritual beliefs are constructed and deconstructed, commented on, analyzed, historicized, criticized, and otherwise run through the gauntlet of humanistic concepts and philosophical wrangling. Even more remarkably than in the sciences, entheogens make it possible to perform experiments in the religion-centered humanities, too—even experiments that promise to increase people's understanding of selected religious and philosophical concepts. By providing direct, personal experiences, entheogens advance what might be called the experimental humanities, informing religious discussions with data-based information.

Experiments on Belief, Ethics, Qualia, and Meaningfulness

Entheogens can move the scientific study of primary religious experience from the anecdotal, descriptive, and correlational stages to the experimental stage (Pahnke & Richards, 1966; Smith, 2000). The Good Friday Experiment is the best example so far. How might empirical metaphysics inform the professional education of seminarians, advanced students of religion, and related fields? How will experiences of experimental mysticism change the research agendas of those who have primary religious experiences? What directions will they give young researchers' professional careers? What questions will they ask? What religious activities may move from church and chancel to entheogenic religious retreats? What questions may move from the scholar's dusty study to the glory of his garden? What methodological questions need to be answered, and what methods of inquiry need to be developed?

How do religious beliefs and philosophical positions depend on whether people have had primary religious experiences? When people experience mystical states, they find some beliefs more credible—for example, perennialism, a common mystical core underpinning world religions, the survival value of PREs, the roles of mind-body states in the origins and history of religion, self-transcendence as a state of grace, a spiritual aspect of human nature, a transpersonal "level" of the human mind. David Toolan (1987) spots the breakthroughs possible for philosophy and religion:

> Even in the universities of the Catholic ghetto in which I grew up, where metaphysical speculation was highly approved, the general assumption was that the noumenal order of things could not be perceived. One got it only by subtle arguments, by "transcendental reductions" and other

such inferential, speculative acrobatics. (The ordinary pious Catholic who prayed before the Blessed Sacrament may have known otherwise, but such pedestrian experience was typically ignored by professors of "natural theology" and theology.) But is metaphysics a matter of "immediate perceptions"? Without argument? The eyewitness of a hack reporter? If true, this would be first-order cultural news. Psychedelics provided the gate-opener for just this announcement. (p. 40)

Just as the physical sciences learn about the material world by experimenting on it, entheogens and other mind-body psychotechnologies allow us to learn about the mental and spiritual worlds by experimenting on them. What personal experiences make various theological positions and topics in religious studies more credible or less credible? Experiment-based evidence will inform these discussions.

People who have undergone ego-transcendent (transpersonal) experiences with entheogens (or otherwise) often shift their values and motivation away from self-gain to community-centered values, or to a cosmic orientation.

Among the predictable characteristics of mystical experience are a sense of the sacredness of all life and a desire to establish a new, more harmonious relationship with nature and with other human beings. There is a corresponding renunciation of the various forms of self-seeking, including the ethos of manipulation and control. (Wulff, 1991, p. 639)

When we visit "the blessed Not-I" (Huxley, 1954, p. 19), it makes perfect sense that I-centered desires will be left behind, or at least put in their motivational place. Early entheogenic research in the 1960s through more contemporary studies confirm this (e.g., Fadiman, 1965; Mangini, 2000; Roberts, 1998). In a 2004 two-continent study, a medical doctor in Israel, Michael Learner, teamed up with a professor from the Department of Psychology at Bond University in Australia, Michael Lyvers, to compare psychedelic users with users of other illegal drugs and with non–drug users (Learner & Lyvers, 2004). Compared to the other two groups, psychedelic users scored higher on life values thought to be associated with spiritual or mystical beliefs such as concern with the environment, concern for others, creativity and spirituality, and manageability of their lives. They perceived life as more meaningful and were higher in empathy. Suppose we believe, "By their fruits you shall know them"; do entheogens yield good fruit?

But, as Learner and Lyvers (2004) caution: "It is possible that the higher levels of spirituality and associated values in psychedelic users were inherent pre-drug spiritual tendencies" (p. 10). In the future, if religious liberty and academic freedom are restored, experimental studies that test groups that are both high-level and low-level to begin with will solve this uncertainty.

If entheogenic mystical experiences produce ego-transcendent states that, in turn, promote these values, then we should expect other psychotechnologies that also produce these states to produce similar results. Looking at the effects of ego-transcendent practices cross-culturally, Roger Walsh (1988) reports:

> the thought of harming "others" therefore makes no sense whatsoever. Rather, the natural expression of this state are said to be love and compassion or *agapé*. Similar unitive experiences have been reported in the West among contemplatives, subjects in exceptionally deep hypnotic states, patients in advanced therapy, experimental psychedelic sessions, and as spontaneous peak experiences. These experiences are under significant voluntary control only in contemplatives, either Eastern or Western, but interestingly, enduring positive after effects on personality have been reported for all these conditions, and the approaches that induce them have therefore been collectively named "holotropic therapies," i.e., growth toward wholeness or unity. (p. 549; Walsh's citations omitted)

Here too, we see the complex of the transpersonal aspect of mystical states, Winkelman's (2001) idea of "psychointegrators," and the enduring changes Doblin (2001) found in his follow-up of the Good Friday Experiment.

But the title of Walsh's (1988) article—"Two Asian Psychologies and their Implications for Western Psychologies"—brings up another clue, one that brings us to contemporary neuroethics. If mystical experiences occurring in culturally different societies lead to similar results, this may be due to the way our brains are structured and the way they work. (This is not to deny other possible reasons for this similarity; that's why this similarity is only a clue, but, thanks to entheogens, it can become an experimental hypothesis.) Michael Gazzaniga (2005) proposes that "intrinsic moral reasoning" may be a capacity of our species: "[T]here could be a universal set of biological responses to moral dilemmas, a sort of ethics built into our brains" (p. xix). Might states of unitive consciousness activate these biological responses? Entheogens and other transpersonal triggers might be the required stimuli, or at least might nourish these brain processes.

By stifling research into entheogens, current drug policies are blocking entheogenic access to "intrinsic moral reasoning." Despite their good intentions, these political decisions prohibit us from becoming more ethical. They lock us into self-centered mind-body states and the self-centered values that reside in them. It is worth noting in this regard that self-importance, Pride, is the kingpin of the seven deadly sins, and his gang of six are all ways of feeding Pride's egoic pleasure. What happens when we knock off Pride? Figure 10.2 is a flow chart of a process of replacing ego-centered, pride-centered desires with higher motivations.

Can we admit some optimistic questions? Has the entheogen revival uncovered a hidden path of moral development? What would it mean to have

Figure 10.2   Moral Development: The Mystical Path

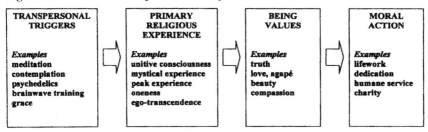

a more virtuous society? The possibilities that entheogens lead to higher values via a transpersonal path are certainly a lead that deserves experimental investigation. I expect it would support the claim that religions (at least their mystical traditions) have survival value.

Is sacredness a qualé? Is it a sensory quality like red, saltiness, or C-sharp, a basic sense perception whose nervous system pathways might be discovered and mapped? During some entheogenic states, sacredness seems to be a directly perceived qualé, and appears to reside in any number of objects, thoughts, or emotions. Perhaps we perceive sacredness simultaneously with these other things but misattribute this quality to them. Similarly, if we were naïve about the rural world, we might see a flowering tree when we are downwind of a pig farm and erroneously attribute the aroma of the pigs to the tree. Do we make a parallel misattribution with sacredness? Is sacredness, say, like dreams, a sort of internal, brain-generated perception? Then do we misattribute sacredness to our contemporaneous perceptions, location, thoughts, or beliefs? That is, do we project (in the psychological sense) our inner perception of sacredness outward onto inappropriate objects? Do we do this always, frequently, sometimes, never? If so, how are we to determine what is or isn't sacred?

Conversely, perhaps everything *is* sacred, and primary religious experiences allow us to perceive what we have missed in our mundane mind-body state. Entheogenic experiments may help answer these questions (or perhaps muddy them). But our failure to examine this topic is nothing less than spiritual cowardliness.

Are meaningfulness, portentousness, adoration, self-transcendence, and awe brain-built spiritual qualia? Are they too directly perceived rather than being cognitive conclusions? During primary religious experiences, some qualities seem to be arrived at through rational cognitive processes. Ineffability, for example, seems like a thought. I experience sacredness, however, as if it were a direct perception. I can imagine someone having this experience and applying "sacred" to whatever he or she is considering at the time.

If this is true, at least for some people some of the time, how is someone to determine what is truly sacred and when is sacredness merely applied? Worse yet, maybe sacredness is only a sense we project onto the world. There goes religion! If this is true of sacredness, what about the other qualities of mystical experiences? Philosophers will have a picnic with this conundrum. Could philosophers design experiments to inform this discussion?

Extending the question, how do everyday recognized qualia vary from one mind-body state to another? Do other qualia reside in other mind-body states? If qualia depend on a self-observer, where do self-transcendent states fit in? Using entheogens for philosophical inquiry, it might become possible to collect subjective reports on these questions and at the same time chart what is going on in our brains.

The president of the psychology of religion division in the American Psychological Association, Israela Silberman (2005), proposed that much of the sometimes-conflicting results that research on religion provides might be resolved by a meaning-system approach. The research she cites is predominantly descriptive, correlational, historical, and survey. The plight of being stuck with these kinds of research is a methodological problem for religious studies, and it's one that entheogens can solve. A common report of people who have had mystical experiences (entheogenic or otherwise) is that they feel a heightened sense of coherence, purpose, and meaning in their lives. Using entheogens as independent variables (if and when this becomes legal) would allow researchers to advance the state of knowledge with experimental studies on meaning. Instead of waiting for religious peak experiences to happen at random, it is possible to greatly increase their occurrence. Instead of using mystics' reports from hundreds—and even thousands—of years ago and questionable translations of their reports, we can study fresh experiences occurring today. Instead of depending on people who may be inclined toward peak experiences, pharmatheological researchers could study a broader sample of the human population. The varieties of substances and their doses, subjects' mindsets, temperaments, personality variables, and belief systems, social contexts, and church affiliations provide practically endless combinations. Instead of making questionable cross-cultural assumptions, we could examine both cultural context and brain processes using standard doses, treatments, and measures. Here again, we see how entheogens could advance the state of the art.

Attraction to the Holy as the Origin of Religion

If one uses any of the transpersonal models of the human mind such as those of Grof or Jung, Buddhism or other Eastern psychologies, or transcendental Christianity, then exploring one's mind is naturally a movement toward its spiritual parts. From this perspective—eventually and taken far enough—the psychological path of self-knowledge turns into a spiritual path to self-transcendence. This turns most twentieth-century psychology, with its antireligion bias, on its head. Is there an inborn desire to take this journey? Psychedelicists' inner voyages often sight spiritual lands. Could this be one reason some people, consciously or unconsciously, want to take psychoactive drugs?

What parts of our brains are involved in this voyage? Is this quest an emergent property of brain-and-body? Since mystical experiences are the most rewarding events a human can experience, how are our pleasure centers involved? Once someone has had a powerful mystical experience, does this establish neural circuits that beg for activation afterward? Do mystical experiences produce some sort of rapid neuroplasticity that establishes mystical circuits and/or activates or connects ones lying dormant? Is our society remiss in providing unhealthy ways to take these quests and not providing healthy ways? Bill Wilson, founder of Alcoholics Anonymous (1984), arrived at this conclusion:

> [It was not] the material itself [that] actually produces these experiences. It seems to have the result of sharply reducing the forces of the ego—temporarily, of course. It is a generally acknowledged fact in spiritual development that ego reduction makes the influx of God's grace possible. If, therefore, under LSD we can have a temporary reduction, so that we can better see what we are and where we are going—well, that might be of some help. The goal might become clearer. So I consider LSD to be of some value to some people, and practically no damage to anyone. It will never take the place of any of the existing means by which we can reduce the ego, and keep it reduced. (p. 370)

We crave oneness, but we live in a society that seldom acknowledges this motivation and provides worthless substitutes and even dangerous social ones such as authoritarianism, consumerism, and ersatz chemical ones such as alcohol. Why are people who have had mystical experiences less likely to be authoritarian, and why do some alcoholics drop their addiction after having a mystical experience? Could we use entheogens to provide healthy ways to oneness, unity, and sacredness? Entheogens move these questions from armchair suppositions to experimental hypotheses.

Bill Wilson "was enthusiastic" about his LSD experience: "he felt it helped him eliminate many barriers erected by the self, or ego, that stand in the way of one's direct experience of the cosmos and of God" (pp. 370–371). Hundreds of clinical-psychotherapeutic studies using psychedelics have been done with alcoholics and for other indications (Mangini, 1998; Passie, 1997). These should help pastoral counseling and supply leads for pharmatheologians.

Historically, did entheogens spark the religious imagination and play a significant role in the origins of religions—shamanic, ancient, and modern? In concert with Barnard's (1966) drug-plant theme, the landmark works of

R. Gordon Wasson stand out in the field of pharmatheology. Wasson (1968) claims to have unraveled the mysterious identity of the god-plant soma from the *Rig Veda*:

> There is I think an inference that we may draw: a plant with properties that could be plausibly named Herb of Immortality responded to man's deepest desires in the early stage of his intellectual development. The superb fly-agaric gave him a glimpse of horizons beyond any that he knew in his harsh struggle for survival, of planes of existence far removed and above his daily round of besetting cares. It contributed to the shaping of his mythological world and his religious life. (p. 210)

Wasson's books track the religious uses of psychoactive mushrooms around the world from the mysteries of ancient Greece (Wasson, 1968; Wasson, Hofmann, & Ruck, 1978) through contemporary uses. In Riedlinger (1990), Brown (1990) lists Wasson's bibliography. So many people have followed Wasson's path in looking at other cultures and other entheogens that he is considered one of the founders of ethnobotany and the father of ethnomycology (Riedlinger, 1990).

While botany is often left out of neurotheology discussions, the work of Wasson and his followers invites this science back into the fold. Determining what roles psychoactive plants played in the origins and development of religions can occupy specialists in this branch of ethnobotany for decades to come. To include the full range of data and to test the validity of their claims, future generations of ethnobotanists and religiobotanists should have personal experiences with these plants.

From an entheogenic perspective, even geology can contribute to understanding brain-religion connections. According to Hale, de Boer, Chanton, and Spiller (2003), the Delphic oracles in ancient Greece were seated above a fissure in the ground that emitted psychoactive gas, thus permitting them to enter altered mind-body states. When an earthquake closed the fissure and blocked the gas, the oracles lost their power. Here we see yet another instance of how an entheogenic perspective allows scientists from a previously excluded discipline to consider new hypotheses and contribute entheogenic insights to religion.

Consilience

Remarkably, entheogens provide an opportunity to study both reductive and emergent causation within a systematic program of interlocking experiments. In the reductive studies, entheogens can be administered and their effects measured on, say, receptor sites and brain structures. At a higher level of organization, we can examine their effects on cognition, beliefs, values, and theology. Looking at downward or emergent causation, we can ask how personality variables, novelty-seeking or harm-reducing temperaments, cognitions and beliefs, theism/atheism, knowledge about entheogens, church acceptance/rejection might affect both entheogens' physiological activity and our interpretations of them. Thus, entheogens and their mind-body siblings provide tools for interlevel studies. They can advance us toward interacting networks of ideas and experiments that integrate the sciences and humanities, thus advancing Edmund O. Wilson's goal of consilience (1998).

The examples of Nichols, Mullis, and Crick in biological studies may reveal parallel strategies for inventing new insights in religious studies and elsewhere. When scientists and humanists can experiment with entheogens and other mind-body techniques, they might solve problems, formulate new questions, refine concepts, and invent new ideas. So far this chapter has sampled entheogenic aspects of mysticism, primary religious experience, neurotheology, the Good Friday Experiment, innate spiritual nature, spiritual healing and psychotherapy, cognitive studies, credibility research, mind-body invention, neuroethics and values, moral development, qualia, meaningfulness, holytropia, the origins of religion, and consilience. To recall Barnard's quotation, do entheogens cause us to think of things we had never thought of before? It is hard to answer "no." But the implications of entheogens reach beyond the sciences and humanities to church and society too. Just as questions in the sciences and humanities meld together, this blend leads to more churchly topics.

QUESTIONS ABOUT CHURCH AND POLITY

Increasing Spiritual Intelligence

Vaughan (1983) describes five kinds of spiritual learning: theological knowledge, interfaith acceptance, personal insight, spiritual practice, and psychological understanding:

> The perennial philosophy and the esoteric teaching of all time suddenly made sense. I understood why spiritual seekers were instructed to look within, and the unconscious was revealed to be not just a useful concept, but an infinite reservoir of creative potential. I felt I had been afforded a glimpse into the nature of reality and the human potential within that reality, together with a direct experience of being myself, free of illusory identification and constrictions of consciousness. My understanding of mystical teaching, both Eastern and Western, Hindu, Buddhist, Christian, and Sufi alike, took a quantum leap. I became aware of all great religions, and understood for the first time the meaning of ecstatic states. (p. 109)

Vaughan (1983) describes increased intellectual understanding and personal insights that her psychedelic experience produced. While most first-person accounts describe psychedelics' perceptual razzmatazz, her thoughtful essay describes spiritual, psychological, and intellectual growth. Vaughan's increased understanding is not just cognitive knowledge *about* these topics, but first hand direct, personal experience *of* them. Subsequently, she obtained a doctorate in clinical psychology, served as president of the Association for Transpersonal Psychology, and wrote and co-edited books on psychospiritual growth (e.g., Vaughan 2001; Walsh & Vaughan, 1993). As is often the case, her personal entheogenic experience contributed meaningful direction to both her professional and personal life.

Have we—unintentionally, even unknowingly—discovered (perhaps rediscovered) a way to increase spiritual intelligence? Two current definitions of intelligence suggest so. Harvard psychologist Howard Gardner (1983) defines intelligence as "the ability to solve problems or provide goods and services of value to a society." By helping her solve problems in the spiritual domain, entheogens boosted Vaughan's spiritual, or existential, intelligence. Robert Sternberg (1988) defines intelligence as "mental self management." By allowing us to manage direct encounter with the holy, entheogens give us greater self-management, higher intelligence, control over the spiritual aspect of our lives.

I find myself stunned by the implications—and excited. Perhaps we have discovered a way to increase spiritual intelligence and can design programs to increase spiritual intelligence. At the very least this would take careful selection of participants, preparation, and follow-up. People to lead entheogenic spiritual sessions would need training in psychospiritual skills. What would it mean to humanity's future to increase spiritual intelligence? I believe it is a moral, spiritual, and sacred duty to examine the feasibility of this idea (Roberts, 2001, p. 237).

The entheogenic use of psychedelics illustrates a more comprehensive theory of the human mind (Roberts, 2006); behind the intelligence of skillfully using each mind-body state lies the metaintelligence of skillfully selecting the most appropriate mind-body program for the purpose at hand.

Entheogen-induced primary religious experiences might also help selected, prepared seminarians and others in religious professions rededicate themselves to their callings. Might a religious order or guild take on this responsibility? Doblin's follow-up study of the Good Friday subjects found more of those who had psilocybin-boosted mystical experiences remained in the clergy than those who didn't, but the small size of the sample doesn't give a statistically significant result. In personal communications, clergy have told me their entheogenic sessions periodically reinvigorate their dedication to their calling.

Would entheogenic spiritual experiences be appropriate for the laity? Could current religions adjust to them? Lawrence Bush (2002) sees Judaism benefiting from entheogens:

> Apart from legal impediments, why shouldn't psychedelic drugs be used in
> Jewish life as they have been in other faith traditions—as a tool for wrenching

open the mind and heart to "God's presence"? Why not embrace the spiritual power of the psychedelic experience and try to elevate it, as we do with sexuality, above the recreational and into the sacramental zone? Why shouldn't the roster of Jewish life-passages include the opportunity to have a psychedelic experience (perhaps after the age of forty, Judaism's traditional age of enlightenment and mystical initiation, or perhaps at an earlier stage of development)—with rabbinic guidance and community approval? If Abraham's Voice and Moses' Burning Bush and the Revelation at Sinai are the archetypal encounters that inform our faith, why not strive to recreate such experiences throughout our "nation of priests"? (p. 91)

Entheogens suggest reinterpretation of religious texts and ceremonies—for example, soma in Hinduism (Wasson, 1968), possible references to entheogens in Judaism and early Christianity (Merkur, 2001), and the ancient Greek mysteries at Eleusis (Wasson, Hofmann, & Ruck, 1978). Entheogens also increase our understanding of anthropological and archeological findings on religion (Rudgley, 1993).

Experimental Chrismation

Bennett (2003) and (Ruck, 2003) contend that the oils used in the ancient Near East anointment ceremonies, including Judaism and early Christianity, contained psychoactive ingredients, particularly cannabis:

> So, did Jesus use cannabis? I think so. The word Christ does mean "the anointed one" and Bennett contends that Christ was anointed with chrism, a cannabis-based oil, that caused his spiritual visions. The ancient recipe for this oil, recorded in Exodus, included over 9lb of flowering cannabis tops (known as kaneh-bosem in Hebrew), extracted into a hin (about 11 pints) of olive oil, with a variety of other herbs and spices. The mixture was used in anointing and fumigations that, significantly, allowed the priests and prophets to see and speak with Yahweh. (Ruck, 2003)

The archeology of entheogens is a growing specialty, and scholars are paying more attention to ancient ways of producing and using psychoactive plants (*Eleusis*, 2001+; Ruck, Staples, & Heinrich, 2001; Rudgley, 1993). Reenactments of these possible historical events under laboratory conditions or in religious settings or clinical laboratories via chrismation experiments could test these claims, supporting or weakening the credibility of this alleged part of religious history. Institutional review boards may need some convincing.

What ideas and interpretations gain credibility for entheogen-informed people? Will existing churches, seminaries, and religious study programs be able to incorporate entheology as Lucas-Caldwell (2001) defines it?

> Entheology is that branch of theology which deals with the experience
> and/or knowledge of the divine, and of the revelation of that divine,
> through the agency of psychoactive substances (used as sacraments), be it
> a revelation of the divine within and/or without the individual. (p. 147)

What religious rituals and practices will evolve from entheogens? The rituals of the syncretic Christian ayahuasca-using churches from Brazil such as the Santo Daime and Uniao do Vegetal are being adapted in churches in the Netherlands and in the United States. Lucas-Caldwell (2001) and Stolaroff (2001) examine whether these, or additional adaptations, are appropriate for followers of other churches. Would existing Eucharistic services gain profundity and real (rather than symbolic) meaning with entheogens?

Because entheogenic peak experiences are only temporary states, it is not clear whether they can be converted into permanent personal traits too and become enduring steps of spiritual development. Smith (1976) raised this issue: "the goal, it cannot be stressed too often, is not religious experiences: it is the religious life" (p. 155). This theme also was addressed by the Council on Spiritual Practices (2001), where Walsh (2001) warned:

> This challenge concerns the limited capacity we seem to have to catalyze
> ongoing development as a result of a single experience. What are the issues
> here? I think we need to distinguish two distinct dimensions of thinking about
> this problem of stabilizing any insights or breakthroughs obtained in drug-
> assisted therapy. We need to think of both the developmental stages and the
> psychological processes that are involved in transpersonal growth. (p. 21)

A swarm of questions arises. Who benefits, and who doesn't? What developmental stages and cognitive processes can help the transition from a transient mystical state to spiritual trait? Are different treatments appropriate for different ages, temperaments, levels of cognitive development, and spiritual stages? Why are some people who have had mystical experiences with psychedelics able to integrate them but others have been unable to integrate them? Can levels of readiness be strengthened by preparation, such as meditation or other spiritual practice? Are there ways to assess readiness?

New Religious Movements

Consider the possible effects that entheogens have already had on current religious practice, ritual, ethics, and the religious community:

> A recent poll of over 1,300 Americans engaged in Buddhist practice
> showed that 83 percent had taken psychedelics . . . and 71 percent believed
> that psychedelics can provide a glimpse of the reality to which Buddhist
> practice points. (Barlow, 1996, pp. 86–87)

How does religiosity—religious activities within established religious structures and outside of them, including attendance at ceremonies, prayer, meditation, religion-motivated service, group or independent study—change with primary religious experience? Are experienced-based religions drawing people away from word-based, belief-based, text-based religions? Psychologically, is perception winning over cognition? Theologically, is primary religious experience outscoring theology? Could mainstream Protestantism revivify itself with entheogens?

With the redefinition (or at least expansion) of religion as experience-based, all the brain-mind-religion questions that researchers have asked about cognition-based religion get re-asked of experiential religion. For example: "What are our brains doing when we have such experiences?" Because our knowledge about our brains and our skill at influencing them are advancing so quickly, scientists may develop new methods of describing brain occurrences. Now, thanks to entheogens, we can add experimental mysticism to that mixture. Now that primary religious experiences can be experimentally induced, their activity in the nervous system can be mapped, their theological effects documented, and resulting shifts in values and social activity described (Pahnke & Richards, 1966; Smith, 2000).

Although seldom organized into religious communities, do entheogenists qualify as a new religious movement but one with dispersed membership rather than an organized church body? If so, it will be hard for them to become visible as most people (mistakenly) think of a system of rituals and beliefs as needing an organization to qualify as a religion.

Democratizing Primary Religious Experience

Perhaps we are experiencing a reorganization in Western religions now, parallel in some ways to the one that occurred around 1500. Before then, religious rites were the main religious activity for the ordinary person (not monks, nuns, or priests). Being religious primarily meant attending mass on Sunday; participating in church festivals, rites, and rituals; praying, and other religious activities and observances.

When the printing press and movable type democratized access to biblical (and other) texts, the emphasis changed from ritual to word. While older religious observances of the previous period sustained, new word-centered activities such as reading texts and interpreting them overlay the older religion-as-rite. New interpretations resulted, new churches flourished, and text became a standard for judging religion. Over time, the locus of Western religion shifted from rites to reading, from observances to Bible, from participation to verbalization. In contrast to pre-1500, we approach religion verbally, as cognitions—through words such as language, texts, speaking, beliefs, catechisms, dogma, doctrines, and theology. This emphasis (perhaps overemphasis) on words shows up today in the way we describe religions—with words. We ask: "What do you believe?" not "What rituals do you perform?" Older, preliterate rites certainly remain and have been updated, but they lie obscured beneath a 500-year blizzard of words.

Is this transition going on today? Are we moving from concept-based religion to experience-based religion, from belief to primary religious experience? Whether this is a major theme in current religious life, it certainly is a leitmotiv. Perhaps Western religion is in the early stages of adding another layer of direct experience on top of word-based religion and rite-based religion. For spiritual guidance, verbalists consult the written word of God; mystics consult their direct experience of God.

A broader, cultural shift away from a single-state view of the human mind toward a multistate view supports this transition in religion (Roberts, 2006). Recognizing our minds' ability to create and manage many mind-body states provides a friendly intellectual context for entheogens, and at the same time entheogens contribute their strand to this larger cultural tapestry. This chapter considers some benefits the entheogen family of psychotechnologies brings to religion. Other mind-body psychotechnologies and the states they produce may offer additional benefits.

Is the reprogrammable brain adaptigenic?

I hope this chapter will catalyze thinking about these questions. Behind these particular questions are some prior questions whose answers will determine how the questions in this chapter will be addressed.

Social and Constitutional Questions about Religious Liberty

As with classic paradigm shifts, entheogens formulate new kinds of questions.

- Are the questions in this chapter religious, spiritual, legal, biological, medical, or political—or all of the above?

- Are entheogen-assisted primary religious experiences authentic? What criteria should be used? Who gets to decide this?

- Who knows most? People who have had these experiences or people who haven't?

- Who has the knowledge, right, and responsibility to decide the answers to the questions in this chapter? Each individual person, churches and clergy, medical doctors and health agencies, politicians, police, legislators, mental health professionals, members of a professional organization?

In a country that is dedicated to individual freedom of conscience and to the separation of church and state, what policy and legal hurdles do entheogens present? Who has the right to decide the future of religion? Can current laws accommodate entheogens? The Center for Cognitive Liberty & Ethics and its publication *The Entheogen Law Reporter* (2005) address these complex social thorns and their legal complexities. Thanks to entheogens, experimental scientific and humanistic research can inform our decisions on the questions in this chapter. Although they won't answer the questions, at least we can be better informed.

SUMMARY—TOWARD PHARMATHEOLOGY

At the beginning of this chapter, we considered Mary Barnard's speculation that psychoactive plants probably had "an almost explosive effect on the largely dormant minds of men, causing them to think of things they had never thought of before." They did, and they still do. For neurotheology, the questions we've considered are the seeds for many more to come. Barnard's (1966) essay ends with these words:

> Looking at the matter coldly, unintoxicated and unentranced, I am willing to prophesy that fifty theo-botanists working for fifty years would make the current theories, concerning the origins of much mythology and theology as out of date as pre-Copernican astronomy. I am the more willing to prophesy, since I am, alas, so unlikely to be proved wrong. (p. 24)

It has been over 40 years since Barnard's essay first appeared. And despite jail, interrogation, and the drug war, the last 40 years has seen remarkable advances in entheogenic studies. When legal, controlled psychedelic studies are resumed in the sciences, humanities, and religion, we can expect "an almost explosive effect on the largely dormant minds of men, causing them to think of things they had never thought of before." Dare we enter this realm? Dare we not?

REFERENCES

Alcoholics Anonymous. (1984). *"Pass it on": The story of Bill Wilson and how the A.A. message reached the world.* New York: Alcoholics Anonymous World Services.

Barlow, J. P. (Fall 1996). Psychedelics and Buddhism: Introduction and Liberty and LSD. *Tricycle: The Buddhist Review.* Retrieved June 13, 2006, from http://www.tricycle.com/issues/tricycle/6_1/special_section/1495-1.html.

Barnard, M. (1966). *The mythmakers.* Athens: Ohio University Press. (Originally published 1963, *American Scholar, 32,* 578–586).

Bennett, C. (2003, February). Was Jesus a stoner? *High Times,* 69–72. Retrieved June 13, 2006, from http://www.420.com/nt/news/content.php?bid=31&aid=2.

Borg, J., Bengt, A., Soderstrom, H., & Farde, L. (2003). The serotonin system and spiritual experiences. *American Journal of Psychiatry, 11,* 1965–1969.

Brown, J. (1990). Appendix II: Bibliography: R. Gordon Wasson and Valentina Pavlovna Wasson. In T. Riedlinger (Ed.), *The sacred mushroom seeker: Essays for R. Gordon Wasson* (pp. 257–263). Portland, OR: Dioscorides Press.

Bush, L. (2002). Drugs and Jewish spirituality. In S. Grob (Ed.), *Hallucinogens: A reader* (pp. 82–93). New York: Tarcher/Putnam.

Center for Cognitive Liberty & Ethics. (n.d.). Retrieved September 1, 2005, from http://www.cognitiveliberty.org/.

Connor, S. (1997). "God spot" in brain found? *Sightings.* Retrieved June 13, 2006, from http://www.rense.com/ufo/godspot.htm.

Council on Spiritual Practices. (2001). Code of ethics for spiritual guides. In T. Roberts (Ed.), *Psychoactive sacramentals: Essays on entheogens and religion* (pp. 250–251). San Francisco: Author.

Doblin, R. (1994). Laying the groundwork. *Newsletter of the Multidisciplinary Association for Psychedelic Studies, 4*(4). Retrieved June 13, 2006, from http://www.maps.org/news-letters/v04n4/04401lay.html.

Doblin, R. (2001). Pahnke's Good Friday Experiment: A long-term follow-up and methodological critique. In T. Roberts (Ed.), *Psychoactive sacramentals: Essays on entheogens and religion* (pp. 71–79). San Francisco: Council on Spiritual Practices.

Eleusis: Journal of Psychoactive Plants and Compounds. (2001+). New Series. Museo Civico di Rovereto (Italy).

Entheogen Law Reporter. (2005). Center for Cognitive Liberty & Ethics, Davis, CA.

Entheology.org. (2005). Retrieved September 1, 2005, from http://www.entheology.org/.

Fadiman, J. R. (1965). *Behavior change following psychedelic (LSD) therapy.* Unpublished doctoral dissertation, Stanford University.

Forte, R. (Ed.). (1997). *Entheogens and the future of religion.* San Francisco: Council on Spiritual Practices.

Gardner, H. (1983). *Frames of mind: The theory of multiple intelligences.* New York: Basic Books.

Gazzaniga, M. S. (2005). *The ethical brain.* New York: Dana Press.

Grof, S. (1975/1993). *Realms of the human unconscious: Observations from LSD research.* New York: Dutton. (Reprinted in 1993 by Souvenir Press, London.)

Grof, S. (1980). *LSD psychotherapy.* Pomona, CA: Hunter House.

Grof, S. (2001). Entheogens as catalysts for spiritual development. In T. Roberts (Ed.), *Psychoactive sacramentals: Essays on entheogens and religion* (pp. 27–45). San Francisco: Council on Spiritual Practices.

Hale, J. R., de Boer, J. Z., Chanton, J. P., & Spiller, H. A. (2003). Questioning the Delphic oracle. *Scientific American,* 66–73.

Hansen, K. (2001). The birthing of transcendental medicine. In T. Roberts (Ed.), *Psychoactive sacramentals: Essays on entheogens and religion* (pp. 207–217). San Francisco: Council on Spiritual Practices.

Hood, R. W., Jr. (1975). The construction and preliminary validation of a measure of reported mystical experience. *Journal for the Scientific Study of Religion, 14*(1), 29–41.

Hood, R. W., Jr., Morris, R. J., & Watson, P. J. (1993). Further factor analysis of Hood's Mysticism Scale. *Psychological Reports, 73*(1), 1176–1178.

Horgan, J. (2005, February 26). Psychadelic medicine: Mind bending, health giving. *New Scientist, 2488,* 36–39. Retrieved June 9, 2006, from http://www.newscientist .com/article.ns?id=mg18524881.400&print=true.

Hruby, P. (2001). Unitive consciousness and Pahnke's Good Friday Experiment. In T. Roberts (Ed.), *Psychoactive sacramentals: Essays on entheogens and religion* (pp. 59–69). San Francisco: Council on Spiritual Practices.

Huxley, A. (1954). *The doors of perception.* New York: Harper & Row.

James, W. (1982/1902). *The varieties of religious experience: A study in human nature.* New York: Penguin Books. (Original work published 1902)

Küng, H., Ess, J., von Stietencron, H., & Bechert, H. (1986). *Christianity and the world religions: Paths to dialogue with Islam, Hinduism and Buddhism.* Garden City, NY: Doubleday.

Kurtzweil, P. (1995, September). Medical possibilities for psychedelic drugs. *FDA Consumer.* Retrieved June 9, 2006, from http://www.fda.gov/fdac/features/795_ psyche.html.

Learner, M., & Lyvers, M. (2004). Cross-cultural comparison of values, beliefs, and sense of coherence in psychedelic drug users. *Bulletin of the Multidisciplinary Association for Psychedelic Studies, 14*(1), 9–10.

Lucas-Caldwell, A. M. (2001). What is entheology? In T. Roberts (Ed.), *Psychoactive sacramentals: Essays on entheogens and religion* (pp. 147–153). San Francisco: Council on Spiritual Practices.

Mangini, M. (1998). Treatment of alcoholism using psychedelic drugs: A review of the program of research. *Journal of Psychoactive Drugs, 30*(4), 381–418.

Mangini, M. V. (2000). *"Yes, Mom took acid:" The sociohistorical influence of prior psychedelic drug use in adults.* Unpublished doctoral dissertation, University of California, San Francisco.

MAPS Bulletin. (1990+). Multidisciplinary Association for Psychedelic Studies, Sarasota, FL.

Merkur, D. (2001). Manna, the showbread, and the eucharist: Psychoactive sacraments in the Bible. In T. Roberts (Ed.), *Psychoactive sacramentals: Essays on entheogens and religion* (pp. 139–145). San Francisco: Council on Spiritual Practices.

Multidisciplinary Association for Psychedelic Studies. (n.d.). Retrieved September 1, 2005, from www.maps.org.

Nichols, C. D., & Sanders-Bush, E. (2002). A single dose of lysergic acid diethylamide influences gene expression patterns within the mammalian brain. *Neuropsychopharmacology, 26*(5), 634–642.

Nichols, D. E. (1999–2000). From Eleusis to PET scans: The mysteries of psychedelics. *MAPS Bulletin, 9*(4), 50–55.

Nichols, D. E. (2004). Hallucinogens. *Pharmacology and Therapeutics, 101,* 131–181.

Pahnke, W. N. (1963). *Drugs and mysticism: An analysis of the relationship between psychedelic drugs and the mystical consciousness.* Unpublished doctoral dissertation, Harvard University.

Pahnke, W. N., & Richards, W. A. (1966). Implications of LSD and experimental mysticism. *Journal of Religion and Health, 5*(3), 175–208.

Passie, T. (Ed.). (1997). *Psycholytic and psychedelic therapy research 1931–1995.* Hannover, Germany: Laurentius.

Rees, A. (2004, August 8). Nobel Prize genius Crick was high on LSD when he discovered the secret of life. *Mail on Sunday* (London), Section FB, 44–45.

Riedlinger, T.J. (Ed.). (1990). *The sacred mushroom seeker: Essays for R. Gordon Wasson.* Portland, OR: Dioscorides Press.

Roberts, T.B. (1998). States of unitive consciousness: Research summary. *San Francisco: Council on Spiritual Practices.* Retrieved June 9, 2006, from http://csp.org/experience/docs/unitive_consciousness.html.

Roberts, T.B. (1999). Do entheogen-induced mystical experiences boost the immune system? Psychedelics, peak experiences, and wellness. *Advances in Mind-Body Health, 15,* 139–147.

Roberts, T.B. (Ed.). (2001). *Psychoactive sacramentals: Essays on entheogens and religion.* San Francisco: Council on Spiritual Practices.

Roberts, T.B. (2005). *Entheogens—sacramentals or sacrilege? Working design for a university course.* Retrieved June 9, 2006, from http://www.cedu.niu.edu/epf/edpsych/faculty/roberts/index_roberts.html.

Roberts, T.B. (2006). *Psychedelic horizons: Snow White, immune system, multistate mind, enlarging education.* Essex, England: Imprint Academic.

Roberts, T.B., & Hruby, P.J. (Eds.). (1995–2003). *Religion and psychoactive sacraments: An entheogen chrestomathy.* San Francisco: Council on Spiritual Practices. Retrieved June 9, 2006, from http://csp.org/chrestomathy.

Roberts, T.B., & Hruby, P.J. (1996). *Entheogens—Return of the ostracized.* Paper sponsored by the Religion and Education Special Interest Group at the Annual Meeting of the American Educational Research Association, New York.

Roberts, T.B., & Winkelman, M. (Eds.). (in press). *Hallucinogens and healing: New scientific evidence for psychedelic substances as treatments.* Westport, CT: Praeger.

Ruck, C.A.P. (2003, January 12.) Was there a whiff of cannabis about Jesus? *Sunday Times* (London). Retrieved June 13, 2006, from http://www.ukcia.org/news/shownewsarticle.php?articleid=5906.

Ruck, C.A.P., Bigwood, J., Staples, D., Ott, J., & Wasson, R.G. (1979). Entheogens. *Journal of Psychedelic Drugs, 11*(1–2), 145–146.

Ruck, C.A.P, Staples, B., & Heinrich, C. (2001). *The apples of Apollo: Pagan and Christian mysteries of the Eucharist.* Durham, NC: Carolina Universities Press.

Rudgley, R. (1993). *Essential substances in society: A cultural history of intoxicants in society.* New York: Kodansha International.

Shanon, B. (2002). *The antipodes of the mind: Charting the phenomenology of the ayahuasca experience.* Oxford, England: Oxford University Press.

Silberman, I. (2005). Religion as a meaning-system: Implications for individual and societal well-being. *Psychology of Religion Newsletter, 30*(2), 1–9.

Smith, H. (1976). *Forgotten truth: The primordial tradition.* New York: Harper & Row.

Smith, H. (2000). *Cleansing the doors of perception: The religious significance of entheogenic plants and chemicals.* New York: Tarcher/Putnam.

Smith, H. (2001). Do drugs have religious import? A thirty-five year retrospect. In T. Roberts (Ed.), *Psychoactive sacramentals: Essays on entheogens and religion* (pp. 11–18). San Francisco: Council on Spiritual Practices.

Stace, W.T. (1961). *Mysticism and philosophy.* London: Macmillan.

Sternberg, R.J. (1988). *The triarchic mind: A new theory of human intelligence.* New York: Penguin.

Stolaroff, M.J. (1994). *Thanatos to eros: Thirty-five years of psychedelic exploration.* Berlin: Verlag fur Wissenschaft und Bildung.

Stolaroff, M. (2001). A protocol for a sacramental service. In T. Roberts (Ed.), *Psychoactive sacramentals: Essays on entheogens and religion* (pp. 155–163). San Francisco: Council on Spiritual Practices.

Tart, C.T. (1969). *Altered states of consciousness.* Garden City, NY: Doubleday.

Toolan, D. (1987). Facing west from California shores: A Jesuit's journey into new age consciousness. New York: Crossroads.

Van Dusen, W. (1961). LSD and the enlightenment of Zen. *Psychologia, 4,* 11–16.

Vaughan, F. (1983). Perception and knowledge: Reflections on psychological and spiritual learning in the psychedelic experience. In L. Grinspoon & J. Bakalar (Eds.), *Psychedelic reflections* (pp. 108–114). New York: Human Sciences Press.

Vaughan, F. (2001). *The inward arc: Healing in psychotherapy and spirituality.* Backinprint.com.

Walsh, R. (1988). Two Asian psychologies and their implications for western psychologies. *American Journal of Psychotherapy, 42*(4), 543–560.

Walsh, R. (2001). From state to trait: The challenge of transforming transient insights into enduring change. In T. Roberts (Ed.), *Psychoactive sacramentals: Essays on entheogens and religion* (pp. 19–24). San Francisco: Council on Spiritual Practices.

Walsh, R., & Grob, C. (Eds.). (2005). *Higher wisdom: Eminent elders explore the continuing impact of psychedelics.* Albany: State University of New York Press.

Walsh, R., & Vaughan, F. (Eds.). (1993). *Paths beyond ego: The transpersonal vision.* Los Angeles: Tarcher/Perigee.

Wasson, R.G. (1968). *Soma: The divine mushroom of immortality.* New York: Harcourt Brace Jovanovich.

Wasson, R.G., Hofmann, A., & Ruck, C.A.P. (1978). *The road to Eleusis.* New York: Harcourt Brace Jovanovich.

Wilson, E.O. (1998). *Consilience: The unity of knowledge.* New York: Knopf.

Winkelman, M. (2000). *Shamanism: The neural ecology of consciousness and healing.* Westport, CT: Bergin and Garvey.

Winkelman, M. (2001). Psychointegrators: Multidisciplinary perspectives on the therapeutic effects of hallucinogens. *Complementary Health Practice Review, 6*(3), 219–237.

Winkelman, M. (2002). Psychointegrators: The psychological effects of entheogens. *Entheos: The Journal of Psychedelic Spirituality, 2*(1), 51–61.

Wulff, D. (1991). *Psychology of religion: Classic and contemporary views.* New York: Wiley.

CHAPTER 11

AN ILLUSION OF THE FUTURE: TEMPTATIONS AND POSSIBILITIES

Keith G. Meador

The previous chapters in this volume provide an intriguing context within which to reflect theologically on substantive conceptual and methodological issues within the "religion and brain" conversation. My comments are far from exhaustive with regard to the thoughtful and notable varied contributions contained in this volume, but will provide some overview of relevant, broad conceptual issues that arise with some regularity and then engage individual chapters as constructive.

Sigmund Freud challenged the religious community of his day with a work titled *The Future of an Illusion* (Freud, 1928) in which he anticipated the "science" of psychoanalysis freeing us from the neurotic needs for religion as he understood them. During the three-quarters of a century since *The Future of an Illusion* was first published, the more illusory dimension of this conversation has proven to be Freud's presumption that psychoanalysis was a science in the fullness of the scientific claims of late nineteenth and early twentieth centuries. The assumptions of explanatory power embodied within the positivistic notions of early psychoanalytic metapsychologies have appeared increasingly naïve and limited in their capacities to explain human nature, motivation, and intention.

While elegant and seductive in their creativity and intellectual lure, efforts to systematize human experience through reified metapsychological structures and theories while isolating understandings of the experiences from contextualized lives that can be intelligibly narrated have proven to be unproductive. As we attempt to engage "religion" in relation to health and behavior we could find ourselves similarly seduced into "illusions" regarding the reducibility of "religion" to a decontextualized biological phenomenon that is amenable to measurement and "scientific" examination independent from a community of spiritual practice and theological interpretation. Although many within the current religion and health conversation would intend to promote a very different endpoint than Freud in regard to religion, efforts to codify human experiences as being "religious" or even "spiritual" that have been abstracted from contexts and communities of interpretation and practice have questionable intelligibility (MacIntyre, 1981).

Even though many participants in the current wave of "religion and brain" research might want to challenge Freud's reductionistic inclinations regarding religion and the implications his work embodied, there may be more in common between the current movement and Freud's agenda than one would initially realize. Freud and the current "religion and brain" studies are genuinely interesting and intellectually intriguing with regard to human experience and the mechanism and significance of neurobiological correlates with these experiences. That said, one substantive question that arises is the issue of what this has to do with "religion" or "spirituality?" What makes an experience religious or spiritual? Is some prior socially and historically mediated context of formation and acculturation not required to provide the language and interpretive capacity through which an experience is narrated? A number of the chapters in this book discuss or allude to these questions and I specifically examine some of their proposed perspectives, but the centrality of the question for all of this work needs to be highlighted for consideration.

Anne Taves (1999) clarifies that "the experience of religion cannot be separated from the communities of discourse and practice that gave rise to it *without becoming something else"* (p. 353). As a historian of religious experience from John Wesley to William James, she offers a comprehensive and thorough account of religious experience as typically considered within the American story of pietistic individualism. The dependency on social and historical context for interpreting and giving meaning to experiential phenomena (Madsen, Sullivan, Swidler, & Tipton, 2002) is a notion broadly acknowledged within much current thought. That does not mean this perspective is without detractors, but the burden is generally considered to be upon the detractors—in particular, those who reject the notion that a socially and historically constructed interpretive capacity is implicit for making meaning and deriving coherence from personal experience. The degree to which an experience mediated through biological substrates (which is a characteristic of all known brain phenomena) is interpreted as being religious or not depends on the history and contextual formation of the person having the experience. This does not limit the potential personal, and perhaps even religious or spiritual, significance of the experience for the person so engaged, but a proper understanding of this delineation does help avoid excessive presumptions regarding the universal meaning and interpretability of neurobiologically mediated phenomena independent of traditions, practices, and cultural context.

Within these considerations, I examine the contributions to this volume, providing conceptual and theological reflection and commentary while appreciating the commitment to thoughtful inquiry evident in all of the chapters. The first section of this essay focuses on Nichols and Chemel's chapter on neuropharmacology in companion to Park and McNamara's chapter on meaning, religion, and the brain. I then attend to the issues of health in regard to the proposed conceptual models considering Newberg and Lee's review of the religion and health relationship in conversation with Magyar-Russell and Pargament's frame for health risk factors and coping, along with Hansen and Norenzayan's engagement with the extrinsic/intrinsic religiosity conversation. Finally, I consider other issues arising within the volume with a review of the temptations and proposal of the possibilities presented by the work in this volume.

NEUROBIOLOGY, RELIGION, AND INTERPRETATION

Nichols and Chemel betray their misguided trajectory of approach with their title of "neuropharmacology of religion," as if they are starting from an acknowledged understanding of "religion" about which they will elucidate a neuropharmacological understanding. When they proceed to state that religion "deals with the supernatural and relies on intuition rather than rationale," and go on to say that "the 'mind' is one place science and religion meet," they frame their notion of religion and its intersection with science in a problematic fashion from the onset. This description of religion as a phenomenon of the "mind" and the "supernatural" leaves limited opportunity to understand religion as anything more than the subjective experience of an individual in relation to the supernatural, which when interpreted exclusively by the individual claiming the experience becomes nonfalsifiable and nonverifiable. While not lacking legitimacy as an empirically discerned, biologically mediated phenomenon, the narration of an experience as being "religious" depends on much more than the absolute "natural processes within the human body." The approach taken by Nichols and Chemel, which they acknowledge to be reductionistic, is intriguing if one acknowledges the inherent limitations with regard to how one describes the neuropharmacologically induced experiences they want to explore. But, without such qualifications, they are prone to appropriate a narrow, excessively interior understanding of religion that does not acknowledge the dependency on context and sociohistorical formation for the interpretation of any experience. They attempt to justify this method by stating that this understanding of religion allows one to proceed with "comparing the various forms of religious experiences, regardless of how they are produced." What they miss is that the crucial junction of adjudication regarding religiousness of experiences is not presumed to be how they are "produced," but rather the context and means by which they are interpreted. The prior formative cultural experiences and contexts, along with the current contexts of the person within which an experience is expressed, will give shape and form to the narration of the experience. Pharmacologically induced experiences may be interpreted as "religious" by an individual whether or not they would be accepted as such by a broader community of observers. The cumulative social and historical experiences of that person provide the capacity for "religious" interpretation and the intelligibility to narrate an experience as being "religious" in their particular place and time.

As Nichols and Chemel acknowledge, current neurosciences consider all such phenomenological experiences as what they name as "religious" to be biologically mediated and produced. If all such experiences are produced through similar neurobiological processes, then how they are interpreted becomes all-important. Whether considering the contextually derived understanding of an experience for an individual formed through prior social and historical formation, or appealing to an argument for a more communally interpreted notion of the discernment of religious experience, the dependence on contextual interpretation for experience to be judged as "religious" is pivotal. Talal Asad (1993) says that "there cannot be a universal definition of religion, not only because its constituent elements and relationships are historically specific, but because that definition is itself the historical product of discursive processes" (p. 29). The attempt to classify a pharmacologically induced experience as being "religious" based on claims of "transcendence of space and time, a deeply felt positive mood, sacredness, a noetic sense of an ultimate truth or reality, paradoxicality, ineffability," while appealing to these as implying some universal religious or spiritual awareness, denies the historical particularity and specificity of religion. That a pharmacologically induced ecstatic experience can be physiologically stimulating, psychologically motivating, existentially heartening, and generally experientially gratifying is not questioned, but whether that experience is most correctly interpreted as being religious or spiritual is a significant point of inquiry. That determination is made in a socially and historically formed context whether acknowledged or not. Attempts to render such determinations separate from their contexts are fraught with reductionistic naïveté and an inadequately formed paradigm for considering the complex interaction of biology, social processes, and cultural formation as interpreters of religion and human experience.

Although employing a different approach, Park and McNamara focus on meaning making in the brain and its relationship to religion with a parallel reductionistic tendency stating that "it is likely that the frontal lobes hold these representations of the religious self." While legitimately linking the neurologically mediated "sense of self" to the prefrontal cortex, they over-reach when they assert that a reified "self" with a religious modifier can be located in some particular domain of the brain. When appealing to the role of a "religious self" for meaning making, Park and McNamara attempt to argue for a neurologically articulated notion of "self." While they reference the apprehension of stories within an "internal set of values and beliefs" when discussing meaning construction, they do not provide adequate development of how and through what process they believe these values and beliefs are derived. They seem to appeal to "innate preparatory or conceptual sche-mas" in conjunction with formative "memories" as the bases for these values and beliefs through which meaning construction will occur. While I find their appeal to a "memory-based conceptual framework" constructive, their assumptions regarding a "hierarchy of motivational constructs" seem overly optimistic in appropriating "costly signaling theory" as a means for relating religion to evolutionary survival through meaning making. Any attribution of motivation is fragile and frequently lacks credibility when observed over time. Excessive dependence on discerning internal motivations and "true believer" status, through costly signaling theory's interpretation of ritual as contributing to evolutionary survival, may be very misleading. This is particularly relevant when trying to understand the meaning of personal sacrifice and commitments to justice within a community of faith unless developed within the context of a particular tradition of faith and practice. Although not intending to do so, these theories have the potential for sub-stantive distortion of traditional understandings of faithfulness and reduce religious ritual to an instrumentalism that distorts worship and practices of transformation.

The memories and motivational constructs to which Park and McNamara attribute meaning making in relation to innate conceptual schemas seem to lack an appreciation of the contingencies of human existence. While claiming that the "meaningless" religious rituals can prove productive through their being "costly," their proposed constructions for meaning making fall short due to the instrumental implications embedded within this argument. They lack a capacity to narrate the compelling nature of religious rituals and prac-tices as a means of bearing witness to a story that gives meaning through its very capacity to narrate suffering, and even death, without any presumption of enhanced survival or perpetuation of themselves. They have a limited abil-ity to incorporate the challenging, and perhaps disorienting, nature of the claim to faithfulness in some religious traditions such as the Christian tradi-tion as noted by David Ford, a Cambridge theologian. He says that,

> the remembering is false if it is not connected with entering more fully into the contingencies and tragic potentialities of life in the face of evil and

death. There can be no quick leap across Gethsemane and Calvary. Here are massive dislocation and disorientation, agonizing loss and the demand to unlearn some of one's deepest convictions and habits. It is therefore very serious if a contemporary celebration of the eucharist dulls instead of sharpening the sense both of exposure to danger and of a God whose way of being God is to be involved in the contingencies in a shockingly complete and painful way. (Ford, 1999, p. 47)

Ford illuminates the Christian theological understanding that God is a God of transformation and redemptive renewal of the tragic, not adaptation and accommodation in service of evolutionary survival. The most powerful potential for faith commitments and religious practices to form meaning through a "memory-based conceptual framework" is compromised when the lack of intelligibility of a ritual or behavior becomes a marker of value to survival greater than its communally remembered and contextually interpreted significance for intelligibly finding meaning within the practice or ritual. The importance of meaning, highlighted by Park and McNamara, is notable and merits continued consideration. Their acknowledged lack of adequate "integrative theories" to support their proposed models of interaction of "religion, meaning, and brain" will benefit from more theologically considered integrative efforts as they continue to push on this frontier. The thoughtful engagement of theological and anthropological implications within this work will be necessary to optimally move this work forward.

RELIGION, HEALTH, AND COPING

Newberg and Lee introduce the relationship of religion and health with a review of the literature and a recounting of some of the most notable findings. They note the increasing interest in this topic reflected by the upsurge of studies reported in this area along with the increased interest of diagnostic and regulatory bodies in the inclusion of religion and spirituality within their criteria for consideration. While noting this increasing acknowledgement and inclusion of religion within mainstream health and medicine, Newberg and Lee appropriately go on to describe the field's current dependence on claims based on associations found within correlational studies and the lack of adequate investigation to establish causal inferences to support hypotheses of mechanism. They appeal for randomized control trials in religion and health, which has some legitimacy, but before proceeding to clinically conceptualized and interpreted randomized control trials in religion and health, the challenges subsequently noted need to be systematically addressed.

The 10 challenges noted by Newberg and Lee for religion and health research are a useful concise articulation of the major conceptual and methodological issues to be considered in this work. Although the temptation to push ahead into randomized control trials regarding the religion and health relationship is luring, adequate attention needs to be given to the issues raised in these 10 challenges prior to proceeding. This approach is needed to avoid compromising the credibility of this work for the future from the perspective of funding institutions and the broader scientific community. Randomized control trials that are inadequately conceived and implemented will be methodologically suspect and limited in interpretability. Adequately addressing these challenges within the religion and health research community should be the top priority at this time so as to optimize the future investments in more elaborate studies to discern causality and mechanisms within this relationship.

Review of the entire list of challenges is not my goal, but reflection on some of the issues embedded within the challenges and their significance for the future of religion and health inquiry may be constructive. The issue of how to define "religion" and "spirituality" is a perpetual issue with many attempts made to varying degrees of success. We have already discussed some points for consideration in regard to this issue from the perspective of the need to provide a contextual interpretation of experience if it is to be legitimately narrated as being religious. Along with the need to avoid excessive explanatory claims regarding reductionistic neurobiological phenomena, we must challenge ourselves regarding the theological significance—and ultimately methodological significance with regard to health outcome claims—of the understanding of religion employed. Shuman, Meador, and Hauerwas (2003) have argued that,

> The most significant *theological* questions about the interrelationship of religion and health is not simply whether being more religious will result in better health but whether the religion in question, that is, the religion that ostensibly improves the health of some, teaches its adherents the sometimes difficult truth about God and God's creation and helps them live well in and as part of that creation—whether they are sick or well . . . questions about the medical utility of a given religion and the practices constituting that religion have to be considered from *within* the boundaries set by that religion's theological tradition, however permeable and elastic those boundaries may be. (p. 45)

When this particularity of religious expression within the boundaries of a theological tradition is not considered in the defining of "religion," the methods of measurement and the ultimate significance of findings with regard to health outcomes are brought into question. The "experiential-expressivist" model of religion as described by theologian George Lindbeck (1984) provides a framework within which to better understand the formulation and implications of the individualistic, experientially dependent understanding of religion that is so prevalent in modernity and typically informs the religion and health conversation.

An alternative understanding of religion offered by Lindbeck (1984) that ultimately allows for a more intelligible and communally verifiable religion and spirituality is the "cultural-linguistic" model. This

> "cultural-linguistic" account of religion, in which "religions are seen as comprehensive interpretive schemes, usually embodied in myths or narratives or heavily ritualized," does not disregard or deny the existence of human religious experience. Rather, it denies the primacy and the priority of *individual* religious experience by showing that myths, narratives, and rituals that make up a particular way of life themselves "structure human experience and understanding of self and world." It is not the naked experience of an individual's believing in something beyond the self that gives rise to the description of that experience and the accompanying religious way of life; it is the way of life of this or that religious community or culture that gives rise to the description and makes possible an individual experience that can be described as religious. (p. 45)

Hall, Koenig, and Meador (2004) frame this issue for religion and health research stating that all worldviews have languages and cultural commitments by which they narrate and give form to the good and ascribe meaning whether what is commonly called "religion" or a more "secular" faith commitment is primary in the formation of the worldview.

The importance of careful definition for informing reliable measurement of religion and spirituality is reflected in these considerations of different theological models of religion. Newberg and Lee allude to some of the varied possibilities when considering proper measurement of religion in this research. Reflected within these possibilities is the need to discern how to most optimally define religion, particularly in regard to health outcome relationships, and how to articulate the demarcation between religion and spirituality, assuming that such a demarcation exists. Hypotheses and disciplines within which religion and health research is pursued frequently affect decisions with regard to definitions of religion. Methods of measurement employed by the fields of sociology, medicine, or psychology somewhat predictably influence standard practices within the respective disciplines of inquiry. Although we may see this as inevitable due to the guilds and intellectual captivity of the disciplines, the implications for religion and health research are substantive. Newberg and Lee rightly point out the need for interdisciplinary engagement to enhance the work in this field. The importance of including theologically informed collaborators who have adequate methodological sophistication to participate in research during the design and interpretation of religion and health research cannot be overemphasized. Systematic initiatives to foster this work needs to be a priority.

The ongoing struggle to thoughtfully differentiate between religion and spirituality consumes much effort on the part of many in this work. Comprehensively addressing this issue is far beyond the scope of this essay, but the "spirituality" to which many persons within contemporary conversations appeal has many of the same hallmarks we have already discussed in regard to decontextualized religion. The more interesting issue with regard to definitions relevant to this conversation may be the boundaries between "spirituality" and "mind/body" practices rather than religion and spirituality. For those whose spirituality and practices are formed within a religious tradition, the split of religion and spirituality has little relevance. Many mind/body exercises are best interpreted as manifestations of the human spirit in service of health and well-being, but with no claim to be part of an interpretable religious tradition. When these mind/body practices are narrated as "spirituality," it is a disservice to all constituents of the current spirituality and health conversation. Appeals to self-referential ecstatic experiences or even transcendental claims within personal and interior experiences not related to any communal context or historically derived interpretation are susceptible to distortion and presumption without means for adjudication or validation. Attribution of "spirituality" to such experiences contributes to a blurring of definitions, and when appropriated within research to an excessively broad set of experiences it distorts the findings and creates potential for misguided research design and funding.

The optimal time frame for observation or measurement in religion and health research links to the persistent issue of discerning causality and mechanism within the abundance of associations found in correlational studies. One's hypothesis regarding the mechanism of the relationship between religion and health inevitably affects how one designs research. Added to this are the inevitable considerations of funding that frequently limit opportunities for more longitudinally designed research. The notion that depth, breadth, and intensity of exposure to religion and spirituality have an impact on the associated health outcomes is consistent with other exposures about which health outcomes might be measured and predicted. Although short-term claims to transformation are common within the history of religious experiences, claims of relationship to health constructed within defensible paradigms for research methodology are necessary. These claims would seem most likely to be justified by models in which the measure of religion as the exposure and health as the effect is intelligible within a model of exposure and effect similar to other types of research. Unless one is going to propose some form of supernatural mechanism that is inherently lacking in falsifiability and vulnerable to discounting by the research community in general, religion and health research needs to offer research designs compatible with mechanisms interpretable within standard paradigms, while not being hesitant to challenge the limitations of those paradigms within the bounds of intelligibility to the broader scientific community. While randomized controlled trials are the gold standard within clinical trials, too quickly attempting to implement such interventions within religion and health research before more adequately understanding the mechanism for the relationship through population-based observational studies exposes the entire area of study to misrepresentation. Efforts prematurely initiated to implement clinical interventions and randomized controlled trials make the field vulnerable to inadvertent negative findings due to misplaced assumptions regarding mechanisms and ethical vulnerabilities due to the nuances inherent to the complexities of religion research.

If the proposed mechanism for understanding religion and health associations is most rightly measured through observing people of faith formed over time through particular practices of communities of faith, there is no substitute for longitudinal studies to optimally better understand this mechanism. Of course, complexity and funding issues inevitably arise, but these concerns should not interfere with clarity regarding hypothesis generation and intentionality directed toward implementing the most intellectually credible methods for this research. A "cultural-linguistically" articulated model of religion in contradistinction to the frequently prevailing "expressivist- experiential" model offers a theologically credible paradigm of religion. A broadly interpreted cultural-linguistic model of religion allows for a more scientifically intelligible religion and health research agenda if appropriated within a research paradigm and model for causal hypothesis that incorporates an adequate sense of depth and duration of exposure to form the basis for an identifiable and measurable mechanism.

Magyar-Russell and Pargament define religion as a "search for significance in ways related to the sacred" in their engagement with health, coping, and "sacred loss." This serves as a good example of the challenges noted by Newberg and Lee with regard to definitions in religion and health research. This definition predisposes Magyar-Russell and Pargament to inadequate differentiation between religion or spirituality and psychological constructs. Their acknowledgement that this definition "rests on the assumption that people are goal-directed beings, motivated to attain value or significance in life" reveals their bias of a highly optimistic view of human nature that is embodied within this definition. The implications of this assumption are further magnified by their dependency on their notion of the internally and individualistically derived "sacred" as a primary determinant of the "religious." While attempting to draw some delineation through this use of the concept of "sacred," their notion of sacred is so broadly construed that it conflates communally practiced expressions of faith and interpreted constructs of God with "seemingly secular parts of life" that are "sanctified" through some form of "association with, or representation of, divinity." This definition falls short of an intelligible understanding of religion or spirituality that would have discernible distinction from whatever the subject might deem worthy of honoring as reflecting their own sense of value and significance. Proposing religion and health research designed using this definition for religion leaves one vulnerable to considerable distortion in measurement of variables and interpretation of findings.

An approach to religion research proposed by Magyar-Russell and Pargament for assessing benefits or harm of religiousness in their chapter is the degree to which a subject's religion is well integrated or poorly integrated. Although some form of this notion permeates a number of commonly used measures of religiosity, there are substantive concerns regarding this practice. The hierarchical implications inherent to this approach and the presumptions of the prerogative to adjudicate among manifestations of religiousness according to health or psychological functioning is methodologically suspect, especially when the discerning process is not vetted through theological lens (Cohen, Hall, Koenig, & Meador, 2005). Hansen and Norenzayan raise parallel concerns in this volume, arguing against the dichotomization frequently found with the use of intrinsic/ extrinsic religiosity measures. The temptation to assign positive valence to what is deemed to be more rational and "mature" while assigning a more negative valence to religion manifested through coping that is depicted as more primitive is common but may be misleading. Comparison of the religious coping of a developing world inhabitant who attends Catholic mass daily as a practice to assuage fears of the future and out of conviction that she is called to a life of such obedience with the rationally verbalized arguments for God's identification with suffering by an academically formed Western intellectual is easily misguided by presumptions of hierarchy of religiosity.

Psychological sophistication and functioning is a legitimate and frequently important axis of assessment in relation to coping skills and health, but taking care to properly discriminate between religious coping and psychological functioning maintains more credibility for the role of both. If the measures for both are inadequately demarcated, the ability to rightly interpret either dimension of a person in relation to his or her health and coping is compromised. The construct of "sacred loss" as used by Magyar-Russell and Pargament depends on the individual's narration of the loss as "sacred," which is subjectively determined and susceptible to predisposing sensitivities that are more psychologically than spiritually mediated. While Pargament's work with negative religious coping and struggles is notable for attempting to better understand an important dimension of the religion and health relationship, the structural overlap between his depictions of "negative religious coping" and psychological struggle challenge the independence of the construct of negative religious coping from maladaptive psychological functioning articulated through religious language. Acknowledgement of this lack of independence would not negate the relevance of the findings but would free the construct from having to carry the burden of claiming an unwarranted conceptual independence and allow for a more unified interpretation of the coping as observed. This acknowledgement would also allow for a more cogent theological interpretation through the lens of the cultural-linguistic understanding of religion as described by Lindbeck (1984).

CONCLUSION

This essay began with reference to Freud's reductionism and its reflection in the current reductionistic tendencies within parts of the religion, health, and brain conversation. Ralph Hood responds in this volume to two poles of work in psychology of religion, one of which he attributes to Freud, by invoking the work of William James as a "middle ground" of dialogue "between various psychological and religious claims." Hood uses James as a basis for his effort at finding a middle ground in his "common core thesis in the study of mysticism." Hood bases his proposal on six stated assumptions that will not be repeated here, but his dependency on these assumptions makes his proposal for a "common core" more of an assertion than an argument. The degree to which he privileges mystical states and appeals to James in asserting that privilege through stated assumptions of "causal indifference," the "ineffability of mystical experiences," insistence on "unmediated experiences of reality," and a "mystical stream" within all religious traditions whose identification and interpretation is independent of context allows him to make an argument without adequately justifying some crucial assumptions. He ultimately claims that unmediated claims of mystical experience can be "reliably measured" through the reports of those having the experiences. Although I am sympathetic to his goal in arguing for the power of narratively derived "data," his position is inadequate to justify the claim of "reliable" measurement. Hood's proposal that mysticism is an "independent type" is ultimately not compelling, and his foundationalist claims in anticipation of empirical expectations regarding mysticism are more illusory than instructive. Hood's effort to claim a "common core" is, in the end, consistent with the neurobiological phenomena described in many of the chapters in this volume, but his effort to circumvent the interpretive context or tradition within which an ecstatic or mystical experience becomes intelligible is misguided.

The limitations and implications of Hood's indebtedness to James is revealed by Stanley Hauerwas (2001) when he says,

> Just to the extent that James denied the creaturely status of human beings, I suspect it is a mistake to take too seriously his arguments against natural theology as the primary objections he had to Christianity.

Those arguments were primarily an expression of James's deep moral objection to Christianity. What really bothered James was not that Christianity seemed to entail false views about the world, but that Christianity challenged the moral and political arrangements necessary to sustain the human project without God. James was profoundly right to see Christianity as the enemy of the world he hoped was being born. That James's world has come into being, a world about which he had some misgivings, makes it all the more important to attend to this aspect of this thought. Many Christians today want the world James wanted, while assuming that they can continue to have the Christian God. But James was right to think that you cannot have both. (p. 78)

We have exponentially advanced our understanding of brain function since William James, and we have made major strides in our understanding of the relationship between religion and health during the last couple of decades. Both of these areas of advance are notable and to be applauded, and the attempts at synthesis and hypothesis generation presented in the chapters in this volume are to be commended for their thoughtfulness. The challenge we all face is how to go forward with methodological integrity embodied within a vision for scientifically rigorous and theologically sophisticated inquiry into these complex phenomena and relationships. The conversations fostered within these chapters offer an opportunity to face that challenge and engage it without illusions of grandeur, but rather with a conviction of the importance of the work. Honoring the complexity of scientific inquiry regarding religion while insisting on theological intelligibility of the inquiry will protect us from many pitfalls and nurture work that will distinguish the field for the future.

REFERENCES

Asad, T. (1993). *Genealogies of religion: Discipline and reasons of power in Christianity and Islam.* Baltimore: Johns Hopkins University Press.

Cohen, A. B., Hall, D. E., Koenig, H. G., & Meador, K. G. (2005). Social versus individual motivation: Implications for normative definitions of religious orientation. *Personality and Social Psychology Review, 9*(1), 48–61.

Ford, D. (1999). *Self and salvation: Being transformed.* Cambridge, England: Cambridge University Press.

Freud, S. (1928). *The future of an illusion.* London: Norton.

Hall, D. E., Koenig, H. G., & Meador, K. G. (2004). Conceptualizing religion: How language shapes and constrains knowledge in the study of religion and health. *Perspectives in Biology and Medicine, 47*(3), 386–401.

Hauerwas, S. (2001). *With the grain of the universe.* Grand Rapids, MI: Brazos Press.

Lindbeck, G. (1984). *Nature of doctrine.* Philadelphia: Westminster Press.

MacIntyre, A. (1981). *After virtue.* Notre Dame, IN: University of Notre Dame Press.

Madsen, R., Sullivan, W. M., Swidler, A., & Tipton, S. M. (2002). *Meaning, and modernity: Religion, polity, and self.* Berkeley: University of California Press.

Shuman, J. J., Meador, K. G., & Hauerwas, S. (2003). *Heal thyself: Spirituality, medicine, and the distortion of Christianity.* Oxford, England: Oxford University Press.

Taves, A. (1999). *Fits, trances and visions.* Princeton, NJ: Princeton University Press.

INDEX

About the Editor and Contributors

EDITOR

Patrick McNamara, Ph.D., is director of the Evolutionary Neurobehavior Laboratory in the Department of Neurology at the Boston University School of Medicine and the Veterans Administration New England Health Care System. Upon graduating from the Behavioral Neuroscience Program at Boston University in 1991, he trained at the Aphasia Research Center at the Boston Veterans Administration Medical Center in neurolinguistics and brain-cognitive correlation techniques. He then began developing an evolutionary approach to problems of brain and behavior and currently is studying the evolution of the frontal lobes, the evolution of the two mammalian sleep states (REM and NREM), and the evolution of religion in human cultures. He has published numerous articles and chapters on these topics pioneering the investigation of the role of the frontal lobes in mediation of religious experience.

CONTRIBUTORS

Kelly Bulkeley, Ph.D., is a visiting scholar at the Graduate Theological Union and teaches in the Dream Studies Program at John F. Kennedy University, both in the San Francisco Bay Area. He earned his doctorate in religion and psychological studies from the University of Chicago Divinity School and is former president of the International Association for the Study of Dreams. He has written and edited several books on dreaming, religion, psychology, culture, and science, including *The Wilderness of Dreams, An Introduction to the Psychology of Dreaming, Visions of the Night, The Wondering Brain, Dreaming beyond Death,* and *Soul, Psyche, Brain: New Directions in the Study of Religion and Brain-Mind Science.*

Benjamin R. Chemel is a doctoral candidate working toward a Ph.D. in molecular pharmacology in the Department of Medicinal Chemistry and Molecular Pharmacology at Purdue University. He is currently researching the role of various dopamine receptor subtypes in the pharmacology of anti-Parkinson drugs, as well as LSD and other hallucinogens. His goal is to unravel the underlying molecular mechanisms that are responsible for the psychoactive effects of shamanically used visionary plants. He earned a B.S. degree with honors in 2001 from The Pennsylvania State University. Prior to beginning his graduate studies, he spent five field seasons as a botanist collecting ecological data on public lands in the western United States.

Ian Hansen is a Ph.D. candidate at the University of British Columbia. Currently conducting research in cultural, social, and political psychology, he earned an M.A. degree in psychology from the University of Illinois at Urbana-Champaign and a B.A. degree in philosophy from Swarthmore College. His thesis is on religion, religious intolerance, and support for religious violence.

Ralph W. Hood, Jr., is professor of psychology at the University of Tennessee at Chattanooga. He is past president of the Psychology of Religion Division of the American Psychological Association and a recipient of its William James Award. He is former editor of the *Journal for the Scientific Study Religion* and former co-editor of *The International Journal for the Psychology of Religion.* He currently co-edits *Archiv für Religionpsychologie.* He has published hundreds of papers on the psychology of religion and has authored, co-authored, and edited nine books.

Bruce Y. Lee is a member of the Department of Medicine, Section of Decision Sciences and Clinical Systems Modeling, at the University of Pittsburgh.

Gina Magyar-Russell, Ph.D., is a postdoctoral fellow in the Department of Psychiatry and Behavioral Sciences at Johns Hopkins University School of Medicine. She earned a doctorate in clinical psychology from Bowling Green State University. Her research and clinical interests include studies of the impact of the loss or violation of what individuals perceive as sacred, religious, and spiritual coping in medically ill patients, and integrating spirituality into psychotherapy with adults suffering from physical illness and injury and traumatic life events.

Keith G. Meador, M.D., ThM, MPH, is professor of the Practice of Pastoral Theology and Medicine at Duke Divinity School, where he teaches pastoral theology and pastoral care. He established the Theology and Medicine Program in the Divinity School and gives leadership to varied programmatic initiatives, one of which is the Caring Communities Program, which seeks to support health ministries and form caring communities throughout the Carolinas through education of clergy, health care providers, and lay leaders in the community. The Theology and Medicine Program also includes academic opportunities for nursing, medical, divinity, and undergraduate students to pursue studies in theology and health and the practice of health ministries. Meador's scholarship focuses on pastoral theology interpreted through practices of caring and their formation within the Christian community, as well as the investigation of health ministries as a manifestation of these practices. A physician and board-certified psychiatrist, his work builds on his clinical, research, and teaching background in mental health, pastoral theology, and public health about which he lectures widely and has published numerous publications, including the recently co-authored book, *Heal Thyself: Spirituality, Medicine, and the Distortion of Christianity.* He is co-director for the Center for Spirituality, Theology and Health in the Duke University Medical Center and holds a joint appointment as a clinical professor of psychiatry and behavioral sciences in the Duke School of Medicine. He also serves as a senior fellow in the Duke Center for the Study of Aging and Human Development.

Andrew B. Newberg, M.D., is assistant professor in the Departments of Radiology and Psychiatry and an adjunct assistant professor in the Department of Religious Studies at the University of Pennsylvania. He graduated from the University of Pennsylvania School of Medicine in 1993. He trained in internal medicine at the Graduate Hospital in Philadelphia and then completed a fellowship in nuclear medicine in the Division of Nuclear Medicine, Department of Radiology, at the University of Pennsylvania. During this time, he actively pursued a number of neuroimaging research projects that include the study of aging and dementia, epilepsy, and other neurological and psychiatric disorders. Newberg has been particularly involved in the study of mystical and religious experiences as well as the more general mind-body relationship in both the clinical and research aspects of his career. His research also includes understanding the physiological correlates of acupuncture therapy, meditation, and other types of alternative therapies.

He has published numerous articles and chapters on brain function, brain imaging, and the study of religious and mystical experiences. He has also co-authored two books entitled *Why God Won't Go Away: Brain Science and the Biology of Belief* and *The Mystical Mind: Probing the Biology of Belief* that explore the relationship between neuroscience and spiritual experience. The latter book received the 2000 award for Outstanding Books in Theology and the Natural Sciences presented by the Center for Theology and the Natural Sciences.

David E. Nichols, Ph.D., is professor of medicinal chemistry and molecular pharmacology in the Purdue University School of Pharmacy and Pharmaceutical Sciences. His research interests focus on drugs and small molecules that affect behavior. He has principally worked in the areas of dopamine and serotonin function in the central nervous system, and his expertise lies in understanding the relationship between molecular structure and biological action. His research has been continuously funded by the National Institutes of Health for nearly 25 years. He has published more than 250 research articles, including book chapters and monographs, holds seven U.S. patents, and has been invited to speak at numerous international symposia. He is recognized as one of the world's top experts on the chemistry and pharmacology of hallucinogens, and his laboratory is one of the few in the world still studying the preclinical pharmacology of the potent hallucinogen LSD. In 2004, he was selected by the International Serotonin Club as the Irwin H. Page Lecturer. In addition to his work on hallucinogens, he also has been a world leader in developing novel drugs for brain dopamine D_1 type receptors for use in treating Parkinson's disease, as well as the memory and cognitive deficits of schizophrenia, and he co-founded DarPharma, Inc., to commercialize his discoveries.

Ara Norenzayan is an assistant professor of psychology at the University of British Columbia. The author of over 25 publications in the area of social and cultural psychology, he received a Ph.D. in psychology from the University of Michigan in 1999. His research interests include cognition across cultures, the psychological foundations of culture and religion, and cultural evolution.

Raymond F. Paloutzian earned a Ph.D. degree in 1972 from Claremont Graduate School and has been a professor of experimental and social psychology at Westmont College (Santa Barbara, California) since 1981. He has been a visiting professor teaching psychology of religion at Stanford University and guest professor at Katholieke Universiteit in Leuven, Belgium. He is a fellow of the American Psychological Association (divisions of general, teaching, social issues, psychology of religion, and international), the American Psychological Society, and the Western Psychological Association, and has served as president of APA Division 36 (Psychology of Religion). The division honored him with the 2005 Virginia Sexton Mentoring Award for contributing to the development of other scholars in the field. He wrote *Invitation to the Psychology of Religion,* and, with Crystal Park, edited the *Handbook of the Psychology of Religion and Spirituality.* Paloutzian is editor of *The International Journal for the Psychology of Religion.*

Kenneth Pargament is professor of clinical psychology at Bowling Green State University. He has been a leading figure in the effort to bring a more balanced view of religious life to the attention of social scientists and health professionals. Pargament has published extensively on the vital role of religion in coping with stress and trauma. He is author of *The Psychology of Religion and Coping: Theory, Research, Practice* and co-editor of *Forgiveness: Theory, Research, Practice.* His awards include the William James Award for excellence in research in the psychology of religion from Division 36 of American Psychological Association (APA), the Virginia Staudt Sexton Mentoring Award from APA for guiding and encouraging others in the field, and two exemplary paper awards from the John Templeton Foundation.

Crystal L. Park is associate professor of psychology at the University of Connecticut. She received a Ph.D. in clinical psychology from the University of Delaware in 1993 and completed a two-year National Institute of Mental Health postdoctoral fellowship in health psychology at the University of California–San Francisco in 1995. Her research focuses on stress, coping, and adaptation—particularly on how people's beliefs, goals, and values affect their ways of perceiving and dealing with stressful events. She has developed a comprehensive model of meaning and meaning making and has been applying this model to a variety of stressful situations. Park has published articles on the roles of religious beliefs and coping in response to stressful life events, the phenomenon of stress-related growth, and people's attempts to find meaning in or create meaning out of negative life events. She is on the editorial boards of the *Journal of Clinical and Consulting Psychology* and *Psychology and Health* and co-edited *The Handbook of the Psychology of Religion and Spirituality.* Park is principal investigator on grants from the Lance Armstrong Foundation, to examine positive life changes in cancer survivors, and the Fetzer Foundation, to examine changes in spirituality and well-being in heart failure patients.

Thomas B. Roberts is the senior full professor in the College of Education at Northern Illinois University, where he has taught a psychedelics course since 1982. His online archive *Religion and Psychoactive Sacraments: An Entheogen Chrestomathy* (www.csp.org/chrestomathy) is the world's largest such compilation, containing excerpts and bibliographic information from over 550 books and dissertations. He edited *Psychoactive Sacramentals: Essays on Entheogens and Religion* and wrote *Psychedelic Horizons: Snow White, Immune System, Multistate Mind, Enlarging Education*. He is expanding the chapter he wrote for this book into a book manuscript tentatively titled *Increasing Spiritual Intelligence: Chemical Input, Religious Output*.

Steven A. Rogers is a postdoctoral fellow in neuropsychology at the University of California, Los Angeles's Department of Neurology and the Semel Institute for Neuroscience and Human Behavior. He earned a doctoral degree in clinical psychology from Fuller Theological Seminary's Graduate School of Psychology, and he has received training in both clinical psychology and neuropsychology from the American Lake VA, the Long Beach VA, and UCLA's Semel Institute for Neuroscience and Human Behavior. He provides psychotherapy in a small private practice and enjoys conducting research focusing on the neuropsychology of dementia and disorders of aging, mental illness, and religion and the relationship between religious coping and mental health. In August 2006, Rogers joined the clinical psychology faculty at Westmont College (Santa Barbara, California).

Michael Winkelman (Ph.D., University of California, Irvine, M.P.H. University of Arizona) is associate professor in the School of Human Evolution and Social Change at Arizona State University. Winkelman has engaged in cross-cultural and interdisciplinary research on shamanism for the past 30 years, focusing principally in the areas of the biological bases of shamanism and altered states of consciousness. He has used cross-cultural research to establish the universals of shamanism and psychobiological research and evolutionary psychology approaches to understand the bases of these universals. He has addressed these universals of religion in *Shamanism: The Neural Ecology of Consciousness and Healing*. He has also co-edited books on *Sacred Plants, Consciousness and Healing*, *Divination and Healing*, and *Pilgrimages and Healing*. He has explored the evolutionary basis of shamanism and the applications of shamanism to contemporary health problems of addiction. He is currently working on a book on the biology of religion.

About the Advisory Board

Scott Atran, Ph.D., conducts research and is centered in the following areas: cognitive and linguistic anthropology, ethnobiology, environmental decision making, categorization and reasoning, evolutionary psychology, anthropology of science (history and philosophy of natural history and natural philosophy), Middle East ethnography and political economy, natural history of Lowland Maya, cognitive and commitment theories of religion, terrorism, and foreign affairs.

The evolution of religion is a topic he explores in his book *In Gods We Trust* (2002). He is based both at the National Center for Scientific Research in Paris and at the University of Michigan. His recent work has focused on suicide terrorism. He has marshaled evidence that indicates that suicide bombers are not poor and crazed as depicted in the press but well-educated and often economically stable individuals with no significant psychological pathology.

Donald Capps, Ph.D., is Princeton's William Harte Felmeth Professor of Pastoral Psychology. He draws on his training as a psychologist of religion in both his teaching and his writing. In 1989, he was awarded an honorary doctorate in sacred theology from the University of Uppsala, Sweden, in recognition of his publications in the psychology of religion and pastoral care and of his leadership role in the Society for the Scientific Study of Religion, for which he served as editor of its professional journal from 1983 to 1988 and as president from 1990 to 1992.

J. Harold Ellens, Ph.D., is series editor for Praeger's Psychology, Religion and Spirituality series. He is a research scholar at the University of Michigan, Department of Near Eastern Studies. He is a retired Presbyterian theologian and ordained minister, a retired U.S. Army colonel, and a retired professor of philosophy, theology, and psychology. He has authored, coauthored, and/or edited 111 books and 165 professional journal articles. He served 15 years as executive director of the Christian Association for Psychological Studies and as founding editor and editor in chief of the *Journal of Psychology and Christianity.* He holds a Ph.D. from Wayne State University in the psychology of human communication, a Ph.D. from the University of Michigan in biblical and Near Eastern studies, and master degrees from Calvin Theological Seminary, Princeton Theological Seminary, and the University of Michigan. He was born in Michigan, grew up in a Dutch-German immigrant community, and determined at age seven to enter the Christian ministry as a means to help his people with the great amount of suffering he perceived all around him. His life's work has focused on the interface of psychology and religion.

Harold Koenig, M.D., M.H.Sc, is an associate professor of psychiatry and medicine at Duke University. He is director and founder of the Center for the Study of Religion/Spirituality and Health at Duke University; editor of the *International Journal of Psychiatry in Medicine,* and founder and editor in chief of *Research News in Science and Theology,* the monthly international newspaper of the John Templeton Foundation. His latest books include the *Handbook of Religion and Mental Health, The Healing Power of Faith: Science Explores Medicine's Last Great Frontier,* and *Religion and Health: A Century of Research Reviewed.*

Koenig completed his undergraduate education at Stanford University, his medical school training at the University of California at San Francisco, and his geriatric medicine, psychiatry, and biostatistics training at Duke University Medical Center. He is board certified in general psychiatry, geriatric psychiatry, and geriatric medicine and is on the faculty at Duke as professor of psychiatry and behavioral sciences and associate professor of medicine. He is also a registered nurse.

Koenig has published extensively in the fields of mental health, geriatrics, and religion, with nearly 250 scientific peer-reviewed articles and book chapters and 26 books in print or in preparation. His research on religion, health, and ethical issues in medicine has been featured on approximately 50 national and international television news programs (including all major U.S. news networks), 80 national or international radio programs (including multiple NPR, BBC, and CBC interviews), and close to 200 national or international newspapers or magazines (including cover stories for *Reader's Digest, Parade* magazine, and *Newsweek*). Koenig has been nominated twice for the Templeton Prize for Progress in Religion. His latest books include *The Healing Power of Faith* (2001), *The Handbook of Religion and Health* (2001), *Spirituality in Patient Care* (2002), and his autobiography *The Healing Connection* (2004).

Andrew B. Newberg, M.D., is director of clinical nuclear medicine, director of neuroPET research, and assistant professor in the Department of Radiology at the Hospital of the University of Pennsylvania. On graduating from the University of Pennsylvania School of Medicine in 1993, Newberg trained in internal medicine at the Graduate Hospital in Philadelphia—serving as chief resident in his final year—and subsequently completed a fellowship in nuclear medicine in the Division of Nuclear Medicine, Department of Radiology, at the University of Pennsylvania. He is board certified in internal medicine, nuclear medicine, and nuclear cardiology.

In collaboration with the Departments of Neurology and Psychiatry, Newberg has actively pursued neuroimaging research projects, including the study of aging and dementia, epilepsy, and other neurological and psychiatric disorders. Additionally, he has researched the neurophysiological correlates of acupuncture, meditation, and other types of complementary therapies.

Newberg has presented his research at national and international scientific and religious meetings; his numerous published articles and chapters cover the topics of brain function, brain imaging, and the study of religious and mystical experiences. In addition to the extensive press he has received, he has appeared on ABC's *World News Tonight* and is coauthor, with Eugene G. d'Aquili, M.D., of *The Mystical Mind: Probing the Biology of Belief.*

Recently, Newberg received a Science and Religion Course Award from the Center for Theology and the Natural Sciences to teach the course titled "The Biology of Spirituality" in the Department of Religious Studies, University of Pennsylvania (spring 2000).

Raymond F. Paloutzian, Ph.D., is a national and international expert in the psychology of religion and spirituality. He received his doctoral degree in 1972 from Claremont Graduate School and has been a professor of experimental and social psychology at Westmont College, Santa Barbara, California, since 1981. He has been a visiting professor teaching psychology of religion at Stanford University and guest professor at Katholieke Universiteit Leuven, Belgium. He is a fellow of the American Psychological Association (divisions of general, teaching, social issues, psychology of religion, and international), the American Psychological Society, and the Western Psychological Association and has served as president of the American Psychological Association's Division 36 (Psychology of Religion and Spirituality). The division honored him with the 2005 Virginia Sexton

Mentoring Award for contributing to the development of other scholars in the field. He wrote *Invitation to the Psychology of Religion* (2nd ed.1996; 3rd ed. forthcoming) and, with Crystal Park, edited the *Handbook of the Psychology of Religion and Spirituality* (2005). He is currently writing chapters on religion and spirituality for handbooks by Oxford University Press and Blackwell Publishers. His current research focuses on religiously motivated child abuse and medical neglect and on a systematic review of the literature on spiritual well-being. Paloutzian is editor of the *International Journal for the Psychology of Religion.*

Kenneth Pargament, Ph.D., has conducted nationally and internationally known research that addresses religion as a resource for coping with major life stressors. His research has also examined how religion can be a source of struggle for people facing major medical illnesses. He has studied the process by which people create perceptions about the sanctity of aspects of their life activities and the various effects of "sanctification" for individual and interpersonal well-being. Most recently, he has been developing and evaluating spiritually integrated approaches to psychotherapy. Pargament won the William James Award for Excellence in Research from Division 36 of the American Psychological Association. He also won the 2000 Virginia Staudt Sexton Mentoring Award from the American Psychological Association for his generous work in encouraging both faculty, undergraduate, and graduate research in the psychology of religion. He has published extensively and his work has received national and international media attention.